Reference Books Bulletin, 2001–2002

A compilation of evaluations
September 2001 through August 2002

*Prepared by the American Library Association
Reference Books Bulletin Editorial Board*

*Edited by Mary Ellen Quinn
Compiled by Keir Graff*

BOOKLIST Publications
Chicago 2002

Copyright 1996, 2002 by the American Library Association.

Permission to quote any review in full or in part must be obtained from the Office of Rights and Permissions of the American Library Association. Permission to quote a review in full will be granted only to the publisher of the work reviewed.

Library of Congress Catalog Card Number 73-159565

International Standard Book Number 0-8389-8219-0
International Standard Serial Number 8755-0962

Printed in the United States of America

Cover design by Jim Lange

Contents

- v   Preface
- vi   Reference Books Bulletin Editorial Board
- vii   Contributing Reviewers
- 1   Encyclopedia Update, 2001
- 5   Special Features
- 29   Reference on the Web

Reviews
- 39   Generalities
- 42   Philosophy, Psychology, Religion
- 47   Sociology, Anthropology, Political Science
- 54   Business, Economics, Resources
- 54   Law, Public Administration, Social Problems and Services
- 60   Education, Commerce, Customs
- 62   Language
- 63   Science
- 70   Medicine, Health, Technology, Management
- 76   Fine Arts, Decorative Arts, Music
- 80   Performing Arts, Recreation
- 84   Literature
- 89   Geography, Biography
- 94   History

Indexes
- 107   Subject Index
- 110   Title Index

Preface

Reference librarians, publishers, and readers of *Reference Books Bulletin* will no doubt look forward to this thirty-fourth annual compilation of RBB reviews as they appeared in the journal *Booklist*. It has been another great year for reference publishing, made so by the depth of coverage and quality of indexing and cross referencing in this year's electronic and printed titles. In addition to reviews from September 2001 to August 2002, this complilation includes the Encyclopedia Update, Reference on the Web, Core Collections, Another Look At, and other RBB features. Reference Books in Brief is not included.

The reviews have continued in the same tradition of high quality which, in this age of tightening budgets, assists librarians in making informed decisions about the books and products that they purchase. I would like to extend my thanks to the conrtibuting reviewers, the Editorial Board, and especially to the editor, Mary Ellen Quinn, and her assistant, Keir Graff. I have met so many wonderful people through *Reference Books Bulletin*, it is a pleasure to work on such a quality publication with such friendly people. I would also like to thank the University of Dayton for its continued support.

Jack O'Gorman,
Chair,
Reference Books Bulletin Editorial Board,
2002–2003

Reference Books Bulletin Editorial Board, 2001–2002

Jack O'Gorman, Reference Librarian, Roesch Library, University of Dayton, Dayton, Ohio, Chair.

Donald Altschiller, History Bibliographer, Mugar Library, Boston University, Boston, Massachusetts.

Barbara Bibel, Reference Librarian, Oakland Public Library, Oakland, California.

Christine Bulson, Assistant Director for Reference and Circulation Services, Milne Library, SUNY Oneonta, Oneonta, New York.

Charlotte Decker, Librarian, Children's Learning Center, Public Library of Cincinnati and Hamilton County, Cincinnati, Ohio.

Susan Gardner, Reference/Instruction Librarian, Leavey Library, University of Southern California, Los Angeles, California.

Nora Harris, Branch Manager, Fairfax Library, Fairfax, California.

Merle Jacob, Director of Library Collection Development, Chicago Public Library, Chicago, Illinois.

J. Sarah Paulk, Head Librarian, TTCPL, Tifton, Georgia.

Linda Loos Scarth, Reference Librarian, Busse Center Library, Mount Mercy College, Cedar Rapids, Iowa.

Cheryl Karp Ward, Penny Alumni Library, East Hartford High School, East Hartford, Connecticut.

Reference Books Bulletin Contributing Reviewers, 2001–2002

James D. Anderson, Professor, School of Communication, Information and Library Studies, Rutgers University, New Brunswick, New Jersey.

Susan Awe, Interim Director, Business and Economics, Parish Memorial Library, University of New Mexico, Albuquerque, New Mexico.

John-Leonard Berg, Reference Coordinator, Karrmann Library, Platteville, Wisconsin.

Ken Black, Director of Teaching and Learning Technology, Dominican University, River Forest, Illinois.

Robert Craig Bunch, Librarian, Coldspring-Oakhurst High School Library, Coldspring, Texas.

Nancy Cannon, Reference Librarian, Milne Library, SUNY Oneonta, Oneonta, New York.

Jerry Carbone, Director, Brooks Memorial Library, Brattleboro, Vermont.

Ann E. Cohen, Assistant Division Head, Information Center, Rochester Public Library, Rochester, New York.

Sharon E. Cohen, Boynton Beach, Florida.

Harold V. Cordry, Baldwin, Kansas.

Carole C. Deily, Reference Librarian, Plano Public Library System, Plano, Texas.

John Doherty, Undergraduate Reference Services Librarian, Cline Library, Northern Arizona University, Flagstaff, Arizona.

Marie Ellis, Librarian IV Emeritus, University of Georgia Libraries, Athens, Georgia.

Stephen Fadel, Public Services Librarian, Everett Community College, Everett, Washington.

Lesley S. J. Farmer, Associate Professor, CSU Long Beach, Long Beach, California.

Jack Forman, Public Services Librarian, San Diego Mesa College Library/LRC, San Diego, California.

Rochelle Glantz, Reviews Editor, Linworth Publishing, Santa Fe, New Mexico.

Susan Gooden, Librarian, Concord High School, Wilmington, Delaware.

Carol Sue Harless, Stone Mountain High School, Stone Mountain, Georgia.

Dona Helmer, College Gate Elementary School, Anchorage, Alaska.

Robin Hoelle, Librarian, Badin High School, Hamilton, Ohio.

Patricia M. Hogan, Administrative Librarian, Poplar Creek Public Library District, Streamwood, Illinois.

Jennifer L. Jack, Reference Librarian, American University Library, Washington, D.C.

Jacqueline A. Jackson, Nelson Poynter Memorial Library, St. Petersburg, Florida.

Merle Jacob, Director of Library Collection Development, Chicago Public Library, Chicago, Illinois.

Sally Sartain Jane, former Head of Adult Collection Development, Lee County Library System, Fort Myers, Florida.

Cynthia Jasper-Parisey, Upper School Library, Cincinnati Country Day School, Cincinnati, Ohio.

Sean Kinder, Humanities/Social Sciences Librarian, Helm Library, Western Kentucky University, Bowling Green, Kentucky.

Dan Kissane, Reference Librarian, Milne Library, SUNY Oneonta, Oneonta, New York.

Jeff Kosokoff, Head of Reference Services, Lamont Library, Harvard University, Cambridge, Massachusetts.

Marlene M. Kuhl, Catonsville Library, Catonsville, Maryland.

Abbie Vestal Landry, Head of Reference Division, Watson Library, Northwestern State University, Natchitoches, Louisiana.

Jan Lewis, Coordinator of Instructional Services, Joyner Library, East Carolina University, Greenville, North Carolina.

Art A. Lichtenstein, Associate Dean, Torreyson Library, University of Central Arkansas, Conway, Arkansas.

Marilyn L. Long, Palma High School, Salinas, California.

Kathleen M. McBroom, Resource Teacher for Library Media and Automation, Dearborn Public Schools, Dearborn, Michigan.

Christopher McConnell, Librarian, SUGEN, Inc., South San Francisco, California.

H. Robert Malinowsky, Manager of Collection Development and Reference, University of Illinois at Chicago Library, Chicago, Illinois.

Arthur S. Meyers, Library Director, Russell Library, Middletown, Connecticut.

Carolyn M. Mulac, Assistant Head, Information Center, Chicago Public Library, Chicago, Illinois.

Clark Nall, Reference/Instruction Librarian, Joyner Library, East Carolina University, Greenville, North Carolina.

Kathryn C. O'Gorman, Director, Johnnie Mae Berry Library, Cincinnati State, Cincinnati, Ohio.

Maren C. Ostergard, Children's Librarian, Bellevue, Washington.

Deborah Carter Peoples, Science Library Manager, Ohio Wesleyan University Libraries, Delaware, Ohio.

Margaret Power, DePaul University Library, Chicago, Illinois.

James Rettig, University Librarian, Boatwright Memorial Library, University of Richmond, Richmond, Virginia.

Deborah Rollins, Reference Librarian, Fogler Library, University of Maine, Orono, Maine.

Diana Donner Shonrock, Science Librarian/Family and Consumer Sciences Bibliographer, Parks Library, Iowa State University, Ames, Iowa.

Esther Sinofsky, Coordinating Field Librarian, Library Services, Los Angeles, California.

Mary Ellen Snodgrass, Hickory, North Carolina.

Kathleen Stipek, Adult Services Librarian, Alachua County Library District, Gainesville, Florida.

Stephen E. Stratton, Social Sciences Librarian, VCU Libraries, Richmond, Virginia.

Martin D. Sugden, Reference Librarian, Florida/Genealogy Department, Jacksonville Public Library, Jacksonville, Florida.

Uri Toch, Corporate and Small Business Liaison, Schaumburg Township District Library, Schaumburg, Illinois.

David A. Tyckoson, Head of Reference, Madden Library, California State University–Fresno, Fresno, California.

Scottie Wallace, Assistant County Librarian, Tippecanoe County Public Library, Lafayette, Indiana.

Sarah Barbara Watstein, Director, Academic User Services, VCU Libraries, Virginia Commonwealth University, Richmond, Virginia.

Ann Welton, Grant Center for the Expressive Arts, Tacoma, Washington.

Christine A. Whittington, Director of Library Services, Greensboro College, Greensboro, North Carolina.

Carolyn N. Willis, Reference Librarian, Joyner Library, East Carolina University, Greenville, North Carolina.

Shauna Yusko, Children's Librarian, Bellevue Regional Library, Bellevue, Washington.

Encyclopedia Update, 2001

Print and Online Encyclopedias
- Compton's Encyclopedia ... 1
- Encyclopedia Americana ... 1
- Grolier Multimedia Encyclopedia Online ... 2
- The New Book of Knowledge ... 2
- New Standard Encyclopedia ... 3
- The World Book Encyclopedia ... 3

CD-ROM Encyclopedias
- Britannica 2002 ... 3
- Grolier Multimedia Encyclopedia Year 2002 ... 3
- Microsoft Encarta Reference Library 2002 ... 4
- World Book Encyclopedia Deluxe 2002 ... 4

Print and Online Encyclopedias

For *Reference Books Bulletin*'s annual encyclopedia update, we reviewed five print sets (*Compton's Encyclopedia, Encyclopedia Americana, The New Book of Knowledge, New Standard Encyclopedia, World Book*), three online versions (*Encyclopedia Americana, The New Book of Knowledge, World Book Online*), and one online title with no print equivalent (*Grolier Multimedia Encyclopedia Online*).

We decided to use the same set of topics as starting points in checking the article content, indexing, search engines, format, and general usability of each encyclopedia: Australian aborigines, cryptography, global warming and the greenhouse effect, the Lewis and Clark expedition, the Middle East, skunks, stem cells, the U.S. presidential election of 2000, and Yugoslavia. These selections proved the point that one should always start with the index, because some of the subjects could only be found as part of more comprehensive articles (*Environment* rather than *Global warming*) or under a completely different heading (*Codes and ciphers* rather than *Cryptography*).

We particularly liked the global "Search Grolier Online" engine, which searches all of Grolier's online databases. Depending on a library's subscription package, these could include *Encyclopedia Americana, Grolier Multimedia Encyclopedia Online,* and *The New Book of Knowledge*, as well as *America the Beautiful, Lands and Peoples, The New Book of Popular Science,* and *Nueva enciclopedia Cumbre en linea*. In many cases, the global search worked better than the search engines unique to each database.

For all the online encyclopedias, added linked content such as dictionaries, news updates, periodical articles, and Web sites was generally well chosen and audience appropriate, and there seemed to be fewer broken links than seen in past years, undoubtedly a result of more frequent checking. Online versions of the encyclopedias were last accessed on July 31, 2001.

This year we've chosen to write shorter reviews of each work than we have in the past and to put pricing and statistical data in a tabular format. Please do let us know whether this approach is useful to you!

—*Barbara Bibel and Deborah Rollins*

Compton's Encyclopedia. 26v. 2001. Success Publishing Group, $649 (0-944262-40-6).

Compton's Encyclopedia has a contemporary, attractive look, with nicely laid-out pages that have numerous color and black-and-white photos, illustrations, maps, diagrams, and drawings. For 2001, 104 color images have been added and 146 maps have been changed or revised. *Compton's* provides fairly current information at a basic level. Articles tend to take a comprehensive approach, rather than going into detail on specific topics or splitting larger ideas into individual entries. For instance, *Skunk* does not merit its own article but is discussed in *Weasel family*, and gene therapy is covered in a paragraph within *Genetic engineering*. *Lewis and Clark expedition* describes the route and participants but does not clearly state the reasons behind the trip. Some of the 57 new articles this year are *Chechnya*; *Human Genome Project*; *Lyme disease*; *Rabin, Yitzhak*; and *Riefenstahl, Leni*; most of the new articles are in volume 20 (Q–R). Among the 15 rewritten articles are *Biological clock*, *Human origins*, *Memory*, *Serbia*, and *Clapton, Eric*. Although some 360 articles have received updates (*Yugoslavia* goes through October 2000), others are not current. The latest reference to events in *Middle East* is 1993 (although more current information can be found in other entries, such as *Israel* and *Jordan*); *Ciphers and codes* does not mention the use of computers in cryptography and has no citations later than 1983 in its bibliography. The latest events mentioned for the aborigines in *Australia* are the right to vote, granted in 1984, and their rejection of the term *aborigine*, since 1988. There is no information about stem cells.

Each volume begins with a section called "Here and There," with key articles grouped by major field, as well as an illustrated section called "Exploring," which posits interesting questions and gives the pages with the answers. These features will encourage browsing among those who happen to see them. Access to articles and information is hampered by the set's Fact/Index volume, which is cumbersome because it functions as both an index and a supplement to the encyclopedia volumes. There are biographies, short articles, and tables of sports champions, celebrity birthdays, and award winners in addition to index entries. The indexing itself needs improvement. The entry for *Zaire* has a cross-reference to *Democratic Republic of Congo*, but neither of these gives a page number for the encyclopedia article, which is under *Congo, Democratic Republic of*. There is no cross-reference to the actual entry. The set includes an entry on *Global warming* and a biography of George W. Bush, but these topics are not indexed.

Compton's is a solid reference, useful for background information on a variety of topics. School and public libraries that need a second or third encyclopedia set because of high usage may want to consider purchase.

Encyclopedia Americana. 30v. 2001. Grolier, $1,049 (0-7172-0134-1).
Encyclopedia Americana Online. [Internet database]. Grolier, pricing from $395 in combination with other Grolier Online encyclopedias. Call 888-326-6546 for pricing details. Visit [http://go.grolier.com] for free 30-day trial.

The *Encyclopedia Americana* (EA) print version continues to offer excellent in-depth, scholarly coverage, especially of American and Canadian topics. There is an ongoing program to update material in the sciences, technology, humanities, and area studies. The 2000 U.S. election results appear in a table, while biographies of Al Gore and George W.

Bush have narrative election-related details. The article *Lewis and Clark expedition* explains the significance of the event. Australian aborigines have their own entry, but stem cells appear in the article *Genetic engineering*. Global warming is covered in a number of places, including *Conservation* and *Environment: environmental issues*. *Cryptography* gets its own article as well as coverage in the article on computer science.

The editors have done well in updating the tables and material in the articles on U.S. states and Canadian provinces, but other articles, such as that on the aborigines, have old statistics. EA is very strong on biography. Topics in the sciences and technology are explained in detail and with advanced vocabulary. For example, in *Skunk*, all species names as well as the chemical composition of skunk spray are noted. For 2001, EA added 45 new entries to the print set, among them *Hadrosaur*; *Lieberman, Joseph Isador*; *Milosevic, Slobodan*; and *Royal Academy of the Arts*, and replaced 33 articles, including *Ethnicity*; *Health insurance*; *Heller, Joseph*; *National Security Agency*; *Olmec*; and *Rauschenberg, Robert*. An additional 1,193 articles were revised. There are 99 new photos, 63 of which are in color.

It has to be said that *Encyclopedia Americana* is rather fusty in appearance. Pages are crowded with dense text relieved by little white space; page number placement jumps annoyingly from header to footer when illustrations bleed to page edges. Many pages have no headwords. Most of the photographs are black and white, and many are quite dark or have high contrast. This more than anything else gives a dated and drab look to the pages, even when the photos are of recent vintage.

On the Web, EA loses its outdated look and seems clean and fresh. Some articles are both timely and unique to the online version, such as *Stem cells*. Although 1,500 color photos have been added, there are different, usually less-detailed maps and fewer illustrations online. *Yugoslavia* in print has two maps: one with eight regions and another of the former Yugoslavia, with an index to towns and populations. Online, there are seven maps (five countries plus the Balkans and Europe) that show less geopolitical detail. Hyperlinks to related Internet sites are usually well chosen, such as the PBS page on Lewis and Clark. EA's links to selected articles from EBSCO periodicals range in quality and quantity: dozens for *Israel* and *Palestine* serve to complement and update encyclopedia articles, but the four for *Skunk* do not really add much to one's understanding. The *Americana Journal* feature, updated weekly, provides information on important current topics with links to relevant encyclopedia articles and maps.

Our major quibble with EA Online is its search engine. The default search is set to article title, meaning that searches for terms such as *Aborigine*, *global warming*, *stem cell*, and *2000 election* that are not article titles all yield zero results. If users read and understand the search instructions they'll be fine, but as we know, most people will simply start typing away in the search box. A full-text search works better. The most essential piece of information for potential subscribers to EA Online: there are many new, replacement, and revised articles from the EA database that are unique to the online edition and not found in print. Some of the more than 1,500 new, replaced, or revised articles found only online are *Atherosclerosis*; *Close, Chuck*; *Davis, Angela*; *Du Pre, Jacqueline*; *Ellis Island*; *Gould, Stephen Jay*; *Gothic Revival*; and *Tamil*.

EA remains a good choice for any high-school, college, or public library collection. Libraries that can afford the online version, updated quarterly, will get the benefit of hundreds of new and revised articles each year that do not appear in the print set, as well as other online features.

Grolier Multimedia Encyclopedia Online. [Internet database]. Grolier, pricing from $395 in combination with other Grolier Online encyclopedias. Call 888-326-6546 for pricing details. Visit [http://go.grolier.com] for free 30-day trial.

Grolier Multimedia Encyclopedia Online (GMEO) provides current information on a broad range of subjects for users from elementary-school age through adulthood. It has an extremely attractive Web page layout, and most articles have pictures, many in color, next to the text. Several current news stories are available right on the home page, a convenient feature. The news topics are of interest to the school and academic community, with links to related encyclopedia articles. GMEO also offers a Research Starters feature that shows users how to find information and write a paper with proper citations. In addition, there are links to periodical articles and Web sites chosen by the editors, as well as a Brain Jam page that explores a new featured topic each month, along with upcoming events and holidays.

GMEO articles tend to be shorter than those in *Compton's*, *Encyclopedia Americana*, and *World Book*. *Lewis and Clark expedition* merits only five paragraphs but touches on the essential points of the trip: the route, the major players, the reasons and results. The article on stem cells has basic scientific information but nothing about the ethical issues associated with research.

This encyclopedia appears to be the most aggressively updated of all we checked. *Aborigines, Australian* has 1996 census figures and rights and survey information from 2000. *Middle East* and *Yugoslavia* are updated through spring 2001. One thing we especially like about GMEO is that it names laws, organizations, etc. (e.g., Intergovernmental Panel on Climate Change, Native Title Act), making it easy to search for further information on them elsewhere. Other encyclopedias often make generic statements such as "an international group recommended" or "legislation was passed that." The default search here is relevancy-ranked keyword, so it is easier to find information than it is in *Encyclopedia Americana Online*.

Among the 570 new articles added to GMEO over the past year are *Addiction*; *Bin Laden, Osama*; *Day trading*; *Falun Gong*; *Immunotherapy*; *Jones, Marion*; *Petroleum industry*; and *Rice, Condoleezza*, plus series of entries on major museums and American ethnic groups. More than 100 replacement articles include *Computers and privacy*; *Conservation*; *Pornography*; and *Yeltsin, Boris*. There are approximately 4,500 major and minor article revisions. Some 500 new pictures have been added.

GMEO is recommended for school and public libraries serving the elementary grades on up to a general adult population.

The New Book of Knowledge. 21v. 2001. Grolier, $699 (0-7172-0532-0).
The New Book of Knowledge Online. [Internet database]. Grolier, pricing from $325 in combination with other Grolier Online encyclopedias. Call 888-326-6546 for pricing details. Visit [http://go.grolier.com] for free 30-day trial.

The New Book of Knowledge (NBK) articles are designed to be engaging to young readers: in *Skunk*, there is information on what to do if and when you meet one, and *Codes and ciphers* shows kids how to make their own secret messages. Sidebars containing "Wonder Questions" " ("What is El Nino?" "What was the Northwest Ordnance?"), "See for Yourself" ("How to make a dew point apparatus"), and other features supplement the text and involve readers in projects designed to help them do hands-on research. *Lewis and Clark expedition* provides good explanations of the reasons for the journey and the results but doesn't say how many miles the explorers logged—something that might make kids marvel.

Some of the material needs updating. The article on libraries still tells students how to use the card catalog, with no mention of OPACs. The Democratic Republic of Congo is still entered under *Zaire*. *Codes and ciphers* makes no mention of computers. Material about global warming is disbursed among various articles about environmental topics, making it difficult for users to find the information. An article on this topic of great interest would be helpful for young users. Drawings, photographs, and maps are colorful, attractive, informative, and plentiful. The placement of guide words at page bottom runs contrary to usual reference publishing practice. The index is helpful in indicating main entries in bold type and listing separate page references under the headings *map*(s), *picture*(s), and *profile* (short biographies). For 2001, more than 40 new and replacement articles include *Ecology*, *Emotions*, *Middle Ages*, *Poetry*, and *Zebras*. Revisions were made to many entries, such as *Clinton, William*; *Drugs*; *Ecology*; *Political parties*; and *Ranch life*. Biographies of 79 "famous people" were added to survey articles, such as *Middle Ages*. Also new are 465 new photos (360 in full color) and 62 pieces of full-color art.

The "Wonder Questions," activities, and teachers' guide that come with the print edition are also part of the online edition. There are links to Web sites and EBSCO periodical articles from magazines like *Ranger Rick* and a searchable children's dictionary and thesaurus. The longer articles have a table of contents, so users may click and go to the section that they need. Articles may also have links to Facts at a Glance, flag (for countries), photos that may be enlarged to show detais and captions, and maps, all of which may be found in the print set (although there are additional illustrations found only in print). NBK News stories and related lesson plans are updated weekly (with one summer update) and tie current events to related encyclopedia entries.

NBK will be useful in libraries serving younger children, although it may not be the first choice when dollars are tight.

New Standard Encyclopedia. 20v. 2001. Ferguson, $499 (0-87392-105-4).

New Standard Encyclopedia's volumes, which are smaller than standard encyclopedia size, cover two letter ranges, with separate pagination for each letter and no pagination on the spine. Most of the material is not covered in depth. Of the major topics checked, only the entry for the *Lewis and Clark expedition* is satisfactory. The coverage of Australian aborigines is odd. Readers looking at the article *Australia* would think that aborigines did not exist because they are barely mentioned there; it is disturbing to see a paragraph under the heading "The People" that begins with "From the time of its settlement in the late 18th century" and focuses on the "British stock" and European immigrants, with aborigines and people of Asian descent relegated to a single brief sentence. The separate article *Australian aborigines* is short, but it does note the 500 tribes and their social organization, as well as the fact that some of their lands were returned.

In the article *Election*, extensive use of the media by candidates is noted. *Cryptology* is too brief to give more than the basics. Global warming is covered in the article *Greenhouse effect*, which mentions the 1992 UN conference and treaty, with no details. Stem cells are discussed in the articles *Blood* and *Cell*, with no information about current medical research and ethics quandaries. Although there are 66 new and extensively revised articles for 2001 (e.g., *Bush, George Walker*; *Hydrothermal vent*; *Rabin, Yitzhak*; *Rowling, J.K.*; *Wal-Mart Stores, Inc.*; *Yahoo! Inc.*), 800 updated articles, and 264 new color illustrations, their number does not make up for the general quality of the set. This is not a priority for libraries.

The World Book Encyclopedia. 22v. 2001. World Book, $819 (0-7166-0101-X).

World Book Online. [Internet database]. World Book, pricing starting at $395. Call 800-975-3250 for pricing details and free 30-day trial.

In *World Book* (WB), articles are accessible and authoritative. The set is easy to use, up-to-date, and extremely well illustrated. One of the things we like best about WB is that topics likely to be sought by students (*Election of* 2000, *Global warming, Greenhouse effect, Stem cell*) are all found under their own entries. *Skunk* has interesting details about the animal's behavior; *Electoral College* has a crystal-clear presentation on the four presidents elected despite not receiving the popular vote. WB is the only print set we examined that provides discussion of the ethical and political issues along with a definition of stem cells (EA *Online* was the only other encyclopedia title that covered both aspects). *Aborigines* gives a balanced view of traditional culture and life today, with a current photo of an aboriginal girl at the computer. *Greenhouse effect* notes use of core samples to study data from the past, a technique not mentioned in other sets in relation to this topic. *Codes and ciphers*, like many complex topics, is written at a more advanced level than other articles. Maps for the Middle East, Israel, and Yugoslavia are easy to read, yet detailed, and clearly show current and historical boundaries and areas of conflict. Longer entries conclude with a list of related articles, outline, questions, and a bibliography. The index is easy to use and detailed, including page numbers for illustrations and maps. The research guide is useful for students who need help organizing a project. Among the 100 new articles this year are *Collectibles*; *Dietary supplement*; *Human rights*; *Potter, Harry*; and SETI *Institute*. *Antibiotic*; *Conservation*; *English literature*; *Peary, Robert Edwin*; *Skateboarding*; and *Vietnam War* are among the 128 articles that were extensively rewritten or revised. There are approximately 300 new photos, diagrams, or other illustrations.

In its online format, WB retains all of its text and adds many other useful and engaging features, including well-chosen Web links, links to periodical articles, a dictionary, "Today in History," "Surf the Millennium" (simulated Web sites from the past 1,000 years), a monthly feature topic (e.g., earthquakes), a teachers' guide, key historical documents and speeches, and "Homework Wizards" to aid students in research and writing. A new option this year, at a slightly higher price, is an integrated Global Edition, with "additional content specific to international English-speaking areas." For example, from *Australia*, there are links to 40 International Edition articles, many of them biographies.

WB *Online* is the most media-rich online encyclopedia, with many of the pictures from the print set plus 3-D Bubble Views (for example, one depicting the Colosseum), sounds, animations, and videos. The search is relevancy-ranked keyword, which is usually successful, but a search for *Australian aborigines* gets no hits. Help recommends typing only one word or using the advanced search for more than one word. This is not how most people accustomed to using *Google* and *Yahoo!* will conduct a search. Article displays are easy to read, with a clickable outline in a frame to the left and the text and illustrations in a frame to the right. Information for citing material appears at the end of each entry, which will be very helpful for students. Typically, between 25 and 50 articles are added each month; among the 395 added between August 2000 and May 2001 are *American Stock Exchange*; *Coleman, Bessie*; *Herbal medicine*; *San Francisco Giants*; and *Seven deadly sins*.

WB is highly recommended for all school, college, and public libraries as well as for home use. Many institutions will find an online subscription more cost-effective and will prefer it for its daily updates, major monthly additions and revisions, multimedia content, and other features.

Encyclopedias on CD-ROM

Here is the follow-up to the Encyclopedia Update that appeared on our September 15, 2001, issue. We were not able to include CD-ROMs with the discussions of print and online versions because the latest editions of the CD-ROMs were not ready in time.

A summary chart is accompanied by a look at each individual CD-ROM product. For purposes of comparison, we looked for information on Afghanistan and stem cells in each title.

Britannica 2002: Deluxe Edition CD-ROM. 2001. Encyclopædia Britannica, $59.99 (0-85229-790-4).

System requirements: For Windows 95, 98, 2000, Me, XP, *or* NT 4.0; 64 MB RAM; 140 MB *free hard disk space (plus* 50 MB *for* IE 5.01).

Britannica 2002 is available in one-and two-disc CD-ROM as well as DVD formats. The DVD ($69.99) has more multimedia features, but the content is the same as that on the two-disc CD-ROM.

Among the 532 new or replaced articles are the biographies of Thomas Jefferson, Pope John Paul II, and Pyotr Illyich Tchaikovsky and entries on Doctors without Borders, the drug Ecstasy, and information theory. More than 3,400 articles have been updated or revised. Disc versions have more than 8,000 articles that do not appear in the print set. Among these are U.S. county entries and new biographies of film actors and mathematicians.

Users may search the encyclopedia using the A–Z index, the search box, or the Knowledge Navigator. The latter offers a group of broad topics in fields related to the search terms. The search mode offers options of expanding or narrowing the search but no Boolean, truncation, or proximity operators. Compared to other CD-ROM encyclopedias, it takes longer for Britannica to display a results list. Information on Afghanistan includes both short and long entries reminiscent of the Micropedia and Macropedia portions of the print version (but no hint in the results list as to which is the more detailed article), "The Year in Review" articles, maps, the flag, and a list of ranked Web sites. A search for material about stem cells produces an article on cell differentiation and a special report from "The Year in Review 2000" called "The Science and Ethics of Embryonic Stem Cell Research," which is a good overview of the major issues in this field. Looking at maps and images requires a great deal of disc switching. The article on dogs lists 80 photographs, 10 at a time. Users must choose the image, change discs, ask to see the next 10 listings, change discs to look at them, and change discs again to see the photographs. When installing the encyclopedia, there is an option for installing the entire work on the hard disk, but this requires a great deal of space and takes 45 minutes.

Britannica 2002 on CD-ROM has the usual dictionary, atlas, time line, and research-organizer features. It also has online updates for articles and outstanding Web links ranked from one to five stars by the editors. It is a good choice for libraries that want to offer *Britannica* content in a CD-ROM format.

Grolier Multimedia Encyclopedia Year 2002: Deluxe Edition. 2001. Grolier, $29.95.

System requirements: For Windows 95, 98, 2000, NT, *or* Me; 16 MB RAM; 25–80 MB *free hard disk space*.

Grolier Multimedia Encyclopedia does a good job of keeping current. There are approximately 560 new articles, including a series on ethnic Americans and several entries on celestial bodies (*Ariel, Umbriel, Vesta*) and on major U.S. and world museums (*Ashmolean Museum, High Museum of*

Art, *Phillips Collection*). Grolier also offers a number of new biographies: *Ashcroft, John; Bin Laden, Osama; Fleming, Renee; Fox, Vincente;* and *Jones, Marion,* to name a few. More than 100 articles, including AIDS, *Gambling,* and *Sex reassignment* have been replaced. Approximately 4,500 articles were revised.

Searching is easy using the tool bar on the left side of the screen. Users may browse by scrolling through the index or search using the simple or advanced mode. In the advanced mode, one may use Boolean operators, truncation, and filters to limit material from the 39,000 articles. Multimedia features include animations, cutaways, panoramas, pictures, videos, sound clips, time lines, tables, and maps.

Grolier Multimedia articles about countries all have fact boxes, which provide a convenient overview with statistics, a map, the flag, and a sound clip of the national anthem. The statistics are current and include useful information such as the literacy rate and the number of physicians and hospital beds as well as the usual population and economic indicator numbers. This is very helpful for students comparing countries. The Afghanistan article describes the major ethnicities and twentieth-century political events clearly; getting to the online article update is very easy. The article on stem cells is strictly scientific, focusing on the types of cells, their culture, and possible uses.

Although the multimedia features are less sophisticated than those of *World Book*, this is still a very nice encyclopedia with current, accessible information. It is a good choice for school and public libraries serving patrons from elementary-school age through adulthood.

Microsoft Encarta Reference Library 2002. 2001. Microsoft, $74.95.
System requirements: For Windows 95, 98, NT Workstation 4.0 with Service Pack 5 or later, 2000 Professional, or Me; 32 MB RAM (64 MB for Windows 2000 Professional); up to 215 MB free hard disk space.

This is a five-disc set with an encyclopedia, dictionary, thesaurus, atlas, a research organizer, and *Africana*, the *Encarta* encyclopedia of black culture. Users may install it on their hard-disk drives and use a great deal of space or switch CDs constantly. The reading level is generally middle school, and there are lots of multimedia features. New to this edition are the pop-up *Encarta* Factfinder, which provides access to ready-reference information such as definitions and business profiles and requires Internet access; streaming media that brings live radio, weather, and MSNBC news (and also requires Internet access); and 3-D Virtual Tours. Some of the multimedia features are better than others: the resolution in the 3-D tours of ancient sites is poor, but the 2-D tours of more modern sites are very clear. Musical sound clips are of superior quality, with original recordings of performers and instruments rather than synthesizer interpretations. Sound clips are also longer than those on other CD-ROM encyclopedias. The atlas has many map overlay choices, including population density, language, religion, rainfall, tectonic, and political. All place-names are indexed and searchable.

Searching can be frustrating. Tiny navigational icons are unaccompanied by explanatory text, and the results list displays undifferentiated entries with the same headings. Content is generally less comprehensive than that of *World Book* or *Grolier Multimedia*, although the article on Afghanistan has an extensive "Peoples" section covering population, cities, ethnic origins and languages, religion, way of life, and more. There is no main entry for stem cells, but the topic is covered in a 1998 Yearbook article as well as in articles on bone marrow and medical ethics. Using online updates and links requires registration with Microsoft and is free through the end of 2002.

Libraries will prefer *Britannica, Grolier Multimedia,* or *World Book* to *Encarta* because of their superior content. *Encarta* has some nice features, such as the atlas and the *Africana*, but it offers more flash than substance.

World Book Encyclopedia Deluxe 2002. 2001. World Book, $22.99.
System requirements: For Windows 95, 98, 2000, NT 4.0, or Me; 16 MB RAM (Windows 2000 requires 64 MB); 40 MB free hard disk space.

The latest *World Book* CD-ROM continues to provide comprehensive coverage that is both accessible and authoritative. The CD-ROM has more than 3,000 additional entries not found in the print set. These include separate articles on all Nobel Prize winners; articles on the capitals of countries; biographies of Laura Bush, Hun Sen, and Laurent Kabila; and entries on literary works such as *Catch 22, Leaves of Grass,* and *Remembrance of Things Past.* Among the 305 new articles this year are *Andromeda Galaxy, Grammy Awards, NASDAQ,* and *Telomere.* Some 128 articles have been extensively revised, including *English literature, Immigration,* and *Sudden infant death syndrome.* There are 242 new maps, 82 new photographs, and 75 new audio clips.

World Book is easy to search. Users may use the topic search mode for keywords or the word search mode to employ Boolean operators, limits, truncation, and proximity operators. Excellent multimedia features, including Bubble views and Simulations, help bring the text to life. Online links offer updates to articles and special features such as topical reports (puberty, bottled versus tap water), Back in Time (year-by-year articles on important topics), and links to 15,000 Web sites that are continuously validated. The Spotlight On feature changes each month to highlight facts about the month. The atlas has a distance calculator and, for some maps, overlays that show population density, average temperatures in January and June, average precipitation, economy, agriculture, and manufacturing. The Time Frame feature allows users to search for events in a given year, decade, century, or millennium.

The article on Afghanistan is fairly short, compared with the other encyclopedias, but covers all the essential points about culture, history, and politics. The update is easy to find, appearing in the left-hand frame. In *Stem cells*, the language is less technical than in *Britannica* or *Grolier Multimedia Encyclopedia* and more accessible for middle school on up. It also notes ethical issues.

With up-to-date coverage and multimedia features that enhance the text, the *World Book* CD-ROM is an outstanding tool for public and school libraries that prefer a CD-ROM source. It is available in single and network-user deluxe (two-disc) versions. The deluxe version comes with supplementary discs containing a stand-alone version of the *World Book Dictionary* and "How to Study," a guide to effective study techniques.

—*Barbara Bibel and Deborah Rollins*

Special Features

American Ethnicity Reference Sources ----- 5
Core Collection: E-Commerce ----- 7
Core Collection: History of Science ----- 8
Core Collection: Urban Studies ----- 9
Dark Reference ----- 11
Horror Reference Shelf ----- 11
More Sites on Sleuths: Women of Mystery ----- 12
Other People's Words: Recent Quotation Books ----- 13
Reference Books in Spanish for Children and Adolescents ----- 15
Top 10 Biography Reference Sources ----- 17
Twenty Best Bets for Student Researchers ----- 17
Where and What: Current World Atlas and Dictionary Roundup ----- 18
A Whole New Environment: Environmental Reference Resources in Print ----- 21
Writer's Tool Kit ----- 22
Another Look At . . .
    Childcraft ----- 22
    The Columbia Granger's Index to Poetry in Anthologies ----- 23
Focus Reviews
    An Encyclopedia of One's Own: Women in World History ----- 23
    Desktop Library: ebrarian for Libraries ----- 24
    Genealogy Gold Mine: Ancestry Plus ----- 24
    Library-in-a-Dorm Room: Questia ----- 25
    Out of the Shadows: Women Building Chicago, 1790–1990 ----- 26
    Sixty-Thousand Page Giant: Oxford Reference Online ----- 26
    Unabridged and Online: Merriam-Webster Unabridged ----- 27
    Wives of the Presidents ----- 27

American Ethnicity Reference Sources

"The nation is much more diverse in the year 2000 [and it is] much more complex than we've ever measured before." Census Bureau official, *Washington Post*, March 12, 2001.

Publishers have responded to the reality of increasing diversity within the U.S. with well-researched, clearly written, reasonably priced reference tools. The following list updates RBB's November 15, 1994, compilation, which covered works produced beginning in 1991. For librarians worrying how to stretch materials budgets, this selection of available resources published since 1995 and costing less than $100 apiece can help in decision making. The list emphasizes general rather than specialized materials, and titles are appropriate for the high-school level and up except where noted.

A to Z of Native American Women. By Liz Sonneborn. 1998. 228p. Facts On File, $44 (0-8160-3580-6).

Well-written brief profiles of more than 100 well-and lesser-known artists, educators, leaders, and others that will also be useful at middle-school level and up.

African American Almanac: Day-by-Day Black History. By Leon T. Ross and Kenneth A. Mimms. 1997. 177p. McFarland, $33.50 (0-89950-675-5).

Arranged by day, and then by year under each day, this is a list of events that were initiated by (or associated with) African Americans and have had a significant impact in U.S. history. It will be especially useful for library displays.

African American Frontiers: Slave Narratives and Oral Histories. By Alan B. Govenar. 2000. 551p. ABC-CLIO, $75 (0-87436-867-7).

The social, economic, and cultural frontiers that developed as runaway and freed slaves migrated west and north are conveyed in these personal accounts, enhanced by biographical details, photos, and other features.

African American Quotations. Comp. by Richard Newman. 1998. 504p. Oryx, $54.95 (1-57356-118-5).

From one-liners to short paragraphs, more than 2,500 mainly twentieth-century quotations from 500 individuals are accessible by name, subject, and occupation indexes.

African-American Writers: A Dictionary. Ed. by Shari Dorantes Hatch and Michael R. Strickland. 2000. 484p. ABC-CLIO, $75 (0-87436-959-2).

A good starting point for information on 500 individuals, movements, publications, and themes. Useful especially for minor writers who are hard to locate elsewhere.

American Ethnic Writers. 2v. Ed. by David Peck and Tracy Irons-Georges. 2000. Salem, $95 (0-89356-157-6).

Drawing from the publisher's *Identities and Issues in Literature* (1997), this set covers 217 works by 136 authors.

Special Features

American Indian Quotations. Ed. by Howard J. Langer. 1996. 260p. Greenwood, $60 (0-313-29121-7).

This work will inform, enlighten, and enrich with its 800 entries from 200 Native Americans ranging from the sixteenth century to the present. Access is aided by author, subject, and keyword indexes.

American Indian Studies: A Bibliographic Guide. By Phillip M. White. 1995. 163p. Libraries Unlimited, $35 (1-56308-243-8).

A very accessible treasury of information for larger libraries, focusing mainly on North America and describing 400 sources, including electronic resources.

American Jewish Desk Reference: The Ultimate One-Volume Reference to the Jewish Experience in America. By the American Jewish Historical Society. 1999. 642p. Random, $39.95 (0-375-40243-8).

Arranged thematically, the 900 mainly biographical entries in 14 chapters cover broad topics, are accessible through an index, and are enhanced by photos and other features.

Arab American Biography. 2v. By Loretta Hall and Bridget K. Hall. 1999. 400p. UXL, $95 (0-7876-2953-7).
Arab American Encyclopedia. By Loretta Hall and Bridget K. Hall. 1999. 200p. UXL, $52 (0-7876-2952-0).
Arab American Voices. By Loretta Hall and Bridget K. Hall. 1999. 233p. UXL, $52 (0-7876-2956-1).

Each title from this imprint for middle-school students provides a different perspective on Arab Americans. The first two offer biographical and topical information, and the third contains excerpts from newspapers, literary works, speeches, and more. May also be purchased as a set.

Atlas of African-American History. By Monique Avakian. 2001. 224p. Facts On File, $85 (0-8160-3700-0).
Atlas of Asian-American History. By James Ciment. 2002. 224p. Facts On File, $85 (0-8160-3699-3).
Atlas of Hispanic-American History. By George Ochoa. 2002. 224p. Facts On File, $85 (0-8160-3698-5).
Atlas of the North American Indian. Rev. ed. By Carl Waldman. 2001. 400p. Facts On File, $49.50 (0-8160-3974-7).

These thematic atlases include many useful tables, graphs, and specially created maps.

Biographical Dictionary of American Indian History to 1900. Rev. ed. By Carl Waldman. 2001. 506p. Facts On File, $71.50 (0-8160-4252-7); paper, $24.95 (0-8160-4253-5).

A well-written first source for quick and accurate information on 1,000 notable Native and nonnative people in the U.S. and Canada, from pre-contact through the nineteenth century.

The Biographical Dictionary of Hispanic Americans. 2d ed. By Nicholas E. Meyer. 2001. 324p. Facts On File, $44 (0-8160-4330-2); paper, $19.95 (0-8160-4331-0).

With articles on 200 Hispanic Americans in a variety of fields, the entries are readable and entertaining. Some include a photo.

Black Americans: A Statistical Sourcebook. Ed. by Louise L. Hornor. 2002. 307p. Information, $55 (0-929960-32-7).
Hispanic Americans: A Statistical Sourcebook. Ed. by Louise L. Hornor. 2002. 280p. Information, $55 (0-929960-33-5).

Demographics, characteristics, vital statistics, education, government, law enforcement, labor force, and other vital data.

Black Authors and Illustrators of Books for Children and Young Adults: A Biographical Dictionary. 3d ed. By Barbara Thrash Murphy and Barbara Rollock. 1999. 513p. Garland, $80 (0-8153-2004-3).

The 274 brief sketches, arranged alphabetically and including much-studied writers as well as currently popular figures, provide a helpful guide for a wide range of users.

Chronology of American Indian History through Time: The Trail of the Wind. By Liz Sonneborn. 2001. 442p. Facts On File, $71.50 (0-8160-3977-1).

Covering the whole history, from the migration across the Bering Strait to early 2001, the entries provide a larger understanding as well as details and are enhanced by photos, illustrations, an index, and other features.

The Columbia Guide to American Indians of the Northeast. By Kathleen J. Bradgon. 2001. 276p. Columbia Univ., $45 (0-231-11452-4).
The Columbia Guide to American Indians of the Southeast. By Theda Perdue and Michael D. Green. 2001. 325p. Columbia Univ., $45 (0-231-11570-9).
The Columbia Guide to Asian American History. By Gary Okihiro. 2001. 352p. Columbia Univ., $45 (0-231-11510-5).

These handbooks combine narrative history with reference features such as a chronology and a bibliography.

Culturally Diverse Library Collections for Youth. By Herman L. Totten and others. 1996. 220p. Neal-Schuman, paper, $38.50 (1-55570-141-8).

Annotated bibliography of 780 books and videos for young adults, with title, author, and subject indexes. A valuable selection tool for school and public libraries.

Distinguished African American Political and Governmental Leaders. By James Haskins. 1999. 314p. Oryx, $54.95 (1-57356-126-6).
Distinguished African American Scientists of the Twentieth Century. By James H. Kessler and others. 1999. 314p. Oryx, $54.95 (1-57356-126-6).
Distinguished African Americans in Aviation and Space Science. By Betty Kaplan Gubert and others. 2001. 336p. Oryx, $59.95 (1-57356-246-7).

Well-researched, clearly organized information. Each volume profiles approximately 100 individuals.

Distinguished Asian Americans: A Biographical Dictionary. Ed. by Hyung-chan Kim. 1999. 430p. Greenwood, $65 (0-313-28902-6).

This compilation of 166 entries highlights a wide range of inspiring persons, whether native or foreign born, and will be valuable in high-school and public libraries.

Encyclopedia of African-American Heritage. 2d ed. By Susan Altman. 2000. 353p. Facts On File, $45 (0-8160-4125-3); paper, $18.95 (0-8160-4126-1).

Brief, well-written, accessible information, including lesser-known subjects. Especially useful for libraries serving junior-high-school students and up.

Encyclopedia of Native American Tribes. Rev. ed. By Carl Waldman. 1999. 312p. Facts On File, $71.50 (0-8160-3963-1); paper, $19.95 (0-8160-3964-X).

Recommended for junior-and senior-high-school students and anyone seeking a basic understanding of North American tribal history for its ease of use, wonderful illustrations, and well-constructed index and glossary.

Global Voices, Global Visions: A Core Collection of Multicultural Books. By Lyn Miller-Lachmann. 1995. 870p. Bowker-Greenwood, $68.75 (0-8352-3291-3).

Thoughtful evaluative annotations of 1,700 recommended works for adults and mature high-school students on groups from all over the world; an excellent source for print materials.

Latina and Latino Voices in Literature for Children and Teenagers. By Frances Ann Day. 1997. 228p. Heinemann, $28 (0-435-07202-1).

Well-organized biographical information combined with summaries of the works, bringing to life this previously ignored community of authors.

Macmillan Encyclopedia of Native American Tribes. 2d ed. By Michael Johnson. 1999. 288p. Macmillan, $115 (0-02-865409-9).

Essential information on 400 tribes, including identity, kinships, cultural characteristics, and other topics; with 300 illustrations and maps.

Making It in America: A Sourcebook on Eminent Ethnic Americans. Ed. by Elliott Robert Barkan. 2001. 448p. ABC-CLIO, $85 (1-57607-098-0); E-book, $95 (1-57607-529-X).

More than 400 biographies of mainly twentieth-century foreign-and U.S.-born ethnic Americans who have made a difference while maintaining an identification with and contributing to their 90 ethnic communities.

Multicultural Resources on the Internet: The United States and Canada. By Vicki L. Gregory and others. 1999. 366p. Libraries Unlimited, paper, $30 (1-56308-676-X).

Although some of the sites are no longer available, many of the the 1,600 resources for 12 ethnic groups, with entries divided into such areas as fine arts, language arts, and science and technology, will still be useful for larger public libraries.

Native North American Firsts. By Karen Gayton Swisher and AnCita Benally. 1998. 263p. Gale, $70 (0-7876-0518-2).

Highlighting first accomplishments from 7,500 B.C.E., beginning with the cultivating the potato and continuing to the appointment of the first Native American archbishop in 1997, this book presents a perspective that until recently was unrecognized.

New Immigrant Literatures in the United States: A Sourcebook to Our Multicultural Literary Heritage. Ed. by Alpana Sharma Knippling. 1996. 386p. Greenwood, $90 (0-313-28968-9).

A clearly written introduction to post–World War II literatures, especially marginalized ones such as Armenian, Pakistani, and Slovak. Covers fiction and nonfiction.

The New York Public Library African American Desk Reference. By the Schomburg Center for Research in Black Culture. 1999. 606p. Wiley, $34.95 (0-471-23924-0).

A comprehensive and accessible ready-reference tool with tables, lists, photos, and quotations. Especially valuable for school and public libraries that cannot afford more extensive resources.

Notable Latino Americans: A Biographical Dictionary. By Matt S. Meier. 1997. 431p. Greenwood, $65 (0-313-29105-5).

Covering 127 persons, with the majority political activists, performing artists, writers, business leaders, and sport figures, the book has useful indexes by activity or profession and then by country of origin or ethnic group.

The Oxford Companion to African American Literature. Ed. by William L. Andrews and others. 1997. 866p. Oxford, $65 (0-19-506510-7).

A distinguished contribution covering 400 authors along with other individuals who have influenced black culture and surveying topics such as children's and young adult literature, film, and folklore.

Puerto Rico Past and Present: An Encyclopedia. By Ronald Fernandez and others. 1998. 375p. Greenwood, $59.95 (0-313-29822-X).

Interspersed with photos, this is a broad overview of the politics, economics, and culture of the island that has been part of the U.S. for a century.

—*Arthur S. Meyers*

Core Collection: E-Commerce

With more than 11 million Web sites on the Net (even after the meltdown of the dot-coms in the past year), IDC, a market intelligence and advisory firm in Framingham, Massachusetts, forecasts that nearly one billion people, or 15 percent of the world's population, will be using the Internet by 2005. And they will fuel a $5 trillion dollar boom in electronic commerce. An Internet survey by the National Federation of Independent Business (NFIB) showed that although more than a third of small businesses had Web sites, 89 percent of those reported that the Web had not improved profits, and 43 percent said it brought in no additional customers. Will the meltdown have the positive effect of forcing businesses to think through and really plan either an online business or integrating online into their total business infrastructure? Only time will tell.

Following are books, electronic journals, and Internet resources that can help business owners and managers and entrepreneurs find the information and tools needed to design and execute a successful business plan in the new economy. Sites were last visited on September 7, 2001.

Books

The E-Commerce Book: Building the E-Empire. By Steffano Korper and Juanita Ellis. 1999. 284p. Academic, $39.95 (0-12-421160-7).

Explains how any company or individual can help build the e-empire. Readers will find the tools needed to build the infrastructure for an efficient, profitable e-commerce venture, including virtual storefronts, e-mail and fax marketing, and secure and convenient transactions.

The E-Commerce Question and Answer Book: A Survival Guide for Business Managers. By Anita Rosen. 1999. 210p. AMACOM, $19.95 (0-8144-0525-8).

An important part of the e-commerce revolution is integrating this transformative force into an overall business strategy. This guide helps business managers understand the basics: What are cookies? Is my product a good candidate for e-commerce? Do I need a programmer to create a Web page? How does encryption technology work?

An IBM Guide to Doing Business on the Internet. By Kendra Bonnett. 2000. 261p. McGraw-Hill, $24.95 (0-07031-8468).

A guide to learning how to anticipate the market, understanding how to apply trends to meet a business's objectives, and determining the most effective way to present online capabilities to customers.

Plunkett's E-Commerce & Internet Business Almanac [with CD-ROM]. By Jack W. Plunkett. 2001. 500p. Plunkett Research, $249.99 (1-891775-21-9).

Profiles 400 major companies that operate at significant levels of revenues and services. This guide provides its overview through easy-to-use tables on all facets of business on the Internet. Industry group information and trends are also included, and some rankings are given.

Pushing the Digital Frontier: Insights into the Changing Landscape of E-Business. Ed. by Nirmal Pal and Judith M. Ray. 2001. 288p. AMACOM, $27.95 (0-8144-0644-0).

Affiliated with Penn State's new eBusiness Research Center, these editors present best-practices models for the strategic challenges confronting companies in the new economy. Measuring return on e-business assets and funds, using Web personalization to develop markets, instigating collaborative commerce, and developing ways to manage technology and its regulation are issues of primary concern.

Scaling for E-Business: Technologies, Models, Performance, and Capacity Planning. By Daniel A. Menasce and Virgilio A. F. Almeida. 2000. 449p. Prentice-Hall, $49.99 (0-13-086328-9).

Introduces a methodology that enables users to approach Web site performance problems in a methodical and quantitative way. An especially important factor is helping to predict how much capacity will be needed as demand grows and changes.

Start Right in E-Business: A Step-by-Step Guide to Successful E-business Implementation. By Bennet P. Lientz and Kathryn P. Rea. 2000. 326p. Academic, $44.95 (0-12-449977-5).

Based on more than 50 e-business implementation projects, each chapter provides detailed guidelines for helping transform a business into an e-enterprise. Highlights include specific actions for e-business implementation, plus a chapter on technology, management, vendors, and organizational issues.

Electronic Journals

E-Commerce Times. 1998–2001. Triad Commerce Group [http://www.ecommercetimes.com].

Free online publication with daily news and feature articles for entrepreneurs and companies.

The Industry Standard. 1995–2001. Internet Industry Publishing [http://www.thestandard.com].

Specializing in the Internet economy, this journal is written for the general business reader. It provides weekly summaries of related news. Special reports look at specific industries in depth, and some reports

Special Features

combine company profiles, recent articles, analysis, and even downloadable PowerPoint slides.

The International Journal of Electronic Commerce. Ed. by Vladimir Zwass. 1996–2001. Sharpe [http://www.gvsu.edu/ssb/ijec].

Devoted to all aspects of e-commerce, this refereed academic journal looks at infrastructure, technology application, globalization, intellectual property rights, social dynamics, and statistics related to Internet communication. Content is not searchable.

Internet Resources

Gateways

About.com: Electronic Commerce. 2001. [http://ecommerce.about.com].

Well-designed and easy-to-use Internet guide to electronic commerce with feature articles, Web site guides, newsletters, discussion forums, and chat. Among the topics that are included are building a Web store, B2B (business-to-business) resources, start-up ideas, banner advertising, portal sites, jobs, and security and privacy.

Business 2.0. 2001. [http://www.business2.com].

Huge megasite containing a large e-business section as well as an E-commerce Web guide. Includes information for manufacturers, retailers, and service businesses developing or expanding a Web presence. The Research and Forecasts section is outstanding.

ecommerce-guide.com. 2001. INT Media Group [http://ecommerce.internet.com].

Many useful links to reviews, news, products and services, columns, and resources are found on this easy-to-use site sponsored by IBM. It helps users locate industry trends and newsletters and check domain names.

Guide to E-Commerce. 2000. Cornell University [http://www.ilr.cornell.edu/library/reference/guides/ecommerce/].

This excellent site from Cornell provides Web pages in general, international, legal, news, and governmental areas. Searchable and well organized but not updated frequently.

Internet and Marketing—E-Commerce. Ed. by Chng Chor Noy. 1999–2000. NTU Library [http://www.ntu.edu.sg/library/mktg/ecomm.htm].

Coming from NTU Library, in Singapore, this site has everything: reports and statistics, journals and newsletters, e-commerce sites around the world, and mailing lists. Great for practical business information as well as academic research.

Yahoo! Business and EconomyElectronic Commerce. [http://dir.yahoo.com/business_and_economy/electronic_commerce/].

Especially important categories are bar codes, digital money, magazines, online shopping centers, organizations, privacy seal programs, software, and tax issues. Covers manufacturing as well as retail industry, with good international coverage.

Law

E-Commerce Law Source.com. Ed. by Michael Sweig. 1999–2001. Mudhouse Management [http://www.e-commercelawsource.com].

This privately funded, comprehensive law and tax resource for e-commerce has links to sites on e-commerce ethics, industry registry, portals, dispute resolution, franchise law, and education. The News section is updated daily and given subject descriptors to group stories. Statistics

CyberAtlas. 2001. INT Media Group [http://cyberatlas.Internet.com].

An outstanding statistics site, with international coverage of demographics, geographics, traffic patterns, and B2B information. Archives extend back to 1998 in most cases.

Internet Economy Indicators. [http://www.internetindicators.com].

Archives here go back to 1998 in this site offering employment and revenue figures on the Internet economy. Full studies done by the University of Texas' Center for Research in Electronic Commerce are available for 1999, 2000, and 2001 in PDF.

Technology

AllBusiness. 2001. [http://www.allbusiness.com].

A guide to everything about the technical aspects of building a business online. Discusses accepting credit card payments, holding online auctions, and designing and building "a killer site."

—*Susan C. Awe*

Core Collection: History of Science

The history of science is the history of human efforts to understand and describe the world and then to control the forces, mechanisms, and characteristics of that world. It is not only a time line of what was or is known in the very specific disciplines of today but also a history of the ways people acquire knowledge. Like other fields of inquiry, science continues to be influenced by philosophers, writers, researchers, and thinkers of the past as well as the present.

Any collection of representative works on the history of science will be eclectic and go beyond those items labeled "history of science." For this bibliography, we have focused on items that highlight key aspects of science history and, taken together, present a broad view. Some items are scholarly, but most are intellectually accessible to the general reader and high-school and beginning college student.

We have divided this basic collection into currently available dictionaries, encyclopedias, a chronology, biographies, guides to the literature, and Web sites to support a history of science collection. Web sites were last accessed on October 1, 2001.

Dictionaries

A Dictionary of the History of Science. By Anton Sebastian. 2001. 373p. Parthenon, $65 (1-85070-418-X).

This recent publication defines scientific terms from antiquity to modern times. The history of medicine is excluded. Brief entries include cross-references in bold and *see* references in italics. Entries reflect the interconnected relationship between scientific pioneers and their fields. Includes some illustrations and photographs. Patrons at all levels will find this source useful in public and academic libraries.

World of Scientific Discovery. Ed. by Kimberley A. McGrath and Bridget Travers. 1999. 1186p. Gale, $105 (0-7876-2760-7).

This guide presents both biographical and conceptual articles in biology, chemistry, agriculture, health, physics, and other sciences and features the men and women who made important scientific discoveries. The 1,083 entries are in alphabetical order, with cross-references in bold. A subject index is included. The audience is general science readers, including high-school and college students.

Encyclopedias

Encyclopedia of the History of Arabic Science. Ed by Rushdi Rashid and Regis Morelon. 3v. 1996. 1,264p. Routledge, $330 (0-415-02063-8).

The history of western European and American science traces its roots back to Arabic science. This encyclopedia chronicles the contributions of Arabic scientists in astronomy, mathematics, physical sciences, technology, and life sciences. Scholarly essays describe the sources of Arabic science and its contributions, translation, and integration into Western thought. Includes indexes for names, subjects, and treatises.

Encyclopedia of the Scientific Revolution: From Copernicus to Newton. By Wilbur Applebaum. 2000. 700p. Garland, $150 (0-8153-1503-1).

This volume chronicles the extraordinary changes in "natural philosophy" from the beginning of the sixteenth century to the end of the seventeenth century. It includes broad coverage of political, religious, and technological factors in the development of medicine, scientific institutions, and social conditions. The 441 clearly written entries include short bibliographies. Also included are a broad topical outline, chronology, and index. Named as a 2001 Outstanding Reference Source by RUSA's Reference Sources Committee.

The History of Science in the United States: An Encyclopedia. By Marc Rothenberg. 2000. 500p. Garland, $125 (0-8153-0762-4).

Upper-level undergraduates, graduate students, faculty, and general readers will enjoy this chronicle of the development of science in the

U.S. The broad spectrum of contributors explores the relationships between American science and American universities, government, and professional societies. Entries cover biographies, scientific societies, and government-sponsored science. Includes recent historical research on the advancement of science in the U.S.

Chronology

The Timetables of Science: A Chronology of the Most Important People and Events in the History of Science. By Alexander Hellemans and Bryan H. Bunch. 1991. 672p. Touchstone, $22 (0-671-73328-1).

The fact that this older chronology is still in print reflects its continued utility. It lists important events in the history of science by year and by discipline, including astronomy, biology, chemistry, earth sciences, mathematics, medicine, physics, and technology. Entries describe who the relevant scientist was and what he or she discovered. Includes sidebars with interesting ancillary stories. Useful for researchers at all levels.

Biographies

The Biographical Dictionary of Women in Science: Pioneering Lives from Ancient Times to the Mid-20th Century. Ed. by Marilyn Ogilvie and Joy Harvey. 2000. 1,499p. Routledge, $250 (0-415-92038-8).

Probing the lives and achievements of women scientists from antiquity to the recent past, this source has broad coverage of nationalities and fields of specialization. The term *scientist* is broadly defined to include some journalists, midwives, and others not always covered in science sources. Each entry offers a short biographical summary; a discussion of education, work history, and accomplishments; and a bibliography of primary and secondary materials. Indexes provide access by subject, country, time period, and occupation.

The Cambridge Dictionary of Scientists. Ed. by Ian Millar and others. 1996. 399p. Cambridge, $17.95 (0-521-56718-1).

This volume of more than 1,300 short biographies focuses on the major contributions of scientists from 38 countries in physics, chemistry, biology, geology, astronomy, mathematics, medicine, meteorology, and technology. Although it is not as extensive as some other works, the people on whom basic information is often requested will be found here. A new edition is anticipated in 2002.

Concise Dictionary of Scientific Biography. 2d ed. 2000. 1,097p. Scribner, $125 (0-684-80631-2).

Libraries that do not own Scribner's vast *Dictionary of Scientific Biography* (1970–1980) may want to add this abridgement. It includes all of the scientists covered in the parent volumes but reduces entry length by about 90 percent. The scientists who are covered died before 1981.

Guides to the Literature

Isis Cumulative Bibliography, 1986–1995: A Bibliography of the History of Science Formed from the Annual *Isis* Current Bibliographies. 4v. Ed. by John Neu. 1997. Science History Publications, $299.95 (0-88135-131-8).

Isis is the quarterly journal of the History of Science Society. Its bibliography appears every January as a special issue. These volumes are the third supplement to *Isis Cumulative Bibliography:* A *Bibliography of the History of Science Formed from Isis Critical Bibliographies*, 1–90, 1913–65 (Mansell, 1971–84). Along with *Current Bibliography in the History of Technology*, the *Bibliografia Italiana di Storia della Scienza*, and the *Wellcome Bibliography of the History of Medicine*, the *Isis* bibliographies form a component of the Research Library Group's *History of Science and Technology Database* (single institution price of $2,750 for one to five users). Whether researchers use it in printed or electronic form, *Isis Cumulative Bibliography* is a comprehensive bibliography of the history of science.

Reader's Guide to the History of Science. Ed. by Arne Hessenbruch. 2000. 934p. Fitzroy Dearborn, $135 (1-884964-29-X).

This volume is an extensive guide to the bibliography of the history of science, technology, and medicine. It includes essays on people, topics, disciplines, and scientific institutions. Entries are listed in alphabetical order, with a thematic list in the front of the book and a list of books cited in the back. There are a general subject index and cross-references at the end of each signed entry. For upper-level undergraduates, graduates, and professors.

Scientific Laws, Principles and Theories: A Reference Guide. By Robert E. Krebs. 2001. 408p. Greenwood, $65 (0-313-30957-4).

The outcomes of science are often laws, principles, and theories. This alphabetically arranged volume summarizes these historically significant ideas briefly and with style. Each entry includes the name of the law, principle or theory, the relevant discipline, complete names and dates of the person(s) credited with it, and the country of origin. The bibliography is made up mostly of history of science books.

Web Sites

Although many colleges and universities have useful Web pages on the history of science, we include these four as exemplars of how such pages might be presented as well as for the wealth of links available on each. All four include some of the same basic links to a fascinating range of information. The annotations note the organization and unique features of each.

History of Science and Ethics Internet Resources. Louisiana State University. [http://www.lib.lsu.edu/sci/chem/internet/history.html].

The LSU page is the shortest of these pages but offers a basic set of links to commonly requested information. The emphasis is on gateway sites. It also includes references to several print books. The alchemy references are of particular interest. This is a good site to use with high-school and lower-level college students.

History of Science and Technology: A Guide to Internet Resources. University of Delaware Library. [http://www2.lib.udel.edu/subj/hsci/internet.htm].

This is a straightforward site of simple design with a table of contents at the top and all sections on a single page. The subheadings speak to the range of resources available electronically: "Topics in the History of Science and Technology"; "Bibliographies and Research Guides"; "Databases and Information Sources"; "Societies, Associations, and Other Organizations"; "Periodicals: Printed and Electronic Magazines, Journals, and Newsletters"; and "Mailing Lists and News Groups" are a few examples.

Internet History of Science Sourcebook. Ed. by Paul Halsall. Fordham University. [http://www.fordham.edu/halsall/science/sciencesbook.html].

This large sourcebook is a subset derived from three even larger ones at Fordham on ancient, medieval, and modern history Internet resources. Its organization revolves around cultures, history, and locales, from the ancient world to the industrial revolution and on to specific modern disciplines. The table of contents is several print pages long. The compiler has included an impressive array of links to materials owned by the university along with individual Web sites and gateways.

Science and Technology Resources on the Internet: Selected Web Resources in the History of Science. By Marianne Stowell Bracke and Paul J. Bracke. [http://www.library.ucsb.edu/istl/99-winter/internet.html].

This site is an article within the online journal *Issues in Science and Technology Librarianship*, so its layout is more reflective of print publications than of a Web page. Each of the resources has a sometimes lengthy description and review. The compilers made biographies a separate heading and point to suggested resources for the history of specific disciplines, from agriculture to physics.

—*Linda Loos Scarth and Jack O'Gorman*

Core Collection: Urban Studies

> What is the city but the people?
> —William Shakespeare, *Coriolanus*

Urban studies, which incorporates aspects of city planning, sociology, municipal government, and demographics, is an attempt to understand the urban environment through narrative, applied research, and statistics. The collection described below is geared toward public libraries

Special Features

and smaller academic libraries without an urban studies program. The emphasis is on American cities, not because of any inherent superiority of the works in this area but in the interest of limiting the scope.

To make an urban studies collection most relevant, it should be somewhat idiosyncratic and reflect the local community. Librarians may consider starting a photograph file of local urban sites, for example, and also should collect city and county annual reports, budgets, and other documents of interest to local citizens.

General Works

The City in History: Its Origins, Its Transformations, and Its Prospects. By Lewis Mumford. 1968. 734p. Harcourt, $25 (0-15-618035-9).

This thorough narrative discusses the origins and development of cities. Although it has not been revised and is therefore somewhat dated, its comprehensive bibliography and index (with some illustrations) make this a valuable addition for students and researchers. In 1999, this book was listed in the Modern Library Top 100. Another book on that list, Studs Terkel's *Working* (Random, 1974), includes first-person testimony of city life and might also be of interest to readers in this field.

The Death and Life of Great American Cities. By Jane Jacobs. 1993. 624p. Modern Library, $18.95 (0-679-60047-7); Vintage, paper, $14 (0-679-74195-X).

Originally published 40 years ago and revised several times, this tome acted as a karate chop to the ethic of urban renewal (large housing projects, highways, etc.). Jacobs admonished planners to help build communities through smaller scale and more interactive design. The book is more literary than scholarly (there is no bibliography, for example), but Jacobs' analysis still packs a powerful punch and is considered a classic.

Encyclopedias and Dictionaries

The City: A Dictionary of Quotable Thought on Cities and Urban Life. By James A. Clapp.1984. 288p. Center for Urban Policy Research, o.p.

A very eclectic group of quotes (from Jane Addams to Oscar Wilde) have been drawn from literature, political speeches, interviews, and other sources. This will be of help to those writing papers and also for those looking for a poetic glimpse of city life. Out-of-print but available from *Alibris* [http://www.alibris.com] for around $35.

Encyclopedia of Urban America: The Cities and Suburbs. 2v. Ed. by Neil Larry Shumsky. 1998. 974p. ABC-CLIO, $175 (0-87436-846-4).

Cities are dynamic places that often defy categorization; still, this A–Z coverage captures and explains the various factors that make cities such complex places. There are about 550 entries, written by 350 contributors. The signed entries are of varying lengths and include detailed descriptions of the important and enduring urban impact of women, immigrants, people of color, and other groups.

Handbooks and Yearbooks

America's Top-Rated Cities: A Statistical Handbook. 4v. 2001. Grey House, $195 (1-891482-68-8).

This four-volume set evaluates 80 cities with populations of more than 100,000 that have been cited in the media as top places to live and work. Each volume covers a different geographic region (Southern, Western, Eastern, and Central). Cities are not "ranked" as they are in the popular *Places Rated Almanac* but are evaluated using statistics, such as average health-care costs, educational attainment, average wages, tax rates, and other criteria.

America's Top-Rated Smaller Cities: A Statistical Profile. 3d ed. 2000. 800p. Grey House, $200 (1-891482-65-3).

Many guides and ranking books describe major metropolitan areas, so this fills a void by focusing on 60 top U.S. cities with populations between 25,000 and 100,000. It covers the same general economic and demographic terrain as its sister publication, *America's Top-Rated Cities*, and will appeal to those interested in life outside the skyscrapers.

Facts about the Cities. 2d ed. Comp. by Allan Carpenter. 1996. 632p. Wilson, $95 (0-8242-0897-8).

This handbook provides basic statistical and economic data for more than 350 U.S. cities. The capsule descriptions and general overview of population, education, housing, and other categories will be of value to students and researchers.

Municipal Year Book: The Authoritative Source Book of Local Government Data and Developments. 2001. International City-County Management Association, $84.95 (0-87326-861-X).

Both a directory of local government and an excellent source of detailed articles on technology, transportation, and other public policy issues. Also includes salary information for police, fire, and other city personnel. Comprehensive subject bibliographies on topics such as planning and public finance make this an ideal research aid.

Places Rated Almanac. 6th ed. By David Savageau. 496p. 1999. Hungry Minds, paper, $24.95 (0-02-863447-0).

This serial always generates press coverage when it is released, as it proclaims the number one place to live in North America. The authors are careful to explain the limits to rankings, but there is always some controversy as people are rankled or pleased with the findings. The book ranks 354 metropolitan areas in nine categories: costs of living; transportation; jobs; education; climate; crime; the arts; health care; and recreation. This sixth edition follows tradition by listing metro areas alphabetically in the final chapter, along with the area's score for each of the categories.

Demographics and Statistics

City and County Extra: Annual Metro, City, and County Data Book. Decennial Census ed. 2001. Bernan, $110 (0-89059-361-2).

A statistical gold mine, this has almost everything demographic that you were afraid a patron would ask. The data are drawn primarily from federal government sources, such as the Economic Census, and the tables provide valuable information, such as local area wholesale and retail trade; housing and employment; and federal funds and city government finances.

The Sourcebook of ZIP Code Demographics. 15th ed. 2000. 1,725p. CACI Marketing Systems, $495 (0-91841-777-5).

This comprehensive work will be of interest to those involved in grants research, market analysis, and other projects requiring detailed data at the micro level. All of the U.S. ZIP codes are represented, with data on income, population, race, spending potential and other categories. Much of this information is derived from U.S. government data, but CACI uses its own models to crunch the numbers. Libraries with larger budgets might also consider the publisher's *Sourcebook of County Demographics*.

Internet Sites

Often, a city's Web site is a good place to get demographic information as well as an overall flavor of the local urban environment. A good portal to link to sites is *Official City Sites* [http://officialcitysites.org]. Other solid urban studies Web sites include:

Smart Growth Network. [http://www.smartgrowth.org].

Although this site has a political agenda in promoting "development that better serves the economic, environmental and social needs of communities," it also provides detailed, full-text documents that describe political and economic issues of vital interest to students and researchers.

The Urban Institute. [http://www.urban.org].

This nonpartisan policy research organization has a wide range of reports and other material on important urban studies topics, such as housing, crime, and child care. Many of the reports are full-text, which will really please patrons.

U.S. Census Bureau. [http://www.census.gov/].

The U.S. government is putting more and more of its data on the Internet, and the Census Bureau has done an admirable job of providing easy access to its vast collection of demographic and statistical information. The 2000 Census is here, as well as the Economic Census and other data. Novices may need a little help in following links the first time around, but this is a user-friendly and very valuable research tool.

—*M. Uri Toch*

Dark Reference

Horror fiction often includes aspects of the occult and the paranormal. The following handful of reference books, all aimed at the general reader, will help libraries that need to reanimate their collections on these topics.

Encyclopedia of Ghosts and Spirits. 2d ed. By Rosemary Guiley. 2000. 448p. Facts On File, $65 (0-8160-4085-0).

This readable compilation of facts pertaining to actual investigations and theories as well as the history of ghosts and hauntings greatly expands the first edition. Many entries are followed by references for further reading, including Web sites. A few illustrations are provided, and *see* references are frequent.

Encyclopedia of Occultism and Parapsychology. 2v. 5th ed. Ed. by Leslie Shepard and Gordon J. Melton. 2001. Gale, $350 (0-8103-8570-8).

The latest edition of this standard source has more than 300 new entries. Readers will find information on persons, organizations, publications, phenomena, mystical beings, and more. Bibliographies are attached to many entries. Discussions of controversial topics are carefully balanced.

Encyclopedia of the Paranormal. Ed. by Gordon Stein. 1996. 872p. Prometheus, $160 (1-57372-012-5).

More than 90 entries exploring various paranormal phenomenon take a decidedly skeptical approach. All entries are followed by a bibliography. This is a good choice for libraries that want to offer balance in collections that contain more middle-of-the-road or blatantly pro-paranormal works.

Encyclopedia of the Strange, Mystical, and Unexplained. By Rosemary Guiley. 2001. 688p. Random, $14.99 (0-517-16278-4).

The author brings together in one comprehensive work a variety of "alternate realities" for the general reader. More than 500 entries are arranged in alphabetical order, with many cross-references. Sources are provided at the end of each entry. Biographies of significant people and a few illustrations and portraits are included.

Encyclopedia of Wicca and Witchcraft. By Raven Grimassi. 2000. 528p. Llewellyn, $24.95 (1-56718-257-7).

Contemporary Wicca and witchcraft traditions are described and arranged in alphabetical listings. Entries vary in length and cover both prominent figures in the history of witchcraft and contemporary practitioners. Mythological characters and creatures are defined in relation to their significance in Wiccan rituals and beliefs.

Encyclopedia of Witches and Witchcraft. 2d ed. By Rosemary Guiley. 1999. 432p. Facts On File, $82.50 (0-8160-3848-1).

Encyclopedia of Wicca and Witchcraft (above) is written for believers, but this volume takes a more neutral tone. More than 500 articles cover the Western tradition from ancient times to the present. An extensive bibliography supplements suggestions for reading given at the ends of articles.

Man, Myth and Magic: The Illustrated Encyclopedia of Mythology, Religion, and the Unknown. 21v. 2d ed. Ed. by Richard Cavendish. 1994. 2,976p. Marshall Cavendish, $714.21 (1-854-35731-X).

This is the second edition of the highly illustrated multivolume set. Articles have been contributed by nearly 200 of the leading authorities in each subject area. The scope encompasses both historical and contemporary aspects of spiritual traditions. The entries vary in length and are designed for the general reader. Cross-references, bibliographies, and a detailed index assist the user in locating information.

Satanism Today: An Encyclopedia of Religion, Folklore, and Popular Culture. By James R. Lewis. 2001. 371p. ABC-CLIO, $85 (1-57607-292-4).

Lewis offers a remarkably evenhanded survey of "contemporary images of the devil"—not only "religious Satanism" but also various satanic organizations, traditions, and personalities. Most articles have a list of further reading. Web sites are also listed because many Satanists have considerable Internet activity.

The Sorcerer's Companion: A Guide to the Magical World of Harry Potter. By Allan Zola Kronzek and Elizabeth Kronzek. 2000. 286p. Broadway Books, paper, $15 (0-7679-0847-3).

This book explores the true history, folklore, and mythology behind the magical practices, creatures, and personalities that appear in J. K. Rowling's Harry Potter books (the third of which, *Harry Potter and the Prisoner of Azkaban*, received a 1999 Bram Stoker Award from the Horror Writers Association in the "Works for Young Readers" category). The entries are detailed and expand on references found within the books.

—*Charlotte Decker*

Horror Reference Shelf

There aren't many reference tools devoted exclusively to horror literature; instead, horror is often lumped together with science fiction and fantasy. But though reference books on horror lit are scarce, there seems to be no end of titles on film. McFarland, in particular, has carved a niche for itself in its coverage of horror films; the full array is listed on its Web site [http://www.mcfarlandpub.com].

Our list is geared more toward fandom and readers' (or viewers') advisory than scholarship. We have not tried to be comprehensive but to let you know about horror-related titles published since 1990 that would be at home on the reference shelves of a medium-sized to large public library. In the interests of space, we have shied away from books that cover the various horror subgenres—Dracula, Frankenstein, slashers, zombies, etc. For more scholarly items, you can refer to "Core Collection: SF/Fantasy Reference Sources" in our May 15, 1999, issue.

Fantasy and Horror: A Critical and Historical Guide to Literature, Illustration, Film, TV, Radio, and the Internet. Ed. by Neil Barron. 1999. 816p. Scarecrow, $85 (0-8108-3596-7).

This is the most complete guide to horror and fantasy, covering almost 3,000 works of fiction in addition to other media. Annotations, the work of a number of contributors, are analytical and detailed.

Hooked on Horror: A Guide to Reading Interests in Horror Fiction. 2d ed. By Anthony J. Fonseca and June Michele Pulliam. 2002. 400p. Libraries Unlimited, $55 (1-56308-904-1).

Even the smallest public library will want to have this readers' advisory tool, which is part of the Genreflecting Advisory Series. In the first edition, books and a few key film titles are listed under a number of subgenres—ghosts, mummies, demonic possession, splatterpunk, and more. Also listed are collections and anthologies, bibliographies of important authors, works of history and criticism, periodicals, organizations, awards, series, and Web sites. We have not seen the second edition, which is scheduled to be published in December 2002.

Horror Film Directors, 1931–1990. By Dennis Fischer. 1991. 877p. McFarland, $95 (0-89950-609-7).

More than 50 "major" directors, such as John Carpenter and David Cronenberg, are covered in extended (7–30 pages in length) biocritical essays, and lesser figures are covered in 48 shorter articles.

Horror Film Stars. 3d ed. By Michael R. Pitts. 2002. 568p. McFarland, paper, $39.95 (0-7864-1052-3).

This revised and expanded edition covers 80 performers, from Lon Chaney Sr. and Bela Lugosi to Jamie Lee Curtis. Entries, which range from 3 pages to more than 20 for Christopher Lee, provide a few biographical details but focus mainly on the performers' horror film careers. Entries for major stars conclude with complete filmographies.

Reference Guide to Science Fiction, Fantasy, and Horror. 2d ed. By Michael Burgess and Lisa R. Bartle. 2003. 598p. Libraries Unlimited, price not determined (1-56308-548-8).

Scheduled to be published in January 2003, this updates the 1992 version of an important resource. If the new edition is anything like the first, it will evaluate hundreds of encyclopedias, dictionaries, bibliographies, and other reference sources in imaginative literature.

Special Features

Science Fiction, Fantasy, and Horror Film Sequels, Series, and Remakes: An Illustrated Filmography, with Plot Synopses and Critical Commentary. By Kim R. Holston and Tom Winchester. 1997. 607p. McFarland, $75 (0-7864-0155-9).

This guide profiles the sequels and remakes of more than 400 movies released between 1931 and 1995. Emphasis is on fantasy and the supernatural and ranges from whimsical family favorites, such as Miracle on 34th Street, to the truly horrific: The Exorcist and Night of the Living Dead.

Science Fiction, Fantasy, and Horror Writers. 2v. 1994. UXL, $95 (0-8103-9865-6).

Eighty writers of interest to young adults are covered in this set, from Mary Shelley to Stephen King and Anne Rice. For each, a 1,500-word biographical essay gives specifics on early life, education, career, and unique characteristics as a genre writer. The essays are accompanied by photos and sidebars

Science Fiction, Horror and Fantasy Film and Television Credits. 3v. 2d ed. By Harris M. Lentz. 2001. 2,261p. McFarland, $195 (0-7864-0942-8).

This edition revises and expands the original 1983 two-volume set and its 1989 and 1994 supplements. Actors and actresses are listed with their credits in volume 1, followed by a similar listing for directors, screenwriters, special-effects technicians, and others who work behind the scenes. A filmography comprises volume 2, and television programs are covered in volume 3.

St. James Guide to Horror, Ghost and Gothic Writers. Ed. by David Pringle. 1998. 746p. Gale, $170 (1-55862-206-3).

More than 400 writers in English and 25 foreign-language writers are profiled here, with biographical summaries, extensive bibliographies, and critical analyses. The names one might expect, such as Stephen King and Bram Stoker, are included, as are some not so closely associated with the genre (Charles Dickens, Edith Wharton) and children's authors Christopher Pike and R. L. Stine.

Supernatural Fiction Writers: Fantasy and Horror. 2v. Ed. by Everett F. Bleiler. 1985. 1,169p. Scribner, $210 (0-684-17808-7).
Supernatural Fiction Writers: Fantasy and Horror. 2v. 2d ed. Ed. by Richard Bleiler. 2002. 760p. Scribner, $240 (0-684-31250-6).

The 1985 volumes are primarily historical, with a small section on contemporary (post-1960) writers such as Ramsey Campbell and Stephen King. The new edition, due out later this year, updates rather than supersedes the first. It has new entries on those contemporary writers covered in 1985 and adds authors, such as J. K. Rowling, who have emerged since the earlier set was published.

Terror Television: American Series, 1970–1999. By John Kenneth Muir. 2001. 685p. McFarland, $75 (0-7864-0890-1).

Beginning with Rod Serling's Night Gallery, Muir offers chronological coverage of 40 series featuring elements of terror. Entries range in length from 3 pages for a program that lasted only a few episodes to more than 40 pages for The X Files.

VideoHound's Horror Show: 999 Hair-Raising, Hellish, and Humorous Movies. By Mike Mayo. 552p. 1998. Visible Ink, paper, $21.95 (1-57859-047-7).

Like other VideoHound titles, this one provides brief information, reviews, and ratings for films from Abbott and Costello Meet Dr. Jekyll and Mr. Hyde to Zombie Lake. Several different indexes aid access. An emphasis on entertainment makes this a good choice for public libraries.

What Fantastic Fiction Do I Read Next? 2d ed. 1999. Gale, $110 (0-7876-4476-5).

This installment in the useful readers' advisory series What Do I Read Next? covers more than 4,800 titles published between 1989 and 1998. Each entry provides author and title; story type, character, time period, and locale descriptors; a short summary; and related title suggestions.

—*Mary Ellen Quinn*

More Sites on Sleuths: Women of Mystery

Our mission for this year's Mystery Showcase was to find some Web sites about women mystery writers. An initial search indicated that there is a veritable treasure trove of information concerning these authors, with Web pages focusing on them as a group as well as individual home pages. Many of the sites have an international scope. There is, of course, some overlapping of information and links, and, sadly, some sites have not been updated recently. The examples given below demonstrate the variety and depth of material available. A delightful aspect of this search was the thread of humor permeating so many of these pages. All sites were last accessed on March 19, 2002.

African American Mystery Page. [http://www.aamystery.com/].

This is a small site that covers mysteries by both male and female authors but that contains a higher number of works by women. In addition to the author information, there is a list of reference materials on black characters, African American detective fiction, and black mysteries.

Feminist Mystery Corner. [http://www.feminist.org/arts/mys_main.html].

This page on the Feminist Majority Foundation Web site has several interesting facets. "Authors and Books" gives an alphabetical list of authors, with many links to home pages. Usually the name of each series' protagonist is provided. "Mystery Reviews" features a small number of titles, most published in 1997 and 1998, and a listing entitled "Online Mystery Resources" that has links not only to other Web pages focusing on female mystery writers' organizations but also to relevant magazines, newsletters, and TV mysteries.

Femmes Fatales. [http://members.aol.com/femmesweb/index.html].

This newsletter covers various professional activities of interest to women mystery writers, with photo essays, news about recent publications, and related Web links.

ID 255: Women Mystery and Detective Fiction Writers and the Rise of Feminism. By Randy Abbott [http://cedar.evansville.edu/~ra2/].

This site has photographs of 10 authors who span the last 150 years, from Anna Katharine Green to Patricia Cornwell, with links to either Web sites with additional information, interviews, or home pages. Abbott also provides connections to bookstores and to Web pages with electronic texts.

Mysterious Strands. By Cindy Silberblatt. [http://home.att.net/~csilberblatt/mystery.htm].

Contains news of Canadian mystery writers (not necessarily women), with an extensive list of authors, reference sources, conventions, organizations, magazines and newsletters, bookstores and publishers, characters, TV mysteries pages, and a collection of online assorted mysterious links.

Mystery Women. [http://www.mysterywomen.freeserve.co.uk/history.HTM].

This is a British group, formed in 1998, which seeks to "raise the awareness and profile of female crime writers, and to provide a forum for the discussion of crime fiction by enthusiastic crime fiction addicts." They produce a newsletter and hold meetings every few weeks with a variety of activities and guests. Their members, many of whom are published authors, hail not only from the U.K. and the U.S. but also from Australia, Canada, Germany, Italy, and South Africa.

Murder She Writes: Washington Women Mystery Writers. [http://www.plu.edu/~egbersgl/murder.html].

A short list of female mystery writers, most of whom are located on the West Coast, giving their occupations and titles of works to date.

Nuns, Mothers, and Others. [http://www.nmomysteries.com/body.htm].

A group of four writers who work together to promote their material. They publish a newsletter as a means of corresponding with their readers and discussing their writing techniques.

Sisters in Crime. [http://www.sistersincrime.org/].

Sisters in Crime is a professional organization that works to facilitate the writing, publishing, and networking of women mystery writers. The group is also dedicated to preventing discrimination within the profession. Sisters in Crime, which was formed in 1986, is international in scope and has a membership of more than 3,300, with chapters in the U.S., Canada, Australia, and Germany. Male members are welcome. Links include mystery organizations, personal Web sites, bookstores, mystery-award sites, mystery presses, and many other mystery-related sites.

Sisters in Crime Internet Chapter. [http://www.sinc-ic.org/].

This subset of Sisters of Crime seeks to provide a forum for those members who do not have a local chapter. Membership information, excerpts from members' recent publications, news of awards, forthcoming conferences, and signing schedules are featured. Other links include members' home pages, a variety of mystery sites, and "Tools and Source Materials for Writers," where writers can find information on such topics as crime-scene investigation, forensic evidence, poison, and law-enforcement procedures.

Women of Mystery. By Dabney Hart [http://www.cosmos-club.org/journals/1999/hart.html].

Hart focuses specifically on female authors and estimates that since 1878 more than 3,500 series mysteries have been written by women. She provides a detailed history with a bibliography.

—Jacqueline Jackson

Other People's Words: Recent Quotation Books

"Of the making of [quotation] books there is no end." Or so it seems. Because the last time RBB focused on collections of quotations was nearly a decade ago [RBB N 15 93], it was time to take another look. Once again the spotlight is on single-subject quotation books rather than general anthologies. Once again the number of available choices is daunting: a quick online search of *Books in Print* using the subjects "reference" and "quotations" yields 2,993 hits. Limiting these to books published between 2000 and 2002 reduces that number to a mere 377. Even a casual search at Amazon.com results in 5,151 items with the keyword *quotations*. This article looks at 20 specialized collections of quotations that were chosen mainly to illustrate the variety of titles available.

African American Quotations. By Richard Newman. 2000. 504p. Checkmark, paper, $18.95 (1-8160-4439-2).
People on People: The Oxford Dictionary of Biographical Quotations. Ed. by Susan Ratcliffe. 2001. 612p. Oxford, $25 (0-19-866261-0).
The Quotable Woman: The First 5,000 Years. 5th ed. By Elaine T. Partnow. 2001. 974p. Facts On File, $75 (0-8160-4012-5).

Quotations about actual people, like biographies, may range in tone from tribute to trashing. This trio of titles includes more tribute than trash, and two of the works represent people usually underrepresented in quotation collections. *African American Quotations* is a compact, solid collection of the words of hundreds of Americans of color, past and present. The quotations are arranged by subject, numbered consecutively, and presented alphabetically by author. Occupation and years of birth and death are provided for each speaker. The layout is clear and attractive. Three indexes—name, subject, and occupation—provide quick and easy access to the riches within. Although narrower in scope than Dorothy Winbush Riley's *My Soul Looks Back, 'Less I Forget: A Collection of Quotations by People of Color* (HarperPerennial, 1995), which quoted people from around the world, this collection's national focus, attractive presentation, and careful organization make it an excellent choice for school and public library collections.

People on People is that rare kind of reference book—one that invites casual browsing as well as serious searching. Comprising quotations by famous people about famous people, it spans the centuries and a few continents as well. Art, literature, politics, and show business are the milieus for both the quoted and those they are quoted about.

Entries are arranged alphabetically by the name of the person referred to in the numbered quotations that follow. Each entrant is described in a single line, and birth and death years are supplied. Quotations about (and sometimes by) a person are presented in a numbered list with the speaker's name and years and the source. An author index allows one to easily locate all the quotations attributed to a person, with keywords and subjects indicated. As is often the case with celebrity biographies, the nasty or negative quotations are among the most memorable.

The first edition of Partnow's *The Quotable Woman* was published a quarter of a century ago, and the latest edition is the biggest and best. As carefully organized and thoroughly researched as one could ask for from a quotation book, this one provides, unlike many others, the title of the work from which the quotation is drawn. The words of some 3,667 women (952 of them from non-English-speaking countries) are presented chronologically. The name of each contributor is numbered consecutively, and within each entry, quotations are also assigned a number. Four indexes (biographical, career and occupation, ethnicity and nationality, and subject) provide not only multiple points of access to the quoted material but additional information on the quoted, such as brief biographical information and classification by occupation or nationality. The subject index is exceptionally thorough and very carefully cross-referenced. In summary, this book sets the standard for quotation books of any kind.

America in Quotations: A Kaleidoscopic View of American History. Comp. and ed. by Howard J. Langer. 2002. 463p. Greenwood, $79.95 (0-313-30883-7).
Quotations on the Vietnam War. Ed. by Gregory R. Clark. 2001. 312p. McFarland, $65 (0-7864-0945-2).
Social Science Quotations: Who Said What, When, and Where. Ed. by David L. Sills and Robert K. Merton. 2000. 437p. Transaction, paper, $39.95 (0-7658-0720-3).

When context is as important as content, a collection of snippets torn from interviews, essays, or news reports will do little to add to an understanding of the past or offer insights into human behavior and organization. The three titles considered here represent a different kind of quotation collection: passages are, on the whole, longer than those found in traditional quotation compilations, and in two of the titles (Langer's and Clark's the arrangement of material provides a chronological look at historical events.

America in Quotations, the newest title examined in this article, offers an interesting approach to American history. Describing it as "a historical anthology," Langer aims to present not only the words of famous historical figures but also those of lesser-known individuals. The work is divided into 18 chapters, from "Before Columbus" to "New World Order—and Disorder." (That last section includes comments on the Bush-Gore election of 2000 and the terrorist attacks of 9-11.) Each chapter begins with a brief explanation that sets the context, and most of the quotations are accompanied by further editorial notes. Sources for the quotations are always indicated (as are the speakers), and these can be anything from court decisions and government regulations to letters and diaries as well as news stories and editorials. Additional features include a selection of brief biographical sketches of those quoted; a chronology of important events in American history; a list of U.S. presidents with years of birth, death, terms, and party affiliations; and a bibliography. More than just a collection of quotations, *America in Quotations* could serve as a textbook or a companion to one.

Quotations on the Vietnam War records a wide range of observations, opinions, recollections, and reactions to that war in a chronology beginning in 1944 and extending to 2000. The passages are numbered consecutively, identify the speaker or writer, often further explain that person's position or identity or the occasion for the remark, and are frequently footnoted. A final section, entitled "The Long View," supplies quotations about war in general as well as Vietnam in particular, along with a number of slogans, graffiti, and anonymous sayings. In addition to a bibliography (including Web sites), source notes are provided for the footnoted quotations. The index cites entry numbers.

Social Science Quotations (originally published in 1991 as *The Macmillan Book of Social Science Quotations: Who Said What, When, and Where*) presents excerpts from the acknowledged classics of the field arranged alphabetically by author. Each author's name is printed in bold type, followed by years of birth and death, an identifying line, and the quoted passage, numbered consecutively under each contributor's entry. In what may be the longest bibliography I have ever seen in a specialized book of quotations, all the works cited are listed, including the dates of first publication. An especially thorough index ties keywords with subentries, under which are listed authors' names and entry numbers.

Biblical Quotations: A Reference Guide. Comp. By Martin H. Manser. 2001. 448p. Facts On File, $45 (0-8160-4654-9); paper, $16.95 (0-8160-4655-7).

A Treasury of Christian Wisdom: Two Thousand Years of Christian Lives and Quotations. By Tony Castle. 2001. 474p. Bantam Books UK; dist. by Trafalgar Square, $29.59 (0-340-78550-0).

Westminster Collection of Christian Quotations. By Martin H. Manser. 2001. 512p. Westminster John Knox, $24.95 (0-664-22258-7).

Manser's *Biblical Quotations* uses several different translations of the Bible, resulting in a richer collection than one drawn from a single version. The translations include the King James Version, the Revised Standard Bible, the New Jerusalem Bible, and several more. The more than 3,000 quotations are organized under themes such as "Angels," "Prophets and Prophecy," and "Worship." Chapter and verse, as well as the translation cited, are provided for each passage. An index of themes gives references to the page numbers of the relevant quotations; an index of Bible references is arranged alphabetically by the name of book, with references to the number of the entry in Manser's text. A fairly extensive keyword index also employs the entry number.

Quotations on religious themes may be found not only in Scripture but also in the writings of believers and others. This is the case with Castle's collection. There are no Bible verses here but, rather, selections from the work of a wide variety of Christian writers, past and present, from each of several different Christian traditions as well as from other sources. Selections are grouped under themes such as "Abandonment," "Leadership," and "Wonder" and thoroughly cross-referenced. The speaker is identified in each, but the title of the work from which the quotation is drawn is not. Anonymous citations are not included but proverbial sayings from a number of different traditions, including Jewish, Hindu, and Chinese are. The quotations form the first part of the book; the rest of it is a collection of brief biographies of prominent Christians from ancient to modern times. These entries supply years of birth and death and range in length from a line or two to a full paragraph. As in the selection of quotations, the persons included here represent a variety of Christian traditions. This book is based on Castle's two previous works, *The Hodder Book of Christian Quotations* (Hodder and Stoughton, 1982) and *The Hodder & Stoughton Book of Famous Christians* (Hodder & Stoughton, 1988).

The *Westminster Collection of Christian Quotations* combines some of the features of both the previously mentioned titles. Several thousand quotations from the Bible as well as from Christian authors and other historical figures are arranged under several hundred cross-referenced topics and presented in alphabetical order. As in Manser's other collection, the translation used is indicated for the Bible quotations; as in Castle's collection, the speaker is identified but not the title of the work from which the passage is drawn. There are an alphabetical index of Bible books quoted and an index of authors listing the topics under which their words may be found. Another alphabetical listing of authors provides years of birth and death and an identifying phrase, such as "Presbyterian minister" or "Mystical poet. "

Cassell's Humorous Quotations. Rev. ed. By Nigel Rees. 2002. 512p. Cassell; dist. by Sterling, $29.95 (0-304-35720-0).

The Oxford Dictionary of Humorous Quotations. 2d ed. Ed. by Ned Sherrin. 2001. 576p. Oxford, $35 (0-19-860289-8).

A humorous quotation or two may mean the difference between a boring speech or essay and one that piques or even keeps our interest. Wit and merriment abound in these two collections, which are both new editions of earlier works. *Cassell's Humorous Quotations* first appeared in 1998; this edition, according to the author, is more than twice the size of its predecessor with more than 5,000 entries arranged under 1,200 themes ranging from "Advertising" and "Advice" to "Comedy, Nonsense" and "Writers and Writing." Many of the quotations are annotated, and most provide references to books, interviews, plays, and more in addition to the speaker's name, years of birth and death, and brief identifying phrase. There is a sizable index incorporating authors' names and keywords.

The Oxford Dictionary of Humorous Quotations is organized in the familiar style of other Oxford collections: quotations, arranged by theme, appear on the left side of each page with the attributions on the right side. Under each theme, the quotations are numbered, so that in the author and keyword indexes, references are to a subject and an entry number rather than a page. The entire work is quite thoroughly cross-referenced, from the subject headings to the index entries. A wide variety of sources is used, and the speakers span the centuries. Subject headings and the names of the quoted are printed in bold type throughout, which helps the eye connect speaker and topic.

Cassell's Movie Quotations. By Nigel Rees. 2000. 431p. Cassell; dist. by Sterling, $29.95 (0-304-35369-8).

A Dictionary of Cinema Quotations from Filmmakers and Critics: Over 3,400 Axioms, Criticisms, Opinions, and Witticisms from 100 Years of the Cinema. Ed. by Stephen M. Ringler. 2001. 248p. McFarland, $45 (0-7864-0849-9).

Tag lines from the latest movie are part of current slang, and quotations from the great classic films are part of popular culture. These two titles have a lot to offer the movie fan as well as the devotee of cinema. *Cassell's Movie Quotations* is an attractively designed production featuring some of the greatest lines from and about the movies as well as the stars in front of and behind the camera, accompanied by stunning black-and-white photos. Entries are arranged alphabetically by film title or, in the case of individuals, surname. The quotations under each name or title are numbered, and entries in the keyword indexes refer to page and quotation number. When quotations are from movies, the year of production and country of origin are noted as well as a few screen credits, mainly writers, directors, and cast. Promotional slogans, catchphrases, and quotations from interviews with actors, directors, and others are also included among the 4,000-plus quotes.

A Dictionary of Cinema Quotations from Filmmakers and Critics concentrates more on the art of the film rather than Hollywood glamour. More than 3,000 quotations are arranged under 31 themes ranging from "Directing" and "Casting" to "Critics," "Montage," and more. The quotations are printed in two columns per page and numbered consecutively. The speaker or writer is identified, and the source—usually a book or a magazine interview—is usually cited. There is an index by quoted name and film title as well as one by keyword, and both use entry rather than page numbers.

Cassell's Sports Quotations. By David Pickering. 2000. 383p. Cassell; dist. by Sterling, $27.95 (0-304-35384-1).

The Ultimate Dictionary of Sports Quotations: From Hank Aaron to the Zone. By Carlo DeVito. 2001. 332p. Facts On File, $45 (0-8160-3980-1).

Sports quotations, like movie quotations, are another part of popular culture and are often employed by nonenthusiasts as well as sports fans. Sports quotations are even used by motivational and organizational experts when speaking about leadership, teamwork, and dedication. These two titles represent sports traditions from both sides of the Atlantic. There is no doubt which side of the pond *Cassell's Sports Quotations* hails from—among the more than 300 subject headings, "Cricket," "County Cricket" "Cricket-Bashing," and "One-Day Cricket," are just a few cricket-related examples. The subject headings are arranged alphabetically, and underneath them the quotations are listed with the speaker's name, year of birth and death, and a brief description, for example, "U.S. baseball player" or "English football referee." Some of the citations include a book title and year of publication or a magazine title and issue date. A single index includes the names of people and sports teams and references' page numbers.

Although *The Ultimate Dictionary of Sports Quotations* may not feature quotations about snooker and greyhound racing, it does include passages about snowboarding, kayaking, handball—and even cricket—among its more than 3,000 entries. The quotations are grouped under alphabetically arranged subject headings and identify the speaker and his or her particular field or sport but not a printed source. There is a bibliography offering a cross-section of sports classics and biographies, past and present. The index helps trace quotations by keyword or subject as well as personal name.

The Concise Dictionary of Foreign Quotations. Ed. by Anthony Lejeune. 2001. 320p. Fitzroy Dearborn, $35 (1-57958-341-5).

Words on Words: Quotations about Language and Languages. By David Crystal and Hilary Crystal. 2000. 580p. Univ. of Chicago, $29 (0-226-12201-8).

All the titles considered thus far have collected quotations in English, although many of the speakers quoted may not have written or spoken it originally. *The Concise Dictionary of Foreign Quotations* supplies English translations of Latin, French, German, Italian, and Spanish quotations alongside the original passages. Each section begins with the selection of quotations, arranged alphabetically by the first letter (so that, for example, *l'homme* will be found in the *l*s instead of the *h*s), original language on the left, and English translation on the right side of each page. The author and source attribution appear in bold type under the original passage. Several indexes are used: keyword indexes in each language, an English index covering all the sections, and an alphabetical index of the authors quoted, noting the page numbers on which they are quoted. This compact handbook has much to offer even the linguistically challenged, and its harvest of quotations gleaned from drama, literature, history, philosophy, and religion will surely increase the erudition of anyone who consults it.

Lovers of the written (and spoken) word have a natural affinity for quotations, and a collection of quotations about words and language is sure to appeal to the literati among us. *Words on Words* is built on a framework of topics such as "Analyzing Language," "Good and Bad Language," and "Genre and Variety," filled out by 65 themes (e.g., under "Good and Bad Language," there are "Keeping Quiet" and "Truth and Lies," to name a few). With quotes drawn from an array of authors from David Abercrombie (British phonetician) to Zeno of Citium (Greek philosopher), this storehouse of word treasures will delight any reader or writer. In one of the hallmarks of an excellent quotation book, indexes (authors, sources and keywords, phrases and concepts) account for half of the book. There is even a postscript offering quotations on the use and abuse of quotations.

Dictionary of Quotations and Proverbs about Cats and Dogs. Ed. by Robert A. Nowlan and Gwendolyn L. Nowlan. 2001.197p. McFarland, paper, $38.50 (0-7864-0801-4).

Quotation Index to Children's Literature. Comp. by Melanie Axel-Lute. 2001. 317p. Libraries Unlimited, paper, $40 (1-56308-809-6).

Vaudevillians may not like to work with children and animals, but books written for children are often the source for some memorable quotations, and even ancient proverbs speak of the bond between humans and animals.

The entries in A *Dictionary of Quotations and Proverbs about Cats and Dogs* are organized into numbered subject sections from "Action" to "Wrong." Author, title, and year of publication (or sometimes just author) are provided for each numbered entry. As the title might indicate, there are more proverbs in this book than in any of the other titles mentioned in this article. Some of the most quoted authors are Desiderius Erasmus, Desmond Morris, T. S. Eliot, Colette, Barbara Woodhouse, and the prolific Anonymous. The proverbs represent American, Danish, German, Irish, and Italian traditions, to name a few. Two indexes are provided, one by author and one by keyword/subject, and in both the references are to a section and a quote rather than a page number.

Children's literature seems to be ignored in literature courses, yet lines from books we read as children often stay with us throughout our lives. *Quotation Index to Children's Literature* offers a way to get back in touch with those reading memories and locate the lines we remember (or at least think we do!). The main section of the book is devoted to quotations from specific authors, arranged alphabetically by name. A wide variety of writers are represented, among them A. A. Milne, Edward Lear, Virginia Hamilton, Madeleine L'Engle, and Lewis Carroll. Under each name the quotations are numbered, so that in the keyword index you will find references to a name and a quote number rather than a page number. The title of a book or poem in which the line appears is also noted in each entry. Another section supplies "Quotations from Traditional Sources," such as fairy tales, rhymes, and folk tales. Citations are made to a particular story or poem, and if that is found in a collection, the title of the collection is also provided. The keyword index is approximately as long as the first two sections of the book, always a good sign in a quotation book. Following that is a title index alphabetically listing all the works referred to in the main part of the book. Finally, there is a bibliography with complete citations for all the works quoted.

The New Penguin Dictionary of Modern Quotations. By Robert Andrews. 2001. 588p. Penguin UK, dist. by Trafalgar, $35 (0-14-029307-8).

The "modern" era here is defined as the period beginning with 1914 and continuing to the present day. Although one might consider this a "general" quotation book because its entries cover a wide variety of subjects, it might also be looked at as a special quotation collection, its subject being the time period indicated. Such compilations function as a kind of time capsule—noting who is quoted and what they are quoted as saying tells us something about an era. There is an alphabetical listing of authors printed in bold type, and beneath each name the quotations are numbered and arranged chronologically. Each entry includes birth and death years; an identifying phrase ("Nigerian novelist," "U.S. essayist and editor"); and a brief description summarizing a body of work or a career. Special features include a "List of Themes," in which broad topics like "Achievement and Failure" or "Law and Disorder" are listed and then broken down into smaller subjects, such as "Luck," "Litigation." Following that is a thematic index in which these terms are used, and under them the names of speakers and quotation numbers are entered. Finally, there is an ample keyword index.

—*Carolyn Mulac*

Reference Books in Spanish for Children and Adolescents

Atlases

Atlas. By Mel Pickering. 2000. 48p. Two-Can, paper, $7.95 (1-58728-656-4). Gr. 2–5.

Through colorful maps and drawings, this well-conceived, large-format atlas introduces young Spanish-speaking children to the world's continents, regions, and countries as it encourages them to search for high-interest sites around the world. Informative sidebars highlight intriguing facts about each region.

Atlas escolar 2000. (Students's Atlas 2000). 1999. 32p. Editorial Everest, paper, $4.95 (84-241-1224-5). Gr. 4–7.

Basic information about the universe, the earth, and the continents of the world is presented through color maps and charts that describe geographical features, population, and such facts as weather and linguistic groups.

Atlas historico. (Historical Atlas). 1999. 153p. Ediciones SM, $35.95 (84-348-4115-0). Gr. 8–12.

In an appealing and concise manner, this large-format historical atlas presents an overview of the most important milestones in the history of the world, with emphasis on Spanish and European history. Especially valuable are the well-done color charts that explain cause-and-effect relationships of particular historical movements.

Larousse gran atlas universal. (Larousse Large Universal Atlas). 2000. 318p. Larousse Editorial, $43.95 (970-607-800-2). Gr. 8–12.

From a general description of the Earth, to satellite images, to recent physical and political maps of every region and country in the world, this beautifully designed, large-format atlas will satisfy every need. Numerous color photos, charts, maps, drawings, and a most complete index make this a first-choice atlas in the Spanish language.

Dictionaries

Diccionario enciclopedico 2001. (Encyclopedic Dictionary 2001). 4v. 1999. 1838p. Ediciones Larousse, $35 (970-22-0140-3). Gr. 7–adult.

Divided in two parts—dictionary of the Spanish language and biographical and geographic entries—and having more than 90,000 entries and 5,000 color illustrations and maps, this encyclopedic dictionary will be most useful to those who can afford only one reference source in Spanish. It is just as attractively designed as the six-volume *Larousse enciclopedico universal* listed on p.502. It is important to note, however, that with the exception of a name index in volume 4, there are no indexes.

Diccionario escolar de la lengua espanola. (Student Dictionary of the Spanish Language). 1999. 674p. Espasa Calpe, paper, $10.95 (84-239-9070-2). Gr. 4–8.

As a practical, easy-to-use Spanish dictionary, this publication with more than 25,000 brief entries will be useful to students. It includes a

Special Features

straightforward grammatical appendix and a well-written prologue by Manuel Seco from the Royal Academy of the Spanish Language.

Diccionario Oceano de sinonimos y antonimos. (Oceano Dictionary of Synonyms and Antonyms). 2001. 1024p. Oceano Grupo Editorial; dist. by Gale, $35 (84-494-1534-9). Gr. 9–adult.

With more than 21,000 entries and 400,000 synonyms and antonyms, this is one of the most comprehensive thesauruses of the Spanish language. Users will appreciate the clear, easy-to-read design as well as the appendixes, which include a dictionary of scientific and technical terms; a dictionary of 10,000 Spanish terms translated into English, French, German, and Italian; idiomatic expressions; neologisms; and proverbs. A CD-ROM is included.

Larousse diccionario School plus espanol/ingles. (Larousse School Plus Dictionary Spanish/English). 1999. 526p. Ediciones Larousse, $21.95 (970-22-0001-6). Gr. 8–adult.

Designed for students of the English language, this well-designed bilingual dictionary includes more than 55,000 words and expressions and 80,000 entries. Serious students will find the chapter, "Como se usa este diccionario," a useful guide as they learn intricacies of the English language including phrasal verbs, prepositional phrases, and idiomatic expressions. With the exception of the British form *colour*, the forms and spelling correspond to the American English and note Latin American and Peninsular Spanish usages.

Webster's New Explorer Spanish-English Dictionary. 1999. 740p. Merriam-Webster/Federal Street, $19.95 (1-892859-08-4). Gr. 7–adult.

More than 80,000 Spanish and English words are included in this bilingual dictionary. Users from the Americas will appreciate the inclusion of American English and the focus on the Spanish spoken in Latin America, along with numerous regional labels. A well-done Spanish grammar section is included.

Encyclopedias

Enciclopedia Mega Junior. (Encyclopedia Mega Junior). Jean-Paul Dupre. 1999. 326p. Larousse, paper, $24.95 (970-607-834-7). Gr. 5–7.

Divided into seven broad areas of learning—history, geography, art and communication, mathematics, physics, natural sciences, language—this encyclopedia highlights significant facts and issues of world knowledge. It includes a brief, easy-to-understand text and colorful photographs, maps, drawings and charts, as well as informative sidebars. It is important to note that this edition, printed in Mexico, emphasizes the history and geography of Mexico.

Enciclopedia milenio. (Millenium Family Encyclopedia). 5v. 1999. Editorial Sudamericana, $99 (970-07-1667-4). Gr. 5–10.

This encyclopedia is made up of 700 one-and two-page articles. Originally published by Dorling Kindersley, London, it includes more than 10,000 clear color photographs, drawings, long with charts and brief, accessible text. Like other reference materials first published in Europe, it emphasizes European history, art, and geography. Despite this caveat, reluctant encyclopedia users will find the appealing design and format an inviting introduction to new ideas and specific information. Volume titles are: volume 1: *Historia de la humanidad* (History of Mankind); volume 2: *La ciencia y el universo* (Science and the Universe); volume 3: *La naturaleza* (Nature); volume 4: *Pueblo y civilizaciones* (People and Civilization); volume 5: *Atlas del mundo* (World Atlas).

Enciclopedia de los paises del mundo. (Encyclopedia of Lands and People). By Sue Grabham. Tr. by Marisa Rodriguez Perez. 10v. 1998. Editorial Everest, $100 (84-241-1980-0). Gr. 5–8.

Originally published by Kingfisher Publications, London, this attractive encyclopedia provides an overview of all the countries in the world through simple text, informative sidebars, and color maps, photographs and drawings on every page. This is not an in-depth study of individual countries; rather, it highlights such aspects as the people, history, geography, economics, and customs that make each country unique. Volume 10 includes geographical facts, a glossary, and an index that refers the user to the other nine volumes, but which is confusing at best. Students in search of basic information about the continents and countries in the world will find these encyclopedias quite appealing.

Enciclopedia Oceano de Mexico. (Oceano Encyclopedia of Mexico). 4v. 2000. Oceano Grupo Editorial; dist. by Gale, $63 (84-494-1412-1). Gr. 10–adult.

Divided into four broad areas, this encyclopedia provides an in-depth overview of the geography, history, economy, and arts of Mexico up to the late 1990s. Despite a dry academic text, serious students will appreciate the detailed information provided. Numerous color and black-and-white charts and maps enliven this compendium of facts. Volume 1 covers the geography, ecosystems, and population of Mexico. Volume 2 covers the economy, history, and international relations. Volume 3 treats the people, science, and popular and fine arts. Volume 4 surveys communication, sports, and the states; and includes a chronology, biographies, and a name index. It is important to note, however, that with the exception of the name index, there are no indexes.

Larousse, el gran libro de preguntas y respuestas. (Larousse, the Big Book of Questions and Answers). 1999. 318p. Ediciones Larousse, $33.95 (970-607-928-9). Gr. 5–7.

In a question-and-answer format, this reference work provides answers to commonly asked questions in the sciences, geography, and history. Originally published by Larousse, London, and adapted for Latin American content, it includes more than 1,300 questions with one-paragraph answers such as, *What is a superconductor? Which is the fastest mammal? How fast do we learn to talk?* and *What are the United Nations?* Numerous color drawings, charts, maps, photographs, and sidebars as well as a glossary and an index invite readers to explore the world of knowledge.

Larousse enciclopedico universal. (Larousse Universal Encyclopedia). 6v. 2000. 1816p. Ediciones Larousse, $280 (970-22-0071-7). Gr. 7–adult.

Attractively designed and easy-to-use, this well-organized resource has more than 90,000 entries and 5,000 color illustrations. Users will find an alphabetical list of words from current technical terms (e.g., *biocombustible, cibernauta*) to commonly used Anglicisms (e.g., *chat, establishment*) and Latin Americanisms. Encyclopedic entries have been updated to 1997. Even though this encyclopedia was published in Mexico, it devotes six pages to Spain, three to Mexico, and one-and-a-half to the U.S. Despite the unbalanced coverage, this is a most useful Spanish-language encyclopedia.

Oceano uno color: Diccionario enciclopedico. (Oceano One Color: Encyclopedic Dictionary). 2001. 1784p. Oceano Grupo Editorial; dist. by Gale, $35 (84-494-1548-9). Gr. 8–12.

More than 80,000 entries and 7,500 color illustrations, maps, and charts make this recently updated encyclopedic dictionary a useful addition to most schools and libraries. Especially noteworthy are the numerous contemporary scientific and technological entries as well as lexical and encyclopedic entries for Hispanic America. The good-quality paper and comprehensive coverage compensate for the cluttered design and small font. A CD-ROM is included.

Other Reference Sources

Diccionario de biografias. (Biographical Dictionary). 2001. 1071p. Oceano Grupo Editorial; dist. by Gale, $35 (84-494-1433-4). Gr. 8–12.

Biographical entries for more than 2,500 outstanding men and women from Biblical times up to Magic Johnson and the Brazilian race car driver, Ayrton Senna, are included. The volume highlights the achievements of monarchs, artists, philosophers, scientists, explorers, athletes, inventors, and others. More than 2,000 color and black-and-white photos, maps, and drawings add to its appeal and usefulness. The scarcity of biographical dictionaries in the Spanish language makes this a unique source for students and casual browsers. A CD-ROM is included.

Gran cronica Oceano del siglo XX. (Oceano's Great Chronicle of the Twentieth Century). 2001. 64p. Oceano Grupo Editorial; dist. by Gale, $28 (84-494-1247-1). Gr. 9–adult.

This fact-filled chronological account provides a year-by-year report on the scientific, technological, political, economic, social, and artistic events of the twentieth century. Through numerous black-and-white and color photographs, maps, and charts, and brief two-to three-page essays, it recounts the major incidents that influenced the 1900s, from the death of Oscar Wilde in 1900, to the effects of globalization in 1999. The lack of an index restricts its use to casual readers or persistent browsers. A compact disc with the music of the century is included.

Grandes personajes. (Great Celebrities). 2000. 808p. Oceano Grupo Editorial; dist. by Gale, $23 (84-494-1689-2). Gr. 8–12.

Beginning with Buddha and ending with British scientist Stephen Hawking, this biographical dictionary describes the lives and achievements of 174 noteworthy men and a few women throughout history, using easy-to-understand narratives and color and black-and-white photos and drawings. As in its four-volume predecessor, *Grandes biografías* (1992), each biography is four to six pages long and includes a time chart. Although the introduction states that there is a slant toward personages from the Spanish-speaking world, users will mainly find notable world scientists, writers, and statesmen as well as popular artists such as John Ford, John Lennon, Marilyn Monroe, and Elvis Presley.

Historia del mundo moderno. (History of the Modern World). 3v. 2001. Oceano Grupo Editorial; dist. by Gale, $125 (84-494-1797-X). Gr. 9–adult.

Highlighting the technical and scientific developments of the last five centuries and the influence of the U.S. in the modern world, this well-written and exquisitely designed encyclopedia reflects the changes in the world's economy, artistic development, and daily life, beginning with Europe in the sixteenth century and ending with the challenges of globalization in the late twentieth century. Serious students of world history will find valuable information and ideas presented in a pleasing format. Unfortunately, indexes are not included—a serious shortcoming that limits use.

Libro de estilo universitario. (University Style Manual). By Carlos Arroyo Jimenez and Francisco José Garrido Diaz. 1997. 556p. Acento Editorial, paper, $19.95 (84-483-0216-8). Gr. 9–adult.

Written for university students, this style manual is also useful for editors, translators, writers, typesetters, and others involved in preparing Spanish-language manuscripts. Divided in five chapters, it includes an alphabetic listing of 8,000 entries on contemporary language issues, rules and recommendations regarding acceptable and unacceptable usage, publishing standards, and a bibliography. There is no index, but a thorough table of contents adds to the value of this manual.

Distributors (unless otherwise noted)

Bilingual Publications, 270 Lafayette St., Ste. 705, New York, NY 10012.
Lectorum Publications, 111 Eighth Ave., Ste. 804, New York, NY 10011-5201.

—*Isabel Schon*

Top 10 Biography Reference Sources

Biography is a big part of reference publishing, so we had plenty of titles from which to choose in compiling this list. Titles were selected based on reviews that appeared in RBB from the January 1 & 15, 2001, to the March 15, 2002, issues. We have added an **HS** following some of the annotations to indicate resources that our reviewers recommended for high-school as well as academic and public libraries.

Baker's Biographical Dictionary of Musicians. 6v. 9th ed. Ed. by Nicolas Slonimsky. 2000. 4,220p. Schirmer, $595 (0-02-865525-7).

With its centennial edition, this reference mainstay moves beyond its traditional classical focus and includes almost 2,000 new entries on popular and jazz musicians. A must for music collections. [RBB Je 1 & 15 01].

Biographical Dictionary of American Indian History to 1900. Rev. ed. By Carl Waldman. 2001. 506p. Facts On File, $65 (0-8160-4252-7).

This useful revision of the author's standard *Who Was Who in Native American History* (Facts On File, 1990) contains updated entries on approximately 1,000 Native and non-Native people in the U.S. and Canada from precontact until the end of the nineteenth century. **HS.** [RBB Ag 01].

Biography Reference Bank. [Internet database]. Wilson, pricing from $2,595. [http://hwwilsonweb.com].

Two Wilson databases, *Biography Index Plus* and *Wilson Biographies Plus Illustrated*, have been combined to produce this reference powerhouse offering book and article citations, photographs, and full text from 1,450 journals and more than 100 Wilson biographical reference sources. [RBB N 1 01].

The Eleanor Roosevelt Encyclopedia. Ed. by Maurine H. Beasley and others. 2001. 628p. Greenwood, $65 (0-313-30181-6).

A number of distinguished and well-known Roosevelt experts contributed to this scholarly yet readable look at the many roles of one of the most influential figures of the twentieth century. **HS.** [RBB My 1 01].

Encyclopedia of the United States Cabinet. 3v. By Mark Grossman. 2000. 1,000p. ABC-CLIO, $275 (0-87436-977-0).

Providing biographical information and analysis of every cabinet secretary from the administrations of George Washington to Bill Clinton, this set is indispensable for history and political science students. [RBB Mr 15 01].

Encyclopedia of Women in the Ancient World. By Joyce Salisbury. 2001. 370p. ABC-CLIO, $75 (1-57607-092-1).

Biographies of women from prehistory to approximately A.D. 500 are enhanced by entries on cultural and historical topics that help put these lives in context. **HS.** [RBB D 1 01].

Encyclopedia of Women Social Reformers. 2v. By Helen Rappaport. 2001. 888p. ABC-CLIO, $185 (1-57607-101-4).

Treats more than 400 individuals, from the French Revolution until the present, from 64 countries. Because many of these women can be found in other biographical resources, the true value of this encyclopedia lies in its emphasis on women in the role of reformers. [RBB Mr 1 02].

Native American Women: A Biographical Dictionary. 2d ed. Ed. by Gretchen M. Bataille and Laurie Lisa. 2001. 384p. Routledge, $85 (0-415-03020-0).

This second edition is much enlarged over the first, published by Garland in 1993. It contains biographies of more than 270 women with diverse roles within their cultures. **HS.** [RBB O 15 01].

Women Building Chicago, 1790–1990: A Biographical Dictionary. Ed. by Rima Lunin Schultz and Adele Hast. 2001. 1,088p. Indiana Univ., $75 (0-253-33852-2).

Profiling 423 women who played a role in the history of Chicago, this work has generated a great deal of interest despite its narrow focus. The very model of a scholarly biographical dictionary. [RBB Ja 1 & 15 02].

Women in World History. 17v. Edited by Anne Commire and Deborah Klezmer. 1999–2002. Gale, $1,395 (0-7876-3736-X).

There is nothing comparable to this encyclopedia's coverage of women from all over the world in all eras and all walks of life. Its sweeping scope makes it the standard against which other biographical reference sources on women will be judged. **HS.** [RBB Mr 1 02].

—*Mary Ellen Quinn*

Twenty Best Bets for Student Researchers

In time for the new school year, here are our top picks from among the many reference books that we reviewed during the past 12 months that would work well for student researchers through the high-school level.

African-American Culture and History: A Student's Guide. 4v. Ed. by Jack Salzman. 2000. 1,082p. Macmillan, $375 (0-02-865531-1).

Based on Macmillan's *Encyclopedia of African-American Culture and History* (1996), this guide covers much of the same material but is written for sixth grade and up. Its articles include "biographies of notable African

Americans, events, historical eras, legal cases, areas of cultural achievement, professions, sports, and places." [RBB Jl 01].

African Literature and Its Times: Profiles of Notable Literary Works and the Historical Events That Influenced Them. By Joyce Moss and Lorraine Valestuk. 2000. Gale, $105 (0-7876-3727-0). [RBB D 15 00].
The second volume in Gale's World Literature and Its Times series, which is designed for the high-school level and up and examines works of literature within their cultural and historical contexts. Other available volumes in the series are British and Irish Literature and Its Times: Celtic Migrations to the Reform Bill (2001); British Literature and Its Times: The Victorian Era to the Present (2001); and Latin American Literature and Its Times [RBB Ja 1 & 15 00].

American Revolution Reference Library. 4v. 2000. UXL, $170 (0-7876-63816-1).
The now-familiar UXL formula of assembling background information, biographies, and a selection of primary material for students in grades five through nine is applied to the American Revolution. Libraries can purchase the three components (Almanac, Biographies, Primary Sources) separately or as a set. With the set comes a free cumulative index. [RBB N 15 00].

Ancient Civilizations. 10v. 2000. 800p. Grolier, $319 (0-7172-9471-4).
People and civilizations of ancient times are the focus of this A–Z treatment. Designed to complement standard elementary-and middle-school curricula, the set's visuals will invite use by its intended audience. [RBB S 1 00].

Aquatic Life of the World. 11v. 2001. Marshall Cavendish. $329.95 (0-7614-7170-7).
Magnificent photos, clear writing, and good organization help make this a winner for grades four through six. [RBB Mr 1 01].

Depression America. 6v. 2001. 768p. Grolier, $319 (0-7172-5502-6).
Designed for high-school students, this set offers an excellent introduction to the Great Depression years. The thematic approach makes for a richer explanation of the 1930s and the events leading to the crash than might be found in a dictionary-style presentation. [RBB Ag 01].

Encyclopedia of the American Civil War: A Political, Social, and Military History. 5v. Ed. by David S. Heidler and Jeanne T. Heidler. 2000. ABC-CLIO, $425 (1-57607-066-2).
The most comprehensive reference source on the Civil War made just about everybody's "best" reference list for 2000 and was a Dartmouth Medal Honorable Mention. High-schoolers should find it eminently accessible. [RBB Ja 1 & 15 01].

Experiment Central: Understanding Scientific Principles through Projects. 4v. Ed. by John T. Tancredi and John Loret. 2000. 773p. UXL, $115 (0-7876-2892-1).
Come science-project time, it seems there are never enough resources on the library shelves. This set offers very detailed presentations of 100 experiments for grades four through six. [RBB O 1 00].

The Facts On File Companion to the American Short Story. Ed. by Abby H. P. Werlock. 2000. 542p. Facts On File. $65 (0-8160-3164-9).
Of the several reference sources on the short story genre that have been published in the past couple of years, this one is probably the most helpful for high-school students. It covers writers, literary terms and theories, influential magazines, important story collections, notable characters and locales, major awards, and subgenres. [RBB S 1 00].

Learning about the Holocaust: A Student's Guide. 4v. Ed. by Ronald M. Smelser. 2001. 1,082p. Macmillan, $375 (0-02-865536-2).
Based on Macmillan's 1990 Encyclopedia of the Holocaust, this set, which has been revised for the school market, has updated material and new entries and resource lists. Entries cover countries most affected by the Holocaust and the primary concentration and extermination camps. [RBB Jl 01].

Macmillan Encyclopedia of Transportation. 6v. 2000. Macmillan. $325 (0-02-865361-0).
Entries provide students with basic information about the historical, economic, scientific, and cultural aspects of transport. There is no other reference work on the market that covers transportation to this degree for the high-school or middle-school audience. [RBB S 1 00].

Peoples of Africa. 11v. 2000. 648p. Marshall Cavendish, $329 (0-7416-7158-8).
Graphic-intensive design and copious indexing make this country-by-country survey an appealing resource for students in upper-elementary and middle-school settings. [RBB F 1 01].

Plant Sciences. 4v. Ed. by Richard Robinson. 2000. Macmillan, $325 (0-02-865434-X).
We called this work "lovely to look at and delightful to read." The inaugural title in the Macmillan Science Library, it is tied to the curriculum and intended for the middle-school grades and up. [RBB Je 1 & 15 01].

Plants and Plant Life. 10v. By Jill Bailey. 2001. 640p. Grolier, $279 (0-7172-9510-9).
A conceptual arrangement and intensely visual approach should make this set a popular resource in school libraries. Although it is geared for middle-and junior-high-school students, high schools might also wish to purchase it for its broad introduction to the complex principles of botany. [RBB Jl 01].

Science and Its Times: Understanding the Social Significance of Scientific Discovery, Volume 5, 1800–1900. Ed. by Neil Schalger and Josh Lauer. 2000. 633p. Gale, $85 (0-7876-3937-0).
This was the first installment in a new seven-volume series for the high-school level and up that examines science history and the impact of developing technologies. All volumes, covering 2000 B.C. to the present, are now available, and a cumulative index is to be released this month. [RBB O 1 00].

U.S.A. Sixties. 6v. 2001. 1,200p. Grolier, $429 (0-7172-9503-6).
Aimed at the high-school level, the A–Z entries and numerous illustrations bring to life the "events, personalities and cultural forces" that defined a tumultuous decade. [RBB Mr 1 01].

UXL Complete Health Resource. 9v. 2000. UXL, $250 (0-7876-3917-9).
The three components of this UXL offering (Body by Design: From the Digestive System to the Skeleton; Healthy Living; and Sick! Diseases and Disorders, Injuries and Infections) can be purchased separately or as a set. Extremely readable, they are invaluable as a health-education reference for topics commonly taught in middle and high school. [RBB O 1 00].

Vietnam War Reference Library. 4v. UXL, $155 (0-7876-4883-5).
As with several other of UXL's publications, the three segments of this title—Almanac, Biographies, and Primary Sources can be purchased separately or as a set. UXL's approach to selecting and presenting information that can be easily digested by a middle-school audience works best when applied to relatively narrow topics such as this one. [RBB Mr 15 01].

World Eras: Classical Greek Civilization. Volume 6: 800–323 B.C.E. Ed. by John T. Kirby. 2001. 395p. Gale, $95 (0-7876-1707-5).
This volume introduced a new series patterned after Gale's popular American Decades and American Eras series. Other titles now available in the series are The European Renaissance and Reformation, 1300–1600 (2001) and Roman Republic and Empire, 753 B.C.–A.D. 476 (2001). [RBB My 15 01].

World Poets. 3v. Ed. by Ron Padgett. 2000. 1,396p. Scribner, $225 (0-684-80591-X).
Both the choice of poets and the writing style are geared to high-schoolers in this appealing set. Poets were selected based on curriculum demands and representation across eras and cultures. [RBB O 15 00].

—Mary Ellen Quinn

Where and What: Current World Atlas and Dictionary Roundup

John Morse, the president and publisher of Merriam-Webster, wrote an article in the July 2001 issue of Library Quarterly in which he noted that publishers live a "hybrid world, part print, part electronic." The same is true of libraries. Although online databases are increasingly becoming the format of choice, dictionaries and atlases are two types of reference sources where the convenience of the book may outweigh the advantages of online. The eye, the book, and the brain will give the quickest, most satisfying result when looking for information in an atlas or dictionary.

Readers of *Booklist* have requested that *Reference Books Bulletin* publish a list of current, recommended atlases and dictionaries. The following sources are recommended for public, academic, and high-school libraries, based on currency, quality, cost, and availability. All have been published from late 1999 to the present except for an unabridged dictionary and major atlas that do not yet have new editions for the new millennium.

The recommended titles are listed by type, and within each type they are ranked in descending order from the best, based on the reviewer's opinion. The purchaser may choose within types depending on individual preferences or needs.

Atlases

The Classic

The Times Atlas of the World. 10th ed. 1999. Times, $250 (0-8129-3265-X).

Although this edition has a 1999 copyright, it is still the pinnacle of atlases. There are 248 pages of digitally produced maps in light hues and clear typeface. For each continent there are at least 10 plates, with increasing definition with each map. The major weakness is the lack of city maps that were included in earlier editions.

Major Atlases

National Geographic Atlas of the World. 7th ed. 1999. 134p. National Geographic, $150 (0-7922-7528-4).

Another late 1999 publication, this rivals the dimensions of the *Times* atlas (at approximately 18 inches by 12 inches) but has fewer pages, fewer index entries, and fewer maps. However, the atlas does a fine job with U.S. maps, which have more entries on each map. Also included is a section of city maps for each continent.

The New International Atlas. 25th anniversary ed. 1999. 1,200p. Rand McNally, $150 (0-528-83808-3).

This is the only major atlas that has text in five languages (English, French, German, Spanish, and Portuguese). The maps have shaded relief that gives a three-dimensional impression. The 160,000 entries in the index use longitude and latitude as the key for location (other atlases use a grid system). A separate section has 65 city maps, including Jakarta, Saigon, and Taipei.

Medium-Sized Atlases

Atlas of the World. 9th ed. 2001. 304p. Oxford, $75 (0-19-521848-5).

This is the newest of the atlases, published in December 2001. It is a major revision, with the addition of a 32-page gazetteer of nations that offers three or four paragraphs of text on each country plus a flag, statistical information, and approximate location of the country in the world. The 176 maps have bright, bold colors depicting topography. As in previous editions, city maps are in a separate section with its own index. Some cities have both a regional and a central city map. Beautiful satellite maps called "Images of Earth," some of which were in previous editions, begin the volume and divide the sections.

Hammond World Atlas. 3d ed. 2000. 312p. Hammond, $69.95 (0-8437-1352-6).

Perhaps in response to criticism in a review in RBB [My 1 00], three items have been corrected in Hammond's largest atlas—the red type in the index has been changed to blue, Nunavut is now listed in the index, and the 16 new administrative divisions of Poland (these are not in the *Hammond Concise*) are on the map. There are more than 150 maps with 110,000 entries in the index. Some of the maps are identical to those in the *Hammond Concise* except they are slightly larger.

Hammond Concise World Atlas. 2000. 238p. Hammond, $45 (0-8437-1386-0); paper, $29.95 (0-8437-1387-9).

Hammond's midpriced atlas has 138 pages of maps with 60,000 entries in the index. There are a number of inset maps and a few pages of maps of metropolitan areas of the world, including some in the U.S. These metropolitan area maps are also included in the *Hammond World Atlas*, listed above.

DK World Atlas. 2d ed. 2000. 354p. DK, $50 (0-7894-5962-0).

DK's first atlas was published in 1997 and has now been revised. Although the publisher maintains that all maps have been completely updated and revised, the number of maps (450) and entries (80,000) in the index remain about the same. A geographical comparisons section has been added, with lists such as the least populous countries (Vatican City is at the top) and richest countries based on GNP per capita (Luxembourg is first; the U.S. is tenth). The maps are smaller than in some other atlases, making room on the page for text, photos, charts, and thematic maps.

The World Book Atlas. 2001. 240p. World Book, $57 (0-7166-2651-9).

World Book uses Rand McNally maps, so the 60 maps are similar to those in *The New International Atlas*. The index lists 54,000 place-names. Because the publishers hope this is purchased in conjunction with *The World Book Encyclopedia* there is little supplementary material.

School or Desk Atlases

Illustrated Atlas of the World. 4th ed. 192p. 2001. Reader's Digest, $26.95 (0-7621-0343-4).

Published by Reader's Digest with 80 maps by Bartholomew and 30,000 place-names, this atlas provides basic continent and country maps. The atlas is enhanced with color photographs on pages with supplementary maps—population, climate, and so forth. Flags and concise country information are also included.

Essential World Atlas. 3d ed. 2001. 232p. Oxford, $24.95 (0-19-521790-X).

Some of the information in this atlas is similar to that in the larger *Atlas of the World*. The *Essential* has a separate city map section and fewer maps overall—less than 15 of the U.S. To make the most of limited space, some of the maps are sideways on the page, so, for example, an area from northern Minnesota to southern Texas is displayed on a double-page spread.

DK Concise Atlas of the World. 2001. 384p. DK, $29.95 (0-7894-8002-6).

Based on the DK *World Atlas*, this one follows the DK format of having lots of information on every page. In addition to maps of continents, there are 75 regional maps accompanied by graphs and tables with supplementary material.

Hammond Citation World Atlas. 2000. 328p. Hammond, $19.95 (0-8437-1295-3).

The arrangement of this atlas differs from other Hammond offerings. There is no comprehensive index or gazetteer, so place-names are included on the same page or adjacent page of the map. This works well only if you know, for example, that Versalles is in Bolivia, not Brazil. The maps do not have the unique shading that the more expensive Hammond atlases use, but individual U.S. state maps show clear county boundaries. State flags are included as well as nickname, state flower, and bird.

Compact Atlases

DK Compact World Atlas. 2001. 192p. DK, $12.95 (0-7894-7987-7).

Described as an atlas for the family, this is a good choice for a library's circulating collection. There are 60 clear, simple maps with 20,000 entries in the index. A fact file contains statistics and flags of countries of the world. A note on the back of the title page provides an URL for updated information.

Rand McNally Premier World Atlas. 2d ed. 2000. 144p. Rand McNally, paper, $15.95 (0-528-83894-6).

This economical atlas has 144 pages of maps, along with a page or two of text about each continent accompanied by colorful photographs. There are individual U.S. state maps.

Hammond Explorer World Atlas. Rev. ed. By Hammond World Atlas Corp. 2001. 132p. Hammond, paper, $12.95 (0-8437-1357-7).

There are 90 pages of maps, with eight pages devoted to the U.S., and two additional pages of U.S. city maps. Also included are country flags and a reference guide.

Special Features

Dictionaries

The Classic

The Compact Oxford English Dictionary: Complete Text Reproduced Micrographically. 2d ed. Ed. by J. A. Simpson and E. S. C. Weiner. 1991. 2,416p. Oxford, $390 (0-19-861258-3).

The Oxford English Dictionary. 20v. 2d ed. Ed. by J. A. Simpson and E. S. C. Weiner. 1989. 22,000p. Oxford, $995 (0-19-861186-2).

The Oxford English Dictionary on CD-ROM: Version 3.0. 2002. Oxford, $295 (0-19-521888-4).

The Oxford English Dictionary Online. 2000. Oxford, pricing from $795 [http://dictionary.oed.com/].

Ideally, any library that can afford it should have some version of this great dictionary. Practically, every library does not have it; but anyone with a college education should be aware that it exists.

Unabridged Dictionaries

Webster's Third New International Dictionary: Unabridged. By Philip Babcock Gove. 1993. 2,783p. Merriam-Webster, $119 (0-87779-201-1).

This famous volume with more than 450,000 entries, the ultimate U.S. unabridged dictionary, was originally published in 1961 and republished in 1993 with an addenda of 65 pages of new words. Merriam-Webster is planning a fourth print edition but not for the near future. However, a new revision of the third edition with an expanded addenda section will be available later this year.

Random House Webster's Unabridged Dictionary. 2d ed. 2001. 2,230p. Random, $49.95 (0-375-42566-7).

This is a slight revision of the *Random House Dictionary of the English Language* (2d ed., 1987). A 1,000-entry new word section begins the volume. COM (as in Comedy Central); *Heaney, Seamus;* and *spam* are listed here, but so is *pyracantha*, which was in *Webster's New International Dictionary*, second edition, published in 1937. The main part of the dictionary still contains 315,000 words with black-and-white illustrations. Ready-reference material is incorporated into the definitions—a list of selected airport codes, Morse Code, members of the United Nations, and more. For many words the approximate date of first use is mentioned.

Comprehensive Dictionaries

New Oxford American Dictionary. By Frank R Abate and Elizabeth Jewell. 2001. 2,064p. Oxford, $50 (0-19-511227-X).

This is the most recent of the comprehensive dictionaries (between an unabridged and a college dictionary in size), with about 250,000 definitions. The entries are structured around "core" senses, with subsenses grouped around the core (e.g., *cowl*—"large loose hood": subsenses include a monk's cloak, a hood-shaped covering of a chimney, the part of a car that supports the dashboard). Definitions, place-names, biographical entries, and proper names are interfiled, so we find Jackson (the city) appearing together with Andrew, Jesse, Mahalia, Michael, and Thomas Jackson (all except Mahalia have photos) as well as Jackson Hole, Jacksonian, and Jacksonville.

The American Heritage Dictionary of the English Language. 4th ed. 2000. 2,116p. Houghton Mifflin, $60 (0-395-82517-2).

The fourth edition of AHD has added color photographs and 10,000 new words, bringing the total to well over 200,000. The editors concentrate on usage, which makes this more prescriptive than other current dictionaries. Notes—regional, synonym, usage, and history—appear in boxes by relevant entries. The illustrations are varied—one two-page spread has pictures of a samovar, Samoyed, sampan, samurai, George Sand, and a sand dollar. An abridged version of AHD is available free of charge.

The World Book Dictionary. 2v. 2001. 2,430p. World Book, $99 (0-7166-0298-9).

The number of entries (225,000) in this set puts it in the comprehensive section, but the price is closer to that of an unabridged dictionary. Because it is to be used in conjunction with *The World Book Encyclopedia*, biographical and geographical entries are not included. In addition, because it supposedly reflects the way people should speak, offensive language is not included. The definitions are clear and concise, with the most common meaning first. Sentences or quotations enhance the meanings, as do numerous line drawings.

College or Desk Dictionaries

The American Heritage College Dictionary. 4th ed. By Houghton Mifflin Company. 2002. Houghton Mifflin, $25 (0-618-09848-8).

This is now the most current college dictionary, with 9-1, 9/11 listed between *nine days' wonder* and *ninepin*. Population figures for U.S. cities are from the 2000 census. The volume has the same attractive format as the larger *American Heritage Dictionary of the English Language*, with photos and line drawings in the outside margin of each page. However, the illustrations are fewer, and they are not in color. AHCD also shares with its parent boxes for usage notes, synonyms, regionalism, and word histories.

Merriam-Webster's Collegiate Dictionary. 10th ed. 2001. 1,600p. Merriam-Webster, $24.95 (0-87779-709-9).

The 10th edition was first published in 1993 but, like other college dictionaries, it is updated annually. The 2001 version contains new words (DVD, *dot-com*) that were not in earlier printings. In most similar dictionaries, biographical and geographical entries are interfiled with word entries, but here they have their own sections. This is the first current dictionary to be available on the Web free of charge [http://www.merriam-webster.com/].

Random House Webster's College Dictionary. 2d ed. 2001. 1,573p. Random, $24.95 (0-375-42560-8).

Described as the dictionary that has the most new words, the 2001 printing includes definitions of *burn* (a CD) and *mouse potato*. The prefatory material lists new words by decades, and a supplement provides a guide for avoiding insensitive and offensive language. Random House concentrates on definitions, so line drawings are few and far between.

Webster's New World College Dictionary. 4th ed. Ed. by Michael Agnes. 2001. 1,716p. Hungry Minds, $23.95 (0-0286-3118-8).

This dictionary, first published by World Publishing, is celebrating its fiftieth anniversary with a revision and a new publisher, Hungry Minds (publishers of the For Dummies series). It is a descriptive source with fewer entries and illustrations than the other college dictionaries, yet it is the dictionary of choice for the AP, *New York Times*, and *Wall Street Journal*. Definitions are arranged historically, and Americanisms are starred. The 2001 printing offers 150 new terms, including *eye candy* and *road rage*.

Microsoft Encarta College Dictionary. Ed. by Anne H. Soukhanov. 2001. 1,678p. St. Martin's, $24.95 (0-312-28087-4).

Editor Soukhanov believes a dictionary should provide help for people who have trouble speaking or writing English. Thus, entries include misspellings (e.g., *suprise*, an incorrect spelling of *surprise*). Technological words are designated by a lightning bolt; *support* is so designated because the eighth definition is "to provide technical support for a computing system." Not surprisingly, new words concentrate on technology—for instance, TTL4N, *tt*. Illustrations are limited to a few small black-and-white photographs and simple line drawings. There are boxes for quick facts, correct usage, and "literary links." The number of entries is greater than in other college dictionaries, but perhaps the misspellings are included in that number.

The Oxford American Dictionary and Language Guide. 1999. 1,330p. Oxford, $35 (0-19-513449-4).

Even though this isn't described as a college dictionary, it fits the bill. The words and definitions are taken from the Oxford database (200 million words). It includes many line drawings and shaded boxes containing spellings, synonyms, and pronunciation tips as well as word history for some words. A language guide and numerous almanac-type lists are also included.

Webster's II New College Dictionary. Rev. ed. 2001. 1,514p. Houghton Mifflin, $24 (0-395-96214-5).

Originally published in 1995 and updated in 2001, *Webster's II* has a definition of *Internet* but not of *chat room*. There are 200,000 entries, with no obscene words and very few illustrations. Biographical and geographical definitions are in separate sections.

—*Christine Bulson*

A Whole New Environment: Environmental Reference Resources in Print

Included here are examples of print reference books on the environment, or with an environmental theme, that were in print as of December 2001. There are many other desirable and even classic reference books on environmental issues that are no longer in print, but because we are offering suggestions for current purchase, they are not included.

Designed to show the breadth of environmental materials available, this selection just touches the surface of print offerings.

AAAS Atlas of Population and Environment. By Paul Harrison and Fred Pearce. 2001. 204p. University of California, $65 (0-520-23081-7); paper, $29.95 (0-520-23084-1).

Essays, maps of environmental issues, charts, tables, and case studies on the effects of population on global change and conditions. Information on natural resources, land use, atmosphere, pollution, biodiversity, etc., is drawn from the United Nations, the Environmental Protection Agency, and other agencies.

American Environmental Leaders: From Colonial Times to the Present. 2v. By Anne Becher and others. 2000. 921p. ABC-CLIO, $175 (1-57607-162-6).

Information on approximately 350 persons whose work has had an impact on the environmental movements of their times. Includes historical figures and young, lesser-known, currently active persons of many orientations—organization leaders, scientists, writers, activists.

Biographical Dictionary of American and Canadian Naturalists and Environmentalists. Ed. by Keir B. Sterling and Richard A. Harmond. 1997. 937p. Greenwood, $190 (0-313-23047-1).

A wide-ranging compilation of biographical information on 445 persons from the fifteenth to the mid-twentieth century. Entries include dates, occupation, education, career highlights, contributions, and short bibliographies. Subjects include explorers, politicians, administrators, mapmakers, scientists, historians, artists, and more.

A Dictionary of Environmental Quotations. By Barbara K. Rodes and Rice Odell. 1997. 344p. Johns Hopkins University, paper, $21.50 (0-8018-5738-4).

Offers 3,700 quotations in 143 categories, from ancient times to the present. Very useful to writers and speakers.

Earth Works: Recommended Fiction and Nonfiction about Nature and the Environment for Adults and Young Adults. By Jim Dwyer. 1996. 507p. Neal-Schuman, $49.95 (1-55570-194-9).

Short annotations on 2,600 works, two-thirds of which are nonfiction. Both fiction and nonfiction are divided into subcategories (e.g., general works, natural history, culture, and issues.).

Encyclopedia of Environmental Biology. 3v. By William A. Nierenberg. 1995. 2,168p. Academic Press, $499 (0-12-226730-3).

Comprehensive coverage of biological terms, concepts, ideas, research, and so on, from acid rain to zoological parks.

Encyclopedia of Environmental Issues. 3v. By Craig W. Allin. 2000. 874p. Salem, $315 (0-89356-994-1).

Eighteen categories of information in which articles on events, persons, topics, history, organizations, issues, etc., are grouped. Very wide collection of topics offering a useful synthesis of information and a good starting place for a wide range of users.

Encyclopedia of Environmental Science. By John F. Mongillo and Linda Zierdt-Warshaw. 2000. 504p. Greenwood, $95 (1-57356-147-9).

Another categorized encyclopedia with 12 broad general groupings, describing basic terminology and concepts for the general reader. Content includes definitions, short biographies, organizations, issues, and bibliographies of print and electronic sources.

The Environment A to Z: A Ready-Reference Encyclopedia. By David Hosansky. 2001. 320p. CQ, $55 (1-56802-583-1).

Basic information on more than 300 terms, people, environmental movements, and legislation.

Environmental Activists. By John Mongillo and Bibi Booth. 2001. 368p. Greenwood, $59.95 (0-313-30884-5).

Biographical information on 60 American activists for general readers. An environmental time line provides a context for the people and activities. Especially accessible to secondary students.

Environmental Disasters: A Chronicle of Individual, Industrial, and Governmental Carelessness. By Lee Davis. 1998. 480p. Facts On File, $45 (0-8160-3265-3).

Covers the major disasters of the last half of the twentieth century that have had significant environmental repercussions. Provides descriptions of events and the context of the major industrial and nuclear disasters. There are also lists of minor disasters and those with short-lived repercussions.

Environmental Literature: An Encyclopedia of Works, Characters, Authors and Themes. By Patricia D. Netzley. 1999. 337p. ABC-CLIO, $75 (1-57607-000-X).

Basic information on a selection of major environmental writers from a broad range of disciplines and philosophies, discussing their works and impact on society.

The Facts On File Dictionary of Environmental Science. By L. Harold Stevenson and Bruce C. Wyman. 2001. 458p. Checkmark, $40 (0-8160-4233-0); paper, $17.95 (0-8160-4234-9).

Broad coverage with approximately 4,000 definitions of environmental terms for the lay reader and professional alike. Entries include some appropriate Web links.

Historical Dictionary of North American Environmentalism. By Edward R. Wells and Alan M. Schwartz. 1997. 226p. Scarecrow, $47 (0-8108-3331-X).

The major, mostly North American, people, places, and events—beginning with the Plymouth Colony in Massachusetts—that evolved into the environmental movement.

Indoor Pollution: A Reference Handbook. By E. Willard Miller and Ruby M. Miller. 1998. 330p. ABC-CLIO, $45 (0-87436-895-2).

Topics include characteristics, health effects, standards, sources, and control of indoor pollution. There are chapter bibliographies and other reference lists including associations and organizations.

Literature of Nature: An International Sourcebook. By Patrick D. Murphy and others. 1998. 512p. Fitzroy Dearborn, $95 (1-57958-010-6).

Looking at the ways nature is represented in the literature of differing cultures, genres, and orientations provides another insight into environmental issues. This volume has sections on geographic regions as well as a section on genres and theories.

Toxic Waste Sites: An Encyclopedia of Endangered America. By Mark Crawford. 1997. 324p. ABC-CLIO, $65 (0-87436-934-7).

Information about the thousands of hazardous pollution sites (location, hazards, chemicals, monitoring actions, etc.) organized by state.

2001 Conservation Directory: A Guide to Worldwide Environmental Organizations. By National Wildlife Federation Staff. 2001. 395p. Lyons, paper, $70 (1-58574-114-0).

More than 3,000 groups, U.S. governmental committees and agencies, educational institutions, and other conservation resources.

Vital Signs 2001: The Environmental Trends That Are Shaping Our Future. By Lester R. Brown and others. 2001. 224p. W. W. Norton, paper, $13.95 (0-393-32176-2).

Yearly statistical snapshots of a wide range of environmental indicators (food, agriculture, energy, atmosphere, economic, transportation, social, and military).

—*Linda Loos Scarth*

Special Features

Writer's Tool Kit

The library reference shelves are crammed with books that could be useful to a writer laboring on that first novel—or on the twentieth, for that matter. These include dictionaries and thesauri for finding just the right word and general and subject encyclopedias for getting the facts straight. In addition, there are a number of directories related to writing and publishing. We've listed a few of the standards that are designed to help writers get it on paper and get it published.

Artists and Writers Colonies: Retreats, Residencies, and Respites for the Creative Mind. 2d ed. Ed. by Robyn Middleton and others. 2000. 352p. Blue Heron, paper, $19.95 (0-936085-62-2).

Offers detailed listings for around 200 opportunities that provide time, space, or money to complete those stalled creative projects.

The AWP Official Guide to Writing Programs. 10th ed. Ed. by D.W. Fenza. 2001. 360p. Dustbooks, $24.95 (0-916685-88-8).

Provides a comprehensive listing of creative writing programs, as well as conferences, colonies, and centers.

Christian Writer's Market Guide. By Sally E. Stuart. 2001. 550p. Harold Shaw, $24.99 (0-87788-189-8).

Directs writers to more than 1,200 potential markets.

Complete Guide to Literary Contests 2001. 2000. 825p. Prometheus, paper, $30 (1-57392-850-X).

Provides information, including criteria, deadlines, entry forms and applications, and contacts, for nearly every open literary contest in the U.S., from small competitions to the Pulitzer Prize and the PEN/Faulkner Award.

Directory of Literary Magazines 2001. 2001. 302p. Moyer Bell, paper, $12.95 (1-55921-288-8).

Contains descriptions, submission guidelines, contact information, and more.

Grants and Awards Available to American Writers. 21st ed. Ed. by John Morrone and others. 2001. 382p. PEN American Center, $18 (0-934638-16-0).

Lists more than 1,000 American and international grants, fellowships, and contests.

International Directory of Little Magazines and Small Presses, 2000–2001. 36th ed. Ed. by Len Fulton. 2000. 960p. Dustbooks, $34.95 (0-916685-78-0).

This classic directory by one of the founders of the small press movement lists more than 500 presses and journals.

Literary Marketplace 2001: The Directory of the American Book Publishing Industry. 2v. 2000. Bowker, $312.50 (0-8352-4346-X).

The standard directory of U.S. publishers, agents, wholesalers, and more.

Novel and Short Story Writer's Market: 2,000 Places to Publish Your Fiction. 2002 ed. 2001. Writer's Digest, paper, $24.99 (1-58297-009-2).

Writer's Market. 2002 ed. 2001. Writer's Digest, paper, $29.99 (1-58297-044-0).

The annual *Writer's Market* listing agents, magazines, and publishers is perhaps the best-known general guide to getting published. *Novel and Short Story Writer's Market* is similar, but takes a more targeted approach.

Writer's Digest also produces a slew of how-to's on everything from ways to build character and write dialogue to "the ABC's of wounds and injuries" for crime and suspense novels to daily life during the Renaissance or the 1800s, for those who want to craft convincing historical fiction. The complete list of titles is available at [http://www.writersdigest.com/catalog/]. These are useful additions to a writer's resource collection, but libraries may already own reference books that serve a similar purpose.

—Mary Ellen Quinn

Another look at . . . :

Childcraft

Childcraft: The How and Why Library. 15v. 2000. 2,880p. illus. index. World Book, $299 (0-7166-0197-4).

When it first appeared in 1934, *Childcraft* was a seven-volume set published in two editions, one for home and one for school. The first three volumes offered poetry and stories, many excerpted from well-known books of the time. The last four volumes were intended to provide guidance to parents and teachers. *Childcraft* evolved from several earlier titles, including *The Foundation Library*, published by W. F. Quarrie and Company, who also published *The World Book*. The review in the October 1935 RBB (or *Subscription Books Bulletin*, as it was called) commented on the first *Childcraft*'s duplication of material already available in many homes and libraries, its representation of books with extracts ("a practice which most librarians and teachers of English feel to be highly undesirable"), and its high price ($39.90). The review concluded: "The chief field for *Childcraft* is perhaps that home or elementary school which is remote from library facilities, or the smaller school where the curriculum is not well defined and teachers lack training."

This generally set the tone for subsequent reviews. In 1940, although *Childcraft* had expanded to 14 volumes, we found that the set still had little to offer the large library, though it might be useful at home and in smaller libraries with few books. (It is difficult now to imagine what "those public libraries and schools where more adequate sources are not readily available" must have been like.) Later on, the tone of the reviews begins to change, reflecting in part the major alterations *Childcraft* had undergone. The idea of two separate editions was dropped, and the selection of literary material was decreased in favor of more coverage of topics such as science. In the 1960s, *Childcraft* incorporated *The How and Why Library*, a somewhat similar set of volumes published since 1913. In an extensive review in 1966, we praised *Childcraft* for its "explanation of complex science subjects," its "high standards of selection of anthological material," and its "generous illustrations." But we found it to have little usefulness for older children and little value as a reference tool. Our last review, in 1990, also found much to praise but noted that *Childcraft* is "only peripherally a reference book." In fact, this has always been the problem with reviewing *Childcraft*. Though often referred to as an encyclopedia, perhaps because of its multivolume format, it does not fit within the standard encyclopedia model.

In its latest incarnation, *Childcraft* retains many of the features of the edition we reviewed in 1990. The amount of literary material, once the heart of the set, has shrunk from three to two volumes, one of poetry and the other of fairy tales, folk tales, and a few excerpts from books for younger children. In 1990 we noted the absence of coverage of art and music, areas now explored in volume 3, *Art around Us*. Volumes 4 through 11 cover science topics: animals, plants, Earth, the universe, basic scientific principles, simple math, and the human body. Volume 12, *Who We Are*, introduces children to "the people and cultures of many nations." Volume 13 focuses on geography, volume 14 covers holidays, and volume 15 is a cumulative index and parents' and teachers' guide. The geography volume, which previously highlighted interesting places, now provides more coverage of topics such as continents, maps, and types of buildings, although there is nothing on cities. Each volume ends with a glossary and an index. Pages are colorful and visually pleasing, with approximately equal amounts of illustration and text. The many activities are coded to indicate their level of difficulty. In 1990 we faulted *Childcraft* for not suggesting additional sources to turn to; now, each volume includes a brief list of other, age-appropriate materials, including some CD-ROMs, videos, and Web sites. The dictionary volume has been dropped, but there are plenty of other children's dictionaries available.

Although there has been tremendous growth in reference publishing for the middle-school level and up, there are few solid resources for children in kindergarten and the primary grades. Childcraft has lasted for all these years because it has adapted to children's changing needs, expanding its factual content while retaining an inviting, picture-book quality. But don't think of it as an encyclopedia. Think of it as an introduction to the wide world of encyclopedias and other reference tools.

—Mary Ellen Quinn

The Columbia Granger's Index to Poetry in Anthologies

The Columbia Granger's Index to Poetry in Anthologies. 12th ed. Ed. by Tessa Kale. 2002. 2,219p. indexes. Columbia Univ., $295 (0-231-12448-1). 016.80881.

There are a handful of reference sources that work so well that we tend to take them for granted. Among these is The Columbia Granger's Index to Poetry, "one of the oldest continuously published reference works in the United States."

Columbia Granger's takes its name from Edith Granger, about whom little is known except that she worked in the poetry department of McClurg's bookstore. A. C. McClurg & Company, a publishing firm that also ran a wholesale and retail book business, was at one time the largest bookstore in Chicago. The poetry department staffers (the idea of a book store with a separate, fully staffed department for poetry conjures up an image of well-mannered people sipping Earl Grey from china teacups while they discuss Wordsworth) needed a tool that would help them locate poems for customers, and so, in 1904, Granger's Index to Poetry was born. To be precise, An Index to Poetry and Recitations: Being a Practical Reference Manual for Librarians, Teachers, Booksellers, Elocutionists, Etc., as the early editions were called, was born. Columbia University Press began editing and publishing the index in the 1940s. Columbia has since turned Granger's into a brand, trademarking the name and spinning off a number of related titles, including The Columbia Granger's Index to African-American Poetry (1999) and The Columbia Granger's Index to Poetry in Collected and Selected Works (1996).

Compared to other reference classics, Granger's has a spotty review history. The appearance of the twelfth edition sent us to the index card file that is the equivalent of the RBB attic, where we discovered that we have reviewed only three editions—the sixth, the eighth, and the tenth. How much is there to say about a volume that is made up of several very long lists? The essential format remains the same, with poems indexed under title, first line, and last line; author; and subject. The news lies in the anthologies that the publisher and its consultants have chosen to include. Like its predecessors, the twelfth edition indexes 400 anthologies, adding almost 150 new ones published from the cutoff date of the eleventh (1997) edition through December 31, 2000. To make way for these, 150 older anthologies have been jettisoned. Among the new poetry volumes are All Shook Up; Collected Poems about Elvis (Univ. of Arkansas, 2001); Chinese Poetry: An Anthology of Major Modes and Genres (Duke Univ., 2000); and Victorian Women Poets: A New Annotated Anthology (Longman, 2001).

Edith Granger created a work waiting for the digital age to happen—the simplicity that makes Columbia Granger's so functional in print also made it an ideal candidate for adapting to electronic formats. Columbia produced a CD-ROM version in 1991 and took Granger's online in 2000. In addition to cumulating content from various editions and titles and multiplying the access routes to poems, the electronic versions add full-text, biographies, bibliographies, commentaries, and other features. With these options available, why do we need Columbia Granger's in print? Because there are still times when the most efficient way to address a reference query is the no-tech approach developed in the poetry department at McClurg's almost 100 years ago.

—Mary Ellen Quinn

Focus Reviews

An Encyclopedia of One's Own

Women in World History: A Biographical Encyclopedia. 17v. Ed. by Anne Commire and Deborah Klezmer. 1999–2002. Gale, $1,395 (0-7876-3736-X). 920.72.

In her essay, "A Room of One's Own," Virginia Woolf notes the absence of women from history. Her own father, Leslie Stephen, was the editor of the Dictionary of National Biography, where men occupy 97 percent of the page space. But times and sensibilities have changed, and now we have a big biographical encyclopedia devoted to exclusively to women.

The roots of Women in World History (WWH) can be traced back at least as far as 1971, when the Harvard University Press published the landmark Notable American Women, 1607–1950. This three-volume encyclopedia was hailed as a significant contribution to biographical dictionaries and the first work of its kind. The project had been proposed as early as 1955 as a companion but also a kind of corrective to Dictionary of American Biography, which, following the pattern of Dictionary of National Biography, included only 706 women among its nearly 15,000 entries. Notable American Women covered 1,359 individuals, and Notable American Women: The Modern Period (Harvard, 1980) added another 442.

A generation's worth of scholarship has gone by, and there is much fuller representation of women in reference materials in general, so any new woman-centered encyclopedia has to offer something unique. WWH's contribution is sheer size, profiling nearly 10,000 women around the world from 3100 BCE to the modern period. Its heft reflects both a greater availability of documentation, and a wider embrace. For example, while the only women admitted to Notable American Women based on their husband's credentials were wives of the presidents, the editors of WWH were "determined not to leave a mother, wife, duchess, or daughter unturned," so we find information not only on presidential wives, but on consorts, royal mistresses, and others generally viewed as appendages to notable men. Here they are examined in light of their own accomplishments. A Madame Pompadour, after all, was by necessity a wielder of influence and power. In addition to looking at such women in a new way, WWH's reach extends far beyond the famous, giving coverage not only to Mary Todd Lincoln but also to Elizabeth Keckley, the ex-slave who was her closest friend.

Entries range in length from a paragraph supplying basic "who's who" information to several pages. Typical of longer entries is the one for Abigail Adams (1744–1818), where a brief summary of facts is followed by more than six pages of discussion, accompanied by a black-and-white portrait, a pull quote, and a brief bibliography. Adams' entry also includes short summaries on her mother and two sisters, as well as her daughter and John Adams' mother—these sidebar entries help rescue thousands of women from oblivion.

One of the things that makes this set an eye-opener is that longer entries are not just devoted to the same women who are routinely covered in other sources. Near contemporaries of Adams who receive multi-page treatment are Louis XV's mistress Madame du Barry; Olympe de Gouges, a French writer whose literary career ended with the guillotine; Catherine Greene, who was not only married to American Revolutionary War general Nathaniel Greene but also helped invent the cotton gin; Mary Jemison, captive of the Iroquois Indians in the French and Indian War; and Englishwoman Joanna Southcott, an illiterate servant who gained a following as a preacher and prophet. Despite the set's awesome breadth, the editors acknowledge that there were many more women who could have been included, and "readers will inevitably find omissions" (one is Rose Bertin, Marie Antoinette's influential dressmaker). But it's hard to quibble when WWH offers so many more women than any reference source before it. This is a landmark publication, and we look forward to its completion (and its indexes).

The past several years have seen a flood of other, smaller biographical encyclopedias and dictionaries devoted exclusively to women. Typically for a maturing discipline, the pool of available resources has become both broader and deeper, the inclusiveness of *Women in World History* complemented by numerous titles that are much more specialized. Below, we've compiled a list of some other women-centered dictionaries and encyclopedias that we've reviewed just in the time since the first volumes of WWH appeared. Citations to RBB reviews are included. There is more to come: Sharpe Reference has a three volume *Encyclopedia of Women in American History* ($299, 0-7656-8038-6), which we will review in a future issue.

American Women in Technology: An Encyclopedia. By Linda Zierdt Warshaw and others. 2000. 384p. ABC-CLIO, $75 (1-57607-072-7). [RBB D 1 00]

A to Z of Women Writers. By Carol Kort. 2000 274p. Facts On File, $40 (0-8160-3727-2). [RBB Je 1 & 15 00]

Biographical Dictionary of Ancient Greek and Roman Women. By Marjorie Lightman and Benjamin Lightman, 2000. 298p. Facts On File, $45 (0-8160-3112-6). [RBB My 15 00]

The Biographical Dictionary of Women in Science: Pioneering Lives from Ancient Times to the Mid-Twentieth Century. 2v. Ed. by Marilyn Ogilvie and Joy Harvey. 2000. 1,499p. Routledge, $195 (0-415-92038-8). [RBB D 1 00]

Encyclopedia of Women: Global Women's Issues and Knowledge. 4v. Ed. by Cheris Kramarae and Dale Spender. 2000. 2,167p. Routledge, $495 (0-415-92088-4). [RBB Mr 15 01]

Encyclopedia of Women in the Ancient World. By Joyce Salisbury. 2001. 370p. bibliog. illus. index. maps. ABC-CLIO, $75 (1-57607-092-1). [RBB Ja 1&15 02]

Encyclopedia of Women's Travel and Exploration. By Patricia D. Netzley. 259p. 2001. Oryx, $65 (1-57356-238-6). [RBB S 15 01]

Extraordinary Women of the Medieval and Renaissance World: A Biographical Dictionary. By Carole Levin and others. 2000. 352p. Greenwood, $65 (0-313-30659-1). [RBB D 15 00]

Handbook of American Women's History. 2d ed. Ed. by Angela Howard and Frances Kavenik. 732p. Sage, $99.95 (0-7619-1635-0). [RBB D 15 00]

Historical Encyclopedia of American Women Entrepreneurs. By Jeanette M. Oppedisano. 2000. 283p. Greenwood, $79.50 (0-313-30647-8). [RBB F 15 01]

International Encyclopedia of Women and Sports. 3v. Ed. by Karen Christiansen and others. 2001. 1,428p. Macmillan, $350 (0-02-864954-0).

Native American Women: A Biographical Dictionary. 2d ed. Ed. by Gretchen M. Bataille and Laurie Lisa. 2001. 384p. Routledge, $85 (0-415-93020-0). [RBB O 15 01]

Notable Twentieth-Century Latin American Women: A Biographical Dictionary. Ed. by Cynthia M. Tompkins and David W. Foster. 2001. 324p. Greenwood, $59.95 (0-313-31112-9). [RBB My 15 01]

Women Building Chicago, 1790–1990: A Biographical Dictionary. Ed. by Rima Lunin Schultz and Adele Hast. 2001. 1,088p. bibliogs. illus. indexes. Indiana Univ., $75 (0-253-33852-2). [RBB Ja 1&15 02]

—*Mary Ellen Quinn*

Desktop Library

ebrarian for Libraries. [http://www.ebrary.com/].

In the months since Reference Books Bulletin started looking at electronic book delivery services, much has changed. NetLibrary went bankrupt and was purchased by OCLC. Questia has a lot fewer employees than it used to. Ebrary [http://www.ebrary.com] is a more recent player entering this market in transition, having recently rolled out ebrarian 2.1 with services targeted specifically to libraries. Ebrary doesn't describe itself as an e-book vendor but rather as a provider of "secure online delivery of authoritative content." According to ebrary, this means that "we provide a platform that enables our publishing partners to distribute copyright protected works to libraries and other organizations."

Ebrarian has nice functionality, with an adjustable framed environment. The coverage seems to have good timeliness. Many recent titles are included as well as some older materials that are out of copyright. Notable publishers are signing up, among them Cambridge University Press, McGraw-Hill, Random House, and Viking Penguin. Ebrary has 6,000 titles currently live and more than 30,000 under contract. Government documents are planned for inclusion into the system.

There did not seem to be any administrative problems with the software. It loaded easily and ran well, with only a few glitches. Documents can be easily navigated, browsed, copied, printed, highlighted, bookmarked, added to a personal bookshelf, and zoomed. Ebrary utilizes something they call InfoTools, which allows word-level linking to various online research tools (a translator, maps, dictionaries, etc.) as well as commands to search all documents, search the Web, and buy the title from amazon.com or Barnes & Noble at www.bn.com. Libraries can link to e-books through their OPAC, either as part of an 856 field linked from the record of a printed book or as a separate catalog entry.

Ebrarian allows access by unlimited simultaneous users. Initially it imposed an access fee to subscribe to the service (for a public library, the annual fee is $0.05 per population served) and a per-page charge of $0.15 to $0.50 to print or copy to compensate publishers. Some librarians may object to paying for this service twice, once to subscribe and once again to print or copy. Whether a library has a cost recovery system in place for printing or allows free printing for its patrons, it will end up subsidizing the additional cost of printing via ebrary. Recently, ebrary adopted a pricing option that they describe as an "all you can eat" model—an annual license fee and a fixed charge based on library type and size, allowing patrons unlimited print and copy transactions.

So far, I've discussed ebrary's good coverage, good software, and workable pricing structure. However, ebrary has an intentionally imposed limitation that seriously jeopardizes its viability.

Ebrary limits the amount of "freely viewable pages" that readers can see on some titles. As their Web site explains, "This is the percentage of the volume that you can view, copy, and print as determined by the publisher. The percentages are based on the total number of pages in the document (for example, if a document is 50 percent viewable, and the document has 400 pages, you can view ANY 200 pages throughout the document). If you have exceeded the viewed pages limit, you can go back to previously viewed pages for copying and printing."

If the reader exceeds this limit, the software informs them, "You have exceeded the limit of freely viewable pages set by this document's publisher." Only 4 publishers out of more than 100 have put these limitations on viewing the material. But in my use of ebrary, I found several titles with this limitation, among them Tom Brokaw's *The Greatest Generation*, published by Random House.

Why should libraries buy or lease a book if their readers are not allowed to read all of it? When I bought my first new car, no one told me that I could only drive it for 20 percent or 50 percent of its usable life. Although 4 out of 100 publishers is a small number, the limit can be frustrating and has the potential to mar an otherwise commendable product. Libraries need to be aware of this restriction before they decide to invest in ebrary for their patrons.

—*Jack O'Gorman*

Genealogy Gold Mine

Ancestry Plus. [Internet database]. Gale, pricing from $2,520 for two users. (Last accessed February 22, 2002).

With "over 1.2 billion records in over 3,000 databases," *Ancestry Plus* is one of the largest andr best-organized online resources for genealogical research. Until recently, the database was available only via personal subscription from *Ancestry.com*. Gale's inclusion of *Ancestry Plus* in its online lineup makes it easy for libraries to license it and to provide access to multiple users. Users who are already familiar with *Ancestry.com*'s organization and search software will find that these are essentially unchanged. Large adds for Ancestry products have been removed, although smaller ads do appear on some results displays.

Most of the individual databases are digitized print resources that have information on individuals and families. Several new databases are added every week. They are a gold mine for genealogists. Some of the major resources include city directories, the *American Genealogical-Biographical Index*, PERSI (*Periodical Source Index* to genealogical and historical periodicals), the *Civil War Pension Index*, and digitized images of the U.S. Census from 1790 to 1920. The contents of Gale's *Biography and Genealogy Master Index* are indexed, but not for persons born after 1920, because Ancestry has a policy of not providing data on living persons. A unique offering, unavailable to personal subscribers, is Gale's *Passenger and Immigration Lists Index*. More Gale content may be added to *Ancestry Plus* in the future. Databases recently added to Ancestry.com, such as *England and Wales, Civil Registration Index: 1837–1900*, may not be available in *Ancestry Plus* until Gale secures distribution rights.

The home page presents an inviting search box, titled "Find Your Ancestors NOW!" It has two blanks, one for given name and one for last name. A location of "any" is the default, but a state abbreviation or "international" may be selected instead. This instant-gratification global search engine often returns hundreds of hits in some or all of the available record categories: Census Records; Birth, Marriage, and Death; Military Records; Biography and History; Court, Land, and Probate Records; Immigration Records; Directories and Memberships; and Periodicals and Newspapers. Users may prefer to select one of these categories to conduct a more focused search. There are also options to use reference and finding aids and resources such as *Ancestry World Tree*, a searchable database of contributed family trees.

Global search results display the number of hits in each record category. When a single category, such as Census Records, is searched, a list of one or more different databases appears, such as the 1830, 1840, or 1850 census. When a database is chosen, entries for personal names are usually displayed 10 at a time. Data fields for entries vary by database. Examples include dates, place-names, military unit, page or microfilm roll numbers from the original source, parents or spouse, and more. Almost all of the data are digitized text transcribed from the original sources, but a View Image link is added to those records for which one is available.

Results for our global search for Amos Bronson Alcott included entries in almost all of the record categories. Of the two records with icons indicating availability of census images, only one was viewable. For the 1810 census, there was no help in interpreting the significance of all the numbers in the columns following Alcott's name. These indicate the numbers of males and females of various age ranges living in a named person's residence, as well as other types of data. Librarians will be able to find explanations elsewhere, but they should be available in the database at point of use.

With Advanced search, the user can specify spelling (exact or Soundex), country, keyword, year range, record type, and proximity (which field or word is proximate to which other thing is not clear). As any genealogist knows, the Soundex search can be extremely useful. It's based on consonant sounds, thus getting around the many spelling variations found in old records: a Soundex search for Mielke would also return such names as Mulkey, Mulcahy, and Milke. Any record category or single database within a record category may be searched on its own. Search screens for individual databases provide a brief description of content and bibliographic source information as well as a keyword search box.

Ancestry Plus and Ancestry's individual subscriber site are on separate servers, they both access the same database when retrieving data. According to Gale, Ancestry is continually monitoring traffic on its site and expanding capacity as needed. There were occasional temporary glitches while searching and displaying results, such as census image views being unavailable because of "regularly scheduled maintenance" or records not showing up even though there were several hits found in the database listing.

Results pages provide a "printer friendly" option for printing without large headers and footers. Another useful feature is the yellow sticky-note icon next to each name on results pages. It's labeled "add comments," and users can both add their own data about the person and read information others have posted. It would be nice if the message changed to "add/read comments" once someone has posted a note. Access to comments was inconsistent.

Even with all the data it offers, *Ancestry Plus* won't be the only place patrons will need to look. Other online resources have a wealth of additional information. And genealogists will add names to many branches of their family tree only after diligent searching by traditional methods—in print and on microfilm, in county courthouses, state archives, libraries, and foreign repositories. That said, *Ancestry Plus* can be a good tool for historians and archivists who want to quickly find information on persons named in collections of letters or other papers, and library users will be thrilled to have access to one of the best and biggest online genealogy databases. The database can definitely be improved with regard to consistency of access to all areas and better explanations where needed. But the quantity and quality of the content itself is outstanding, and any library that subscribes to *Ancestry Plus* will have waiting lines and very grateful patrons!

—Deborah Rollins

Library-in-a-Dorm Room

Questia. 2001. Questia Media, Inc., $19.59/mo., $149.95/yr. (http://www.questia.com).

Since it was launched in January 2001, Questia has created a stir in the library world. Unlike other e-book business models, such as netLibrary, libraries cannot subscribe to it. From Questia'ss marketing, it appears that college students who have a paper to write are their audience. (Hey, wait a minute; I thought college students with a paper to write were our audience.) Librarians may feel that Questia is more like a competitor than a product they can recommend to students. However, if we are concerned that our customers will be shopping at another store, we don't have to worry yet. Though the interface and site design have improved, the content is still uneven.

According to the *Questia* Web site, "Questia is a scholarly online library that augments and complements your academic library collection." *Questia* states that they have more than 40,000 complete books and journal articles online. The books and articles come from more than 170 publishers, many of which are university presses. Emphasis is on the liberal arts. The content includes both new materials (e.g., *Humor in British Literature* [Greenwood, 1997]) and older, out-of-copyright materials (e.g., *History of French Literature* [Oxford, 1912]). There are several ways to search. Quick Search offers simple searching by author, title, subject, or keyword; Power Search allows more specific searching, including by publication date. The Explore a Topic option is a browse search, based on 28 broad academic subject areas. Searches can be conducted across (or limited to) media type: books, articles, and the sixth edition of *The Columbia Encyclopedia*. Results can be sorted by relevancy, publication date, contributor, title, publisher, or media type. A frame to the left of the results screen displays relevant subject headings that the user can select to refine a search, a helpful feature for those whose search terms are too broad.

Currently, the journal articles component of *Questia* does not have the depth of coverage of other periodical databases, such as *Ingenta* (which recently merged with *UnCover*) and OCLC's *ArticleFirst*. Entering *Civil War* in Quick Search retrieves more than 300 books but only two articles.

The automatic creation of footnotes and bibliographies are useful features, but will *Questia* really help students write better research papers (as the company claims) or to understand the research process? Why should students pay to get access to resources and assistance they already get as part of their tuition if they go to the campus library? For those who are intrigued by the e-book concept, the library may well offer other options, such as *netLibrary* [RBB Mr 1 01] or ABC-CLIO's electronic publishing program [RBB Ap 15 01]. Libraries also provide access to electronic journals.

A more pressing question for libraries is just how *Questia* will augment and complement our services. In an interview in the February, 2001 issue of *Information Today*, company founder, president, and CEO Troy Williams offered this vision of the library/*Questia* partnership: "*Questia* has an unlimited number of copies of a text . . . A librarian could say: 'That copy is checked out. You could request it on ILL from another university, or if you need it tonight, you can get it on *Questia*.'" This is not likely to strike many librarians as an ideal model for promoting library use. Students may appreciate having a one-stop, 24 x 7 service that enables them to pull together a research paper without having to leave their dorm rooms, especially if the collection grows to the targeted 250,000 items in three years. For libraries, Questia might be a harder sell—but it's not for sale to us, anyway.

—Jack O'Gorman

Out of the Shadows

★**Women Building Chicago, 1790–1990:** A Biographical Dictionary. Ed. by Rima Lunin Schultz and Adele Hast. 2001. 1,088p. bibliogs. illus. indexes. Indiana Univ., $75 (0-253-33852-2). 305.4.

If size alone were an indication of a reference book's value, this one, with more than 1,000 pages and weighing nearly seven pounds would top every "best" list. A reference book, however, is much more than the sum of its pages; and in this case, the subject covered, the way it is covered, and even the way the book itself came to be are more reliable indicators of worth.

In 1990 the Chicago Area Women's History Conference (CAWHC) launched the Historical Encyclopedia of Chicago Women Project. Two years later a proposal was sent to the National Endowment for the Humanities under the auspices of the Center for Research on Women and Gender at the University of Illinois at Chicago. Editorial and advisory boards were formed, and the task of assembling an account of the lives of women integral to the history and development of the city of Chicago began.

Several criteria were established for the selection of biographees. Entrants had to have been deceased prior to December 31, 1990; played some kind of role in the history of the city; and attained some degree of accomplishment or expertise in her particular field or left writing reflecting the effects of historical events on her or on those around her. In addition, enough background information for a sizable reference entry was deemed essential. Research in the early stages of the project used *Women's History Sources: A Guide to Archives and Manuscript Collections in the United States*, by Andrea Hinding and Ames S. Bower (Bowker, 1979), to identify primary sources of information. The editors also gathered names from their own research, from historians and practitioners in various fields, and from members of ethnic communities. These efforts resulted in a database of about 3,000 names. The editorial board soon selected the first hundred names and conducted workshops for potential contributors. Contacts were made with local scholars in a variety of disciplines, professional associations, women's studies and history groups, and ethnic organizations. Even at this stage, contributors were asked to verify the existence of sufficient background material on their subjects. The entire board would eventually select 423 entries, with choices ranging from scholar and social reformer Edith Abbott (1876–1957) to pianist and teacher Fannie Bloomfield Zeisler (1863–1927). The resulting book is a fascinating collection of the life stories of a group of remarkable women, and the source notes after each entry (listing published and unpublished sources that were consulted) make it a valuable aid to further research in women's history.

An extended essay by editor Schultz—her survey of the history of women in Chicago is substantial enough to serve as a minicourse on the subject—opens the book. Rather than simply reciting the facts about each entrant, entries set each woman in historical context; and because many of the biographees are not particularly well known, this is an essential and welcome feature and one of the strengths of this work. The signed entries are arranged alphabetically, with the biographee's name in bold type followed by birth and death dates and occupations or roles in capital letters. The length of the entries varies with the subject, but most are from 2,000 to 5,000 words. Within the entries cross-references to other women included in the book are printed in capital letters the first time they are mentioned. In addition, color plates feature the work of Chicago women artists and craftswomen, and more than 100 black-and-white illustrations, ranging from formal portraits to news photos, are distributed throughout the text.

Although some of the women included here are well known, most of the entries are accounts of the lives of women who are not. Page after page tells the story of women's participation in the history of Chicago: the contributions of women to the commercial and social development of Chicago from 1790 to 1860; women's relief work in the Civil War; the movement for women's rights; women's contributions to labor, education, journalism, medicine, law, the fine arts; and more. Here one will find not only Harriet Monroe, the founder of *Poetry* magazine, but also Othelia Mork Myhrman, a Swedish American community activist. Charlemae Hill Rollins, eminent children's librarian and author, is represented, as is Ida Gray Nelson Rollins, the first African American woman to establish a dental practice in Chicago. Rosa Raisa, operatic soprano, and Margaret Dreier Robins, labor and social reformer, each have an entry, as do Bozena Salara, Czech missionary and teacher, and Sister Dolores Schorsch, educator and author. Famous names in broadcasting, like Fran Allison, of *Kukla, Fran and Ollie* fame, and Irna Phillips, creator and writer of soap operas, are profiled, as are Alice M. Peurala, trade unionist and civil rights activist, and Maria Diaz Martinez, social worker and one of the founders of Mujeres Latinas en Accion (Latin Women in Action). The index lists entries by names as well as occupation, race, ethnicity, and religion, so the reader can easily locate notable women in any of those categories. There is also a list of entries by year of birth.

Elizabeth Janeway once wrote that, "Like their personal lives, women's history is fragmented, interrupted; a shadow history of human beings whose existence has been shaped by the efforts and demands of others." *Women Building Chicago*, 1790–1990 gathers those fragments into a wonderful mosaic depicting the women of Chicago, whose efforts and demands have shaped life in the city as we know it today.

—Carolyn Mulac

Sixty-Thousand Page Giant

Oxford Reference Online. [Internet database]. 2002. Oxford, pricing from $325 [http://www.oxfordreference.com]. (Last accessed May 3, 2002).

Having already produced online versions of *American National Biography* and *The Oxford English Dictionary*, Oxford University Press has recently adopted a more integrated approach to delivering content online and launched *Oxford Reference Online* (ORO), a database made up of content from around 100 OUP titles. According to Oxford, this is the equivalent of a reference work of 60,000 pages. Though the quotes we found on the home page ("A giant reference work that dwarfs any book in history"; "The giant Oxford Reference Online will eclipse any general knowledge source on the Web or in print") may be overstatements, there is no doubt that this is a resource with lots of potential.

Among the titles are many that will be familiar to librarians—*The Concise Oxford Guide to Classical Literature*, *The Concise Oxford Guide to English Literature*, *The Oxford Guide to United States Government*, *The Oxford Guide to United Stated Supreme Court Decisions*—plus works on art, mythology, religion, science, language (including some bilingual dictionaries), quotations, and more. Users are offered three word searches: Quick Search, Advanced Search, and Search Within a Subject, which lists 23 broad subject categories. In addition, one can search within an individual book. There is also a global browse search that lists each and every database entry along with its source, from A*algorithm (in A Dictionary of Computing) all the way to ZZ Ceti star (in A Dictionary of Astronomy). Users can also browse by subject or by book.

In Advanced Search, searches can be limited to entry headings, people, and dates and also by subject. Additional options are Standard search (which will find plurals and derivatives), Boolean search, and Pattern search. Search results can be sorted by relevance ranking, by subject, by book, or alphabetically; and results can be displayed by up to 100 per page. Each result provides a few lines of text and the source. A nice feature is the Refine by Subject option. When we entered *Salisbury* as a search term we got 24 results, from *Salisbury Cathedral* to *Salisbury steak*. Displayed along with the results were a list of subject headings and the number of results within each heading—six hits from titles in the Food and Nutrition category, 12 hits from the History category, and so on. Clicking on Food and Nutrition brought a revised results list showing just the occurrences for *Salisbury steak*. If one is already searching within a subject category, the search can be refined by book instead of by subject.

From each entry one can access previous and next results, select from an expanded list of adjacent entries (within the same book), and e-mail. Every entry includes information on how to cite. Cross-references are hyperlinked, although only within books. Inevitably, we found some rigidity that tends to occur in the absence of a human hand. There is an entry for *Salisbury steak* in *A Dictionary of Food and Nutrition* that describes the dish, and an entry in *A New Dictionary of Eponyms* that tells us how the dish got its name, but there are no direct links between the two. Oxford has attempted to provide a way around this by offering a cross-reference icon that can be clicked after the user highlights a term, bringing up a list of all the entries in which the term appears.

Like many other databases, Oxford offers external links, in this case from each individual title. For example, there are links from *The Concise Oxford Companion to the Theatre* to 10 related Web sites and links to 13 sites from *A Dictionary of World History*. It is not clear how frequently the links will be updated, but new books and new editions will be added to the database every year. Between now and 2004, Oxford expects to add around 30 new and revised works.

The ORO home page contains another quote—"the world's most respected reference publisher"—which comes from the pages of this magazine. Given Oxford's reputation for high-quality reference material and the ease of use, convenient features, and reasonable cost of its new database, libraries should certainly take a look. *Oxford Reference Online* may lack the overriding editorial vision that shapes general subject encyclopedias and works such as *American National Biography* and *The Oxford English Dictionary* but the lack of an overriding vision is a hallmark of the Web anyway.

—Mary Ellen Quinn

Unabridged and Online

Merriam-Webster Unabridged. [Internet database]. Merriam-Webster, institutional pricing from $295 [http://www.MerriamWebsterUnabridged.com/mwol-1b.htm]. (Last accessed April 8, 2002).

The trade name many people associate with the phrase "unabridged dictionary" has at last launched a Web version of its most famous work. *Merriam-Webster Unabridged* (MWU) contains all entries from *Webster's Third New International Dictionary, Unabridged* (Merriam-Webster, 1993) and the six addenda that have been published and presents it within an easy-to-use interface at a reasonable price. It also comes with links to a "Reference Library" featuring an online atlas as well as the *Merriam-Webster Collegiate Dictionary* and *Thesaurus*, an online monthly newsletter, various word games, and the ability to submit a new word. A seventh addenda section will be available on the site in September 2002.

MWU's opening screen offers eight types of searches: Main Entry, Begins With, Ends With, Crossword, Definition, Rhyme, Etymology, and Jumble. Each is self-explanatory with the exception of Crossword, which allows the use of a question mark for a single-character wild card and an asterisk for any number of letters. (Actually, the same search works in the Main Entry search; typing in "th?o*t" for either Main Entry or Crossword retrieves 32 entries, including *theocrat* and *throughput*). Main Entry searches automatically retrieve any inflected forms, variant spellings, homographs, and phrases derived from the main entry. For example, a search for *put* retrieves *feed bag*, which contains the phrase *put on the feed bag*, as well as the entry *put down*. Help is available in several places from the main entry screen. If there is an illustration (and there aren't many—only 1,000 or so according to the User's Guide), it is available via a hyperlink at the end of an entry.

Any search brings up a scrollable menu of results listing the relevant entries. Clicking on a term in the results list brings up the full definition and entry, with all parts clearly labeled (main entry, pronunciation, function, inflected forms, etc.). A Pronunciation Guide link near the headword opens a separate window listing the most common pronunciations and also provides the only place in the unabridged work where one can hear audio pronunciations—though only for the sample pronunciation and not for the entry itself. The results list is limited to 400 entries, though the total number of results is always indicated ("2639 entries found, of which 400 are in list"). Cross-references to other entries are hyperlinked. Each entry also contains hyperlinks allowing one to search the entry in the *Collegiate Dictionary* or in the thesaurus. In addition to a Get Help tab, each main entry also has tabs enabling one to bookmark the entry, print it in a printer-friendly format, e-mail it, or browse the dictionary by opening a separate window listing 20 entries alphabetically before and 20 entries alphabetically after the entry being examined. At any point while in the site, the same eight search types featured on the main page are available via a drop-down menu at the top of the screen, making it easy to start a new search.

The Advanced Search screen features 11 search boxes: Main Entry, Definition, Function, Etymology, Usage Note, Usage Example, Author Quoted, Synonym Paragraph, Rhyme, Homophone, and Cryptogram. Any box may be filled in for a combined field search. However, more than one word in a box gets mixed results depending on the field searched and does *not* constitute a phrase search. For example, a search for *old English* in the Etymology field retrieves not just Old English but also English, Middle English, Old French, and Old Norse. Fair enough—it's an implied *and* within the field. On the other hand, an Advanced Search in the Author Quoted field for *Joseph Conrad* retrieves nothing. The same search omitting *Joseph* does retrieve quotes, but some of these are from a Barnaby Conrad. Although in most retrieved entries search terms are easy to find because they are highlighted in bold red type, inflected forms of the search term are not. A search in the Definition field for *house* will retrieve any definition that contains the words *houses*, *housing*, or other forms, but only *house* is highlighted.

As the User's Guide points out, search results "might actually be organized in two sections: words from the base dictionary arranged alphabetically, followed by words from the addenda sections arranged alphabetically." For example, a search in the Definition field for *code* retrieves 296 entries. One must scroll through this list, past the entry for *zulu*, to discover that the listing begins anew with AC and continues through *zip-code*, because this latter group all came from the addenda. Dictionary and addenda entries should have been combined. More disheartening is the complete lack of neologisms. One must rely on the link to the *Collegiate Dictionary* for terms such as *cyberspace*, *flatline*, Internet, *newbie*, or *velociraptor*. A search on *spam* brings up the term in the unabridged work, but one must click on the *Collegiate Dictionary* link to retrieve its e-mail use. Such terms should have been incorporated within the unabridged version's lexicon. The final shortcoming is the lack of audio pronunciations, which is another area where the user must remember to link to the Collegiate version.

Merriam-Webster will need to incorporate some changes in MWU to take full advantage of its new online environment. It is hoped that the current reliance on the *Collegiate Dictionary* for neologisms and audio pronunciations does not cause the smaller work to get yanked from its present free status on the Web and get folded into the paid unabridged site.

Shortcomings aside, public and academic libraries should certainly add MWU to their collections if budget allows, if only because of the Merriam-Webster name. Merriam-Webster at least offers its premier unabridged work on the Web. While some other dictionary publishers may claim to be more up to date, most have yet to mount *any* Internet version—for free or fee. Will the next war of unabridged dictionaries be fought on the Web?

—Ken Black

Wives of the Presidents

Although reference books on U.S. presidents are plentiful, sources that consider First Ladies in their own right have been harder to come by. Four recent publications, three new and one revised, help fill the gap. All share some features, such as arranging entries chronologically and introducing each entry with a portrait and vital statistics. But each book has characteristics that that distinguish it from the rest.

American First Ladies. Ed. by Robert P. Watson. 2002. 439p. bibliogs. illus. index. Salem, $135 (0-89356-070-7). 973.

This companion to *American Presidents* (rev. ed., 2000) presents 44 entries on women who were married to or, like Patsy Jefferson Randolph and Angelica Singleton Van Buren, served as hostesses for American presidents. Entries are signed by a variety of contributors and range in length from five to ten pages, with the longest generally devoted to women from Jacqueline Kennedy on. Each entry adheres to the same format: a brief overview followed by discussions of early life, marriage and family, the White House years, and legacy. Sidebars offer information on each president and highlight a significant aspect of the first ladyship. Each entry offers at least one illustration and concludes with a bibliography. Nine additional entries examine such topics as family life at the White House and the involvement of First Ladies in policy issues. The volume winds up with a chronology of First Ladies; a chronology of presidents; a list of libraries, museums, historic sites, and Web sites; and an extensive general bibliography.

American First Ladies: Their Lives and Their Legacy. 2d ed. Ed. by Lewis L. Gould. 2001. 468p. appendixes. bibliogs. illus. index. Routledge, $95 (0-415-93021-9). 973.

The work of almost 30 historians, this volume is an update of a 1996 publication. Laura Bush makes a debut appearance, and there are new entries on Abigail Adams, Frances Cleveland, Lou Hoover, Bess Truman, Mamie Eisenhower, Rosalynn Carter, and Nancy Reagan. Other entries have been revised. Coverage is restricted to the 39 women who were married to U.S. presidents during their terms, thus excluding those like Martha Jefferson who died before their husbands took office. Because of this, there are some presidential administrations that are not represented. Entries provide several pages of detailed biographical information followed by a bibliographic essay, each of which has been updated for this edition. Entry length varies from six (Letitia Tyler) to eighteen (Eleanor Roosevelt) pages. Two appendixes follow the text: the Siena College First Lady Polls for 1982 and 1993, and a chronology.

First Ladies: A Biographical Dictionary. By Dorothy Schneider and Carl J. Schneider. 2001. 406p. bibliog. illus. index. Facts On File, $65 (0-8160-4195-4). 973.

The same 39 women who have entries in Routledge's *American First Ladies: Their Lives and Their Legacy* are spotlighted here. Entries average between seven and eight pages (the longest treatments, 12 pages, go to Dolly Madison and Lady Bird Johnson), with biographical essays followed by chronologies specific to each woman and lists of resources for further reading. Occasionally there is another illustration in addition to the portrait. Several appendixes provide information on presidential spouses who did not live to be first ladies; women who were not first ladies but acted as White House hostesses; "First Lady Firsts" (Lucy Hayes was the first with a college degree; Lou Hoover was the first to deliver a radio address); and some reflections by First Ladies on their role. In addition to a very useful general index, entries are indexed by place and by date of birth.

First Ladies of the United States: A Biographical Dictionary. By Robert P. Watson. 2001. 327p. appendixes. bibliogs. illus. index. Lynne Rienner, $49.95 (1-55587-907-1). 176.2.

Forty-four women are treated in the volume—but not the same forty-four that are found in Salem's *American First Ladies*. There is an entry, for example, for Emily Tennessee Donelson and Sarah Yorke Jackson, who both served as hostesses for Andrew Jackson; but not for Rachel Jackson, his wife, who died several weeks before his inauguration. This small volume provides the most in terms of introductory information: birth and death dates and places; presidential birth and death dates, political party, and terms of office; dates and places of marriage; and names and dates of children. Biographical essays are shorter than those in the other First Lady volumes. Each includes a portrait and a brief bibliography. Appended are lists of First Ladies' formal education, states of birth, and ages on becoming first lady; as well as information on the four women who predeceased their husband's terms. A subject index is supplemented by an "Index of First Ladies and Presidents."

Which to choose? Salem's *American First Ladies* is the most attractive of the four titles, leavening its text with sidebars and more and larger illustrations. Other pluses are the topical essays and Salem's usual uniform approach to organizing content. Routledge's scholarly *American First Ladies: Their Lives and Their Legacy* and Facts On File's *First Ladies* offer the most in-depth discussions, although in both cases readers may be put off by long stretches of dense text unbroken by subheadings or illustrations. The smallest book, *First Ladies of the United States: A Biographical Dictionary*, has some unique features, but $49.95 seems a lot to pay for a volume this size (9 1/4" x 6") when there are other options. Consider this a supplemental purchase. Academic libraries will want the Routledge volume for its research-oriented bibliographical essays. High-school and public libraries should consider the accessible Salem publication. The Facts On File entry is a solid, less expensive alternative.

—*Mary Ellen Quinn*

Reference on the Web

American Ethnicity - 29
Dictionaries - 29
Digitizing Black History - 30
Environmental Resources - 30
Exploring Antarctica - 31
Horror - 32
Keeping Up with What's New - 32
Lives of the Presidents - 33
Military History - 33
Nupedia - 33
Quotations - 34
Religion - 34
Science Q&A - 35
Shakespeare - 35
Sites for Writers - 35
Staying Healthy - 36
Urban Legends - 36
Web Site Miscellany - 37
Women's History - 37
xreferplus - 38

American Ethnicity

This small sample of the Web sites highlights the increasing diversity of the U.S. population. For print sources covering the complexity and diversity of U.S. citizenry. All sites were last accessed on April 22, 2002.

American Family Immigration History Center. [http://www.ellisislandrecords.org].
A fabulous glimpse into the "Golden Door," providing facts on 22 million people who entered the country through Ellis Island.

American Memory: Historical Collections for the National Digital Library. Library of Congress. [http://memory.loc.gov].
A rich gathering of digital and print collections. Examples include a photo of an Asian American baseball coach with his school team, probably taken in Denver around 1910 to 1920, and a 1940 Jacksonville, Florida, recording of a Lebanese lullaby. Other resources at [http://lcweb.loc.gov/] include a guide for the study of black history and culture.

American Muslim Council. [http://www.amconline.org/].
The council seeks to increase the effective participation of American Muslims in the political and public policy arenas.

Chinese American Librarians Association, Midwest Chapter. 1996–2002. [http://www.uic.edu/depts/lib/projects/resources/calamw/].
This is a fine example of a library organization using the Internet to disseminate information such as cultural observances and festivals in different midwestern states.

Islamic Assembly of North America. [http://iananet.org/].
The Web site of an umbrella group of organizations that provides North American Muslims and others with accurate, relevant information on Islam.

Mapping Census 2000: The Geography of U.S. Diversity. 2001–2002. [http://www.census.gov/population/www/cen2000/atlas.html].
Maps that illustrate demographic patterns and changes in population, including race and ethnicity, down to the county level.

Queens Borough Public Library. [http://www.queenslibrary.org/].
A good example of the many public and academic library gateways to resources, this site provides a list of local newspapers in international languages and links to bilingual Hispanic Web sites.

Voices from the Gaps: Women Writers of Color. [http://voices.cla.umn.edu].
Several hundred famous and some lesser-known writers are covered on a site that is user-friendly, accurate, and current, making it a good stop for high-school and undergraduate students.

—*Arthur S. Meyers*

Dictionaries

Although Merriam-Webster's new site, *Merriam-Webster Unabridged*, is fee-based, there are still plenty of free dictionary sites for word lovers and definition seekers. Some, like *Merriam Webster's Collegiate Dictionary* at *Merriam Webster Online* [http://www.merriam-webster.com/] and *Encarta World English Dictionary* [http://dictionary.msn.com] aren't so different from their print counterparts, except that they may have audio pronunciations and hyperlinked cross-references. We've selected a few sites that can supplement the dictionaries sitting on your ready-reference shelf. All were last accessed on April 4, 2001.

The American Heritage Dictionary of the English Language, Fourth Edition. [http://www.bartleby.com/61/].
American Heritage does not have its own site but is available at Bar-

tleby. The researcher will find more than 90,000 entries, 70,000 audio pronunciations, and 900 color illustrations. Besides entry word and full text, several types of additional searches are available, including Definition, Etymology, and Articles. There is also an Entries with Notes search that lists all the entries containing synonym notes, usage notes, word history notes, and so on. The Illustrations Index is another nice feature, providing thumbnails that correspond to the pictures in the print dictionary and can be expanded for full-page views. But though the illustrations are linked to their definitions, there does not seem to be a way to link directly from a definition to its illustration.

OneLook Dictionaries. [http://www.onelook.com/].

Instead of a single dictionary, *OneLook* indexes 750 dictionaries and more than four million words. Titles include subject dictionaries, from banjo terms to wine glossaries, as well as foreign-language lexicons. Users can select individual titles or search the entire database.

Pseudodictionary: The Dictionary for Words That Wouldn't Make It into Dictionaries. [http://www.pseudodictionary.com].

Here is a classic kind of Web site—anyone can submit a term to this slang dictionary, which currently consists of almost 10,000 words. Another 63 are "waiting approval," presumably until someone makes sure they meet the site's guidelines—no overly sexual terms, no terms related to drugs or bodily functions, no racist or sexist terms, no "words and definitions that make absolutely no sense." Each word has a brief definition and usage example. Recent additions include *dweezil* ("to name one's child inappropriately") and *namestorm* (to brainstorm names for a company or product"). Many of these terms will never make it out of *Pseudodictionary*; but others just may show up some day in *Merriam-Webster Unabridged*.

The Word Spy. By Paul McFedries. 1991–2002. [http://www.logophilia.com/wordspy/].

This is a good place to look for definitions of words that haven't made it into the dictionaries yet (and might never do so). There is a word of the day (*cinematherapy* when we looked at the site), but users can search definitions for more than 1,500 previous "recently coined words, existing words that have enjoyed a recent renaissance, and older words that are now being used in new ways." Recent examples include *de-proliferating*, *going plural*, and *man in the middle attack*. Words are indexed alphabetically and by subject. Entries provide pronunciations (no audio), parts of speech, examples of use, and earliest found occurrences.

—Mary Ellen Quinn

Digitizing Black History

A growing number of archival materials, previously accessible to just a few researchers, are being digitized and made available to a much wider audience via the Web. Listed here are some good digitization projects that highlight aspects of black history. All sites were last accessed December 20, 2001.

African American Women Writers of the Nineteenth Century. 1999. The New York Public Library. [http://digital.nypl.org/schomburg/writers_aa19/].

Images of African Americans from the Nineteenth Century. 1999. The New York Public Library. [http://digital.nypl.org/schomburg/images_aa19/].

These two collections are from Digital Schomburg, which is part of the New York Public Library Digital Library Collections. *African American Women Writers of the Nineteenth Century* contains electronic editions of more than 50 works published before 1920. The entire database is cross-searchable by keyword and also browseable by title, author, and genre. Complementing the texts are brief biographies of the 37 women whose work is represented. *Images of African Americans from the Nineteenth Century* offers a variety of images made by artists, engravers, and photographers, both black and white, drawn from 21 different collections at the Schomburg Center. The collection is searchable by keyword and broad topic area.

Born in Slavery: Slave Narratives from the Federal Writers' Project, 1936–1938. 2001. Library of Congress. [http://lcweb2.loc.gov/ammem/snhtml/].

This page of the Library of Congress' exemplary American Memory online collection is the electronic version of 2,300 first-person accounts of slavery collected in the 1930s as part of the Federal Writers' Project of the Works Progress Administration. The narratives and 500 accompanying photographs are searchable by keyword and state. The narratives can also be searched by narrator and by print volume.

Powerful Days: The Civil Rights Photography of Charles Moore. By John Kaplan. 1998. [http://www.civilrightsphotos.com/].

Moore was a freelance photographer based in Florence, Alabama. Most of his landmark civil rights photographs were originally published in *Life Magazine*. More than 50 of those photographs are available here, organized under topics such as "Birmingham" and "Martin Luther King." Other material includes photo captions and a biographical essay on Moore.

Through the Lens of Time: Images of African Americans from the Cook Collection. Virginia Commonwealth Universities Libraries. [http://www.library.vcu.edu/jbc/speccoll/cook/cook11.html].

The Cook Photograph Collection at the Valentine Museum/Richmond History Center consists of more than 10,000 photographs taken in Virginia and the Carolinas from the 1860s to the 1930s. More than 400 of these photographs documenting African American life have been digitized by Virginia Commonwealth Universities Libraries. The collection can be searched by keyword or subject.

—Mary Ellen Quinn

Environmental Resources

This collection of free databases on the Web, including links to several governmental agencies and environmental organizations, will be useful to a wide range of information seekers. Many of these databases are part of the so-called invisible, or deep, Web, which is not indexed by the well-known search engines and directories. All sites were last accessed November 21, 2001.

EarthTrends: The Environmental Information Portal. [http://earthtrends.wri.org/].

From the World Resources Institute. Excellent source of data on country, issue, ecosystem, population, energy, agriculture, and more.

Electronic Green Journal. [http://egj.lib.uidaho.edu/index.html].

Peer-reviewed online journal on international environmental issues. The December 1999 issue had an article on environmental Resources Web [http://egj.lib.uidaho.edu/egj11/shrode.html]. Many of the links to good basic resources are still active.

Energy Trends: Energy Research and Development, Global Trends in Policy and Investment. [http://energytrends.pnl.gov/].

Site sponsored by the Pacific Northwest Laboratory examines trends in energy research, development, and investment around the world.

EnviroLink Network. [http://envirolink.netforchange.com/].

This site is being developed as a comprehensive resource for individuals, organizations, and businesses working for social and environmental change. Many useful links.

Environmental Defense. [http://www.edf.org/].

Another gateway site by an important organization to information on environmental hot topics and more.

Environmental Fate Data Base. [http://esc.syrres.com/efdb.htm].

Searchable databases on what happens to specific chemicals in the environment.

Environmental News Network. [http://www.enn.com/].

Online newspaper with news stories, in-depth accounts, significant press releases, and other information.

Environmental Quality Statistics. [http://ceq.eh.doe.gov/nepa/reports/statistics/].

From the U.S. Department of Energy. Statistical tables from the annual report of the Council on Environmental Quality.

EnviroZine: Environment Canada's Online Newsmagazine. [http://www.ec.gc.ca/EnviroZine/english/home_e.cfm].

Online environmental issues magazine from the Canadian Ministry on the Environment.

Global Invasive Species Database. [http://www.issg.org/database/welcome/].

Searchable information provided by the Invasive Species Specialty Group, Species Conservation Commission of the World Conservation Union.

Global Trends 2015. [http://www.odci.gov/cia/publications/globaltrends2015/index.html].

A paper from the National Intelligence Council, which includes environmental issues.

Global Warming: Early Warning Signs. [http://www.climatehotmap.org/].

Information on various indicators, references, and teaching resources.

Know Your Environment. [http://www.acnatsci.org/erd/ea/index.html].

Article database from the Academy of Natural Science of Philadelphia.

MapCruzin.com. [http://www.mapcruzin.com/index.html].

Home page of the Clary Meuser Research Network, which is an example of a small activist group providing links to relevant information on environmental issues.

Pew Center on Global Climate Change. [http://www.pewclimate.org/].

Access to many reports on various issues.

Pilot Environmental Sustainability Index. [http://www.ciesin.org/indicators/ESI/pilot_esi.html].

The Environmental Sustainability Index is a project of the World Economic Forum's Global Leaders of Tomorrow Task Force at the Yale Center for Environmental Law and Policy and the Center for International Earth Science Information Network (CIESIN) of Columbia University.

Second Time Around. [http://www.epa.gov/seahome/housewaste/src/recycle.htm].

Information from the EPA and Agricultural and Biological Engineering, Purdue University, on aluminum, batteries, glass, motor oil, paper, plastic, steel, yard waste, etc.

Superfund: 20 Years of Protecting Human Health and the Environment. [http://www.epa.gov/superfund/action/20years/index.htm].

Report published online with links to all relevant agency home pages.

U.S. Department of Energy, Office of Environmental Management. [http://www.em.doe.gov/program_data.html].

Office on Environmental Management online databases.

U.S. Environmental Protection Agency. [http://www.epa.gov/].

Gateway to resources from the EPA. Among their pages is the EnviroFacts [http://www.epa.gov/enviro/index_java.html], an excellent data source.

Water Quality Information Center. [http://www.nal.usda.gov/wqic/].

National Library of Agriculture page on water and agriculture.

World Resource Institute: Facts and Figures. [http://www.wri.org/facts/index.html].

Links to numerous environmental reports.

The World's Water. [http://www.worldwater.org/default.htm].

Information on the world's freshwater resources from the Pacific Institute for Studies in Environment, Development and Security.

Yearbook of International Cooperation on Environment and Development. [http://www.greenyearbook.org/].

Links to international agreements, nongovernmental organizations, country profiles, environmental performance articles, and more.

—*Linda Loos Scarth*

Exploring Antarctica

The story of Ernest Shackleton's *Endurance* expedition has been the subject of several recent books, a museum exhibition, a public television program, and an IMAX movie. The Web provides an alternate route for students and armchair explorers to learn more about Shackleton and other giants of the "heroic age" of Antarctic discovery (1901–17). We found most of these links in the "Resources" section of *Antarctica and the Arctic: The Complete Encyclopedia*. All sites were last accessed on March 15, 2002.

The AAP Mawson's Huts Foundation. [http://203.63.165.141].

Douglas Mawson, leader of the Australian Antarctic expedition (1911–14), oversaw the building of four huts at his base camp at Cape Denison. The huts are among the most enduring physical traces of the heroic age of Antarctic exploration and a significant historic site. This Web site documents ongoing preservation and restoration efforts.

Antarctic Philately. [http://www.south-pole.com].

More than a site about stamps, this Web destination offers very detailed information about Antarctic exploration. Shackleton is covered, of course, but the user can also read here about other heroic age explorers such as Roald Amundsen and Robert Scott as well as earlier and later voyagers. A 1519–1959 time line is linked to the explorer essays.

The Endurance: Shackleton's Legendary Antarctic Expedition. [http://www.amnh.org/exhibitions/shackleton].

This is the online companion to an exhibit mounted by the American Museum of Natural History in 1999. Users will find a very good summary of the events of the Imperial Transarctic Expedition of 1914–1917, which was Shackleton's attempt to make the first crossing of the Antarctic continent. It was during this expedition that his ship, *Endurance*, became icebound, stranding his team on the ice floes.

The James Caird Society. [http://www.jamescairdsociety.com].

Named after one of the *Endurance* lifeboats (which was itself named after one of Shackleton's sponsors), the James Caird Society was founded in 1994 "to preserve the memory, honour the remarkable feats of discovery and commend the outstanding qualities of leadership associated with the name of Sir Ernest Shackleton." The site offers a fairly detailed account of Shackleton's life and polar exploits.

Kodak: The Endurance. [http://www.kodak.com/US/en/corp/features/endurance].

Because of Frank Hurley, an Australian postcard photographer who talked his way onto Douglas Mawson's Antarctic expedition of 1911–14 and later became part of Shackleton's team, we have many haunting images of *Endurance* and its crew. Kodak capitalizes on the fact that Hurley used Kodak equipment and film to offer this page on its corporate Web site, describing his role in the expedition and providing insight into his innovative working methods. Many of the images are here as well, courtesy of the Royal Geographic Society and the Scott Polar Research Institute, where they are housed. Another useful site is *Frank Hurley* [http://frankhurley.com], which offers links to Hurley photos taken before and after his trip to the Antarctic with Shackleton.

Shackleton's Voyage of Endurance. [http://www.pbs.org/wgbh/nova/shackleton].

In 1999 and 2000 NOVA sent film crews to the Antarctic region to acquire footage for a PBS program and an IMAX movie on the *Endurance* expedition. This companion Web site offers a time line of the expedition, thumbnails on all of the members of Shackleton's team, and excerpts from a previously unpublished journal kept by one of the team members.

—Mary Ellen Quinn

Horror

The first edition of the readers' advisory guide *Hooked on Horror* (Libraries Unlimited, 1999) offers a number of carefully chosen Web sites, but, as is the way with the Web, several of these sites are now static or defunct. *The Cabinet of Dr. Casey* is closed, *Fiona's Fear and Loathing* is no longer being updated, and the content of Universal Studios' *Horror Online* has been incorporated into *DarkEcho Horror* (see below). Using *Hooked on Horror* as a starting point, we went in search of sites that are currently active. Many horror sites are—well, horrible; but we did find some that offer useful content with a minimum of scary clutter. Also worth bookmarking is *The Literary Gothic* [http://www.Litgothic.com], which we discussed in our March 15, 2002, issue. All sites were last accessed on June 21, 2002.

Classic Horror and Fantasy Page. 1997 [http://www.geocities.com/Area51/Corridor/5582/index2.html].

In an effort to give attention to classic authors, this site offers links to stories and novels by Ambrose Bierce, H. P. Lovecraft, and Nathaniel Hawthorne, to name just a few. In addition, the site's author has written fairly extensive articles on a handful of neglected writers, such as Algernon Blackwood and Robert W. Chambers, with bibliographic information and links to texts and related material. (Because no information is provided about the sources used, it is difficult to verify the authority of these.) A reading list of recommended writers is organized into separate sections for fantasy, horror, vampire material, folklore, and poetry and includes links if they are available.

Dark Side of the Net. By Carrie Carolin. 2002. [http://www.darklinks.com].

Created in 1994 and originally called *Dark Side of the Web*, *Dark Side of the Net* boasts "over 10,400 working, hand-picked links." The entire universe of horror seems to be included—literature, music, movies, TV series, zines, chat rooms, art, shops, and a good selection of sites on Halloween. Among the recently added links are *Dead at Last*, "a good resource for Goths in Japan," and *Gothic Decor*, "a new Yahoo group for gothic home decoration ideas."

DarkEcho Horror. By Paula Guran. 2002. [http://www.darkecho.com].

This site, referred to in *Hooked on Horror* as the premier horror site on the Web, offers interviews, articles and essays, reviews, and an online workshop for horror writers. From 1994 to 2001 Guran produced *DarkEcho*, a weekly e-mail newsletter for horror writers, and the emphasis at *DarkEcho Horror* is also on writing and literature. The Dark Links page connects to author sites, awards, booksellers, organizations, publishers, writer's aids, and more. The site was completely redesigned and relaunched in May 2002.

Horror World. By Andy Fairclough. [http://www.horrorworld.cjb.net].

The primary lure of *Horror World* is the community it is building. It contains forums where fans of dark fantasy and horror can interact with the authors and editors they like. Other forums are available for buying and selling, talking about movies, poetry, comics, and more. *Horror World* also offers upcoming publication lists for major presses in the industry and has links to a good portion of the independent presses.

The site's book review database, maintained by a staff of about four reviewers, is its major failing. Several of the reviews are nearly impossible to read because they are so poorly written. Those that are better written are rife with typos, spelling errors, and minor grammatical problems. One major addition to the site is "Andy Fairclough's A to Z of Horror Fiction," which is slowly but surely going online. It was "seven years in the making," and some of the information is obviously seven years old, but if you're looking for something about authors in this emerging field, this is a great place to start.

Horror Writers Association. [http://www.horror.org].

"Dedicated to promoting the interests of writers of Horror and Dark Fantasy," the Horror Writers Association was founded in the 1980s. The Web site offers several public areas designed to encourage interest in good horror fiction. Among these areas are reading lists, links, and lists of present and past Bram Stoker Award winners and nominees.

—Shane Hoffman and Mary Ellen Quinn

Keeping Up with What's New

The daily proliferation of Web sites makes keeping current a challenge. Fortunately, a few individuals have made it their mission to help the rest of us be better-informed users of Web-based resources. The following is a selection of directories, newsletters, and more that regularly announce new sites. For added convenience, we've listed only those that offer free e-mail updates. All were last accessed September 17, 2001.

Academic Info. By Michael Madin. 1998–2001. [http://www.academicinfo.net/].

This independent site "aims to be the premier educational gateway to online college and research-level resources." Sites are organized into three sections: a subject list of 13 broad academic areas, a compilation of sites that might be useful at the reference desk, and a collection of resources for students. Browsing by subject and searching by keyword are available. Several hundred sites are added to this directory each month, and users can sign up under What's New to receive free monthly updates. The updates are archived back to June 2000.

Digital Librarian: A Librarian's Choice of the Best of the Web. By Margaret Vail Anderson. 1996–2001. [http://www.digital-librarian.com].

Anderson's list of links is organized by subject area. Annotations are minimal, and we could not find a selection policy. (But Anderson is a librarian, so we trust her.) The user can sign up to receive weekly e-mail notification of new sites.

Neat New Stuff I Found on the Web This Week. By Marylaine Block. [http://marylaine.com/newtnew.html].

Block is a professional who describes herself as "your librarian without walls." She lists and minimally annotates around a dozen sites each week, looking for variety among those that are authoritative and easy to use but also including some that are just fun. A number of her picks are library related. Previous weeks are archived for six months. Block also edits *Ex Libris*: A *Weekly E-Zine for Librarians*, which she will e-mail to subscribers along with *Neat New Stuff*.

ResearchBuzz. By Tara Calishain. 2001. [http://researchbuzz.com/].

While other services provide information about Web sites, Calishain offers updates on search engines, data managing software, browser technology, Web directories, metasites, and more. She explains her selection process this way: "If in doubt, the final question is, 'Would a reference librarian find it useful?' If the answer's yes, in it goes!" There are three sections: News, Articles, and ResearchBuzz Weblog ("things that have very little to do with research but are interesting"). In the Articles section are in-depth looks at various aspects of Internet research, generally based on Calishain's own hands-on experience. News and Articles are archived, and the site is searchable. Even those who aren't fascinated by some of the more arcane details of Internet searching will find the chatty *ResearchBuzz* informative and interesting to read. The weekly newsletter is delivered to subscribers free, but an enhanced version called *ResearchBuzz Extra* is available for $20 ($15 for teachers, students, and librarians).

The Scout Report. Internet Scout Project. 1994–2001. [http://scout.cs.wisc.edu/report/sr/current/].

Many librarians are familiar with this weekly report published by the Internet Scout Project, which is located at the Department of Computer Sciences, University of Wisconsin at Madison. Each issue lists a diverse collection of sites arranged under several categories—Research and Education, General Interest, and Network Tools. Another category, In the News, assembles sites related to a topic of current interest. All selections are carefully chosen and very well annotated. A new report is published every Friday. If you subscribe to just one Web update service, this should be it.

—Mary Ellen Quinn

Lives of the Presidents

Our March 1 issue featured a Focus review of reference books on First Ladies. For Booklist's Spotlight on Biography, we decided to use this issue's Reference on the Web to give equal time to their husbands. Being familiar with general sites such as POTUS: *Presidents of the United States* [http://www.ipl.org/ref/POTUS/] and *The Presidents of the United States* [http://www.whitehouse.gov/history/presidents/], we went in search of a few good resources on individual office holders.

Like so much else on the Web, coverage of U.S. presidents is hit-and-miss. There are several good sites devoted to Ulysses S. Grant but no single comprehensive one for either George Washington or Abraham Lincoln. We chose the sites listed below because they have particularly interesting features. All were last accessed on February 13, 2002.

Franklin D. Roosevelt Library and Digital Archives. [http://www.fdrlibrary.marist.edu/index.html].

The "K–12 Learning Center" section of this site offers the most biographical information, including fairly lengthy essays and time lines for both Franklin and Eleanor. More than 1,000 copyright-free photos of the president and First Lady are available, searchable by keyword and date. The site also offers access to several thousand documents from the Roosevelt-era White House safe files.

Monticello: The Home of Thomas Jefferson. 1996–2001. Thomas Jefferson Foundation. [http://www.Monticello.org/index.html].

As the name implies, the focus here is on Jefferson's life at Monticello. A fascinating "Day in the Life of Jefferson" describes his activities and surroundings on a typical sunrise-to-evening period during his retirement. Hyperlinks lead to additional information on the house, the gardens, and more. Readers will also find a brief biography, a chronology of Jefferson's life, and a clickable floor plan of Monticello, with room-by-room descriptions of the architecture and features. Also useful are the numerous links to other Jefferson-related sites.

Truman Presidential Museum and Library. 2001. [http://www.trumanlibrary.org/].

The Truman Presidential Museum and Library does a good job with this searchable site, which offers chronologies, access to an extensive collection of archival materials, multimedia, and links to sites related to all of the president's Cabinet members, among other useful resources. The site seems to be updated regularly; one recent addition to the Archival Collections is Truman's appointment calendar, which can be searched by date as well as keyword.

Ulysses S. Grant Home Page. By Candace Scott. 1997–2000. [http://www.mscomm.com/~ulysses/page152.html].

This is one of several sites devoted to rehabilitating a controversial U.S. president. It assembles a rich and well-documented collection of images, interviews, and more related to his early years, his private life, his military career, and his presidency. There is also a lengthy discussion, replete with quotes from people who knew him, of whether or not Grant had a drinking problem. Other Grant sites are *The Ulysses S. Grant Association* [http://www.lib.siu.edu/projects/usgrant/index.html] and *Ulysses S. Grant Network* [http://saints.css.edu/mkelsey/gppg.html].

—Mary Ellen Quinn

Military History

With the exception of *War, Peace and Security Guide*, which is a directory, we selected the following sites because they are good sources for images. Compiling this list underscored the Web's role in providing greater access to information—some U.S. government facilities, such as the Naval Historical Center and the U.S. Army Ordnance Museum, have been closed to the public since September 11, so the only way to get to their collections is online. All sites were last accessed on November 27, 2001.

Map Library. [http://www.dean.usma.edu/history/dhistorymaps/MapsHome.htm].

The U.S. Military Academy's Department of History is making available online a series of more than 1,000 maps and atlases developed over the years for a course called "History of the Military Art." The collection can be searched by topic, from *Ancient Warfare* to *Wars and Conflicts since* 1958. Download times can be considerable, as some of the files are quite large.

Naval Historical Center. [http://www.history.navy.mil/].

This site, maintained by the U.S. Navy, is a good source for, among other things, online images related to naval and maritime history. The site's arrangement is a bit confusing, but the Frequently Asked Questions page pulls together materials on popular topics, such as *African Americans in the U.S. Navy*.

Photos of the Great War. [http://listproc.cc.ukans.edu/~kansite/ww_one/photos/greatwar.htm#TOP].

There are more than 1,800 photos in this database, part of the WWI/WWW project at the University of Kansas and Brigham Young University. Images have been "scanned from contemporary photohistories (c. 1916–1920)" and are organized by topic. The site also offers links to documents and other World War I sites.

U.S. Air Force Museum. [http://www.wpafb.af.mil/index.htm].

Like the Naval Historical Center listed above, this site is rich in images, especially of weapons, equipment, and uniforms.

U.S. Army Ordnance Museum. [http://www.ordmusfound.org/].

Still another useful (though still quite small) collection of images, in this case focusing on the evolution and development of American military ordnance materiel.

War, Peace and Security Guide. [http://www.cfcsc.dnd.ca/links/milhist/].

Affiliated with the Information Resource Centre, Canadian Forces College, this site offers an extensive collection of links on military history. Users can search for online resources by time period, subject (e.g., *Aviation History, Military and Diplomatic Biography*), or war. A clickable time line offers another alternative. Though there are many useful links here, the site has not been updated since July 2000, and numerous links are dead. Selecting Search or Help sends one off into *D-net*, the Web site for the Canadian Department of National Defense, with no apparent way to get back.

—Mary Ellen Quinn

Nupedia

Nupedia [http://www.nupedia.com]. (Last accessed July 18, 2001).

We first visited *Nupedia*, the "open content" Web-based encyclopedia, in our May 15, 2000, issue. For a time, we received frequent mail updates on its progress. It's been awhile since we'sve heard anything, however, so we decided to have another look.

The first news we have to report is that *Nupedia* is still alive, now calling itself "the free encyclopedia." Editorial policies remain the same. The goal is "to create an open content encyclopedia, usefully cross-referenced, arranged, and searchable, freely available on the web and in various other inexpensive formats, and with a greater amount of content than any encyclopedia has had in history." Articles are "peer-reviewed and academically respectable, translated into various non-English languages, and will offer both practical and theoretical information."

Nupedia has now achieved several goals. They have "a functioning web-based editorial process" and some 20 articles now appear on the Web site. Among these are *Irish traditional music, New Zealand, Polymerase chain reaction,* and *Vergil*. These are brief, one-to five-paragraph articles; presumably, longer versions will appear in the future. Users are invited to read and comment upon the almost 70 articles that are currently in various stages of the editorial process, including *Amino acid*; *Bach, Johann Sebastian*; *Beer in antiquity*; *Foot-and-mouth disease*; and *Source code*. Completed articles can be viewed in printable or text-only versions and always note review group, editor, lead reviewer, and lead copy editor, in addition to author. Further reading lists are appended, although these are sometimes sparse (just two titles for *New Zealand*, the most current a 1998 statistical source). As of now there are no cross-references, and the search engine is not functional; until the content is fuller, searching and hyperlinking would be of limited value anyway.

For the near term, *Nupedia* hopes to fully staff all the review groups and put at least one article from each subject on the Web site. It will naturally take time for this site to even approach its goal of being the largest encyclopedia in history, and the rigorous editorial policy is almost guaranteed to slow things down. But we are glad to see the project is still moving forward, and we continue to be intrigued.

—Mary Ellen Quinn

Quotations

In the never-ending search for that half-remembered quotation, reference librarians may find themselves trolling cyberspace for a reliable Web site. Here are a dozen quotations sites found on that lifeline of today's reference desks, the Librarians' Index to the Internet [http://www.lii.org]. All were viable as of May 17, 2002.

Advertising Quotes. [http://advertising.utexas.edu/research/quotes/].
Assorted thoughts on the field and its impact from the University of Texas at Austin. Advertising *slogans* may be found at [http://advertising.utexas.edu/research/slogans/].

Aphorisms Galore! [http://www.ag.wastholm.net/home].
Intended "to store an abundance of aphorisms along with information on their origin, and make this all available with an easy to use interface."

Bartlett's Familiar Quotations. [http://www.bartleby.com/100/].
An old (10th ed., 1919) favorite in print is now a new one online. Perhaps one day later editions will be launched into cyberspace.

Creative Quotations. [http://creativequotations.com].
Searching for a quotation can be *fun*! Browse through a menu featuring indexes by keyword, author, subject, month and day, profession, and much more.

Mouthpiece: Lawyerly Quotations from Popular Culture. [http://tarlton.law.utexas.edu/pop/quotes.htm].
No dry legal terms here—just some memorable lines from movies, books, television programs, plays, and more.

Mysticism in World Religions. [http://www.digiserve.com/mystic/].
A look at the mystical traditions of seven faiths (Taoism, Hinduism, Buddhism, Sufism, Islam, Christianity, and Judaism) through quotations from the representative literature.

Quoteland. [http://www.quoteland.com/].
A surfeit of sayings on dozens of subjects searchable by author, topic, and special occasion. Ignore the commercial tie-ins for T-shirts, mugs, and books if you can.

Quoteworld.org. [http://quoteworld.org].
Thousands of quotations by people ranging from Kareem Abdul-Jabbar to Zig Ziglar searchable by topic, author, and more. You can even e-mail a quote to a friend.

Rockwisdom.com. [http://www.rockwisdom.com/].
In the words of its creator, "The main purpose of this collection of quotes from Rock and Roll music is to celebrate and provide a documented reference to an under appreciated form of literature."

The Samuel Johnson Sound Bite Page. [http://www.samueljohnson.com].
Search or browse through a collection of the words of one of the most quoted men in the English language.

A Short Dictionary of Scientific Quotations. [http://naturalscience.com/dsqhome.html].
Complete citations to key quotations about science from scientists as well as other notable writers.

Simpson's Contemporary Quotations. [http://www.bartleby.com/63/].
The folks at Bartleby.com bring the 1988 edition of this useful work to a computer screen near you.

—Carolyn Mulac

Religion

We thought we would make things easy for ourselves by focusing on a fairly narrow topic for our contribution to *Booklist*'s Spotlight on Religion only to find out that the Web is awash in sites about mythology. As with just about any other topic one cares to name, these sites are compiled by a motley crew of students and teachers from the elementary through graduate levels, scholars, enthusiasts, and crackpots, and it's a challenge to find material that is both authoritative and accessible. We've selected two examples that offer different approaches to the topic. Both were last accessed on July 31, 2001.

The Encyclopedia Mythica: An Encyclopedia on Mythology, Folklore, and Legend. By M. F. Lindemans. 1995–2001. [http://www.pantheon.org/mythica.html].
We last looked at this site in our August 1998 issue. At that time, it had around 4,300 entries on gods and goddesses, legendary and supernatural beings, places, texts, real and imagined objects, and concepts. Since then, entries have grown to 5,700. Articles can be retrieved by browsing one of the content areas (Mythology, Folklore, Bestiary, Heroes, Image Gallery, and Genealogy Tables). With the April 2001 update (the first in more than a year), the Mythology articles are now arranged by continent, and a drop-down menu displays cultural groups or regions, such as Celtic or Korean. A useful index in the left frame lists all articles related to the broader topic. A search engine is available for those interested in approaching the material in other ways; a search for *dragon*, for example, yields 18 results.

Back in 1998, we stated that *The Encyclopedia Mythica* "is not the rigorous, scholarly treatment of its subject area that one might expect in a published work of the same magnitude." Among our concerns were the facts that anyone could contribute, no authorship was attributed in most cases, and most entries were undocumented—all still true. None of this has kept the site from having between ten and twenty thousand visitors each day, winning almost 100 awards, and showing up as a link all over the Web.

Mything Links: An Annotated and Illustrated Collection of Worldwide Links to Mythologies, Fairy Tales and Folklore, Sacred Arts and Sacred Traditions. By Kathleen Jenks. 1998–2001. [http://mythlinks.org].
Developed for graduate students in mythology and psychology at Pacifica Graduate Institute, *Mything Links* organizes its extensive collection of links by theme. An example of what the researcher will find here is the page on creation myths, listing sites on African, Australian, classical Greek and Roman, Hindu, Japanese, ancient Mesopotamian, Native American and Mesoamerican, and Norse origin stories. Another page arranges links by geographical region. There are also seasonal links (for festivals and celebrations such as Beltane and Day of the Dead), resources for primary and secondary school teachers, cross-cultural and interdisciplinary collections, and a search engine. The site is a little confusing to navigate, but it is well maintained and visually appealing, with annotations that strike just the right balance between authority and informality.

—Mary Ellen Quinn

Science Q&A

While trawling for sites for the Spotlight on Sci-Tech, we came across some that have question-and-answer formats. Here are a few of our favorites. All sites were last accessed October 15, 2001.

Ask Dr. Math. 1994–2001. [http://mathforum.org/drmath/dr-math.html].

A project of the Math Forum at Drexel University, this site "answers questions from students and their teachers, often (but not exclusively) about the mathematics people usually learn before they're 18 years old." Answers are provided by Swarthmore College math students. Users can browse the Frequently Asked Questions or search the archives, where questions and answers are organized by age group (elementary school, middle school, high school, and college and up) and topic.

How Things Work. By Louis A. Bloomfield. 1997–2000. [http://howthingswork.virginia.edu/].

Bloomfield, professor of physics at the University of Virginia and author of How Things Work: The Physics of Everyday Life (2d ed., Wiley, 2001), answers such questions as "Why is it easy to stay on a bike while moving, but impossible once it stops?" He describes this site as "a radio call-in program that's being held on the WWW instead of the radio." Past questions and answers are searchable by date, topic, and keyword. Bloomfield's Q&A can also be found at [http://www.PhysicsCentral.com] and [http://www.wiley.com/college/howthingswork].

MadSciNet: The Twenty-four Hour Exploding Laboratory. 1995–2001. [http:// www.madsci.org/].

Based at Washington University Medical School in St. Louis, Mad Sci Network "represents a collective cranium of scientists providing answers to your questions." Questions are vetted by graduate students or area specialists (only 40 percent make it through the review process), then passed along to at least two scientists. Each question is given an identification number so that the person who submitted it can track its status. The questions and answers themselves are somewhat buried. The most common questions are grouped by topic in MadSci FAQs. Others can be found in the searchable archives, where they are indexed by topic and by grade level.

New Scientist: The Last Word Science Questions and Answers. [http://www.newscientist.com/lastword/].

Here is the online counterpart of "The Last Word," a regular feature of the British publication New Scientist that provides "questions and answers on everyday scientific phenomena." Older questions and answers are organized by topic. Not only can anyone submit a question but users are invited to send in answers. This raises a few authority issues in our mind, but the site is fun to look at anyway. Typical questions are "Do giraffes ever get hit by lightning?" and "Why is house dust always grey?"

Scientific American: Ask the Experts. [http://www.sciam.com/askexpert/].

Users are invited to e-mail questions, and the "most interesting" are answered by scientists and other experts. When we visited, we found four questions: "How do planets acquire rings?" (Earth is acquiring a set made up of space junk); "What is the origin of zero?" "How do seedless fruits arise and how are they propagated?" and "How do water softeners work?" An archive of previous questions and their answers is arranged by broad scientific discipline. Some of the answers include links to related Web sites.

—Mary Ellen Quinn

Shakespeare

William Shakespeare Mr. Shakespeare and the Internet. 1995–2001. By Terry A. Grey. [http://Shakespeare.palomar.edu].
Shakespeare Online. 1999–2001. By Amanda Mabillard. [http://www.shakespeare-online.com].

Among the thousands of Internet sites on Shakespeare, we came across two that provide a good case study for the need to train students to critically evaluate material they find on the Web. Both sites were last accessed on July 18, 2001.

Mr. Shakespeare and the Internet is primarily an extensive collection of scholarly links. With so many possible links available, good organization is critical, and the site is well-arranged, with a menu offering "Works," "Life and Times," "Theatre," "Criticism," "Renaissance," "Sources," "Educational," "Best Sites," "Other Sites," and "Searching," which covers Shakespeare Internet research tools. These menu areas are further subdivided. "Works," for example, has links not only for collected and individual editions of the plays but also for study guides, Charles and Mary Lamb's Tales from Shakespeare, non-English-language editions, quotations, bibliographies, and more. "Life and Times" offers "Introduction and Explanations," "Primary Documents," "Biographical Links," The Authorship 'sProblem,'s" and "Elizabethan Era." Many of the links are critically annotated, and throughout the pages the researcher will find explanations for why the links were selected and discussions of various problems related to doing Shakespeare research online. Mr. Shakespeare and the Internet suffers from the problem that plagues so many noncommercial sites—lack of time for regular updates and revisions. Although, given the subject matter, timeliness is not a major concern, the fact that the site was last modified in May 2000 means that newer resources are missed, and an increasing number of links may be inactive.

More frequent updating can be found at the slickly designed Shakespeare Online, which, in fact, had been last modified approximately five minutes before we wrote this sentence. Like Mr. Shakespeare and the Internet, this commercial site is well organized. However, although it offers some links, particularly to texts of plays and poems, its emphasis is on original analysis and essays on Shakespeare's life and sources, Elizabethan theater, and more, nearly all written by Amanda Mabillard, who is also "the Shakespeare guide on About.com." Everything she writes may be perfectly valid, but we did not find any references to the sources she used in producing the site's content. Both Mr. Shakespeare and the Internet and Shakespeare Online offer Shakespeare time lines, but only the Mr. Shakespeare and the Internet time line is supported by a bibliography of works that were consulted.

So, which site is better? Students may prefer Shakespeare Online as a one-stop resource, but they need to understand its limitations as an authoritative research tool. Although they will have to work harder if they use Mr. Shakespeare and the Internet, they will learn far more.

—Mary Ellen Quinn

Sites for Writers

Here are just a few of the many Web-based resources aimed at writers. All sites were last accessed on October 2, 2001.

The Author's Guild. [http://www.authorsguild.org/].

The Author's Guild describes itself as "the nation's largest society of published authors" and "a leading advocate for fair compensation, free speech, and copyright protection." Besides information on the organization and its services, the Web site offers recent news, such as the Supreme Court decision on electronic rights.

Writer's Conferences and Centers Online. [http://www.awpwriter.org/direconf.htm].

Writer's Conferences and Centers is a division of Associated Writing Programs, an organization founded in 1967 "to support the growing presence of writers in higher education." The Directory of Conferences contains detailed listings for workshops and programs held by Writers' Conferences and Centers members, such as the Iowa Summer Writing Festival and the Kenyon Review Writer's Workshop.

Writersdigest.com. [http://www.writersdigest.com].

Writer's Digest maintains a Web site that complements its print publishing program by offering market updates, a searchable database of submission guidelines, and more. A considerable amount of the content is free, but the nominal subscription fee of $2.99 per month or $29 per year puts market contact information, standard pay rates and sub-

Writing-World.com. By Moira Allen. 2001. [http://www.writing-world.com/].

Another commercial site, with articles, monthly columns, calls for submissions, and information on markets, freelancing, rights and contracts, author services, contests, and more. The fiction section offers advice on writing and marketing children's literature, science fiction, horror, and romance. Articles are accompanied by author credentials.

The Zuzu's Petals Literary Resource. [http://www.zuzu.com].

An attractive and continuously updated site, home of *The Zuzu's Petals Quarterly* as well as almost 1,700 categorized links to arts-related Web resources, including writer's conferences, commercial and literary magazines, and e-zines.

—*Mary Ellen Quinn*

Staying Healthy

Now that there is so much information available on the World Wide Web, it is important to distinguish the reliable sources from those that are useless and possibly dangerous. Finding the best information may seem difficult, but knowing where to search and how to evaluate what is available will make the process easier.

When searching for medical information, it is important to find sources that are accurate and up-to-date. Because anyone can publish anything on the Web, check the credentials of the author and the origin of the Web site. Academic and government sites are usually reliable. Those with dot-com addresses often have something to sell. Drug companies frequently sponsor medical sites. Proponents of unorthodox therapies also publish many pages. This is not inherently bad, but it is something to think about, especially when doing research on treatment options. When using commercial Web sites, make sure that the advertising is differentiated from the textual content.

These Web sites will help librarians and patrons find accurate health and medical information. All were last accessed on October 26, 2001.

The Alternative Medicine Home Page. By Charles B. Wessel. Updated September 2001. University of Pittsburgh. [http://www.pitt.edu/~cbw/altm.html].

The Falk Library of Health Sciences at the University of Pittsburgh offers this gateway site with information on complementary, alternative, innovative, and integrative therapies.

CAM on PubMed. The National Center for Complementary and Alternative Medicine and the National Library of Medicine. [http://www.nlm.nih.gov/nccam/camonpubmed.html].

The National Institutes of Health are studying complementary and alternative therapies. This Web site offers excellent information and directories of further resources.

CAPHIS. 2001. Medical Library Association. [http://www.caphis.mlanet.org].

The Consumer and Patient Health Information Section of the Medical Library Association's site provides information about developing and managing consumer health collections, bibliographies of current books on consumer health topics, a newsletter with book reviews, and discussion groups.

The Cochrane Collaboration Consumer Network. Updated August 23, 2001. The Cochrane Collaboration. [http://cochraneconsumer.com].

This Australian organization helps people understand research reports and clinical studies by explaining how they are conducted and what the statistics mean.

Go Ask Alice. Columbia University. [http://www.goaskalice.columbia.edu].

Health educators from Columbia University School of Public Health have created an excellent site with health information for young adults.

Healthfinder. U.S. Department of Health and Human Services. [http://www.healthfinder.gov].

The Department of Health and Human Services produces this site for consumers, with links to online publications, support groups, and other agencies. The basic health information offered here is available in English and Spanish.

Healthinfoquest. Revised March 30, 2001. National Network of Libraries of Medicine. [http://www.nnlm.nlm.nih.gov/healthinfoquest].

The National Network of Libraries of Medicine has put together an excellent tutorial for reference librarians seeking medical information. The site offers sample searches on common questions, pathfinders, help with reference interviews, and links to good health sites.

MayoClinic.com. 1998–2000. Mayo Foundation for Medical Education and Research. [http://www.mayoclinic.com].

A respected clinic offers general health information and news.

MEDLINE. U.S. National Library of Medicine. [http://www.nlm.nih.gov].

The National Library of Medicine's site offers a wealth of information. PubMed indexes the world's largest collection of academic medical journals. MEDLINEplus provides consumer health information in several languages. There are links to government agencies, such as the various departments of the National Institutes of Health, the Centers for Disease Control and Prevention, and the Food and Drug Administration, and resources about the history of medicine.

The National Women's Health Information Center. U.S. Department of Health and Human Services. [http://www.4woman.gov].

This is a federal government resource with current information about women's health issues in English and Spanish.

NOAH. 1995–2001. New York Online Access to Health. [http://www.noah-health.org].

The New York Academy of Medicine provides consumer health information on a wide variety of topics in English and Spanish.

Nutrition Navigator. Tufts University. [http://www.navigator.tufts.edu].

Tufts University reviews and rates sites offering nutrition information on the Web.

Oncolink. 1994–2001. University of Pennsylvania Cancer Center. [http://www.oncolink.upenn.edu].

The University of Pennsylvania Cancer Center provides up-to-date information about cancer and links to relevant sites.

Rosenthal Center for Complementary and Alternative Medicine. Columbia University Health Sciences. [http://cpmcnet.columbia.edu/dept/rosenthal].

This center at the Columbia University School of Medicine offers assistance with integrating alternative therapies into medical treatment. There are special pages devoted to pediatric and adult cancers.

YourSurgery.com. 1998–2001. Animation Education Group. [http://www.yoursurgery.com].

This site explains surgical procedures, patient preparation, recovery, possible complications, and treatment alternatives. The graphics are excellent.

—*Barbara Bibel*

Urban Legends

Urban Legends Reference Pages. By Barbara Mikkelson and David P. Mikkelson. 1995–2001. [http://www.snopes2.com/].

Is it true that Coca-Cola first became carbonated by accident? Is there any basis for the Nordstrom tire refund story? Over the years, many libraries have put together bar-bet, trivia, and urban legends files to help with questions like these that are almost impossible to answer but won't go away. If all the files were ever consolidated we would have a fascinating and valuable resource; but in the meantime, we can turn to *Urban Legends Reference Pages*.

The Mikkelsons define urban legends as "trivia, rumors, hoaxes, common misconceptions, [and] odd facts." They have organized these pages into 29 categories, some fairly broad (Humor, Radio and Television) and some more specific (Disney, *Titanic*). The site can be searched by selecting one of the categories or by entering a word, phrase, or group of words in a search box. Colored bullets are used to rate the individual entries, indicating those that are plausible but of indeterminate origin, those that are demonstrably true or based on real events, those for which "the available evidence is too contradictory or insufficient to establish as either true or false," and "claims which cannot be established as true by a preponderance of (reliable) evidence." Entries vary from section to section, but generally users will find a description of the custom, legend, or claim; a discussion of its origins; and a list of sources. Many entries are cleverly illustrated and quite detailed.

Also available on the site are a page of recent additions and updates, a page on net lore currently circulating through e-mail, a message board for registered users, and a few annoying features, such as ads. There is music, but this, fortunately, can be turned off. Updating is regular, and some of the new additions are up-to-the-minute, dealing with misinformation regarding stories just recently in the news.

This is not an academic site like the ones we tend to favor; but then, neither is its subject matter. Try it out the next time you are plagued by an impossible-to-answer reference question.

—*Mary Ellen Quinn*

Web Site Miscellany

Several of the books reviewed in this issue of RBB cite Web sites as important sources for information or were based in part on research conducted on the Web. Here are a few that we found particularly interesting. All were last accessed February 1, 2002.

Chicago Jazz Archive. [http://www.lib.uchicago.edu/e/su/cja].

We discovered this site by way of *The New Grove Dictionary of Jazz*. The Chicago Jazz Archive was founded at the University of Chicago in 1976. Besides providing information about the archive itself, the Web site offers links to a wide variety of jazz research materials—bibliographies, discographies, musician pages, sound files, oral histories, other archival collections, and more. It also reaches beyond the university community to offer guidance to students working on jazz-related history fair projects. A nice feature is the "constantly updated" map of Chicago jazz clubs, 1915–1930.

Discovering Lewis and Clark. 1998. VIAs, Inc. [http://www.lewis-clark.org].

Of the several Lewis and Clark Web sites listed in *Mythical West: An Encyclopedia of Legend, Lore, and Popular Culture*, we were most taken with this site from "a non-profit entity devoted to the production of interactive educational programs." It offers a 19-part "synopsis" by a professor of history at the University of Montana, combining background text with maps, journal selections, images, animations, videos, and sound files. There are also thematic "Discovery Paths" that explore topics such as natural history and native nations as contemporary issues as well as from the perspective of the early nineteenth century. A final navigational route is provided by excerpts from Meriwether Lewis' journals. The site is searchable, and new material is added monthly. There is a shopping feature, but it is not obtrusive. Help and Quick Tour were being rebuilt when we last checked; presumably, they would have been useful for those occasions when we found it hard to figure out where we were in the site and how to get from one thing to another.

The Literary Gothic. By Jack G. Voller. 1995–2002. [http://www.Litgothic.com].

This impressive collection of author information, research advice, links, and electronic texts maintained by an associate professor of English at Southern Illinois University at Edwardsville is listed in the bibliography of *Gothic Writers: A Critical and Bibliographical Guide*. The site's scope encompasses classic Gothic fiction, ghost stories, and "related pre-and-post-Gothic and supernaturalist literature written prior to the mid-C20." Author pages provide brief background information, as well as links to related Web sites and e-texts. Many of the texts made their online debut on this site, and some can be found nowhere else on the Web. An extensive and well-organized research tool and a good source for scary stories (though not indexed by topic).

—*Mary Ellen Quinn*

Women's History

If you are looking for general directories of Web-based women's history resources, good places to start are *Women's History* [http://www.iisg.nl/~womhist/vivalink.html], part of the World Wide Web Virtual Library; and *Women's History Resources* [http://www.library.wisc.edu/libraries/WomensStudies/hist.htm], maintained by the University of Wisconsin System Women's Studies Librarian. We've listed some additional sites that we found to be particularly interesting and well organized. All were last accessed on January 10, 2001.

AFSCME Labor Links: Women's Labor History. [http://www.afscme.org/otherlnk/whlinks.html].

Provides links to bibliographies, biographies, and other resources. There are special sections on "Mother Jones and Other Women in the Mines," "Women and Labor in the Textile and Garment Industries," and "Wobbly Women," as well as a collection of lyrics from women's labor songs.

American Women's History: A Research Guide. By Ken Middleton. [http://www.mtsu.edu/~kmiddlet/history/women.html].

We always like to see sites maintained by a librarian, as this one is, because librarians generally do a meticulous job of gathering and organizing information. This site is a kind of pathfinder to various types of resources on women's history, including reference materials, primary documents, state and regional history sources, journals, and dissertations. Citations are to Internet as well as print resources. In addition to general items, Middleton has compiled lists of materials under a broad range of specific subjects, such as "Advice Literature," "Music," and "Settlement Houses." Useful both as a research guide and a collection development tool for academic and large public libraries.

Diotima: Materials for the Study of Women and Gender in the Ancient World. By Ross Scaife. 1995–2001. [http://www.stoa.org/diotima/].

We looked at this academic site once before, for our March 1, 2000, issue. Much has been added to its collection of primary texts, course materials, links to images and to online articles, and searchable bibliography related to Greek, Roman, Egyptian, and other ancient cultures.

Internet Women's History Sourcebook. Ed. by Paul Halsall. 1998. [http://www.fordham.edu/halsall/women/womensbook.html].

An impressive collection of online documents and secondary materials related to women. This page is a subsidiary of the well-known Internet History Sourcebooks Project, and material is drawn from three other databases: *Internet Ancient History Sourcebook*, *Internet Medieval Sourcebook*, and *Internet Modern History Sourcebook*.

Women and Social Movements in the United States, 1775–1940. By Thomas Dublin and Kathryn Kish Sklar. 1997–2002. [http://womhist.Binghamton.edu/index.html].

This project of the Center for the Historical Study of Women and Gender at the State University of New York at Binghamton offers more than 600 documents and images organized around 30 learning modules designed by undergraduate and graduate students. Each module addresses a theme, such as "The Nineteenth Century Dress Reform Movement" and "African American Women and the Chicago World's Fair": and includes a substantive introduction to put the documents and images in context, as well as a bibliography and links to related sites. A Teacher's Corner encourages use of the modules in classroom setting.

—*Mary Ellen Quinn*

xreferplus

xreferplus. [Internet database]. 2001. xrefer, pricing starting at $1,500. [http://www.xrefer.com].

Normally we reserve this column for free Web sites, but this time we decided to use the space to look at *xreferplus*, a new subscription site that is based on the well-known (and free) *xrefer* reference engine.

xrefer combines content from more than 40 reference titles from seven publishers, most of them British. Users can search by word or phrase or by one of 13 broad topics, from Art to Sci-Tech. What puts the "plus" in *xrefer* is the addition of more titles (a total of 80, 100, or 120, depending on what one is reading); more publishers (23 in all); and more ways to search. Titles from a number of publishers, among them Blackwell and Cambridge University Press, are only available via the paid site. (On the other hand, titles from Oxford University Press are available only on the free site.) Currently, the Art and Biography areas are the most heavily represented, with 11 titles each.

Searching is very easy. Keyword searches can be conducted across all topics and all titles or across selected topics and selected titles. Unlike *xrefer*, *xreferplus* has an advanced search option that allows the user to search entry headings instead of full text and also offers a few other refinements, such as specifying exact phrases and "spelt and sounds like." One of the things we liked about *xrefer* was the "magic ingredient" of cross-referencing. All of the titles in the database are linked, so that a search not only yields expected results, but also leads the user down some circuitous and surprising byways. With more titles at its command, *xreferplus* offers even greater linkage. This also means that simple terms such as *Beethoven* or *stained glass* can deliver several hundred hits, so refining searches is a good strategy. Results are displayed as relevancy-ranked lists of entry headings, along with 200 characters from each entry. Search terms are highlighted, and sources are noted. Delivery options include printing and e-mailing. *Xrefer* provides subscribers with monthly usage statistics by book, top searches, and number of searches performed.

For school and public libraries, in particular, the fact that so many of the titles have a British slant might be a drawback, and the subscription price seems high to us. But librarians who like *xrefer* will want to take advantage of the free *xreferplus* trial. For institutions with particular subject interests, the "specialty data sub-sets" that are promised for the future may offer a more economical alternative than subscribing to the full database.

—*Mary Ellen Quinn*

Reviews

Generalities

World of Computer Science. 2v. Ed. by Brigham Narins. 2002. 668p. bibliog. illus. index. Gale, $150 (0-7876-4960-0). 004.03.

In his introduction, the editor states that it is necessary for "all citizens to have a practical, theoretical, and historical understanding of computers and the major issues regarding information and communication technology." This reference work, aimed at the student and nonexpert, succeeds in providing that understanding.

Nearly 800 entries are arranged in alphabetical order. The topics are primarily related to computer languages, innovations, and specific types of commands; but there are many entries on the people who made significant contributions to the field. Examples include Marc Andreessen, Bill Gates, Kurt Godel, and An Wang. Many of these entries include photographs of the individuals, but other types of illustrations are few. Writing is clear, with plentiful examples that help provide a better understanding of computer programming structure. Related entries are indicated by boldface text, and each entry concludes with *see also* references.

Volume 2 contains a historical chronology that outlines the history of computer science from 1500 B.C. through 2001 and a bibliography. The bibliography lists many excellent Web sites on all facets of computers and also provides an excellent tool for updating this fast-moving part of the reference collection. Recommended for high-school, public, and college libraries.

booksinprint.com. [Internet database]. 2001. Bowker, pricing from $1,495. [http://www.booksinprint.com]. (Last accessed September 10, 2001).

Bowker's *booksinprint.com* is actually a conglomeration of numerous Bowker products, including *Books in Print*, *Books Out of Print*, *Bowker's Complete Video Directory*, *Children's Books in Print*, *Forthcoming Books*, *Subject Guide to Books in Print*, *Subject Guide to Children's Books in Print*, *Words on Cassette*, and others. As a result, *booksinprint.com* contains more than four million titles, including more than 50,000 e-book entries.

Users can choose from six search screens listed on a menu bar located at the top right-hand side of the home page—Search, Browse, Publishers, Awards, Bestsellers, and Bio's. Clicking once on Search displays the primary search screen. Located at the top of the Search page is Quick Search, which consists of a drop-down index menu (Keyword, Author, Title, or ISBN/UPC), a text-entry box, and a search button. Quick Searches are not case sensitive, and word order does not matter.

Advanced Search, located below Quick Search, provides five text boxes linked by Boolean operators. A drop-down index menu listing 30 options, such as Keyword in Subject and Author/Contributor, accompanies each text box. Search results can be easily sorted by Author, Date, ISBN/UPC, Price, Publisher, Relevance, or Title. Other advanced limit options include Format (book, audio, or video), Status (in-print, out-of-print, or forthcoming), Book Limiter (e.g., large print, e-book, best-sellers), Audience, Publication Year, Price Range, Binding, Reviewed In, and Vendor. Another search option is Boolean Search. In a large text box, expert users can type in their search using *booksinprint.com* command language. To assist users with command language, a drop-down menu adjacent to the Boolean text box lists all 32 index abbreviations.

Browse Search offers 17 browsable indexes (such as Audiobook Subject, Language, and Series Title), Awards (a searchable index of more than 300 awards, arranged alphabetically and in 33 subject categories), Publishers (information on more than 165,000 publishers), Bestsellers (best-sellers from 1998 to the present, plus 100 years of top-10 best-sellers for each year from *Publishers Weekly*), and Bio's (short biographies on 6,000 authors).

Results can be added to lists and printed or e-mailed. Downloading is available in several formats, including ASCII, CSV (comma separated values), MARC, or vendor-specific formats, to facilitate ordering.

In addition to the six options available from the search menu bar, three rooms—Children's Room, Fiction Room, and the Forthcoming Book Room—offer additional search features. For example, the Children's Room enables limiting a search by grade and provides access to the fifth edition of the reference source *A to Zoo: Subject Access to Children's Picture Books* (Bowker, 1998).

The advantages of using *booksinprint.com* instead of Bowker's print sources include currency (there are daily updates) and the ability to search several Bowker titles in one swoop. Additional features such as Hooks to Holdings (links to library holdings with Z39.50 compliant catalogs), book covers illustrations, and jacket descriptions are further enhancements. Access to more than 600,000 full-text reviews from 15 review sources is available but at extra cost.

Some libraries use bookstore Web sites, such as *amazon.com*, to assist in collection development and reference service. However, compared to bookstore Web sites, *booksinprint.com*'s clear-cut design, extensive search interface, and commitment to providing comprehensive and accurate bibliographic data ensures reliable reference service and expedites collection development. *booksinprint.com* is highly recommended for academic, public, and school libraries.

Bearing Witness: A Resource Guide to Literature, Poetry, Art, Music, and Videos by Holocaust Victims and Survivors. By Philip Rosen and Nina Apfelbaum. 2002. 210p. index. Greenwood, $49.95 (0-313-31076-9). 016.94053.

Rosen and Apfelbaum have collected a diverse group of more than 800 works into a resource designed for librarians, teachers, and students. Each of the works' creators is a Holocaust victim or survivor. Some were in camps, others in partisan groups, and others spent years in hiding. Many of the names are easily recognizable, others not known at all.

Five chapters cover memoirs, diaries, and fiction; poetry; art; music; and videos. Following an overview, entries within each chapter are arranged alphabetically by the creators' names. Age-level suggestions are provided for narratives and videos, although many of these reach ages younger than those for which the piece is actually intended. Entries include biographical information and noncritical summaries of each title. Where applicable, poetry entries include anthology citations, art entries include institutions where the work can be viewed, and music entries give sources for obtaining the music.

Persons are unevenly cross-referenced if they appear in more than one chapter. Often the reference is only from one chapter to another. For example, although Elie Wiesel appears in both the memoirs, diaries, and fiction chapter and the poetry chapter, the cross-reference appears only in the latter. Under some headings the index provides an unwieldy and hard-to-read list of names and page numbers; under others only a long string of page numbers is offered. Some broad categories in the index, such as *artworks* and *poetry*, might have been better placed in appendixes.

In spite of these flaws, this volume will be valuable to all who are researching the Holocaust. Its strength lies in the inclusion of materials not often found elsewhere. Even the most knowledgeable Holocaust educator may not be aware of some of the works that are represented.

The Biography Book: A Reader's Guide to Nonfiction, Fictional, and Film Biographies of More Than 500 of the Most Fascinating Individuals of All Time. By Daniel S. Burt. 2001. 640p. indexes. Oryx, $74.50 (1-57356-256-4). 016.92.

Filling a niche in the readers' advisory collection, this book lists more than 10,000 biographical sources, including nonfiction, fiction, books for young readers, and both documentary and dramatic films. The subjects are more than 500 of "the most written-about historical figures." They must be deceased and have had at least 30 books chronicling their lives and achievements. Since the author based his selections on numbers of titles in the libraries of his home state of Connecticut, it is not surprising that the overwhelming majority of individuals who are covered are American or English. The titles that are included "are meant to reflect what most readers could expect to find or at least easily retrieve from their linked library systems through interlibrary loan."

Arrangement is alphabetical by name of biographee, beginning with Abigail Adams and ending with Émile Zola. Entries range in length from a half page to more than three pages. A typical longer entry is that for Eleanor Roosevelt. A brief biographical description is followed by "Autobiography and Primary Sources," "Recommended Biographies," "Other Biographical Studies," "Biographical Novels," "Fictional Portraits" (such as the Eleanor Roosevelt Mystery series written by Elliot Roosevelt), "Recommended Juvenile Biographies," "Biographical Films and Theatrical Adaptations," and "Other Sources." All titles are briefly described and evaluated. Listings are quite current; for example, Tracy Chevalier's *Girl with a Pearl Earring* (Dutton, 2000) appears in the entry for Jan Vermeer, and Anne Edwards' *Ever After: Diana and the Life She Led* (St. Martin's, 2000) shows up in the entry for Diana, Princess of Wales.

Thorough indexing is crucial in readers' advisory guides, and this volume provides several indexes to facilitate access to the listings. The first and most extensive is the "Author Index," which is followed by an "Index of Books and Other Works by Title," "Index of Figures by Nationality," "Index of Figures by Occupation" (*writer* is the biggest category), "Index of Figures by Time, Period, and Place," and "Subject Index." This last is useful but not very detailed, and some headings, such as *religion*, are overly broad. Missing are indexes by genre, format, and reading level.

Though there are numerous guides to meet the needs of fiction readers, biography is less well served. Burt, who also wrote *What Historical Novel Do I Read Next?* (Gale, 1997), has provided librarians with a valuable tool. For broader coverage of women, one might turn to Linda G. Adamson's *Notable Women in American History* (Greenwood, 1999) and *Notable Women in World History* (Greenwood, 1998), which together list biographical and autobiographical material on 1,000 women.

Eugene O'Neill: An Annotated International Bibliography, 1973 through 1999. By Madeline C. Smith and Richard Eaton. 2001. 248p. indexes. McFarland, $55 (0-7864-1036-1). 016.812.

According to the introduction, this work is an update of Jordan Miller's *Eugene O'Neill and the American Critic: A Bibliographical Checklist* (Archeon, 1973). The authors have picked up where Miller left off but also include some earlier works that Miller skipped. In addition, they have expanded the scope of the bibliography to encompass material in English but not necessarily American and material in foreign languages. Presumably, the volume also updates Smith and Eaton's *Eugene O'Neill: An Annotated Bibliography, 1973–1985* (Garland, 1988).

All of O'Neill's plays are referenced by abbreviated titles (e.g., *Iceman* for *The Iceman Cometh*; *Mansions* for *More Stately Mansions*). Content is divided into sections covering English-language periodicals, books and parts of books, and dissertations; foreign-language scholarship and criticism; reviews of English-language productions of the plays; reviews of foreign-language productions; and primary works. Arrangement is alphabetical by author except in the sections on English-language and foreign-language productions, where reviews are grouped chronologically under each play. Most of the citations are annotated. The section on primary works includes translations—one can find listings for *Desire under the Elms* translated into Arabic, Chinese, Czechoslovakian, French, Greek, Italian, Korean, and Spanish. A final brief "Miscellaneous" section references an eclectic mix of film and audio versions of the plays, operas based on the plays, plays in which O'Neill appears as a character, and so on. The volume concludes with three indexes: authors, plays, and subjects.

Reflecting O'Neill's growing "internationality," this is a good resource for research collections.

Feature Films, 1960–1969: A Filmography of English-Language and Major Foreign-Language United States Releases. By Harris M. Lentz III. 2001. 694p. bibliog. index. McFarland, $95 (0-7864-1100-7). 016.79143.

This is a catalog of English-language movies made during the 1960s that were released in theaters (as opposed to made-for-television movies), as well as major foreign films exhibited in the U.S. Lentz has compiled several other film-related reference works, including *Science Fiction, Horror & Fantasy Film and Television Credits* (2d ed. McFarland, 2001) [RBB Ap 15 01], and *Western and Frontier Film and Television Credits: 1903–1995* (McFarland, 1996).

The 4,307 entries are listed in alphabetical order by film title. Each includes the year of release, nation of origin (if not from the U.S.), production or distribution company, black and white notation (if not in color), running time, genre, production credits, cast and characters, and a one-or two-sentence synopsis. Although the entries contain abbreviations within the production credits ("Spfx" for "special effects"), there is no directory of abbreviations or explanatory material. Alternate titles and English translations of foreign titles are cross-referenced. There is a one-page bibliography of books and periodicals the author consulted in his research. He also acknowledges using *The Internet Movie Database* [http://us.imdb.com] and *All Movie Guide* [http://allmovie.com] Web sites to compile factual data.

Feature Films, 1960–1969 complements two other McFarland reference titles: *Feature Films, 1940–1949: A United States Filmography* (1994) and *Feature Films, 1950–1959: A United States Filmography* (1999), both by Alan G. Fetrow. Fetrow's works contain slightly different content and also include listings of Academy Award winners and nominees, but as this information is easily accessible from the Academy of Motion Picture Arts and Sciences Web site [http://www.ampas.org], the value of Lentz's filmography is not lessened by this omission. This specialized reference tool is accessible to almost any audience and is recommended for comprehensive academic collections and performing arts or film libraries.

The Films of the Nineties: A Complete, Qualitative Filmography of Over 3,000 Feature-Length English Language Films, Theatrical and Video-Only, Released between January 1, 1990, and December 31, 1999. By Robert A. Nowlan and Gwendolyn L. Nowlan. 2001. 720p. index. McFarland, $95 (0-7864-0974-6). 016.79143.

Two established film authors follow up *The Films of the Eighties* (McFarland, 1991) with their new book on films of the nineties. This volume contains 3,268 entries for films released in theaters between January 1, 1990, and December 31, 1999. Aside from excluding pornographic, documentary, and experimental films, the authors endeavor to be exhaustive but admit that some films may have been missed. However, they believe that they have captured all of the films that were "deemed worthy of being reviewed by some critic in some periodical."

Each entry (arranged in alphabetical order) contains the year of release, production company, country of origin, director(s), producer(s), screenwriter(s), awards (if any), lead players and their character names, and a critical summary. These summaries range in length from 30 to 200 words and can be scathing (see the entry for *The Quick and the Dead*). In addition to the main entries, the book offers a four-page introduction that addresses the highlights and lowlights of the decade in film. The index is a master list of names and is more than 100 pages long.

So why, with free Web sources like *The Internet Movie Database* [http://www.imdb.com/], would a library buy this book? The IMDb provides more information, many more search options and, based on a sample, covers all of the films listed in this title. What it does not provide, besides the Nowlans' commentary, is the 1990s perspective, which places each film within the context of other films of the decade. *The Films of the Nineties* is recommended for academic and public libraries that support a film studies curriculum.

The Grey House Directory of Special Issues: A Guide to Business Magazines. 2001. 624p. index. Grey House, $200 (1-930956-41-X); paper, $175 (1-930956-40-1). 016.051.

This first edition identifies 1,833 magazines in 95 industry categories—"Amusement and Entertainment," "Art and Antiques," "Fishing Industry," "Gifts," "Internet," "Shoes," "Travel," and "Water Supply," to name a few. "Special issues" are generally published annually and can be fact books, yearbooks, buyers' guides, directories, reviews, forecasts, statistical reports, rankings, marketing studies, convention and trade show reports, and membership rosters.

Within each category, entries are arranged alphabetically by magazine name. Each entry offers the name of the magazine, address, phone and fax numbers, and Web site and e-mail addresses if available. Key contacts, a brief description, and a list of special issues follow. Sometimes a subscription price is given, although special issues are often available priced individually. Information provided for the special issues includes name, frequency of publication, and publication month. At the end of every chapter are entries for additional industry-specific magazines that do not have special issues. These listings include address, phone and fax numbers, and Web site and e-mail addresses.

The volume has two indexes. The "Entry and Publisher Index" includes all 4,601 magazines, with publishers in bold type and magazines with special issues identified with an asterisk. The subject index lists more than 400 terms, from *accessories* to *wood and wood products*, to provide more access points to the entries.

This comprehensive new business reference, with information verified by research and phone interviews, will meet the needs of advertising agencies, career-planning services, entrepreneurs, inventors, market researchers, and public relations personnel, as well as business-school students and faculty. Library business collections will want to add it to their shelves.

Dictionary for School Library Media Specialists: A Practical and Comprehensive Guide. By Mary Maude McCain and Martha Merrill. 2001. 219p. Libraries Unlimited, paper, $40 (1-56308-696-4). 020.

Once in a while a reference work appears that pleasantly surprises a reviewer. This is the case with this work, which is much more than a boring addition to the professional shelf. The authors are distinguished members of the library media profession with a combined service record of more than 55 years. They know school library media programs, and they know what other professionals need to know to communicate effectively with other colleagues.

Because the target audience is the building-level library media specialist of any range of experience, the authors have included basic and more sophisticated terms, and historical (*record*: "a sound recording made on a vinyl disc") as well as contemporary definitions. While concentrating on the terms that are most important to the field of school library media, the authors included the words they and their advisory committee felt would be most beneficial from other disciplines, such as instructional design, computer science, technology, literature, educational psychology, educational administration, educational testing, and even special education—in other words, not just the terms of a specialized profession but the terms needed to talk to others outside the field. For example, on a single page one finds definitions for *base number*, B*atchelder Award*, *baud rate*, *beast tale*, and *behavior modification*.

The book defines more than 375 terms. There are two types of definitions—shorter glossary descriptions (*capital outlay*, *reboot*) and longer, more detailed treatments (*poetry*, *proximity operators*). *See* references (especially from acronyms and abbreviations) and *see also* references facilitate use.

Except for the fact that there are no pronunciation guides, this is a near-perfect book. Browsing through it is like taking a class. Library professionals and students of library media programs will want to keep it on their own shelves. School libraries and academic libraries that serve schools of education and library media programs will need copies in their collections.

Internet Resources and Services for International Finance and Investment. By Qun G. Jiao and Lewis-Guodo Liu. 2001. 540p. indexes. Oryx, $49.95 (1-57356-346-3). 025.06.

Because of the tremendous array of resources on the Internet today, professors Jiao and Liu intend to save investors time by helping them find relevant sources to increase their financial opportunities in a global environment. Covering 216 countries, regions, and territories and listing more than 3,000 Web sites, this work is organized into six main sections. The first section, "Global Finance and Investment Resources," arranges Web sites under subject areas like "International Trade Associations" and "Emerging Market Resources." The rest of the volume is arranged by continent. For each, a section on "General Finance and Investment Resources" is followed by an alphabetical country list with the best sites specific to each country.

The Web resources include sites on real estate, taxation, government agencies, trade regulations, country profiles, privatization programs, and business, personal, public, or corporate finance. Under each country, sites are grouped under four categories: "Government Agency," "Stock Exchange," "Business and Investment Sites," and "Business and Financial/Economic News." Each entry includes the title, URL, and a descriptive paragraph highlighting the content of the site. Most sites are free, in English, and were last checked in September 2000. Three indexes complete the volume: an alphabetical Web site index, a country index, and a huge subject index.

Most business collections will want to add this timely, easy-to-use resource. Buy two copies, one for reference and one to circulate.

International Dictionary of Library Histories. 2v. Ed. by David H. Stam. 2001. 1,053p. index. Fitzroy Dearborn, $175 (1-57958-244-3). 027.009.

These two handsome volumes contain 271 essays by library historians on the great contemporary libraries of the world. Some 224 essays focus on individual libraries, 34 provide overviews for various types of libraries, and 13 deal with "library development in regions of the world sporadically represented elsewhere in these volumes."

The A–Z topical and geographical surveys, which are confined to volume 1, vary in length from less than a page (*Circulating libraries and reading rooms*) to nearly eight pages (*Iberian libraries*). Each concludes with suggestions for further reading. Topics include types of institutions (A*rchives*, P*ublic libraries*, S*pecial libraries*); libraries focusing on special topics or formats (B*uddhist libraries*, M*ap libraries*, M*edical libraries*); libraries for special clientele (P*rison libraries*, W*omen's libraries*); and libraries originating in the past (M*edieval libraries*, R*enaissance libraries*). There is also an essay on O*nline catalogs*.

Following the introductory surveys, library essays appear in alphabetical order under the names of owning institutions, so that the Bodleian Library is not in the Bs, but in the Us, under U*niversity of Oxford Libraries*. Library entries range from less than one page for N*ational Library of Pakistan* to as many as six pages for L*ibrary of Congress of the United States* and B*ritish Library*, or seven pages for N*ew York Public Library*. Each entry begins with the library's name in English and its own language if different, address, Web address if available, year of founding, holdings statistics, and a list of special collections. Like the topical and geographical essays, the library essays also conclude with further reading suggestions. The set concludes with a detailed index of 80 pages, largely devoted to headings for organizations (with cross-references from their acronyms), libraries (by name and by type), countries, continents, persons, and publications. A geographic index of the library entries would be helpful for readers who might be interested in exploring the great libraries of New York or China.

All academic and large public libraries interested in library history will want to add this one-of-a-kind compilation to their collections.

World Almanac Reference Database@FACTS1. Facts On File News Services, $225. [http://www.2facts.com]. (Last accessed September 10, 2001).

A new addition to FACTS.com is the *World Almanac Reference Database* (WARD), which consists of the complete 2001 *World Almanac and Book of Facts*, with updates from the upcoming edition, and the *World Almanac Encyclopedia*, made up of 26,000 articles from the *Funk & Wagnalls New Encyclopedia*.

The Almanac portion of the database is the default opening screen, with tabs for switching between the Almanac and the Encyclopedia. Both offer a Custom Search option as well as Menu Access. Among other things, Custom Search allows the user to search the Almanac and Encyclopedia (as well as other FACTS.*com* databases to which a library might subscribe) simultaneously. Menu Access in the Almanac includes an A–Z table of contents and World Almanac Favorites, described as "instant access to the coolest stuff," including feature topics, top news stories, and historical information. In addition, the opening screen contains links to special features arranged under broad headings, such as "Nations of the World" and "Arts and the Media." Almanac entries consist of the familiar lists, statistical tables, and other content one finds in the print *World Almanac*. In addition, there are links to related content from the Encyclopedia and other FACTS.*com* databases.

The Encyclopedia has three search menus: Table of Contents, with A–Z access to encyclopedia articles; Biographies, which offers the user a quick way to locate the biographical entries; and Special Reports. Encyclopedia entries are displayed in a no-nonsense way. Longer articles have their own tables of contents, but there are no illustrations and in some cases no hyperlinked cross-references. Special Reports offers a cumulative index to monthly features related to news events. One of the featured stories for August was Lance Armstrong's victory in the Tour de France. The story was linked to related content in both the Encyclopedia (*cycling*, *France*) and the Almanac as well as to news stories from Facts On File News Services. There were also links to relevant Web sites, such as the official Web site of the Tour de France. Special Reports are available going back to 1997.

The tables of contents and index pages seem more efficient for searching than does the current search engine, which ranks hits based on frequency of the term(s) in the article. Carefully selecting and combining terms using Boolean operators is necessary to search efficiently. The Help section explains and offers useful search suggestions. The Search History button lists all searches done, but one must toggle between databases to repeat a search from the list. The site uses frames on its explanation, index, and search pages. The article pages have wide margins with sidebar menus of links, and use more paper to print than necessary. A "reformat for printing" feature would be desirable.

With material from *The World Almanac* updated regularly and intertwined with the *World Almanac Encyclopedia*, this is a nice addition to a school or library's online reference collection, especially if the library already subscribes to FACTS.com.

The World Book Encyclopedia Estudiantil Hallazgos. 13v. 2001. 2,500p. illus. index. maps. World Book, $359 (0-7166-7405-X). 036.

This Spanish-language version of *The World Book Student Discovery Encyclopedia* is a useful resource for elementary-school students who are learning to do research. With more than 3,500 illustrations (including over 400 maps), pages with ample white space, and thin volumes easily grasped by small hands, the set welcomes young users.

The alphabetical entries are brief—one page maximum—with very basic information, but the scope is broad. There are articles on the countries of the world, all of the Canadian provinces, and every state in the U.S. Biographies of major athletes (Henry Aaron, Pele), authors and poets (Jorge Luis Borges, Rita Dove), all of the U.S. presidents, scientists (Luis Alvarez, Louis Pasteur), and other people of interest (Marian Anderson, Elvis Presley) address a wide range of interests. Entries about living and extinct animals, scientific and technical concepts, folklore and mythology, holidays, and religions explain basic ideas well. The articles about countries, states, and provinces have fact boxes with brief statistical information, a flag, a small map, and useful facts (e.g., state flower and bird). The historical information about countries is often sketchy and not current. The article on Afghanistan stops in 1919 when it became independent.

The use of many brief entries can be a disadvantage. The article on the human body would be stronger if the few sentences devoted to individual organs in separate entries (even the appendix has one!) were incorporated into it. Separate articles for New Year, Chinese New Year, and Jewish New Year could also be combined effectively. The longer articles, such as those on national parks, Native Americans, and animation, do a better job of presenting subject matter. Hands-on projects such as mask making, dyeing carnations, and preparing mint-yogurt dip give students a chance to apply concepts described in the text.

The *World Book Enciclopedia Estudiantil Hallazgos* has instructions for use in every volume. The alphabetical arrangement makes locating information easy, but volume 13 contains an index as well as a small atlas for those who wish to use it. This set is a good choice for public library children's collections and school libraries serving a Spanish-speaking population.

The World of Learning Online. [Internet database]. Europa, pricing from $540. [http://www.worldoflearning.com/]. (Last accessed February 27, 2002).

Europa Publications introduces the online version of *The World of Learning* (WOL). This international directory lists more than 30,000 academic institutions and includes colleges, universities, schools of art and music, libraries, learned societies, international organizations, research institutes, museums, and art galleries. Updates are promised quarterly.

WOL packs plenty of powerful yet intuitive search options. Users can type their search term(s) in a single text-entry box, browse contents, or choose to use one or more of the advanced search options. The browse categories are Countries, Institutions, or Subjects (which groups academic staff under areas of specialization). Browse screens are designed in bite-sized chunks for quick loading. For example, selecting Countries initially displays a short country list extending from Afghanistan to Azerbaijan. A clickable alphabet as well as a Go To text box enables the user to easily advance through the alphabet.

The Advanced Search screen provides more than a dozen search options. Users can choose to do a full-text search with additional limit options such as Institutions and People. A Geographical Search and an Institution Search are also available. Geographical Search limits include World Region, Country (198 listed), State or Region, and Town or City. Institution Search options include Institution, Institution Type (Learned Societies, Research Institutes, Libraries and Archives, Museums and Art Galleries, Universities and Colleges, International Organizations), Year of Foundation, and Publications. Equipped with these search options, the user will find that custom searches are a snap. For example, a search for universities and colleges in Havana, Cuba, quickly retrieved 17 entries.

As in the print edition, information is gathered primarily through the use of questionnaires returned from institutions. Type of information provided includes address, phone number, fax number, e-mail address, year founded, institution description, number of students and instructors, and list of key personnel. URLs are also included, although we came across several prominent institutions without an accompanying Internet address. These included M.V. Lomonosov Moscow State University, Cairo University, and Stockholms Universitet.

Similar print resources include the *International Handbook of Universities* (16th ed., Palgrave, 2001) and *The World List of Universities and Other Institutions of Higher Education* (23d ed., Palgrave, 2002). However, both are narrower in scope and are currently offered only in print every two years. Although time-consuming, gathering information freely off the Internet, either by visiting an institution's Web site or by visiting a free online directory such as *Braintrack University Index* [http://www.braintrack.com/], will offer further competition to WOL. However, for users seeking a quick, easy-to-use, one-stop source for information on academic institutions located around the world, the online version of *The World of Learning* will prove to be popular and useful. Recommended for academic and public libraries.

Philosophy, Psychology, Religion

Encyclopedia of Prophecy. By Geoffrey Ashe. 2001. 291p. bibliogs. illus. index. ABC-CLIO, $75 (1-57607-079-4); e-book, $100 (1-57607-528-1). 133.3.

According to this volume's preface, the term *prophecy* has two meanings. One is "inspired utterances" —an unseen being, usually a god or goddess, speaking through a mortal. The other meaning refers to predicting future events. In light of the interest in New Age phenomena such as crystals and astrology, an encyclopedic study of prophecy is timely. This work brings together information on prophets, psychics, symbols, methods, and even a study of theories of prophecy.

Some 134 entries are arranged alphabetically and cover people (*Cassandra*; *Cayce, Edgar*; *Elijah*; *Nostradamus*), places (*Delphi, Glastonbury*), techniques, and symbols of prophecy. Many of the articles are accompanied by an illustration, portrait, or photograph. Most entries end with *see* references to other articles and a list of titles for further reading. Well-known prophecies such as the sinking of the *Titanic* are covered in several articles as well as in an individual entry under *Titanic*. The volume concludes with a bibliography of approximately 130 sources and an index.

Some individuals are included (Saint Augustine, for example), not necessarily because they made prophetic statements but because of their views on prophecy. Although the volume does not specifically cover science fiction, some writers who present a compelling view of the future, such as Aldous Huxley and George Orwell, were selected for inclusion. One obvious omission is the psychic the Amazing Criswell, who was a popular figure on late-night television and noted for his outlandish predictions.

Much of the information included in this work can be found in other reference works dealing with the paranormal, psychic phenomena, astrology, and even religion, but no work pulls together all the different facets of prophecy in one volume. Recommended for public, school, and academic libraries with collections in these areas or where patron demand is anticipated.

The Greenhaven Encyclopedia of Witchcraft. Ed. by Patricia D. Netzley. 2002. 288p. bibliog. illus. index. Greenhaven, $74.95 (0-7377-0437-3). 133.4.

This book from the student-tailored Greenhaven Encyclopedia Of series brings together all aspects of witchcraft: traditions, rituals, concepts, and magical tools as well as important personages both historical and modern, deities, and historical events. Occult topics that do not have a function for witches have been omitted. The author has organized the information in an alphabetical arrangement. Articles vary in length, from just a paragraph to several pages (*Salem, witch trials of*; *Traditions, Witchcraft*). When appropriate, the article ends with *see also* references. The table of contents and index assist the user in finding topics quickly and efficiently. The text is easy to comprehend.

There are illustrations scattered throughout the text. Some are portraits of historical persons accused of being witches or of denouncing witchcraft. Others are illustrations from early books or photographs of modern practitioners. All are in black and white. There is one unfortunate error: the two tarot cards that are pictured are incorrectly identified as "King, or Emperor" and "Queen, or Empress." In fact, these cards represent the Pope and Popess. The bibliography lists many classic and recent titles for anyone interested in learning more about the general topic of witchcraft.

This title is very similar in coverage to Rosemary Guiley's *Encyclopedia of Witches and Witchcraft* (2d ed., Facts On File, 1999), which remains the witchcraft reference source of choice. Considering the perennial interest in the topic, even those public and high-school libraries that already have Guiley's book may want to add the accessible Greenhaven offering to their collections.

Satanism Today: An Encyclopedia of Religion, Folklore, and Popular Culture. By James R. Lewis. 2001. 371p. appendixes. bibliog. index. ABC-CLIO, $85 (1-57607-292-4); E-book, $95 (1-57607-759-4). 133.4.

Proposing "to survey contemporary images of the Devil," this book examines not only "religious Satanism" but also various satanic organizations, traditions, and personalities. The general focus is on the Christian-Jewish-Islamic tradition of Satan, but there are articles discussing Buddhism and Taoism and their somewhat different demons and hells. Lewis also explores the contribution of Zoroastrianism to both Satan and the concept of hell in the three great monotheisms and the influence of Aleister Crowley and Anton LaVey on the modern satanist movement.

Several entries address satanic ritual abuse, both in individual cases and as a broader topic. One of the appendixes to the book is the 1992 FBI report on satanic ritual abuse that generally demolished the concept. Other appendixes contain samples of contemporary satanic writings and a survey Lewis did of satanists.

The book is in dictionary format. Articles range from a few sentences to several two-column pages in length. Most articles have *see also* references and a list of further reading, much of it recent. Where appropriate, Web sites are also listed, as many satanist organizations have considerable Internet activity.

There are some errors. In the article on *Fantasia*, several composers but not the right one (Mussorgsky) are credited for the music in the film's final sequence. In the article *Magic and magical groups*, the creator of Wonderland (as in *Alice's Adventures in Wonderland*) is identified as Reverend Charles Ludwig (instead of Lutwidge) Dodgson. The name "Lucifer" is translated as "light giver" in the *Lucifer* article and "light bearer" (correctly) elsewhere.

Still, this is a useful book. It is remarkably evenhanded. The bibliography and list of nonprint resources are valuable, and many of the titles can be obtained at larger public libraries. The FBI report and the survey of satanists are almost worth the price of the book. Most larger public and academic libraries will want to consider this for purchase.

A Dictionary of Psychology. By Andrew M. Colman. 2001. 864p. appendixes. illus. Oxford, $39.95 (0-19-866211-4). 150.3.

In recent years, a number of dictionaries of psychology have been published, among them David Statt's *The Concise Dictionary of Psychology* (3d ed., Routledge, 1998), Raymond J. Corsini's *Dictionary of Psychology* (Brunner/Mazel, 1999), Arthur Reber's *Penguin Dictionary of Psychology* (3d ed., Penguin, 2001), and Jon Roeckelein's *Dictionary of Theories, Laws, and Concepts in Psychology* (Greenwood, 1998). This latest addition carves a spot for itself by increasing coverage of the technical terminology of neuroanatomy, neurophysiology, psychopharmacology, and statistics, not always covered in previous psychological dictionaries. It also continues the traditions of earlier psychology dictionaries in covering the more widely used terms.

Entries include parts of speech, numbered senses (with the sense that is most common in psychology literature appearing first), synonyms, alternate forms, and cross-references. Etymological or word origin information is provided for many terms. When a term was coined by an individual or originated with a person's name (*Weber's law, Purkinje cell*), the individual's birth and death dates are noted. British spellings are employed.

Physically, this is an attractive and comfortable dictionary to use. Even with 10,500 entries, or an average of 11 and one-half per page, the pages do not appear crowded. Dictionary entries are followed by two appendixes. The 20-page "Phobias and Phobic Stimuli" lists phobias by their technical names, noting their stimuli and etymologies, and also lists stimuli (*ageing, spiders*) for those unsure of the technical terms. Appendix 2 defines 700 abbreviations and symbols. The list of principal sources is more than three pages long and includes subject dictionaries, companion volumes, research methods, statistics, subject encyclopedias, and more. This list in itself would be useful as a benchmark against which a research library might judge its reference collection in psychology and related areas.

This dictionary is a required addition to larger public and academic libraries where users seek information in the social, biological, and medical sciences. It is both classic and futurist, bringing together theory and practice and physical, emotional, and historical concepts used within the widening scope of psychology. It is a great value for the price and would also be a welcome addition to any social scientist's personal library.

Encyclopedia of Ethics. 3v. 2d ed. Ed. by Lawrence C. Becker and Charlotte B. Becker. 2001. 1,800p. bibliog. indexes. Routledge, $350 (0-415-93672-1). 170.

Since the publication of the first edition of this work, in 1992, the number of general and specialized reference works in philosophy has significantly increased. Examples include two general works—Salem's three-volume *Ethics* (1994) and the *Encyclopedia of Ethics* (Facts On File, 1999), which serves as a basic introduction to the subject—and the more specialized four-volume *Encyclopedia of Applied Ethics* (Academic, 1998). Scholars, university students, and readers with a serious interest in ethical theory will be pleased to find that this second edition of the *Encyclopedia of Ethics* distinguishes itself in aim and coverage from these other works.

The coverage of ethical theory as pursued among English-speaking philosophers remains the scope of this set. Entries are listed in word-by-word alphabetical order. A list of entries gives a convenient overview of headwords and *see* references. A subject index provides a guide to subjects discussed in the text of the entries, including persons; and a citation index provides an author-by-author listing of writers, and some editors, cited in the bibliographies of all 581 entries.

In their introduction, the editors note that the second edition has been both revised and expanded by more than 30 percent. They also claim that almost all of the 435 entries from the first edition have been retained but that many have been substantially revised; "where appropriate and possible," bibliographies have also been updated. In this new edition more than 300 specialists are responsible for 581 signed entries, 150 of which are new. A list of contributors and editors provides brief biographical information about these individuals.

Although entries are consistently highly accessible and readable, a careful comparison of entries across editions reveals two principal shortcomings. First, revisions are not always "substantial"—even when substantial revision may have been warranted. The article *Abortion* is an example. Second, most bibliographies have not been updated. The bibliography accompanying the entry *Academic freedom*, for example, includes only one reference published in the 1980s and none from the 1990s. Likewise, the bibliography accompanying the entry *Ethics in government* has no references published in the 1990s. On the other hand, the entry on genocide has been updated to include mention of Bosnia and Rwanda, and the accompanying bibliography lists several resources published in the 1990s. The real value of this edition lies in the 150 new entries, among them *Cheating, Gay ethics, Genetic engineering, Islamic ethics, Multiculturalism, Political correctness*, and *Racism, concepts of*, to name just a few.

Is this encyclopedia an essential purchase? Yes, despite the shortcomings noted, especially for large public and academic libraries. Libraries that own the first edition will want to replace it with the second.

Encyclopedia of Ethics in Science and Technology. By Nigel Barber. 2002. 386p. appendix. illus. index. Facts On File, $60 (0-8160-4314-0). 174.

From stem cell research to the Kyoto Treaty to land mines, our lives are intertwined with science and technology and the social and ethical controversies surrounding them. This work attempts to give a broad overview of the ethical issues surrounding the development of science and the deployment of technology. Although the goal is admirable, the choice of topics is somewhat random and superficial and often focuses more on debunking pseudoscience than on ethics.

The more than 400 entries range in length from 25 to more than 1,000 words and fall into five general categories: biography, legal aspects, specific technologies or theories, events, and movements and organizations. Some entries include brief lists of further reading, most of which is taken from secondary popular literature. The entries on philosophical concepts, such as *Utilitarian ethics* or *Dualism*, do not provide a better or more relevant explanation than one would find in a basic philosophical or ethical reference work. Some biographical entries (e.g., *Mendel, Gregor Johann*) discuss ethical issues, but others offer only simple biographical information with little or no explicit ethical discussion. Other types of entries that are not well integrated into the theme of the book include one on UFOs, a very lengthy entry on the history of science, and entries that simply describe an event or experiment (e.g., *Hubble Space Telescope, Catalytic converter*).

The strength of the encyclopedia is its coverage of specific technologies and events and their controversial aspects. The author has done a good job of treating many of the technologies—such as contraception and genetic engineering—that we see in the daily news. The coverage is fairly evenhanded in addressing the claims of both the opponents and proponents of the technology in question. Useful cross-references to related articles also add value here. There is a helpful appendix listing organizations (with contact information) that treat ethical issues in science and technology.

Overall, this volume provides a decent introduction, and high-school and public libraries may want to consider adding it to their collections as a supplement to other resources. Academic libraries will find that larger, scholarly works such as *The Encyclopedia of Ethics* [RBB Ja 1 & 15 02] have adequate coverage of science and technology issues.

Encyclopedia of Asian Philosophy. By Oliver Leaman. 2001. 669p. bibliogs. indexes. Routledge, $160 (0-415-17281-0). 181.

The reference literature for Asian philosophy is scant, probably because philosophy and religion are viewed in the West as more inextricably linked in Asian cultures. Many reference works address Asian religious traditions, but the *Encyclopedia of Asian Philosophy* aims to treat only philosophy, including "religion only in so far as it relates to philosophy."

Alphabetically arranged entries are signed by the scholars who wrote them and conclude with bibliographies. They range from ancient times through the twentieth century and include individuals (Gandhi, Mencius), schools of thought (*Kagyu school, Yoga*), texts (*Bhagavad Gita, Upanishads*), and concepts (*Free will, Subject and object*). Topics are drawn from the traditions of Buddhism, Confucianism, Hinduism, Islam, Jainism, Shinto, and Zoroastrianism and cover the geographic areas of China, India, Japan, Korea, Melanesia, and Tibet. Given their proximity to Asia as well as their experience with indigenous cultures, there are entries for Australia and New Zealand, too. There is also coverage of Western influence on Asian philosophy, an example being *Western learning in Japan*. Extensive cross-referencing and *see also* recommendations are used throughout. The encyclopedia begins with a lengthy general bibliography and a thematic outline of entries by religious tradition and geographic area and ends with separate name and subject indexes.

Two other sources treat Asian philosophy fairly exclusively. The first is the *Companion Encyclopedia of Asian Philosophy* (Routledge, 1997). Its drawback is that it consists of lengthy, thematic essays and not discrete entries. *Key Concepts in Eastern Philosophy* (Routledge, 1999) follows a dictionary-like format, but compared to this new encyclopedia, the entries are fewer in number and shorter in length, with no individuals treated in separate entries. The *Encyclopedia of Asian Philosophy* is a valuable resource for readers interested in both Western and Asian philosophy, Asian religions, and Asian culture and civilization and is recommended for academic and large public libraries.

Encyclopedia of American Religious History. 2v. Rev. ed. Ed. by Edward L. Queen II and others. 2001. 868p. bibliogs. illus. indexes. Facts On File, $137.50 (0-8160-4335-3). 200.

With more than 800 alphabetically arranged entries, this revision of the 1996 edition gives students and general readers an excellent source of information on American religious history. Individual religions, denominations, religious theory and doctrine, religious movements, major personalities, and geographical regions are covered. Entry topics include *African-American religion, Church of God, Hinduism, Identity movement, New France, Scottish Common Sense Realism,* and *Washington, Booker T.* The set includes a 36-page general index as well as a "Synoptic Index," which lists related articles under broad categories such as "Feminism" or "New Religious Movements." The entries, which range from one paragraph to more than four pages and are written by scholars of religious studies, offer cross-references and bibliographies (now including Web sites). Many entries are complemented by black-and-white photographs.

This source offers a unique and convenient ready reference compared to other reference publications in the field. The *Encyclopedia of the American Religious Experience* (Scribner, 1988) consists of topical essays rather than short, focused entries. The *Encyclopedia of American Religions* (6th ed., Gale, 1999) doesn't include biographical information. The currency of the *Encyclopedia of American Religious History* is also an advantage. Many entries covering the period since the original 1996 publication have been added. New entries include *Heaven's Gate, Hsi Lai Temple,* and *Waco*. An effort has been made to expand coverage of religious pluralism. According to the publishers, 30 percent of the material is new or revised.

Encyclopedia of American Religious History is an excellent and readable resource for the study of the history of religion in the U.S. The coverage is extensive and reliable, and the indexes and cross-references allow for easy access. Recommended for public and academic libraries, especially where the first edition has been heavily used.

Encyclopedia of Fundamentalism. Ed. by Brenda E. Brasher. 2001. 512p. bibliogs. illus. index. Routledge, $125 (0-415-92244-5). 200.

Part of Routledge's Religion and Society series of reference sources that cover various aspects of religious experience from a cross-cultural perspective, this encyclopedia discusses and analyzes the concept of fundamentalism in American Protestant Christianity and other religious traditions and cultures.

In her introduction, editor Brasher treats fundamentalism primarily as "a widespread, populist, socio-economic movement that emerged in twentieth-century Christian Protestantism." But she defines the scope of this encyclopedia broadly, noting that the term *fundamentalism* can be applied to movements within different religious traditions. "These movements," Brasher states, "attempted to blockade religious authority from most, if not all, outside critique, and fence off adherents from the influence of contemporary culture beyond their religion."

The clearly written, alphabetically arranged entries range in length from one to seven pages, and each ends with an author byline and a short bibliography. Some of the longer articles also include sidebars with textual excerpts from documents related to the topic of the entry. There are a few marginally relevant black-and-white photos interspersed throughout the book. Entry topics include major fundamentalist movements and sects (there are long entries on Catholic, Hindu, Islamic, and Jewish fundamentalism but none on Buddhist or Confucian Fundamentalism); significant creeds (*Creationism, Cult of Mary, Westminster Confession*); historical events (*Azusa Street Revival, Great Awakening*); and social and political issues that are important to fundamentalists (*Abortion, Antifeminism, Militia*). Biographical information on key figures in the history of fundamentalism is interwoven into the text of many of the entries.

Entries such as *Bible study, Evil, Free will, Miracles, Prophecy,* and *Sin and sinners* are exclusively or mostly discussed in a Protestant fundamentalist context. Information in entries dealing with topics related to Judaism is sometimes set in a Christian context, for example, the Hebrew Bible is called the "Old Testament," the Western Wall is called the "Wailing Wall," and an entry on *Elohim* (one of the words for God used in the Hebrew Bible) discusses its interpretation by Christian fundamentalists but not their Jewish counterparts.

Although most elements of this encyclopedia are covered adequately in a combination of other broader reference works (e.g., *Encyclopedia of Religion* [Macmillan, 1995] and *Encyclopedia of American Social History* [Macmillan, 1993]) the *Encyclopedia of Fundamentalism* provides the most comprehensive and accurate coverage of Protestant Fundamentalism; its entries of non-Protestant Fundamentalism are less complete. Recommended for academic libraries, large public libraries, and seminary libraries.

Philosophy, Psychology, Religion

The Oxford Guide to People and Places of the Bible. Ed. by Bruce M. Metzger and Michael D. Coogan. 2001. 355p. bibliog. index. Oxford, $30 (0-19-514641-7). 220.9.

This dictionary is a spinoff from *The Oxford Companion to the Bible* (1993), from which the compilers have extracted the articles about people and places. Many of the more than 300 articles in *People and Places* are exactly the same as those in the larger *Companion*, except that the frequent parenthetical references to biblical passages have been deleted. Some articles are extracts from longer articles in the *Companion*.

Articles range in length from a short paragraph, such as the nine lines devoted to *Gethsemane*, to as many as nine pages (for *Jerusalem*) or thirteen pages (for *Jesus Christ*). Longer articles are divided into sections, each with a topical subheading. The accompanying 14 biblical maps, plus the separate index to these maps, are slightly smaller reproductions of the maps and index in the *Companion*. The bibliography has been updated to include references as recent as 2000.

Like the *Companion*, *People and Places* is selective, covering only the "major" figures and places of the Bible, in contrast to *Harper's Bible Dictionary* (1993), which includes an entry for every person mentioned three or more times in the Bible. However, the rather comprehensive subject index does provide access to topics, persons, and places lacking their own entries, and also to discussions of major persons and topics within other articles. The index is generally well done with generous subdivisions for the more important headings. The publisher, however, has neglected to insert continuation lines when subheadings carry over to a new twopage spread, forcing the user to consult the previous page.

Except for the updated bibliography, there does not appear to be any material in *People and Places*. Thus, libraries that own the *Companion* may not wish to purchase this spinoff, unless their users would find a smaller volume devoted only to people and places a useful reference work.

Dictionary of Popes and the Papacy. Ed. by Bruno Steimer and Michael G. Parker. 2001. 268p. bibliogs. indexes. Herder and Herder, $50 (0-8245-1918-3). 262.

Lexikon fur Theologie und Kirche (LTK) (Herder and Herder, 1993–1999) has long been recognized as a standard academic reference tool for Christian theology and church history, with emphasis on Roman Catholicism. The *Dictionary of Popes and the Papacy* is the first in a series of thematic dictionaries containing translated articles from LTK as well as supplemental information "that give[s] greater attention to the Anglo-American historical and theological context."

The volume is divided into two sections. The first provides biographies on the popes and antipopes. The second part addresses the "institutional, canonical, and theological aspects of the papacy." All articles are alphabetically arranged within their respective sections, signed, and conclude with supplemental bibliographies. Although the dictionary aims to make information about popes and the papacy available to an English-language public, the citations in the supplemental bibliographies are to very scholarly sources, the overwhelming majority in languages other than English. A subject index concludes the work.

The biographical entries are straightforward. The entries on the papacy itself range from details about the ring and tiara worn by the pope to longer articles on topics such as infallibility, how popes are elected, and the process of canonization. Historical entries include treatment of the Roman Curia, ecumenical councils, and the Vatican itself. The only attention to the Anglo-American context appears to be an entry for Vatican-U.S. relations.

There isn't much here that can't be found in the *New Catholic Encyclopedia* (McGraw-Hill, 1967) and its supplements. A more recent title, *Encyclopedia of the Vatican and Papacy* (Greenwood, 1999), extends beyond the religious and theological, addressing the political, diplomatic, social, and cultural roles of the papacy as well. Biographical information can also be found in the *Oxford Dictionary of Popes* (Oxford, 1988). Besides providing non-German readers with access to part of LTK, the *Dictionary of Popes and the Papacy* charts little new ground. Academic and large public libraries lacking other resources on the topic, or those in need of comprehensive coverage of the papacy, should consider purchasing this work.

Historical Atlas of Christianity. 2d ed. By Franklin H. Littell. 2001. 440p. appendixes. glossary. illus. index. maps. Continuum, $35 (0-8264-1303-X). 270.

This is a revised and expanded edition of *The Macmillan Atlas History of Christianity*, published in 1976. The original text has been reworked, new maps have been added, and the time line has been expanded. Littell, who also authored the first edition, is Emeritus Professor of Religion at Temple University, and the work grew out of his teaching.

Some 200 maps and 240 illustrations portray the expanding nature of Christianity and are accompanied by readable narratives. The material is arranged under three major headings: "Early Christianity in Its Setting," "The Christian Roman Empire," and "The Age of Personal Decision." The middle section, which extends from approximately A.D. 313 through the nineteenth century, received the greatest repositioning and editing. Equal and fair treatment is given to varying denominational viewpoints within Christianity and between Christian, Jewish, and Muslim religions.

The revised edition has several new chapters, among them "Centers of Interfaith Dialogue," "Mega-Churches," and "Christianity and the Holocaust." Four appendixes of marginal consequence have been added (for example, "Countries Recently Limiting Religious Liberty" simply lists the names of 77 countries, with no additional information) and a list of illustrations has been deleted. A short glossary of "Selected Persons and Concepts" and an index complete the volume.

Unfortunately, there are no bibliographic references supporting the text. The maps, all of which are black and white, can be difficult to read, and the illustrations, most of them hand drawn even when a photograph would certainly be available (for example, the portrait of Billy Graham), do not add visual interest. Libraries that own the 1976 edition may want to update, but for others, this is a secondary purchase.

A Dictionary of Asian Christianity. Ed. by Scott W. Sunquist. 2001. 947p. bibliog. maps. Eerdmans, $75 (0-8028-3776-X). 275.

Christianity is generally regarded as a Western tradition, its history linked to Europe. This view omits a long and rich relationship of Christianity and Asian cultures. Although some scholarly attention of late has been paid to Christianity in Asia, there is now a reference work that gives an overview of how Christianity has shaped and been shaped by many Asian cultures.

The 1,260 entries are alphabetically arranged, signed, and conclude with supplemental bibliographies. Worthy of mention is the fact that the majority of contributors are scholars or religious leaders in Asia, intimately associated with the topics about which they write. Many of the articles are short biographies of Asian religious leaders and missionaries from Europe and North America. Political leaders influenced by Christianity (e.g., Katayama Tetsu, in Japan) or whose policies affected Christians (e.g., Sukarno, in Indonesia) are also included. Survey articles on countries provide nice overviews of the history and development of Christianity there. Other entries describe the history of Christian denominations (e.g., *Anglican Church*, *Seventh-day Adventists*) in Asia. Roman Catholic and Orthodox religious orders in Asia are discussed, as are such Protestant religious communities such as the Methodist *Sitiawan Christian Settlement*, in China. Specific Asian approaches to Christian theology are treated in the entries for *Minjung Theology*, in Korea, and *Homeland theology*, Taiwan. Finally, issues such as *Family*, *Poverty*, *Racism*, and *Secularization* are all discussed in their Asian contexts.

See and *see also* references are useful, but they are no substitute for a thorough index. However, given that this work charts new territory, with no competition on reference shelves, the lack of an index is probably a minor complaint.

The *Dictionary of Asian Christianity* makes the reference literature for Christianity more complete and is recommended for academic and public libraries that want to add depth to their religion reference collections. It will be a welcome resource for Asian history and cultural studies, too.

The Encyclopedia of Saints. By Rosemary Ellen Guiley. 2001. 402p. appendixes. glossaries. illus. index. Facts On File, $82.50 (0-8160-4133-4); Checkmark, paper, $24.95 (0-8160-4134-2). 282.

This alphabetical compendium profiles more than 400 saints recognized by either the Catholic or the Orthodox Church. Entries range from a brief paragraph to several pages and provide complete name, alternative names and spellings, biographical information, summation of religious experiences, reports of miracles or apparitions, and, when available, noteworthy dates: beatification, canonization, and feast day. Each saint's area of patronage is also noted. Some longer entries feature further reading citations listing books, journal articles, and Web sites. Occasional black-and-white illustrations—photographs, woodcuts and reproductions—appear throughout.

Twelve appendixes supplement the data. Three list Doctors of the Church, Fathers of the Church, and canonized popes. Others identify patron saints by topic or place, provide a chronological calendar of feast days, or explain the processes of beatification and canonization. Three are devoted to the Blessed Virgin Mary: feast days, authenticated apparitions, and unauthenticated apparitions. There is one glossary of general terms and another glossary of heresies. A detailed index completes the work.

Written for the general public, the readable entries establish social and historical context and do not shy away from identifying controversial or unsubstantiated claims. In her introduction, the author tells that she was motivated to produce this work by a personal mystical experience. Despite this, she does not attempt to interpret or proselytize. Instead, she allows the facts to speak for themselves, as she has in her previous Facts On File publications, including *Encyclopedia of Angels* (1997) and *Atlas of the Mysterious in North America* (1994).

Readers seeking inspiration through the lives and examples of historical figures have a multitude of titles to choose from. Recent offerings range from Richard P. McBrien's *Lives of the Saints: From Mary and Francis of Assisi to John XXIII and Mother Teresa* (Harper, 2001) to *Heaven Help Us: The Worrier's Guide to the Patron Saints*, by Alice La Plante and Clare La Plante (Dell, 1999). Public libraries in need of a basic, accessible resource for the reference collection, or collections that need to update (Guiley includes saints canonized as recently as 2000), will be well served by this volume.

The Papacy: An Encyclopedia. 3v. Ed. by Philippe Levillain. 2001. 1,780p. bibliogs. index. Routledge, $495 (0-415-92228-3). 282.

This new encyclopedia is in large part a direct translation of the French work *Dictionnaire historique de la papauté* (Librairie Artheme Fayard, 1994). However, events that have occurred since the publication of the French edition have been included here, developments in the pontificate of John Paul II being a good example. Bibliographies have also been updated to include recent and English-language sources.

In addition to biographical articles on popes and antipopes, the alphabetically arranged entries offer historical information on a wide variety of topics. Some describe attributes of the pope, such as his teaching authority (*Magisterium*) and when that magisterium is infallible (*Infallibility*). Others treat institutions associated with the papacy (*Curia, Synod of Bishops*). The papacy vis-a-vis important historical events (*French Revolution, Reformation, World War II*) is described. Intellectual movements such as Renaissance humanism and Marxism and the papacy's engagement with them are discussed. The papacy has been important to the history of Western art and architecture, and this importance is reflected in articles on *Museums, Vatican; Painting; Patronage, papal;* and specific churches. There is a substantial survey on Judaism, offering a look at the treatment of Jews and the views of Judaism held by the papacy. Historical throughout, this encyclopedia is nevertheless contemporary, with entries for *Modernism, Modernity,* and even the *Cinema, popes and*. The set concludes with a very substantial index.

There are several smaller, less comprehensive treatments of the papacy, including *Dictionary of Popes and the Papacy* [RBB Mr 15 02] and *The Pope Encyclopedia: An A to Z of the Holy See* (Crown, 1995). Although a three-volume encyclopedia may seem a large undertaking for such a specialized topic, the papacy is not just an important religious institution of interest in Western Europe. Rather, the Holy See is an extremely important player on the world's religious, political, and diplomatic stage. The detailed and substantial treatment of the subject matter, along with the scholarly approach taken, make this reference title appropriate for academic and large public library collections. Researchers in religion, art, and history will find much of use here.

Handbook of Norse Mythology. Ed. by John Lindow. 2001. 365p. illus. index. ABC-CLIO, $55 (1-57607-217-7); e-book, $75 (1-57607-573-7). 293.

Edited by a professor in the Scandinavian Department at U.C. Berkeley, this handbook covers all periods and aspects of Scandinavian mythology.

Opening with a lengthy introduction followed by a chapter on the concept of time in Norse mythology, Lindow presents an overview of the history, literature, language, and culture of Scandinavia. Although these two sections provide a large amount of information, their scholarly approach may make them inaccessible to some readers.

By far the longest chapter is the dictionary-style "Deities, Themes, and Concepts." More than 200 entries range in length from one paragraph to four pages. The entries for well-known figures and concepts such as *Thor* and *Valholl* (Valhalla) receive the most discussion, but lesser-known figures and concepts like *Hod* (Odin's blind son) and *Jotunheimar* (the world of giants) are also listed. Each entry contains a very brief description or definition followed by a more detailed account. Most of the entries have *see also* references, and all but the shortest include a "References and Further Readings" list. Several entries include photographs of relics.

The fourth and final chapter surveys print and a few nonprint sources and is intended to "give the reader a general picture of important background materials, as well as print resources pertaining more generally to the mythology itself." A discussion of primary sources is included, particularly important because the field of Scandinavian mythology has relatively few primary source materials.

Many of the dictionary entries can be found in general encyclopedias of mythology. A treatment of Scandinavian mythology is included in the standard Larousse *World Mythology* (Gallery Books, 1969–1989). However, Lindow has produced a single volume that provides both a comprehensive overview and a listing of concepts and figures that is more detailed than *Cassell's Dictionary of Norse Myth and Legend* (1997). This source makes a significant contribution to the fields of mythology and Scandinavian studies and is highly recommended for large public and academic libraries.

The Illustrated Encyclopedia of Hinduism. 2v. By James G. Lochtefeld. 2002. 876p. bibliog. illus. index. Rosen, $212.95 (0-8239-2287-1). 294.5.

The Illustrated Encyclopedia of Zen Buddhism. By Helen J. Baroni. 2002. 426p. bibliog. illus. index. Rosen, $119.95 (0-8239-2240-5). 294.3.

These encyclopedias cover festivals, texts, doctrine, rituals, practices, biographies, deities and heroes, architecture, mythology, sects, and institutions of the religious traditions covered. Examples of the more than 2,500 entries in *The Illustrated Encyclopedia of Hinduism* include *Bhagavad Gita, Brahma, Cow slaughter,* and *Stages of life*. Among the more than 1,700 entries in *The Illustrated Encyclopedia of Zen Buddhism* are *Dogen Kigan, Filial piety,* and *Shikhin Buddha*. Much of the content of the Zen Buddhism volume consists of short, dictionary-type definitions, although some (for example, *Bodhisattva precepts, Buddha, Pilgrimage*) are more expansive. Entries in the Hinduism volumes tend to be longer, with some (for example, *Asceticism; Bhagavad Gita; Dance; Gandhi, Mohandas K.; Sita*) extending for more than a page. The illustrations are all black and white, occur on approximately one-quarter of the pages, and usually cover less than half a page. The entries include extensive cross-references, and the "Contents by Subject" at the beginning of each encyclopedia aids the reader in locating thematically related entries. The coverage of the subject areas is good.

Both encyclopedias could have been greatly improved with the inclusion of glossaries giving the terms in the various languages involved. In the case of *The Illustrated Encyclopedia of Hinduism*, Sanskrit and English would be the obvious minimum. For *The Illustrated Encyclopedia of Zen Buddhism*, a glossary of Sanskrit, Chinese characters, pinyin and Wade-Giles Chinese transliteration methods, and transliterated Japanese would significantly increase the utility. Although the volumes are adequate for the general reader, this conspicuous omission limits their usefulness for the more serious researcher.

Libraries that already have common religion reference sources, such as Eliade's *The Encyclopedia of Religion* (Macmillan, 1987), will probably find no reason to add these new encyclopedias to their collections. Some other subject encyclopedias may also be more useful. For example, *Japan: An Illustrated Encyclopedia* (Kodansha, 1993) includes the Chinese characters with Japanese transliterations along with far superior illustrations and gives good coverage of religious themes. However, academic libraries supporting large religious studies departments may want to buy these for the added coverage. Public libraries that have no other resources on Hinduism and Zen Buddhism might also consider them.

Sociology, Anthropology, Political Science

Encyclopedia of Communication and Information. 3v. Ed. by Jorge Reina Schement. 2002. 1161p. bibliogs. illus. index. Macmillan, $375 (0-02-865386-6). 302.2.

We may live in the information age, but information and communication have been creating culture and society since ancient times. Cuneiform symbols, Chinese characters, Egyptian hieroglyphics, and, later, alphabets allowed people to preserve ideas that had been expressed orally. Today, newspapers, cellular telephones, and the World Wide Web transmit ideas all over the world as quickly as they are conceived. Macmillan's *Encyclopedia of Communication and Information* attempts to "summarize what we know about communication and information in all of their manifestations."

The encyclopedia has 280 alphabetical entries written by an international group of scholars with academic appointments. The signed articles cover eight broad fields: careers (*Librarians*; *Television broadcasting, careers in*); information science (*Human-computer interaction*; *Retrieval of information*); information technologies (*Cable television, system technology of*; *Digital communication*); literacy (*Computer literacy*; *Traditional literacy*); institutional studies (*Broadcasting, government regulation of*; *Telephone industry, history of*); interpersonal communication (*Organizational communication*; *Rhetoric*); library science (*Cataloging and knowledge organization*; *Libraries, functions and types of*); and media effects (*Advertising effects*; *Tobacco and media effects*). There are also biographies of influential people such as Nellie Bly, Andrew Carnegie, Thomas Edison, and Marshall McLuhan.

The interdisciplinary approach allows coverage of hot topics such as violence in the media, censorship, and pornography. The articles objectively present major points of controversy such as freedom of speech versus the protection of children. All articles have short bibliographies of print and electronic sources. The comprehensive subject index is very useful because the table of contents does not include all of the subject matter. Readers searching for information about censorship will not find the term in the table of contents, but the index refers them to the articles *First Amendment and the media* and *Intellectual freedom and censorship*.

The *Encyclopedia of Communication and Information* will be a useful source for public, academic, and high-school libraries because it provides a good overview of these vast subject areas and serves as a starting point for deeper research. With articles on minorities and the media, soap operas, major legislation, and pirate media, it has information of interest to a broad range of users.

Encyclopedia of Women Social Reformers. 2v. By Helen Rappaport. 2001. 888p. appendix. bibliog. illus. index. ABC-CLIO, $185 (1-57607-101-4). 303.48.

Women have been in the forefront of social reform and often made their mark in history in their efforts to improve society. This encyclopedia includes over 400 reformers from the French Revolution until the present, from 64 countries.

In order to include a number of women from different nationalities and ethnic backgrounds, the author took a very liberal view of "reformer," encompassing writers and philanthropists. Even so, the majority of the women included are American or British. Among them are many names one would expect to find such, as Mother Teresa, Princess Diana, Eleanor Roosevelt, and the three Pankhursts; but also many less familiar individuals, such as Mehrangiz Kar of Iran and Lee Tai-Young of Korea. There is a wonderful entry on Afghan women social reformers, who are mostly anonymous. Women engaged in violent activities such as armed conflict and destruction of property (except for some of the major suffragists) were excluded.

The encyclopedia is arranged alphabetically by last name. Lists of women by country and by cause as well as by name introduce the work. The articles generally vary in length from one to five pages, and many are accompanied by black-and-white illustrations. Cross references to entries for women who shared similar concerns are included along with up-to-date and often extensive references and further reading. The work concludes with an appendix of the organizations cited most often in the book, giving their founding dates and names in original language other than English; a chronology from 1789–2001; and a 44-page bibliography.

Since many of these women can be found in other biographical resources, the true value of this work lies in the emphasis on women in the role of reformers. It is a valuable addition to any collection on women, social welfare, or reform movements. The selected bibliography is an excellent collection development tool. Recommended for public and academic libraries.

American Immigration: A Student Companion. By Roger Daniels. 2001. 303p. appendixes. bibliogs. illus. index. Oxford, $40 (0-19-511316-0). 304.8.

The Civil War and Reconstruction: A Student Companion. By William L. Barney. 2001. 368p. appendixes. bibliogs. illus. index. maps. Oxford, $40 (0-19-511559-7). 973.7.

These titles are the newest in Oxford's Student Companions to American History, written for the junior-high-school through adult audience. Arranged alphabetically, each book in the series focuses on a major historical period or theme, with authoritative articles on key issues, events, and individuals.

American Immigration surveys its subject from the sixteenth century to the present, with entries covering topics such as *Artists, immigrant*; *Ellis Island*; *Hinduism*; *Naturalization policy*; *Nicaraguans*; *Picture brides*; and *Slave trade*. Entries for most ethnic groups include data on numbers of U.S. citizens claiming ancestry in each group (according to 1990 Census figures), the numbers who arrived during the period from 1986 to 1996, the major periods of immigration, and the major areas of settlement. Examples of entries in *The Civil War and Reconstruction* include *Confederate policies*; *Desertion*; *Election of 1876*; *Impressment Act of 1863*; *Ku Klux Klan*; *McClellan, George B.*; and *Railroads*. Biographies begin with fact summaries that provide birth and death dates and places, political affiliation, and details about education and career. In both volumes, most entries range in length from one-half to three pages in length and are accompanied by excellent cross-references and further readings, as well as period illustrations, photographs, and maps with informative captions. Laws and legislation are well covered. Chronologies, bibliographies, and lists of museums and Web sites conclude each volume. Indexing is thorough.

For general information as well as background reading, these two titles will find readers and researchers within high-school and public libraries and are recommended for these audiences. The variety of topics that are covered surpasses many other single volumes on similar subjects.

The Encyclopedia of American Immigration. 4v. Ed. by James Ciment. 2001. 1,638p. bibliog. illus. index. maps. Sharpe, $399 (0-7656-8028-9). 304.8.

This encyclopedia examines the immigrant experience and how it continues to change America. From the first people to migrate to North America approximately 12,000 to 15,000 years ago to the people who are arriving as you read this, the movement of people into America, and the response to that movement, is detailed in a series of well-written essays and a compendium of immigration documents.

The set is made up of four major parts: "Immigration History," "Immigration Issues," "Immigrant Groups in America," and "Immigration Documents." "Immigration History" chronologically examines each new wave of immigration to the U.S. and explores the causes, the reaction, how the immigrants were or were not assimilated, and how they affected mainstream American culture. This part includes discussions of such topics as the slave trade, Japanese internment, and the collapse of Communism. "Immigration Issues" concentrates on 13 broad topics as they relate to immigration, among them, legislation, labor, and religion. Human smuggling and illegal immigration, impacts on health care, and English as a second language are some of the specific issues that are explored. There is also a section on the major U.S. destinations of immigrants and another that discusses immigration to other areas of the world (Australia, Canada, Israel, Japan, and Western Europe).

"Immigrant Groups in America" discusses the immigrants and immigration patterns of people from Africa, the Americas, Asia, the Pacific, the Middle East, and Europe. The final part, "Immigration Documents," includes the texts of laws and treaties, executive orders, directives and statements, Supreme Court cases, referenda, political platforms, debates, government reports and rulings, and nongovernmental documents such as historical articles and letters. Among them are the immigration planks of both the Republican and Democratic parties from 1856 to 1996, President Roosevelt's Executive Order 9066, and rulings on the return of Haitian refugees in 1992. Throughout the set, there are explanatory charts, graphs, and photographs. Each essay concludes with a bibliography and references to other pertinent essays in the set.

Each volume contains a general index, a geographical index, and a legal and judicial index. The fourth volume includes a glossary.

This set will be essential in academic libraries and extremely useful in large and medium-sized public libraries for both students and the general public. Libraries already holding the *Gale Encyclopedia of Multicultural America* (2000) will find that *The Encyclopedia of American Immigration* complements it very well.

Facts about American Immigration. By David M. Brownstone and Irene M. Franck. 2001. 818p. appendixes. glossary. illus. index. Wilson, $95 (0-8242-0959-1). 304.873.

Facts about Retiring in the United States. Ed. by Steven S. Shagrin. 2001. 761p. bibliog. index. Wilson, $95 (0-8242-0969-9). 646.7.

These two publications illustrate Wilson's continual focus on editorial quality and provision of thorough, up-to-date reference sources.

Beginning with the earliest Americans, who crossed the Bering Land Bridge to Alaska between 12,000 and 15,000 B.C.E., *Facts about American Immigration* focuses on who came and from where, why they came, the nature of their journeys, where they settled, and the many efforts to stop them. An overview, which includes extensive statistical data, places the process of immigration in a wide historical and global context. The main text delves into immigration experiences, numbers, and motives by region of emigration including Europe, Africa, Asia, the Americas, and Oceania. Each of these sections contains a brief introduction to the region and a series of articles on specific countries or groups of countries. Articles include tables and graphs as well as lists of additional Internet and print resources. "Annual Immigration Statistics," generated from U.S. government records, are presented in a section of tables. Six appendixes provide information on general immigration resources, legislation, estimates of emigration and illegals, tips on genealogical research, and two guides on using the National Archives and Records Administration. A detailed index completes the volume.

Part 1 of *Facts about Retiring in the United States* delivers guidance in four major areas: housing, health care, and financial and legal concerns. Part 2, "State-by-State Retirement Housing Options," presents alternatives on a state-by-state basis, including facts about climate, cost of living, taxes, major transportation, and cultural attractions. Lists of elder hostels and other travel-related agencies, retirement counselors and consultants, and additional resources and organizations are listed in part 3. The planning tools and forms in the final section include "Five Wishes" (a document from the Commission on Aging with Dignity) and "Checklist for Choosing an Assisted Living Community." A glossary, bibliography, and index complete the work.

Both of these informative and practical guides are recommended in particular for public libraries. *Facts about American Immigration* will be useful in high-school and undergraduate libraries as well.

Adolescence in America: An Encyclopedia. 2v. Ed. by Jacqueline V. Lerner and Richard M. Lerner. 2001. 924p. bibliog. illus. index. ABC-CLIO, $175 (1-57607-205-3); e-book, $235 (1-57607-571-0). 305.235.

Much of this information is available in other sources, but it is handy to have it collected in one spot. The editors, from Boston College and Tufts University, sought "to present the best information currently available about the adolescent period and the ways in which scientists and practitioners understand the period and, as well, take actions to successfully promote positive development among youth."

About 200 alphabetically arranged articles, most by university-affiliated authors, range from two to five pages in length. All are accompanied by *see also* references and short lists of "Further readings," mainly from professional journals from the 1990s. A complete bibliography is found at the end of volume 2. Black-and-white photos are scattered throughout, illustrating multicultural male and female teens.

The variety of writers means that there are some inconsistencies. Terms (e.g., *modality, school engagement*) are not always defined, and length and scope of articles could have been more uniform. Better entry headings and indexing would have improved usability. Many of the entry headings are obvious for a work dealing with adolescence, such as *Body image, Dating, Inhalants, Shyness,* and *Standardized tests*; but there are also some odd headings, such as *Bumps in the road to adulthood* and *Why is there an adolescence?* Readers looking for information on working mothers will find nothing in the index to refer them to *Maternal employment*. There is no reference in the index from *Indian* to the entry heading *Native American adolescents*, even though both terms are used in the article.

Less scholarly than *Encyclopedia of Adolescence* (Garland, 1991) and more focused on the period between childhood and adulthood than *Gale Encyclopedia of Childhood and Adolescence* (1997), this one will be used, despite its flaws. It presents a wide range of topics that will be useful for school reports as well as interesting for high-school, college, and general readers.

Boyhood in America: An Encyclopedia. 2v. Ed. by Priscilla Ferguson Clement and Jacqueline S. Reiner. 2001. 845p. bibliogs. illus. index. ABC-CLIO, $185 (1-57607-215-0). 305.23.

Infancy in America: An Encyclopedia. 2v. Ed. by Alice Sterling Honig and others. 2001. 768p. bibliogs. illus. index. ABC-CLIO, $185 (1-57607-220-7). 305.232.

Boyhood in America and *Infancy in America* are the fourth and fifth members of a series from ABC-CLIO, The American Family, following *Parenthood in America* (2000), *Adolescence in America* [RBB O 15 01], and *Girlhood in America* (2001).

The volumes of *Boyhood in America* include about 150 articles by approximately 120 experts in their fields. A check of the credentials of the authors shows a breadth of knowledge and expertise. The editors define boyhood as the "stage of the life cycle in terms of time, beginning at birth and continuing until the individual reaches some definition of self-sufficiency" at around age 20. Topics span a period from the seventeenth century to the present and take into account regional, class, racial, and ethnic differences. Examples include *Fathers, adolescent; Films* (which discusses portrayal of boys in films ranging from Charlie Chaplin's *The Kid* to *The Sixth Sense*), *Fire companies, Fishing, Foster care, Fraternities,* and *Frontier boyhood.* Each entry includes a list of suggested readings that appear to be both timely and to the point. In addition, at the end of volume 2 there is a 75-page bibliography that would make the set worth its price. If this pair of volumes suffers from anything it is the same thing as the other encyclopedias in this series: the small number of photos and the total lack of color.

Infancy in America has over 600 entries, but only 29 contributors, almost all of them faculty at one academic institution. Entries are unsigned. The set is narrower in focus than *Boyhood in America*, for although some entries provide a historical perspective, emphasis is on "the latest findings on the mental, emotional, and physical life of the human infant." The audience is defined as "parents, practitioners, and professionals." Articles range from *Abortion* and *Afterbirth* to *Toileting* and *Toys for Tots,* varying in length from a single sentence (*Brain structure, Conscience*) to more than 10 pages (*Emotion*).

The preface states that one use for the set is to read the description of an area of interest and then "follow up with the references provided to gain more information," but citation of references and further reading is uneven. For example, the further reading list for *Grandparents* includes several resources on Down Syndrome, but the entry *Genetic disorders,* where Down Syndrome is discussed, has no resource list at all. Volume 2 contains appendixes: "Resources on Infants and Toddlers" (Internet sources, books, and videos) and "Popular Songs for Infants and Toddlers" plus a bibliography. The bibliography is adequate and the resources seem potentially useful, but the 20 or so songs are in no order and add nothing to the usefulness of the volume.

Boyhood in America serves as a good introduction to an emerging area of study and is recommended for high-school, public, and academic libraries. *Infancy in America* is recommended only for libraries that have no coverage in this area or wish to have all the parts of this series in their collection.

Child Development. Ed. by Neil J. Salkind. 2002. 487p. appendixes. bibliogs. illus. index. Macmillan, $130 (0-02-865618-0). 305.21.

This title launches the new Macmillan Psychology Reference Series. The volume has an alphabetical arrangement that includes four types of entries: overview articles of 3,000 words that serve as an in-depth look at specific topics (*Cognitive development, Heredity versus environment, Parenting*); introductions to important topics of about 1,500 words each (*Autism, Domestic violence, Resiliency*); definitions of 150 words or so of terms that should be familiar to most people interested in child development (*Cliques, Developmental norms, Standardized testing*); and biographies of around 400 words of leading people in child development (*Apgar, Virginia; Ginott, Haim; Spock, Benjamin*). There are 289 articles in all.

The intended audience is described as "anyone who wants to know more about the field of child development," and the volume does a good job of having something for most reader groups. Each entry has a bibliography of items for further reading that are current and often include Web sites. The volume concludes with two appendixes: one containing a variety of statistical tables and a second with a list of Web resources. The index that follows the appendixes seems accurate and easy to use; main article page numbers are in bold type for ease of recognition, and table page numbers are in italics.

The nearest competitor would be *The Gale Encyclopedia of Childhood and Adolescence* (Gale, 1998), but the Macmillan volume is more focused on young children and contains more up-to-date Internet information. In general the two titles complement each other, and larger collections should have both. *Child Development* is a welcome addition to general information in this field and highly recommended for public and undergraduate libraries.

Encyclopedia of Russian Women's Movements. Ed. by Norma Corigliano Noonan and Carol Nechemias. 2001. 424p. bibliogs. glossary. index. Greenwood, $100 (0-313-30438-6). 305.42.

To varying degrees, Marx, Engels, Lenin, and Stalin all wrestled with "the woman question." Women in Russia and the Soviet Union have walked, and continue to walk, the tightrope of accommodation, resistance, and transformation. This volume traces their stories and the stories of their movements. Alphabetically arranged entries are organized into three parts corresponding to three distinct periods that encompass almost 200 years—the nineteenth and early-twentieth centuries prior to the Bolshevik Revolution of 1917; the Soviet period, 1917–1991; and the transitional and post-Soviet periods, 1985–2000. The first two parts include only representative groups, movements, or individuals, reflecting the editors' desire to focus primarily on the post-Soviet era.

Readers will find this to be an invaluable source for information on a broad range of topics, such as Russian peasant women, Soviet family policy, early Russian feminism, and women's activism in contemporary Russia. The editors have chosen a comprehensive definition of women's movements, encompassing *Decembrist women active in Siberia in the 1830–1850s*; *Women's periodical publishing in late imperial Russia (1860–1905)*; *Professional Union of Home Employees (1917–1920)*; *Women in the Communist Party of the Soviet Union (1922–1991)*; and *Gender/Women's Studies in Russia (1990–)*. Also covered are women (Raisa Gorbacheva, Natal'ia Herzen, Nadezhda Krupskaia) who played a role in supporting or advancing the status of women. Introductions to each of the three parts provide good overviews of the periods covered. The signed entries conclude with cross-references and lists of suggested readings. Additional features include a chronology, a glossary of abbreviations and major terms, and a selective bibliography.

Kudos to editors Noonan and Nechemias for tackling this complex subject matter and holding their contributors to high standards. Useful in academic and research libraries with reference collections on women or Russia and the Soviet Union, this title is also recommended for large public libraries.

Encyclopedia of Women and Gender: Sex Similarities and Differences and the Impact of Society on Gender. 2v. Ed. by Judith Worell. 2001. 1,256p. bibliogs. indexes. glossaries. Academic, $300 (0-12-227245-5). 305.403.

In the past several decades, the term *gender* has been reexamined from a variety of scholarly perspectives. The use of *gender* was introduced in the behavioral and social sciences to distinguish it from the concept of sex which is understood to be biologically defined, while gender is culturally constructed. This set fills a unique niche and succeeds in providing students, researchers, and practicing clinicians with comprehensive coverage of current research and scholarship on the psychology of women and gender in all its diverse manifestations. The goal is "to explore . . . how social and cultural influences have structured and shaped the gender-related roles, behaviors, well-being, life events, and opportunities afforded to diverse groups of women and men."

Androcentrism, Entitlement, Hate crimes, Recovered memories, Social constructionist theory, Test bias, and *Work-family balance* are some of the themes that are represented. The encyclopedia also examines such topics as *Body image concerns, Depression, Divorce and child custody, Friendship styles, Gender stereotyping,* and *Midlife transitions.* Signed A–Z articles cover topics in depth. Each includes an outline, a glossary of relevant concepts, cross-references, and a suggested reading section. To aid the reader, an alphabetical outline of contents appears at the beginning of each volume, and an author and subject index conclude the set.

This is an excellent resource that provides well-organized and clearly expressed information on one of the most fascinating constructs that has shaped, and continues to shape, contemporary society. Highly recommended for academic libraries of all sizes; large public libraries will want to consider its purchase as well, especially in locales in which access to local college libraries is limited for those outside the campus community.

Encyclopedia of Women in American History. 3v. Ed. by Joyce Appleby. 2002. bibliog. illus. indexes. Sharpe, $299 (0-7656-8038-6). 305.4.

Encyclopedia of Women in American History, written in eminently readable prose by 41 subject experts with university affiliations, includes not only biographical entries but also topical information to "help readers situate women's lives and accomplishments within the larger structures of society." Each of the three volumes treats a discrete time period. Volume 1 deals with colonization to the beginning of the national period (1585–1820); Volume 2 with the Civil War, western expansion, and the Industrial Revolution (1820–1900); and Volume 3 with the beginnings of the suffrage movement to the present (1900–2002).

Each volume begins with an annotated time line and between 8 and 10 signed essays, each three to five pages in length. These serve not only to give an overview of the time period but also to investigate specific issues relevant to defining women's roles in society during the era under consideration. Names, issues, or incidents mentioned in the essays in small capitals can be found as entries in the body of the alphabetically arranged encyclopedia. Each essay is followed by a short list of further resources, all print works.

Arranged alphabetically within each volume, the more than 900 entries are brief, running generally between half a column to three columns in length. Approximately half of the entries are biographical; others treat topics ranging from *Frontier life, Indentured servitude,* and *Seminole household economy* to *Glass ceiling, Miss America Pageant,* and *Planned Parenthood.* Related articles are listed as *see also* references at the entries' ends. Frequently, lists of print works for further reading are also appended. Sidebars titled "Trailblazers" or "Women's Firsts" highlight women who were trendsetters or those who were first in some particular way; for instance, the first English child to be born on American soil or the first black woman public speaker. Clear black-and-white reproductions and photographs are well placed and extend the text ably. A final section of relevant and representative primary source documents concludes and enhances each volume.

All volumes contain detailed tables of contents, volume-specific bibliographies, and biographical indexes. Volume 1 contains a comprehensive table of contents for the entire set, volume 3 has the cumulated general index, and both are accurate. Broader in scope than *What American Women Did, 1789–1920: A Year-by-Year Reference* (McFarland, 2001), this title gives some stiff competition to the one-volume *Handbook of American Women's History* (Sage, 2000), which lacks the inherent chronological arrangement and is somewhat less readable. Attractively laid out, clearly written, current through 2001, and easy to use, the *Encyclopedia of Women in American History* is a sound purchase for colleges and universities with women's studies programs and is suitable for use in high schools as well.

Encyclopedia of Women in the Ancient World. By Joyce Salisbury. 2001. 370p. bibliog. illus. index. maps. ABC-CLIO, $75 (1-57607-092-1). 305.4.

This world as defined here is the ancient Mediterranean world, with Persia and a little of northern Europe and the British Isles added. The period covered is from prehistory to approximately A.D. 500. The cutoff date means that Theodora, who ruled the Byzantine world with Justinian in the mid-500s and is one of the best known "women of the ancient world," is not included. However, there are more than enough other interesting women to make the work useful.

The approximately 230 A–Z entries range from a few paragraphs to several double-columned pages, with the average being about three columns. They cover individual women, whether historical (Aspasia, Boudicca, Hatshepsut, Livia), mythological (Artemis, Isis), or biblical (Eve, Ruth), and a number of cultural and social topics, including *Contraception, Jewelry, Prostitution,* and *Work.* There are entries devoted to various groups, including *Jewish women, Persian women,* and *Roman women.* Each entry includes *see also* references and suggestions for further reading. Some articles are illustrated with photographs of statues, coins, or frescoes. The volume also contains maps and genealogical charts. A list of "Entries by Category" complements the index by grouping entries under cultural group or region.

One error was noted. In the entry *Danae*, Acrisius is referred to as Perseus' father, when he was in fact the hero's grandfather. Variant spellings, especially from non-Roman alphabets (e.g., *Rebekah* instead of *Rebecca*), may cause confusion.

This volume should be helpful to high-school students, undergraduates, and general readers. Other titles, such as *Biographical Dictionary of Ancient Greek and Roman Women* (Facts On File, 2000), cover some of the same ground, but *Encyclopedia of Women in the Ancient World* is broader in scope.

Encyclopedia of Women in the Middle Ages. By Jennifer Lawler. 2001. 287p. bibliog. glossary. index. McFarland, $45 (0-7864-1119-8). 305.4.

Lawler's contention is that while much has been written about the Middle Ages, if you ask the average person to name women of this time period, the usual answers are Joan of Arc and Eleanor of Aquitaine. Beyond these noted individuals, only queens and famous mistresses rate any mention in standard texts. In correcting this underreporting of half of the population, Lawler delved deeply into historical records and archives. As might be expected, hers was not an easy task given the absence of women in the historical records.

Lawler profiles women from 500 to 1500 C.E., among them Amalasuntha (d.535), Ostrogothic queen of Italy; Herrad of Landsberg, twelfth century abbess and mystic; Peretta Peronne, fifteenth century surgeon; and Shiko, sixth century empress of Japan. Also included are women from legend and literature, such as Griselda and Guinevere. But coverage goes beyond a compilation of brief biographies to provide information on women's issues and concerns during this time period—*Hospitals*, *Marriage and family*, *Social class*, and *Witchcraft and the arcane arts* are examples of contextual entries, which range in length from a few lines to six or seven pages. Encyclopedia entries, many of which include suggested readings, occupy just over half the book. The remainder of the work consists of genealogical charts (approx. 60 pages), a 9-page glossary, a 28-page bibliography, and an index. There are no illustrations.

There are other resources in which readers might find information about many of the women covered here, including *Extraordinary Women of the Medieval and Renaissance World* (Greenwood, 2000) and Gale's nearly completed *Women in World History*. What sets this volume apart is the juxtaposition of biographical material with information on some of the conditions and circumstances that shaped medieval women's lives. Recommended for high-school, public, and academic libraries.

Girlhood in America: An Encyclopedia. 2v. Ed. by Miriam Forman-Brunell. 2001. 760p. bibliogs. illus. index. ABC-CLIO, $175 (1-57607-206-1); e-book, $235 (1-57607-550-8). 305.23.

Edited by a history professor from the University of Missouri, *Girlhood in America* is the third title in The American Family series. This set aims "to provide a solid basis for understanding American girls" by examining their histories and cultures over the past 400 years. More than 90 scholars (mostly women) contributed the 120 entries.

Arranged in alphabetical order and averaging six pages in length, each entry is fully documented with a "References and Further Reading" list. Most entries are written in a style that is more popular than scholarly, making the information accessible to the general public. They cover a variety of topics ranging from *Clothing*, *Fan clubs*, and *Prom* to *Acquaintance rape*, *Birth control*, and *Substance abuse*. Articles on organizations for girls are included, from the well known (*Girl Scouts*) to the less familiar (*Saturday Evening Girls*). Although this is not intended as a biographical source, there are three entries on particular girls—Mary Pickford, Pocahontas, and Shirley Temple. *Asian American girls*, *Catholic girls*, and *Mennonite girls* are among the articles that highlight religious or ethnic diversity. Though the introduction states that the work treats all ages of girlhood, there is greater concentration on the adolescent and teenage years.

An extensive cumulative bibliography appears at the end of volume 2. Each entry includes at least one photo or drawing; however, some of the illustrations seem to merely fill a space rather than lend support to the article. *See also* references and an index facilitate access, although the index misses some topics. For example, there is no index entry for Madame Alexander, even though the doll maker is mentioned in at least two articles.

The articles provide a more in-depth treatment than those in other encyclopedias, such as *Gale Encyclopedia of Childhood and Adolescence* (1998). The study of girls, separate from the study of childhood and adolescence in general, is relatively new. As a result, little has been published in the area. For this reason, regardless of any shortcomings, this work is recommended for public and high-school libraries. Academic and research libraries with gender studies or women's studies programs will also find it useful.

Statistical Handbook on the World's Children. By Chandrika Kaul. 2002. 544p. appendixes. glossary. index. Oryx, $69.95 (1-57356-390-0). 305.23021.

Kaul, who is also responsible for other titles in the Oryx Statistical Handbooks series, provides a portrait of the state of the world's children. Statistics were drawn from international sources such as the United Nations, World Health Organization, United States Census Bureau, and International Criminal Police Organization. The volume is organized into eight chapters covering such topics as "Education," "Health and Nutrition," and "Crime, Violence and War." Each chapter begins with an introduction and explanation of indicators, followed by tables. Examples of topics addressed in the tables include worldwide mother and infant mortality rates, public spending on education, malnutrition, and child labor. Because there is no internationally accepted definition of *child*, the age ranges provided in the tables vary, depending on the source.

The well-formatted layout and large size of this book make the statistics easy to read and use. Citations to the sources are accompanied by the location of their related Web sites, so the researcher may locate revised information when it becomes available. Appendixes containing the texts of documents such as "Declaration of the Rights of the Child" and "C182 Worst Forms of Child Labour Convention, 1999" are an excellent addition. This volume is recommended for academic and large public libraries.

W. E. B. Du Bois: An Encyclopedia. Ed. by Gerald Horne and Mary Young. 2001. 252p. bibliogs. illus. index. Greenwood, $85 (0-313-29665-0). 305.896.

A brief preface notes that "this book seeks to provide new insight into the protean life of W. E. B. Du Bois by examining individuals, occurrences, themes, places, organizations, and the like." Entries are arranged alphabetically, from *Accommodations versus struggle* to *World War I*. Each is signed and includes a list of suggested further reading. A chronology provides historical perspective. The general bibliography not only leads to selected writings of Du Bois, including his poetry, but also offers additional resources on issues of concern to Du Bois, such as birth control, colonialism, and anti-Semitism.

The encyclopedia aims to offer "entries that point to the leading influences on his rich and instructive life." Subjects include family members; such supporters as James Weldon Johnson and Paul Robeson; and those who, like Booker T. Washington, did not share Du Bois' views. Various aspects of Du Bois' activism are fleshed out in *Pan-Africanism* and *Socialism/Communism*, to cite two examples. There are entries on his writings and scholarly pursuits (*The Crisis*, *Encyclopedia projects*) and his relation to the arts (*Drama*, *Poetry*). Historic events, such as the Brownsville Raid and the cold war; world leaders, such as Mao Zedong and Theodore Roosevelt; and places, such as Africa and China, are included; but discussions always center on their influence on Du Bois' attitude and involvement.

This highly readable work is suitable for public and academic libraries. It is a tool that provides both facts and the sinew that joins those facts into a comprehensive portrait of Du Bois and his many roles.

Beacham's Encyclopedia of Social Change: America in the Twentieth Century. 4v. Ed. by Veryan B. Khan. 2001. 1,999p. bibliogs. illus. index. Beacham; dist. by Gale, $350 (0-933833-62-8). 306.

Beacham's Encyclopedia of Social Change "traces American history through forty-one key indicators of social change." Each chapter is devoted to one gauge of social history and discusses changes throughout the twentieth century. To provide historical background, there is also some coverage of events in earlier centuries.

The 41 chapters are arranged in alphabetical order by topic and range from 25 to 135 pages in length. Among the topics are "Advertising and Consumerism," "Family Life," "Fashion," "Law Enforcement," "Science," and "War." Each is divided into decades and is heavily supplemented by graphs, photographs, and sidebars with tidbits of information. Those wanting more information will find considerable chapter bibliographies (including Web resources). The comprehensive index in volume 4 is well done. A 40-page time line, also in volume 4, lists important events in social history dating from 1492 to September 11, 2001.

In appearance and coverage this set will remind users of Gale's American Decades and American Eras series, which it is supposed to complement. While *Beacham's* begins at the topic level and then takes a decade-by-decade perspective, the two Gale series start their examination of U.S. society at the chronological level, exploring various topics within each decade or era. Overall *Beacham's* would be accessible to a somewhat younger audience, and Gale covers topics in greater detail, but which one a student will prefer depends on whether the topic or decade approach is more useful.

Although high-schoolers are the intended audience for *Beacham's*, it is also a useful general reference source for social history. Both high-school and public libraries will find it a worthwhile addition to their reference collections. Academic libraries will find the *Encyclopedia of American Cultural and Intellectual History* (Scribner, 2001) [RBB S 15 01] a more appropriate choice.

Countries and Their Cultures. 4v. Ed. by Melvin Ember and Carol R. Ember. 2001. 2,608p. bibliogs. illus. maps. Macmillan, $425 (0-02-864950-8). 306.

In 1996, G. K. Hall published the 10-volume *Encyclopedia of World Cultures*, prepared under the auspices of the Human Relations Area Files (HRAF) at Yale University and focusing on the cultures studied by anthropologists. This new set, from the same editors, looks instead at "countries and their usual multiplicity of cultures." Emphasis is on "widely-shared behavior and values, as well as on cultural variations within the country."

A total of 225 countries are alphabetically arranged. Most are politically independent entities, but there are also entries for dependents (such as Bermuda and Guadeloupe) and for Hong Kong. In addition, the divisions of the United Kingdom—England, Northern Ireland, Scotland, and Wales—are treated separately. Entries range in length from six or seven to twenty pages, with discussions organized under headings such as "History and Ethnic Relations"; "Urbanism, Architecture, and the Use of Space"; "Social Stratification"; "Gender Roles and Statuses"; and "The State of the Physical and Social Sciences." Although the headings are standard, the contributors vary widely in approach. Where some devote several paragraphs to topics such as etiquette or child rearing, others deal with them in a terse sentence or two. It is difficult to distill a nation's cultural complexities into a few pages, and there are some broad generalizations and oversimplifications: "Americans consider it impolite to talk about money and age"; "Chinese people are nonconfrontational." Each entry concludes with a fairly extensive bibliography, often including Web sites. Bibliography items are generally scholarly.

The similar sounding (and looking) *Worldmark Encyclopedia of Cultures and Daily Life* (Gale, 1998) covers some of the same ground, but its arrangement, like that of *Encyclopedia of World Cultures*, is based on cultural group rather than national boundary. *Countries and Their Cultures* complements both titles by offering a different perspective and is recommended for high-school, public, and academic libraries.

Encyclopedia of Death and Dying. Ed. by Glennys Howarth and Oliver Leaman. 2001. 560p. bibliog. illus. indexes. Routledge, $135 (0-415-18825-3). 306.9.

The editors see this encyclopedia as an introduction to the broad interdisciplinary area of the study of death and dying, aiming at both professional and academic audiences as well as general readers. There has been, as noted in the introduction, an increase in both scholarly and public literature on the subject as well as development in focus areas of professional occupations—in response to the hospice movement, for example.

In dictionary format, topics in historical, social, cultural, and technical areas are presented—from brief treatments on *Autopsy*, *Pyre*, and *Rigor mortis* to lengthier articles on *Euthanasia*, *Graves*, *Hell*, and *Life support*. Biographical entries and information on important associations and journals are also included. Most of the close to 100 contributors are from the United Kingdom or Australia; a British emphasis can be seen in vocabulary (e.g., "cot death," not "crib death"), spelling, and emphasis of many entries.

The terminology, selection, and tone of articles and coverage of topics do not seem to be consistently planned. For example, articles are included on some of the leading causes of death—stroke and cancer—but not coronary disease or Alzheimer's. The inclusion of some entries seems curious—why a fairly substantial article on solvent abuse when there are not other articles on various substance abuses? There are entries for Judaism, Islam, Hinduism, Shintoism, and Buddhism but none for Christianity (although Christian practices are covered in many entries). There is an index by name and topic that can help with finding topics within articles. A bibliography accompanies the volume, and there are also suggested readings with articles.

Despite the introduction's claim that there are no reference works published on this topic, there have been a few others, notably *Encyclopedia of Death*, by Robert Kastenbaum and Beatrice Kastenbaum (Oryx, 1989). However, because the Kastenbaum title is now more than 10 years old, large public and academic libraries may want to consider the newer title to update information in this area.

Wimmin, Wimps & Wallflowers: An Encyclopaedic Dictionary of Gender and Sexual Orientation Bias in the United States. By Philip H. Herbst. 2001. 322p. bibliog. Intercultural, $39.95 (1-877864-80-3). 306.74.

Herbst's first book, the acclaimed *The Color of Words* (Intercultural, 1997), identified and explored racial and ethnic slurs. In *Wimmin, Wimps & Wallflowers*, Herbst applies the same thorough and fascinating analysis to more than 1,000 terms currently used or recognized in the U.S. pertaining to gender and sexual orientation. Alphabetically arranged entries survey the words' etymology, provide insightful commentary on their current and historical usage, including examples from literature and popular culture, and discuss their frequently complex and conflicting meanings. Some terms require only brief explanations (*billy goat*, *damaged goods*), but Herbst devotes entries longer than a page to terms that merit them, such as *babe/baby*, *dog*, *queen*, and *transsexual*. Terms range from the familiar to the obscure and from the blatantly sexist to those many of us use without a second thought as to their meaning (*honey*, *nag*, *old hat*, *shrinking violet*). Herbst also includes controversial neologisms, such as *womyn* and *herstory*, that have "provoked a questioning of our gender standards and relations."

Not every term included is necessarily always off-limits. In some cases, only certain contexts or usages are unacceptable. Herbst addresses the complexity of the usage of some terms, such as those that are acceptable when used by "insider" groups but not by others (e.g., *dame*, *queer*), and examines terms, such as *crone*, from positive as well as negative points of view. A few terms are missed, probably because our culture invents them faster than they can be published in books. Among those not included are *arm candy*, *babelicious*, *mommy track*, *soccer mom*, and the use of *twinkie* as a condescending term for female journalists. *See* references and cross-references are plentiful, though there are so many variations for terms that Herbst does not include *see* references for all possibilities.

A similar title is *The Dictionary of Bias-Free Usage: A Guide to Nondiscriminatory Language*, by Rosalie Maggio (Oryx, 1991), which Herbst acknowledges as a source for his own book. Although there is some overlap between the two books, Herbst includes many terms not listed in Maggio (e.g., *goldbrick*, *ho*, *lavender menace*). Maggio, on the other hand, more consistently offers usage guidelines and suggests alternatives.

Wimmin, Wimps, & Wallflowers is a fascinating compendium that is unique in its coverage and its detailed treatment of the terms included. It should find a home in all academic and larger public libraries.

Encyclopedia of Political Thought. By Garrett Ward Sheldon. 2001. 342p. appendix. bibliogs. illus. index. Facts On File, $66 (0-8160-4351-5). 320.

This is an enjoyable, though somewhat limited, work that will be helpful to students and those looking for brief descriptions of political ideas. Though international in scope, it favors ideas and concepts related to U.S. and European history. The author is a professor at the University of Virginia who has written other books on political philosophy and theory.

The book contains about 400 entries touching on the range of political ideas that have influenced governments and individuals over the last several hundred years, with an emphasis on the twentieth century. Overall, the author handles controversial topics, such as abortion, with tact and fairness. Most of the entries are brief descriptions; there are few full-length survey articles, such as those that abound in *The Blackwell*

Encyclopaedia of Political Thought (Oxford, 1987). The writing style seems geared toward a high-school reading level. Although some of the illustrations enhance the narrative, many are simply photographs of a person, adding little to the drama of the political thought contained in the entry. Many of the reading suggestions that follow each entry are somewhat dated. For example, the *Communitarian* entry only recommends a 1974 book although much has been written on that topic in the last decade. More liberal use of cross-references would help to connect ideas and the personalities, such as *Abolition* and *Douglass, Frederick*.

Many entries seem to focus on Christian themes, and some do not really cover political thought. For example, there are entries on the Christian writer C. S. Lewis, Lollards (an early Protestant group in England), Pat Robertson, Knights of Labor (a Catholic labor union in the U.S.), and the Christian Right but none for Che Guevara and Samuel Gompers, to name two from other sides of the political spectrum. Additionally, entries such as *Prayer in school* and *Commandments* discuss the Christian point of view without discussing the views of other religious and nonreligious groups.

There are few encyclopedias on political thought, so this work should find an active readership among school and public library users despite its limitations.

Electronic Encyclopedia of American Government. [Internet database]. 2000. Congressional Quarterly, pricing from $800 [http://library.cqpress.com]. (Last accessed September 10, 2001). 320.

CQ's *Electronic Encyclopedia of American Government* is a handy source for background information on U.S. politics. Drawn from the publisher's A to Z Encyclopedia series (*Congress A to Z*, *The Supreme Court A to Z*, etc.), the more than 1,200 articles describe events, operations, concepts, and personalities that have had an impact on the U.S. government from the American Revolution to present times. Anyone can examine this database, browse its indexes, perform searches, and view GovLinks (live links to federal Web sites), but only paid subscribers have access to the encyclopedia entries and the more than 600 drawings, cartoons, and photos.

Searching, either by browsing or by specified words or phrases, is simple and intuitive. The four primary search areas of the database (Presidency, Congress, Supreme Court, and Elections) can be refined, so that opening the H folder in the Congress folder leads to topics like *Hispanics in congress*, *Hubert Humphrey*, and *House bank and post office scandals*. The user can also approach subjects via Quick Search Guides (Who's Who, What's What, Who Does What, When, and Why and How). Who's Who, for example, brings up a list of biographies and group profiles where one can read about *Bilingual voters*, *Former presidents*, and *Jesse Jackson*. Articles are hyperlinked and can be e-mailed and put into a printer-friendly format.

One section, called "More Resources," includes items such as the text of the U.S. Constitution and a detailed index to it, numerous lists ("Chief Justices of the U.S."; "Democratic Conventions, 1832–1966"; "Blacks in Congress, 41st–106th Congresses, 1869–2001," for example), explanations ("How to Read a Court Citation," "How to Write a Member of Congress"), and fiscal information (such as justices's salaries and campaign contribution limits). An area that might appeal to homeschoolers and teachers is Click and Quiz. Under Presidency there is a group of questions called "For the record" that could be used to test one's knowledge of presidential firsts, such the first to be heard on radio, the first to get a pension, and the first to serve without having been elected to that office or to the vice presidency.

In addition to the materials produced by CQ, this product includes links to many federal Web sites that offer additional, current information. This is important to note, because, although we did find information on the results of the 2000 presidential election, the database is not routinely updated. For example, in recent weeks the American political scene has offered several stories that might prompt research: questions about Gary Condit's relationship with an intern, the death of Floyd Spencer, and Jesse Helms's decision not to run again. There are no biographical entries for any of the three, much less any updates; there are references to Senator Helms in four articles, all dealing with the committee system. Entering *scandals* as a search term yields 53 hits, including *Edward M. Kennedy*, *Teapot Dome*, and *Libraries* (the article on presidential libraries notes that these institutions downplay scandal) but nothing recent.

Libraries that own most of CQ's fine print publications on American government will find no new information here, but the convenience of the electronic version makes it worth consideration, especially for remote users and for simultaneous access in multiple sites.

The Oxford Companion to Politics of the World. 2d ed. Ed. by Joel Krieger. 2001. 1,018p. bibliogs. index. maps. Oxford, $60 (0-19-511739-5). 320.

The second edition of this ambitious, informative, but unevenly written reference source originally published in 1993 covers people, political concepts, forms of government, organizations, events, and issues related to world politics. Some 87 new entries have been prepared for this edition, including two new features: 23 "interpretative essays" on themes like globalization and nationalism and 6 pairs of essays offering opposing viewpoints on topics such as affirmative action and sustainable development. These additions focus attention on important issues of world politics.

Most of the almost 600 remaining entries are at most only slightly revised. In many, a paragraph or two has been tacked on to the end of the original entry. And in the entry on Mexico, where more substantial revisions have been made, the subheading of the section where the revisions are located does not reflect the changes: the election of Vincente Fox last year is discussed under the subheading "The Elections of 1988, 1994 and 1997." There are also some entries where revisions are already two or three years old. The entry on Russia does not mention Vladimir Putin at all and discusses Yeltsin very generally while concentrating on events happening before 1997. (A separate entry for Yeltsin refers to Putin only briefly.)

The entries are arranged alphabetically and contain cross-references as well as a short list of sources and an author byline at the end of the entry. The main body concludes with a confusing set of maps and a very useful and complete index. The five pages of black-and-white regional maps are small, sketchy, and disorganized. Most of the maps show a broad outline of countries and identify capital cities, although the geographic placement of these cities is very approximate. In at least one instance, the map misplaces a capital city: a small insert map of the Middle East locates Jerusalem, the capital of Israel, in a shaded area labeled "West Bank—Palestinian Authority." (The book's first edition omitted Jerusalem completely, mistakenly identifying Tel Aviv as Israel's capital.)

The book is intentionally broad in scope and overlapping in structure, resulting in some inevitable inconsistencies, some missing coverage (e.g., international slavery), and some repetitive information. Despite these factors—the relatively few entries that have been updated substantially and the poorly designed maps—academic and most public libraries will continue to find this compendium useful. Libraries owning the first edition need to weigh the outdatedness of some entries in the 1993 edition against the weaknesses in the second edition. Smaller libraries (including high-school libraries) may find that current editions of general encyclopedias provide adequate and more current coverage.

The Oxford Guide to the United States Government. Ed. by John J. Patrick and others. 2001. 640p. appendixes. bibliog. Oxford, $35 (0-19-514273-X). 320.473.

In this alphabetical encyclopedia on topics relating to both the present activities and history of the U.S. government, entries include biographies of presidents and vice presidents, selected First Ladies and members of congress, and all Supreme Court justices who have ever served. Other types of biographical entries are those of unofficial groups of people who have played important roles in American government and history, such as *Carpetbaggers*. There are also articles on the various departments of the federal government; important historical events (*Camp David peace talks*, *Watergate*); issues and concepts (*Capital punishment*, *Freedom of speech*); laws and decisions; and Supreme Court cases. In addition, the volume covers the various powers, procedures, and practices of the president, congress, and the courts. There are some miscellaneous entries as well, including one for *Bean Soup*, which describes (complete with recipe) the tradition of serving bean soup every day in the House and Senate restaurants. Results of the 2000 presidential elections are included.

Entries run from several paragraphs to several pages. Each includes bulleted high points related to the event or person, as well as *see also* references and a list of sources used. There are six appendixes which cover the U.S. Constitution; presidents and vice-presidents in chronological order (ending with Bill Clinton); presidential election results; tables of congress giving majority and minority parties; terms of

Supreme Court justices; justice appointees and their presidents; tips on visiting the branches of the federal government; and a list of presidential historic sites and libraries.

Although most of the information may be found elsewhere in encyclopedias and almanacs, having it in one, inexpensive, convenient volume recommends purchase for most libraries.

America at the Polls: 1960–2000: John F. Kennedy to George W. Bush, A Handbook of American Presidential Election Statistics. By Alice V. McGillivray and Richard M. Scammon. 2001. 1,091p. maps. CQ, $200 (1-56802-604-8). 324.973.

Atlas of American Politics 1960–2000. Ed. by J. Clark Archer and others. 2002. 242p. bibliogs. index. maps. CQ, $115 (1-56802-665-X). 320.973.

Prolong your millennial celebration with the 2000 update of a reference classic and a new look at U.S. politics from the perspective of geography scholars.

The latest volume of America at the Polls extends the coverage of this venerable publication through the end of the century. Following its established format, the front section contains summary tables of the state-by-state popular and Electoral College vote for each election from 1920 to 2000. A chapter for each state and the District of Columbia follows. Each chapter includes a summary of the statewide popular and Electoral College vote for all elections from 1920 to 2000, a handy county outline map that will be useful for homework assignments and other reference needs, and the county-by-county details of each election from 1960 to 2000. (Detailed returns for 1920 to 1956 are covered in a separate volume.) A separate section on presidential primaries provides the primary vote totals for all candidates by state and a chronological list of votes for all Democratic and Republican candidates who received at least 10,000 votes nationwide. America at the Polls is a handy compendium of presidential election statistics and is an essential reference source for political researchers at all levels. The small amount of new content added every four years for the hefty price is a concern. Perhaps CQ will begin a third volume, with a proportionately smaller price tag, with the 2004 elections.

Four geography professors collaborated on Atlas of American Politics, which examines U.S. government and politics at the congressional district, state, and national levels from a combined historical, geographical, and political perspective. More than 200 maps from a variety of governmental and private sources show the relationship between the nation's geography and its political life. Topics include presidential elections, party affiliation, votes on significant legislation, voter turnout, participation in politics by women and minorities, foreign aid, trade, health, education, crime, and the environment. Visual learners will be attracted by the maps, while the accompanying text provides details and numbers as well as a historical context. Even though much of the information is available elsewhere (e.g., U.S. Census Bureau, National Center for Health Statistics), this book provides a unique look at U.S. politics during the last 40 years and will be useful to students and researchers from the high-school level up.

A Statistical History of the American Electorate. By Jerrold G. Rusk. 2001. 708p. appendix. bibliog. index. CQ, $75 (1-56802-364-2); paper, $45 (1-56802-363-4). 324.973.

With this title, CQ further cements its place as publisher extraordinaire in the area of election statistics. CQ's America at the Polls and America Votes have long been two of the most heavily used sources for reliable voting statistics. This volume adds a historical perspective to the offerings, as it presents the electorate's vote for president, House, Senate, and governor from 1788 (if data are available) to 1999. Essays at the beginning of each chapter explain the data, put it in context, and expand upon the author's premise, introduced in the preface, that state and local politics play a larger role in America's political history than presidential races and other national influences.

Chapters devoted to the presidential, House, Senate, and gubernatorial elections show raw vote counts and percentages at the national, regional, and state level for Democratic, Republican, and "Other" categories. Additional tables on topics such as reelection rates for incumbents and vote shifts needed to change election outcomes provide interesting detail. Chapters and accompanying tables also address election laws that limited the eligible electorate and female suffrage acts; voter eligibility percentages for presidential elections; national, regional, and state voter turnout and mobilization percentages for presidential and congressional elections; and party competition at the national, regional, and state levels. A chapter is also devoted to considering inaccuracies that can occur when collecting election data. Explanatory notes and a list of sources accompany each table; these sources, along with those noted in the essays, are included in a bibliography.

Recommended for academic libraries that support political science departments.

Encyclopedia of American Foreign Policy. 3v. 2d ed. Ed. by Alexander DeConde and others. 2002. bibliogs. index. Scribner, $350 (0-684-80657-6). 327.73.

Much about the world has changed since 1978, when this encyclopedia's first edition appeared. The Soviet Union has dissolved, Yugoslavia has become a jigsaw puzzle of smaller states designed to keep ethnic conflict in check, an oil war raged briefly in the Persian Gulf, Eastern Europe has been freed to find its own way, Israeli and Palestinian leaders met on the White House lawn to sign a peace accord that is fading into memory, and China has experienced both brutal political repression and significant economic reform. The U.S. has had to adjust its foreign policy to fit this post–cold war world.

The revised Encyclopedia of American Foreign Policy reflects the challenge the nation has faced in several ways. The most evident change is the updating of articles such as Balance of power (now briefly discussing George W. Bush's rapid shift in September 2001 from unilateralism to collaboration); Cold War evolution and interpretations (noting the continuity between interpretations of the forces that fueled it and interpretations of its end); and Dissent in wars (noting the ambivalence of the U.S. and its political leaders toward the 1990s conflicts in the Balkans). Indeed, it now takes four articles to cover the complexities of the origins and end of the cold war, whereas the first edition managed with just one. Thorough updating of history and the collateral changes in U.S. foreign policy theories and strategies is evident throughout.

The expanded encyclopedia also reflects changes through 48 new essays, among them African Americans, Cultural imperialism, Gender, Multinational corporations, Outer space, Refugee policies, and, of course, Terrorism and counterterrorism. Others have been dropped, including those dealing with conscription, detente, the Fourteen Points, the Truman Doctrine, the King Cotton theory, and missionaries. This list argues in favor of retention rather than disposal of the old edition.

Bibliographies have been thoroughly updated to account for new scholarship and thinking on enduring topics as well as to provide leads to additional resources on new ones. Most items include informative, brief descriptive annotations. See also references at the conclusion of each article also provide pointers for further exploration.

By covering the somewhat specialized concerns of the foreign policy "establishment" (e.g., Deterrence, Extraterritoriality, Protectorates and spheres of influence) as well as those forces the public observes in foreign relations (e.g., Nationalism, Race and ethnicity, Religion), the encyclopedia meets the needs of both academic users and the curious citizen seeking greater understanding of foreign affairs. The academic specialists who wrote the articles kept this latter audience in mind.

The broad topical essays in the revised Encyclopedia of American Foreign Policy complement the country-by-country treatment and biographies of diplomats and statesmen that predominate in the Encyclopedia of U.S. Foreign Relations (Oxford, 1997). Both are essential to academic collections, and the former merits exposure to the broader audience public libraries serve.

The Encyclopedia of World War II Spies. By Peter Kross. 2001. 371p. bibliog. index. Barricade, $24.99 (1-56980-171-1). 327.12.

Much of the information provided in The Encyclopedia of World War II Spies was researched from recently declassified OSS (Office of Strategic Studies) documents obtained from the National Archives, known as "Record Group 226." According to the author, it would take several lifetimes to review all of the material. What Kross has done in this work is put in an A–Z alphabet a selection of the unsung heroes, villains, organizations, terms, and spy rings of the U.S., German, Italian, and Japanese espionage industry of the war years.

Entries include well-known spies, such as professional baseball player and scholar Morris "Moe" Berg, who worked for the OSS in the 1940s and in his most important assignment almost killed Werner Heisenberg, one of the lead German scientists working on the atomic bomb in Germany. There is also an entry on James Bond's creator, Ian

Fleming, a commander in the British navy who, with his own band of raiders, carried out espionage missions behind the lines.

Other entries include *Venona*, a project begun during the war to break the code of all of the Soviet diplomatic messages being sent from the U.S. to Moscow. A major achievement of this project was the discovery that the Soviets had penetrated the Manhattan Project. More examples of entries are: *Enigma machine, Navajo code talkers*, and OSS *truth drug project*.

Although other titles, such as *Spy Book: The Encyclopedia of Espionage* (1997), cover all aspects of espionage, this is the only one that focuses on World War II. Although its value as a reference tool is somewhat hampered by the lack of cross-references, it is a recommended purchase for public libraries where an interest in World War II and spies is evident.

Peace Movement Directory: North American Organizations, Programs, Museums and Memorials. By James Richard Bennett. 2001. 310p. bibliog. illus. index. McFarland, paper, $49.95 (0-7864-1006-X). 327.1.

This directory of organizations and monuments was published before the attacks of September 11th. Over the past few months, the issue of peace has been in the public's hearts and minds more than ever.

Bennett collaborated with "officers of the organizations, programs, museums, and memorials" to compile this directory of 1,170 organizations (including museums) and 230 peace memorials in the U.S., Canada, and Mexico.

Entries are arranged within sections on the U.S., the Canada-U.S. border, Canada, the Mexico-U.S. border, and Mexico. Each entry provides the name and type of organization, the year founded, address, phone number, and e-mail and Web addresses. Entries range in length from a few lines to a few paragraphs. Some include black-and-white photographs (e.g., Maya Lin's eloquent Elizabeth Baker Peace Chapel at Juniata College).

Although several peace-related reference sources have been published in recent years, Bennett's encompasses many peacemaking activities in a single directory. The Board did note a few omissions; for example, the U.S. chapter of the Pugwash Conferences on Science and World Affairs, located in Cambridge, Massachusetts. Pugwash received the Nobel Peace Prize in 1995.

The index includes cites many entry numbers for some terms. It is not clear which entry number leads to the national headquarters of an organization. For example, the index entry *Physicians for Social Responsibility* is followed by six main entry numbers, only one of which is for the national chapter in Washington, D.C. Boldface entry numbers indicating national headquarters would save users the frustration of having to look up multiple entries before finding the correct one. The index entry *Lown, Bernard*, MD does not lead to the main entry for International Physicians for the Prevention of Nuclear War (IPPNW), which won the 1985 Nobel Peace Prize and of which Lown is the founding copresident.

The *Peace Movement Directory* is recommended for public, academic, and theology libraries. The Board hopes that future editions will be even more useful and inclusive.

Business, Economics, Resources

Endangered Animals. 10v. Ed. by Penelope Mathias. 2002. glossary. illus. index. maps. Grolier, $409 (0-7172-5584-0). 333.95.

This 10-volume set, designed for the elementary and middle school level but suitable for students of all ages, provides information for over 400 extinct or threatened animals all over the world, including all the major animal groups—fish, amphibians, reptiles, insects, invertebrates, mammals, and birds—with special emphasis on the latter two groups. Although the sheer number of endangered and threatened species precludes the set from being exhaustive, its coverage is nonetheless comprehensive, including a number of rare and obscure animals, and a selection of species representative of the various causes of endangerment.

Organization of the set adds to its value and usability. Volume 1 acts as a general introduction to the subject, explaining to users what constitutes an endangered animal, the classification process, reasons for endangerment, and conservation efforts initiated to address the situation. The remaining volumes contain entries that are alphabetically arranged by the species' common names, from *Addax* to *Zebra, mountain*.

Each entry comprises two pages that include a large color photo or artistic rendering; textual information; a locator map showing the geographical range of the species; and a data panel presenting information such as the scientific name, world population, distribution, habitat, diet, size, form, and breeding characteristics. Cross-references enhance individual entries, and each volume boasts a glossary of terms, lists of useful publications and Web sites, and a full set index that is searchable by the species' common and scientific names.

This set has much to recommend it. The writing is solidly researched, highly accessible, and imbued with a clearness of purpose. The textual information is strengthened by a copious amount of supplementary material and further enhanced by the exquisitely beautiful photography. Among comparable titles, UXL's *Endangered Species* (1999) covers both plants and animals, but includes only 200 species altogether. Both Marshall Cavendish's *Endangered Wildlife and Plants of the World* [RBB Je 1 & 15 01] and *The Grolier World Encyclopedia of Endangered Species* (1993) are aimed at an older audience. *Endangered Animals* is highly recommended for school libraries, media centers, and public libraries.

The Environmental Resource Handbook: 2002. Ed. by Laura Mars-Proietti. 2001. 998p. glossary. indexes. Grey House, $180(1-930956-05-3); paper, $155 (1-930956-04-5). 333.7.

This handbook is a directory and a data source, with extensive coverage both of U.S. organizations of many types and of environmental statistical information. Section 1, "Resources," has contact information (names, addresses, telephone, e-mail, URL, executive officer, and sometimes a brief description) for 6,988 entries in 15 categories ("Associations," "Consultants," "Environmental Law," "Green Product Catalogs," etc), some of which have subdivisions. Some of the same resources are found in more general directories such as Gale's *Encyclopedia of Associations*, but most are not.

Section 2, "Tables" has more than 100 tables in 20 categories (e.g., "Energy," "Land Use," "Waste"). Most of the tables come from U.S. government sources such as the Department of Energy and the Department of Transportation. Although there are entry, geographic, and subject indexes for the directory content, tables are not indexed and would need to be browsed to find particular information. For example, the "Energy" group has a table on the estimated number of alternative-fueled vehicles in use by the state, but this table is not cited under *alternative fuels* in the subject index. The book also offers a 50-page glossary of terms and phrases and 14 pages of abbreviations and acronyms.

Although this volume contains much valuable information, the lack of detailed indexing for 280 pages of tables diminishes its usefulness. Nevertheless, the address directory and the intrinsic value of the information make it worth consideration by libraries with environmental collections and environmentally concerned users.

Law, Public Administration, Social Problems and Services

Great Debates at the United Nations: An Encyclopedia of Fifty Key Issues, 1945–2000. By Robert F. Gorman. 2001. 452p. appendixes. bibliogs. glossary. illus. index. Greenwood, $65(0-313-31386-5). 341.

This important work conveys the crucial concerns the United Nations has tackled in its first half-century. The debates are arranged chronologically "based on the time when they first appeared on the U.N. agenda," from "Disarmament (1946)" to "Kosovo Situation (1998)." Each entry consists of an initial paragraph on the significance of the issue; a page or so background information; several pages on the history of the debate, including events before and after the date; and outcome of the issues in later years. Suggestions for further reading at the end enable the user to continue the quest for information.

The entries are sometimes on a broad topic, such as human settlements or U.N. reforms, but more often on a particular regional or national dispute. The issues are described objectively, and information is reasonably current; for example, "East Timor Question (1975)" mentions events in February 2000. The information was found to be accurate when checked against the Library of Congress Country Studies. The writing about the complex issues is cogent and lively.

Following the entries are several helpful sppendixes, such as "General

Assembly Special and Emergency Sessions" and "Peacekeeping Operations"; a glossary; and an extensive bibliographic essay that includes many Web sites. The index is detailed. Most entries include a well-chosen and -captioned photograph depicting some aspect of the issue being discussed.

The value of this work is that it brings information on the "great debates" together objectively, succinctly, and clearly. It will be useful in academic and large public libraries.

Constitutional Amendments: From Freedom of Speech to Flag Burning. 3v. By Tom Pendergast and others. 2001. 528p. glossary. illus. indexes. UXL, $130 (0-7876-4865-5). 342.73.

There are numerous reference sources on the U.S. Constitution, but few are designed, as this one is, to be accessible to middle-school users. Presentation is very clear. A chapter is devoted to each amendment, beginning with the wording of the amendment presented in a block. A sidebar contains the ratification data, including the states that voted for the amendment and the year. The text provides historical background, details about the drafting and ratification processes, a chronological summary of significant court cases, and a discussion of how the amendment has affected Americans in their everyday lives. Sidebars provide information about related individuals or events. Each chapter ends with a bibliography of both print and electronic resources. A glossary and index are repeated in each volume, and teachers will appreciate the suggested discussion ideas found in the introductory material.

There are some puzzling editorial decisions and errors that may confuse student users. The subtitle is misleading; at first glance the work appears to be only about the First Amendment because flag burning has been determined to be a free-speech issue. The cover of volume 3 indicates that it encompasses amendments 18 to 26, when in fact it also includes Amendment 27. Including the text of the Constitution in each volume, instead of only in volume 3, would have been helpful. These are minor flaws that do not detract from the overall quality or usefulness of the work. The price might be a problem for some school library budgets, but this is definitely a set that belongs in school and public libraries. Gale's *Constitutional Amendments, 1789 to the Present* (2000) and Macmillan's *The Constitution and Its Amendments* (1999) are good choices for an older audience, and libraries that own one or both of these may not need to add the UXL set unless they are looking for a middle-school resource.

Encyclopedia of Crime and Punishment. 4v. Ed. by David Levinson. 2002. 1,876p. appendixes. bibliogs. illus. index. Sage, $600 (0-7619-2258-X). 346.

Closely following the publication of the second edition of Macmillan's *Encyclopedia of Crime and Justice* [RBB Ap 15 02] comes Sage's encyclopedic look at crime and efforts to control it. Sage's work focuses on the field of criminal justice, while the Macmillan set's primary focus is on criminology. As such, the Sage encyclopedia is more practice oriented and application based, as seen in entries on programs like "Scared Straight"; specific prisons, including Devil's Island and San Quentin; and alternative punishments like boot camps and house arrest.

The 439 signed entries cover 13 major themes: crimes and related behaviors, law and justice, policing, forensics, corrections, victimology, punishment, social and cultural context, international aspects, concepts and theories, research methods and information, organizations and institutions, and special populations. Articles are arranged alphabetically and vary in length from one page for *Interpol* and *Singapore* to more than nine pages for *Firearms identification* and *Terrorism*. All entries include a list of further readings and in some instances citations to court cases. Most also include a simply written summary paragraph that beginning researchers will find helpful. Many have sidebars (ranging from carjacking security tips to excerpts from novels and court cases), interesting facts presented in "Did You Know . . ." shaded boxes, photographs, drawings, or tables. A "Reader's Guide" groups articles by theme, and appendixes list criminal justice careers, organizations, and Web and print resources.

With entries for *Drug millionaires* and *Women who kill*, this work is less scholarly than the Macmillan encyclopedia. It is nonetheless a valuable source for high-school, public, and undergraduate libraries. Students and the general public will find its background discussions, definitions, and explanations of important issues and future trends easy to understand and useful for beginning research in the field of criminal justice.

Homosexuality and the Law: A Dictionary. Ed. by Chuck Stewart. 2001. 429p. appendixes. bibliogs. index. ABC-CLIO, $55 (1-57607-267-3). 346.7301.

More than 120 entries are included in this volume, from *Absurd sex laws* to *Wills*. Many are quite lengthy, such as *Students' rights*, *Domestic partnership*, and *Transsexual*, which run five, six, and ten pages, respectively. An introduction offers a concise history of the gay rights movement that will prove useful for individuals just beginning their research. The well-developed index will be most helpful in ferreting out specific terms, especially for people new to this topic.

A closer look at the 10-page *Family* helps illustrate the structure of the entries. Under *Family* may be found a number of subheadings, including "Same-Sex Couples," "Marriage and Domestic Partnerships," "Child Adoption and Foster Care," and "Procreation and Parenting." As with most of the dictionary's entries, references are placed at the end, and in this instance, they occupy nearly a full page. Words in bold type signal to the reader that definitions are located elsewhere in the dictionary as separate entries. Case law references are visible throughout.

Appendix A, "State and Local Laws," offers general descriptions of such concepts as sex statutes and domestic partnership benefits and registries, in addition to specific state, county, and city legislation, codes, and ordinances. Appendix B, "Resources," lists advocacy groups, books and journals, and state Equal Employment Opportunity Commission and Human Rights Commission offices. Court cases referred to in the body of the dictionary may be found in the "Table of Cases."

This is a book to which one might turn for help in placing specific ideas, myths, or points of view concerning homosexuality into American social and legal context: What does the essence of public accommodation have to do with the Boy Scouts or with marching in a St. Patrick's Day parade? What does, or doesn't, "opposite sex" mean for someone who is intersexed? *Homosexuality and the Law* would be very appropriate in public libraries of any size, as well as high-school and academic libraries.

Biographical Directory of the Federal Judiciary 1789–2000. 2001. 864p. Bernan, $225 (0-89059-258-6). 347.

This volume is much more than its title implies. Certainly, it is a useful directory to the more than 2,800 men and women who have served on the federal judiciary. Alphabetically arranged entries provide vital statistics and summarize each person's education, professional history, and federal judicial service. They also contain references to manuscript collections for those justices and judges whose primary source material has been collected, making this a valuable reference work for researchers. But in addition to biographical material, the book includes legislative histories, lists of judicial appointments, and a bibliography for each district court, court of appeals, circuit court, and the Supreme Court. The location of each court's official records and Web sources for its opinions are noted. This information is also provided for federal courts of special jurisdiction established under Article III of the U.S. Constitution but not for those that, like the Court of Federal Claims, were created under Article I. One editorial error is puzzling: the introductory section on courts of special jurisdiction states that "biographies of the judges follow the description of their respective courts." No such biographies appear either here or in the main biography section. In fact, neither judges of courts of special jurisdiction nor bankruptcy judges are included in the directory.

The book also discusses and reproduces landmark judicial legislation and, in a section called "Topics in Judicial History," lists interesting facts such as the oldest and youngest judges, first women judges, first minority judges, judges who have been impeached, etc.

Judges of the United States (Judicial Conference of the United States, 1978) provides similar biographical information, but despite plans for periodic revision, it apparently has not been updated. Because the Bernan volume provides 22 additional years of biographical coverage in an easy-to-read format while also offering information useful to serious researchers, law libraries, state libraries and archives, and large academic and public libraries will want to purchase it. Biographical information about current federal judges (including bankruptcy and magistrate judges) can be found in *Almanac of the Federal Judiciary* (Aspen Law and Business 1984–).

Justices of the United States Supreme Court. 2001. 443p. bibliog. glossary. illus. index. Macmillan, $80 (0-02-865634-2). 347.73.

This volume from the Macmillan Profiles series designed to complement the high-school curriculum is a compact, readable work giving information on the 108 individuals who have been justices of the U.S. Supreme Court. Presented in alphabetical order, entries include a photo of each justice plus one to four pages (usually two) on his or her family, career, political leanings, and major decisions. One nice feature is a highlighted quote from each biographee, often from a written opinion. Entries also include a time line of events of each life. Some terms (*capital punishment, presidential elector*) are defined in the margin, and some specific cases (*Gregg v. Georgia, South Dakota v. Dole*) are explained in sidebars. Following the entries are a "Time Line of Events Surrounding Justices of the Supreme Court," a list of resources, and a glossary. The "Additional Resources" section includes general resources as well as materials specific to each justice. Controversial people (Roger Taney, Clarence Thomas) and issues get balanced treatment.

Indexing is awkward. There are entries for every state birthplace but not enough subject headings—no *censorship* or *obscenity*, for example. Although sidebars are listed in the table of contents, they are not indexed, so a reader looking in the index for information on the nominating and approval process will not find anything, even though these matters are discussed in a sidebar in the Clarence Thomas entry.

Most of this information is readily available elsewhere, particularly in *American National Biography* (Oxford, 1999) and on the Cornell Law School (LII: Supreme Court Collection at [http://supct.law.cornell.edu:8080/supct]) and Oyez Project [http://oyez.nwu.edu] Web sites. However, if patrons, especially at the high-school level, have individual Supreme Court figures to research, they may be delighted with this one-stop source.

The Supreme Court of the United States: A Student Companion. 2d ed. By John J. Patrick. 2001. 398p. appendixes. illus. index. Oxford, $45 (0-19-515008-2). 347.73.

Designed for students 12 years of age and older, this resource contains information related to many aspects of the Supreme Court, including its structure, history, origins, development, composition, functions, duties, and objectives. In this second edition, content has been expanded and updated to reflect recent rulings and to describe the current status and significance of certain controversial topics, such as abortion and affirmative action. The alphabetically arranged entries tend to fall into one of the following categories: biographies; decisions of the court; core concepts, ideas, and issues; legal terms and phrases; and procedures, practices, and personnel.

Readers encounter few surprises in the entries devoted to biographies and decisions. Personal information is provided for all justices—both chief and associate—and each entry contains a short section detailing the individual's contribution to important decisions and cases. One hundred significant cases are profiled, among them *Brown v. Board of Education, Plessy v. Ferguson,* and *Roe v. Wade,* and each is accompanied by background information, the official citation from *United States Reports,* voting results for the case, concurring and dissenting opinions, and how this decision has affected constitutional law.

Those entries that would be best described as core concepts, ideas, and issues discuss fundamentals of constitutionalism and certain rights and freedoms that have dramatically altered American notions of liberty and justice—for instance, *Bill of Rights, Civil rights, Freedom of speech and press*. This information would be incomplete, however, if not for the entries that treat terms, procedures, and practices. With terms such as *Decision days, Habeas corpus,* and *Per curiam,* readers gain helpful insights into the Court's processes, routines, and daily operation.

Overall, this resource is excellent and will be a boon to students wanting a more introductory guide than titles such as *Encyclopedia of the U.S. Supreme Court* [RBB F 15 01]. Readers will appreciate the balanced, well-researched entries and the book's organization and structure, both of which are very user-friendly. Photographs, several appendixes—one listing relevant Web sites—and an index enhance an already fine reference tool that is highly recommended for all high-school and public libraries.

Encyclopedia of American Law. By David Schultz. 2002. 542p. appendixes. illus. index. Facts On File, $75 (0-8160-4329-9). 349.73.

Encyclopedia of American Law "is written in a style that demonstrates that the law need not be mysterious and confusing, but that instead it should be open to all of us." Often books concerning legal information are difficult to follow, but the person who reads this volume will not find it necessary to have a legal background or a legal vocabulary. Definitions for terms such as *Assault and battery* are stated clearly. Landmark cases such as *Brown v. Board of Education* are summarized with only the most important facts.

Noted scholars in the field of law have written more than 400 alphabetically arranged entries, each of which includes a brief list of further readings for those who wish to do more research. From half of a page to three pages in length, entries address terms, issues, concepts, institutions, and court cases. Individuals who are covered include a selection of Supreme Court justices, presidents, and others (Martin Luther King Jr., Rodney King).

The appendixes at the end of the book contain the Declaration of Independence, Articles of Confederation, the Constitution of the United States, the Bill of Rights, other amendments to the Constitution, and the Emancipation Proclamation. It is useful to find all of these documents in one volume. A list of U.S. Supreme Court justices from John Jay through Stephen Breyer is also included. Other helpful appendixes are "Locating Court Cases and Laws," "How Cases Reach the United States Supreme Court," and "The Stages of a Criminal Case."

For a similar audience, the three-volume *Magill's Legal Guide* (2000) offers more comprehensive coverage. Schultz's *Encyclopedia of American Law* is a user-friendly resource that would be a good addition to high-school, public, and academic libraries looking for a one-volume introduction to the American legal system.

Historic U.S. Court Cases: An Encyclopedia. 2v. 2d ed. Ed. by John W. Johnson. 2001. 1089p. bibliog. illus. index. Routledge, $195(0-415-93019-7). 349.73.

Historic U.S. Court Cases offers 201 signed essays by political scientists, historians, and legal scholars that highlight major legal issues in five thematic areas: crime and criminal law; governmental organization, power, and procedure; economics and economic regulation; race, gender, sexual orientation, and disability; and civil liberties. Essays generally focus on one or two U.S. Supreme Court cases, although influential cases decided by lower federal courts, the colonial courts, and state courts are also covered. These range from the 1692 Salem witchcraft trials to the O.J. Simpson criminal and civil trials in California state court in the mid-1990s. Landmark cases are the subject of a number of the essays (e.g., *Miranda v. Arizona, Roe v. Wade*), but many lesser-known cases that are representative of a large body of litigation are included, as well as some, like Jerry Tarkanian's suit against the NCAA, that show "eccentricities in the American legal past."

Essays are arranged chronologically within each thematic area and provide the historical and social context, as well as the case's legal significance. Each essay begins with "the case in brief," which outlines the date, location, court, principal participants, and significance of the case. The essays vary in length from 1,000 words for "lesser" cases to 2,000 words for cases of "medium-level significance" and 5,000 words for cases of "monumental importance." Each concludes with a brief bibliography. Following the entries are an index of cases and a subject and name index.

This edition contains 43 new essays, half treating cases decided since the publication of the first edition in 1992 and half analyzing older cases. *United States v. Microsoft Corporation, Bush v. Gore,* and *Clinton v. Jones* are among the topics of new essays. Most of the essays included in the first edition have been updated by the authors. Format changes in the second edition make it more readable, and the new "Case in Brief" feature offers the user a quick overview. Students and researchers in political science and history, as well as law, will find the encyclopedia useful, and it is recommended for public, academic, and law school libraries. A similar title, Gale's *Great American Court Cases* (1999), treats 800 cases and is appropriate for high-school as well as academic and public libraries.

America's Military Adversaries: From Colonial Times to the Present. Ed. by John C. Fredriksen. 2001. 621p. bibliog. glossary. illus. index. ABC-CLIO, $85 (1-57607-603-2). 355.

America's Military Adversaries covers enemies of the U.S. government, from Native Americans defending their land and rights to Saddam Hussein (but not Osama bin Laden). Other examples include Filipino guerilla Emilio Aguinaldo, Japanese submarine captain Mochitsura Hashimoto, Adolf Hitler, Stonewall Jackson, and Pancho Villa. Among the few women represented are Margaret Arnold (wife of Benedict), Belle Boyd, and Tokyo Rose.

Each of the 223 alphabetically arranged entries is a readable essay containing personal as well as historical information. Cross-references refer readers to related items. The bibliographies that follow each entry are extensive, offering a mix of primary and secondary materials. The volume concludes with appendixes that group entries by occupation and by conflict.

This volume complements the author's previous book, *American Military Leaders: From Colonial Times to the Present* (ABC-CLIO, 1999). Aimed at secondary students, it is useful for high-school and college libraries. Public libraries might also consider it for their military reference collections.

Magill's Guide to Military History. 5v. Ed. by John Powell. 2001. 2,024p. bibliogs. illus. indexes. maps. Salem, $450 (0-89356-014-6). 355.

In more than 1,500 entries, this set surveys "the wars, battles, people, groups, and civilizations that played an important role in worldwide military history from ancient times to the twenty-first century." Coverage ranges from Megiddo, where Egyptians and Syrians clashed in 1469 B.C.E., to Desert Storm; from Assyrian general Ashurnasirpal II (915–859 B.C.E.) to Colin Powell; from Pontiac's Rebellion (1763–1766) to World Wars I and II. Articles are the work of more than 350 contributors, most of them affiliated with universities in the U.S.

Like other Salem multivolume sets, this one is well organized, and the organization is clearly spelled out in the "Publisher's Note." Entry length varies from 150-word definitions to 3,000-word surveys. There are approximately 350 essays on major wars and conflicts and another 395 on battles, sieges, and campaigns. Some 514 of the entries are biographical. Other entries cover various aspects of military history including weapons and equipment (*Chariot*, *Dreadnought*, *Firearms*), organizations (*Coast Guard, U.S.*; *French Foreign Legion*), and moral and legal questions (*Religion and war*, *War crimes*). Finally, there are definitions of terms such as *Infantry*, *Reparations*, and *Search and destroy mission*. Entries on military actions generally begin with brief ready-reference information detailing the issues involved, the dates, the location, the combatants, the principal commanders, and the result. For biographical entries, this list provides birth and death information, principal wars and battles in which the individual was involved, and his or her (there are a handful of women) military significance. Most entries conclude with lists of resources and ample cross-references.

Each volume has its own table of contents and a comprehensive list of maps. The extensive bibliography found in volume 5 cites and annotates standard general sources, and then goes on to list other resources under broad subject headings. Volume 5 also offers a "Time Line of Wars and Battles" and lists of "Wars and Battles by Geographical Area" and "Military Leaders by Geographical Area." Finally, indexes by category, personages, and battles and wars supplement the general index. It would be useful if all of the volumes referred the reader to these added features; as it is, they are listed only in volume 5's table of contents.

Other military reference sources cover specific wars, concentrate on a single nation, or treat military leaders. The value of this set lies in the fact that it offers convenient access to such a wide range of topics as a starting point for further research and also allows the reader to examine those topics in a broad context. Recommended for high-school, public, and academic libraries.

The Oxford Companion to Military History. Ed. by Richard Holmes. 2001. 1,048p. bibliogs. illus. maps. index. Oxford, $60 (0-19-866209-2). 355.003.

Holmes is professor of Military and Security Studies at Cranfield University and the Royal Military College of Science. He has presented two popular BBC Television series on military history and authored six monographs on the subject.

Although this reference work surveys all military services from ancient to modern time periods, it emphasizes land warfare in Europe and North America from the eighteenth through the twentieth centuries. It contains approximately 1,300 entries arranged in an A–Z format written by some 148 contributors from Great Britain, Europe, and North America. There are 31 feature articles of two or more pages on topics such as *Artillery*, *Infantry*, *Logistics*, *Peacekeeping*, *Tactics*, and *Women in the military*. Appropriately placed throughout the text are 70 black-and-white maps and 15 black-and-white illustrations. Entries are cross-referenced and signed, and many contain a short bibliography of one to five items at the end.

There are numerous single-volume reference tools with coverage similar to that of *The Oxford Companion to Military History*. One recent example is Cowley's *Readers Companion to Military History* (Houghton Mifflin, 1996), which has more than 600 entries, 40 maps, and 89 black-and-white illustrations. All entries are signed, and most have short bibliographies. Holmes compares favorably with Cowley, with more entries and maps but fewer illustrations. *The Oxford Companion to Military History* should be considered by high-school, public, and academic libraries that need a convenient military history guide.

Reader's Guide to Military History. Ed. by Charles Messenger. 2001. 948p. bibliogs. index. Fitzroy Dearborn, $135 (1-57958-241-9). 355.009.

Messenger, a former British military officer, and approximately 200 advisors and contributors have compiled a critical annotated bibliography of the latest scholarship on military topics. Intended for scholars, the work covers topics from ancient to modern times and attempts to be universal in coverage, although there is some Western European and North American emphasis. Topics include land, sea, and air services; conflicts; types of warfare; military theory; prominent military leaders; and national armed services. There is no coverage of hardware.

More than 500 entries are arranged alphabetically, from *Abyssinia: British and Italian expeditions*, 1867–1896 to *Zhukov, Georgii*. A typical entry begins with a bibliography of monographs and articles, primarily in English. This is followed by a page or more of text discussing the cited sources. All entries are signed and include *see also* references. In the front of the book are an alphabetical list of entries; a thematic list by region, chronology, and topic; and a chronological list of individuals. Following the entries, a "Booklist Index" refers to the sources that are discussed in the entries and is organized by author. This is followed by a general index.

There are very few similar resources. *The American Historical Association's Guide to Historical Literature* (Oxford, 1995) does have annotated bibliographies to assist scholars, but military coverage is fragmented. The *Reader's Guide to Military History* is a unique, well-designed reference tool that will be useful to academic, large public, and specialized libraries.

Who's Who in Twentieth-Century Warfare. By Spencer C. Tucker. 2001. 384p. Routledge, $29.95 (0-415-23497-2). 355.020.

Tucker is the John Biggs Chair of Military History at the Virginia Military Institute. He has authored or edited nine books, including *The Encyclopedia of the Korean War* (ABC-CLIO, 2000) and *The Encyclopedia of the Vietnam War* (ABC-CLIO, 1998).

As the title suggests, this is a who's who type of biographical reference. It is worldwide in scope. Coverage includes army, navy, and air force personnel who served during the twentieth century. Most are high-ranking military leaders, but a few are individuals better known for their heroism, such as Alvin C. York. Also included are politicians (*Roosevelt, Franklin Delano*), explorers (*Byrd, Richard E.*), physicians (*McIndoe, Archibald*), writers (*Remarque, Erich Maria*), and others who played an important role in military history.

Most of the approximately 1,000 entries are 250 words in length or less. Information covered includes birth and death years, schooling, commands, battles, and promotions. Assisting users are a short preface and a list of abbreviations and terminology, the latter especially helpful as the author has used many abbreviations to save space and allow for more entries.

There are numerous biographical references of military people. Most of these are specialized according to time period, nationality, or service. Despite some overlapping coverage, *Who's Who in Twentieth-Century Warfare* is itself unique because of its worldwide scope. This would be an appropriate reference for military enthusiasts in academic and public libraries.

★Encyclopedia of Public Health. 4v. Ed. by Lester Breslow. 2002. 1,480p. appendix. bibliogs. index. Macmillan, $475 (0-02-865354-8). 362.1.

Subsequent to 9-11, information is increasingly available in the news media about essential public health functions, including, for example, environmental protection; the prevention, surveillance, and control of communicable diseases; occupational health; and specific public health services, such as emergency disaster services. With deep historical traditions, the field of public health encompasses a wide array of intellectual disciplines, professions, trades, and practical skills.

Arranged in alphabetical order and written by experts, this set's more than 900 clearly written, well-organized entries provide an excellent source of background information for the lay reader, college student, and professional. Length ranges from a hundred words or so for basic definitions to several thousand words for "each of the most important sectors and disciplines" of the field. Some entries include charts, graphs, and tables. It is disappointing that no Web sites are included in the brief bibliographies that conclude each entry. See also references point the reader to related topics. Adding considerable value, back matter consists of core documents in the field (for example, "The Oath of Hippocrates," "World Scientists' Warning to Humanity"), an annotated bibliography of historical and modern works, and a topical outline of contents.

Arms control, Child mortality, Filth diseases, Homicide, Medical waste, Oil spills, Race and ethnicity, and Street violence are examples of some of the entries in this work. More than 40 entries are biographical, covering such individuals as Joseph Lister, Walter Reed, and Margaret Sanger. Readers looking for information on public health administration and agencies will not be disappointed; neither will others looking for information on the history, philosophy, and ethics of public health. Here too is information on communicable and noncommunicable diseases and conditions, injury related to acts of individual and mass violence, epidemiology, environmental health, behavioral and community health issues, personal health services, nutrition, and public health and the law. The editor and contributors clearly understand the field's breadth and depth, and the diverse entries reflect their appreciation of the field's vitality.

Over the past decades the availability of works on medicine and health has surged, and today the reference output in both print and electronic formats in these fields continues to grow. Most other sources emphasize the health of individuals rather than the health of populations, so this work fills a gap in the reference literature. The Board extends an unqualified "thumbs up" to the editor and his contributors for successfully imparting to the reader an understanding of the extraordinary progress of the field of public health. Strongly recommended for academic libraries and medium-sized and large public libraries.

Censorship: A World Encyclopedia. 4v. Ed. by Derek Jones. 2001. 2,891. illus. index. Fitzroy Dearborn, $395 (1-57958-135-8). 363.31.

This work provides a wide-ranging view of censorship, spanning ancient Egypt to present times and covering art, literature, music, newspapers and broadcasting, and the visual arts, among many other topics. In addition, the work provides country surveys and discussions of major controversies for specific movies, books, and television shows. Some 1,550 entries, arranged in alphabetical order by subject, were written by about 600 contributors from 50 countries. Entries are enhanced by occasional illustrations, a name-subject index, and an alphabetical and thematic list of entries at the beginning of each volume.

The editor offers a broad—even elastic—definition of censorship to cover "formal and informal, overt and covert" methods by which "restrictions are imposed on the collection, display, dissemination and exchange of information." The set especially aims to provide a comparative study of the topic, an approach not taken in the few other reference works on censorship. Readers will find an enormous amount of useful and unique information—censorship in Iceland, suppression of a Kyrgyz folk epic, the banning of Mahler's music, and the influence of Red Channels, a newsletter that blacklisted individuals during the McCarthy era, to give just a few examples. Each entry concludes with a list of further reading, and in many cases these readings will help broaden one's understanding of the topics being discussed. An exception is the bibliography following the entry on Columbia University professor Edward Said, which suffers from omission of two well-publicized works containing critical comment about him.

With so many contributors, it is inevitable that inconsistencies would arise regarding the comparative length of entries. For a U.S. audience, treatment of some topics that have received substantial U.S. press coverage, such as Hate speech, might seem too brief at just over a page, especially when there is half a page devoted to Ice-T in New Zealand. Access can be a problem—a reader will only come across the discussion of the controversy over public television's airing of the documentary Days of Rage: The Young Palestinians by looking in the entry for Jo Franklin Trout, the program's director, because Days of Rage is not listed in the index.

Questions about balance in what is included and what is omitted are inescapable in a multivolume encyclopedia, especially when it deals with so many controversial topics. The Encyclopedia of Censorship (Facts On File, 1990) is the most similar work, but entries there are usually very cursory and always unsourced. Because of its broad coverage, Censorship: A World Encyclopedia is recommended for large academic and major public libraries.

Dangerous Planet: The Science of Natural Disasters. 3v. By Phillis Engelbert. 2001. 446p. bibliog. glossary. illus. index. UXL, $130 (0-7876-2848-4). 363.34.

This new set for young adults from UXL is sure to be popular. It explores 16 natural disasters, including avalanches, earthquakes, floods, landslides, tornadoes, and wildfires. Each of the 16 chapters is divided into sections that tell of one or two major disasters in history, explain the scientific nature and short-term and long-term consequences of each type of disaster, and discuss how humans can cause and prevent the disaster or mitigate its effects. Fact boxes with primary source material and further information are placed throughout the text, as are black-and-white photographs. There is a glossary specific to the type of disaster at the beginning of each chapter, with important safety tips and a bibliography at the end. Each volume has a general glossary as well as a bibliography and index for the set. The bibliographies are divided by type of source and include a wealth of Web sites. The pages are consecutively numbered throughout the set, but the index includes the volume numbers.

The stories about particular disasters, such as the East Coast blizzard of 1888, the dust bowl, and the Bangladesh monsoon floods of 1998, will be fascinating to readers of many ages. The science is accurate, and the technical terms are explained well. The illustrations are clear and well placed, but some are too small to convey the magnitude of the disaster. Some readers may be distracted by the three different typefaces used.

Most school and public libraries will want to add this excellent and useful set. For an older audience, Salem's three-volume Natural Disasters (2001) also takes a disaster-by-disaster approach but describes more examples.

Encyclopedia of Birth Control. By Vern L. Bullough. 2001. 347p. appendixes. bibliogs. illus. index. ABC-CLIO, $75 (1-57607-181-2); e-book, $100 (1-57607-533-8). 363.9.

Birth control has a long and colorful history. Since the beginning of time, humans have sought a way to enjoy their sexuality while avoiding pregnancy. This encyclopedia written by a medical historian specializing in the history of sex provides a fairly detailed overview of a fascinating subject. The 130 alphabetical entries cover the historical and sociological aspects of birth control as well as the key figures in the birth control movements in the U.S. and Great Britain.

The articles range in length from 1 paragraph to 10 pages. They cover a wide range of topics: Abortion; Comstock, Anthony and Comstockery; Demography and population control in early modern Europe; Herbal contraceptives and abortifacients; and Witchcraft, contraception and abortion. There are also entries about countries (France and birth control) and biographies of pioneers in the birth control movement: George Drysdale, Emma Goldman, Margaret Sanger. Readers may wonder why Gregory Pincus, inventor of the birth control pill, has an entry while Carl Djerassi, whose research helped form the basis for Pincus' work, and John Rock, the physician involved in early tests of the pill, do not. The articles have references at the end, and many contain illustrations. There are see also references but no see references. Users looking for information about "the Pill" will have to search for the article Oral contraceptives. The index does not solve this problem, because pill is not an index entry.

Two appendixes provide further information. Appendix 1 is a "World Survey of Birth Control Practices," with country-by-country statistics from the International Planned Parenthood Federation Web site. Most statistics are from 1998. Appendix 2 is a list of print and nonprint resources.

Although the author may exaggerate when he calls this the "most comprehensive historical survey of birth control, contraception, and abortion available," he does present information on relatively obscure topics, such as African slaves in the United States and birth control and Self-help literature in the nineteenth century. This will be a good companion for Marian Rengel's Encyclopedia of Birth Control [RBB F 15 01], which emphasizes the scientific and medical aspects of contraception. Bullough's work will be useful in academic and large public library collections.

Environmental Activists. Ed. by John Mongillo and Bibi Booth. 2001. 353p. Greenwood, $50 (0-313-30884-5). 363.

This volume profiles more than 60 Americans who have worked to save the environment. Arrangement is alphabetical. Articles are generally three to five pages in length, and most are followed by a bibliography, often with Web sites.

The editors admit that not everyone who has been involved in saving the earth has been included. They tried to provide a balance of historical and current, male and female subjects. Historical personages include those we associate with environmental issues—such as Audubon, Muir, and Theodore Roosevelt—as well as names better known in other fields—such as George Catlin (art) and Frederick Law Olmsted (landscape architecture). Among more contemporary activists are the familiar Roger Tory Peterson and Karen Silkwood and the less-familiar Nevada Dove, a youth organizer for Concerned Citizens of Los Angeles, and Catherine Sneed, director of the Garden Project in San Francisco. In some cases, profiles were written by the subjects themselves.

Following the biographies is an "Environmental Timeline" that begins with colonial America and continues through the year 2000. When a person is mentioned on the time line and also appears in the text, the name appears in bold type. This feature puts environmental problems and the attempts to solve them in historical perspective. A table of contents would have been a useful addition, giving a snapshot of the volume's range.

Although it is easy to find information on Edward Abbey and Rachel Carson, this volume is valuable for its inclusion of individuals who are less well known. The message to the reader is that these were ordinary people who cared enough about some environmental issue or some place to dedicate themselves to publicizing or preserving it. This book will be useful for the general reader as well as middle-and high-school students who need information for reports.

The Environment Encyclopedia. 11v. Ed. by Ruth A. Eblen and William R. Eblen. 2001. 1,547p. bibliogs. glossary. illus. indexes. Marshall Cavendish, $459.95 (0-7614-7182-0). 363.7.

This encyclopedia is an update and repackaging of the Houghton Mifflin *Encyclopedia of the Environment* (1994), which was among the first resources to focus on the human and social aspects of environmental issues. In its new incarnation, the encyclopedia has expanded from 1 to 11 volumes and incorporates many more illustrations and photographs. Although adults will find it useful, the layout and presentation seem most suitable to middle-school through senior-high-school students.

The editors selected and updated or commissioned 400 articles, arranged alphabetically over a broad range of topics. The breadth goes beyond the expected coverage of *Carson, Rachel; Clean Air Act;* and *Climate change* to include *Migrant labor, Suburb,* and *Wright, Frank Lloyd*. Most entries are signed and vary in length but are usually several pages long. They may have sidebars called "Linkups" to refer readers to other entries dealing with related concepts. Other type of sidebars may include definitions, tables, or several paragraphs of related information. Entries conclude with *see also* references and short bibliographies. Most of the photographs and illustrations are in color.

Each volume has own its table of contents and index. The first volume contains a complete table of contents of all volumes as well as a "Thematic Outline of Contents." Volume 11 contains the set index as well as seven thematic indexes, among them an "Index of Places" and an "Index of Persons." The indexes, which reference illustrations and other graphics as well as text, are a valuable part of this work and should be well used. Volume 11 also includes a glossary, a 12-page "Environmental Time Line," and a valuable "Resources for Further Study" that includes an essay on using libraries and their resources (including librarians) well.

As with any work, there are small quibbles. The article *Wildflowers* features a photograph of cosmos, described as "native to North America." But in fact, most cosmos are specifically native to Mexico and are considered invasive aliens in many parts of the U.S.

This is an expensive work, but because of its breadth of information and accessibility it is recommended for school and public libraries. It may also be useful in undergraduate libraries as an introduction to the topic.

Food Safety Information Handbook. By Cynthia A. Roberts. 2001. 312p. bibliog. glossary. index. Oryx, $52.50 (1-57356-305-6). 363.19.

Written by the coordinator of the USDA/FDA Foodborne Illness Education Information Center, this volume provides an overview of the field of food safety and aims to serve as a resource for a broad audience of parents, students, health professionals, educators, and librarians. The volume is divided into two parts. Part 1, "An Overview of Food Safety," contains an introductory chapter that discusses food hazards, such as viruses, pathogenic bacteria, natural toxins, and pesticides. There is also a short history of the discoveries in food safety and techniques for making foods safer. The next chapter introduces hot topics related to food safety, including the cases for and against genetic engineering, irradiation, and the use of pesticides. Following this chapter is a lengthy chronology of events related to food safety, including inventions, discoveries, and legislation, beginning with 6000 B.C.E., when techniques for drying and smoking food were developed. Part 1 concludes with a history of laws and legislation in the U.S., starting with the Massachusetts Meat and Fish Inspection Law of 1641 and ending with the 1996 Food Quality Protection Act. Each chapter includes lists of resources, many of which are government documents available via the Web.

Part 2, "Resources," is dedicated to various information sources related to food safety, with chapters listing reports and brochures, books and newsletters, Internet resources and electronic products, educational materials, and state and national organizations and agencies. The book concludes with a glossary that is easy for the layperson to understand yet specific enough for teachers, undergraduates, and librarians. The index is well constructed and accurate, although not thorough. For example, the index entry *peanut* cites the discussion of peanut allergies in part 1 but does not capture the various resources related to peanut allergies listed in part 2.

Although food safety is a very timely topic, few materials published in recent years are intended for the same broad audience. This unique and well-rounded book is highly recommended for high schools and public libraries and for academic libraries' general reference collections.

Forbidden Films: Censorship Histories of 125 Motion Pictures. By Dawn B. Sova. 2001. 350p. appendixes. bibliog. index. Facts On File, $55 (0-8160-4017-6); paper, $16.95 (0-8160-4336-1). 363.3.

When most people think of censored films, they assume that the work offends because of sexual content. But *Forbidden Films*, which traces censorship efforts against 125 films, demonstrates that from silent to modern cinema, films have also been banned for religious, social, and political reasons.

The book "analyzes representative films and the mechanism by which they (and other movies) have been suppressed." Focus is on censorship in the U.S., although some entries discuss efforts in other nations. The films that have been selected include such expected titles as *Last Tango in Paris* and *Caligula*, but the reader may be surprised to learn that *Martin Luther, The Spirit of 76,* and *Birth of a Nation* were banned in certain cities. Even *Schindler's List* was banned in some countries for its so-called Jewish propaganda and several scenes of cruelty. Entries are arranged alphabetically by film title and include production details such as country and date of production, distribution, format, running time, director, writer, awards, genre, and cast. A summary of the film's plot is followed by a description of its censorship history. Each entry concludes with a short bibliography for further reading.

The volume ends with a bibliography of books and articles and three appendixes. "Directors' Profiles" offers brief information on directors of banned films. "Reasons for Banning" groups films under five categories, such as "Sexual Films." The index interfiles personal names, titles, and subject headings.

This resource provides an interesting approach to the issues of censorship in the twentieth century and is recommended for high-school, public, and academic libraries.

Murders in the United States: Crimes, Killers and Victims of the Twentieth Century. By R. Barri Flowers and H. Loraine Flowers. 2001. 226p. bibliog. index. McFarland, $45 (0-7864-1037-X). 363.15.

This volume aimed at "researchers, writers, scholars, students, criminal justice professionals, laypersons, and others with an interest in the crime of murder" covers selected homicides from 1900 to 1999.

The book is arranged in three parts. Part 1, "A Century of Murders," surveys each decade from the 1900s to the 1990s, beginning with the assassination of President McKinley and ending with the killings at Columbine High School. Part 2, "A Century of Murderers," is an alphabetical listing organized by types of killers (male, female, juvenile), subdivided by categories such as "Serial Killers," "Caretaker Killers," and "Killers of Celebrities." There are also categories for group murders, hate crimes, and murders in U.S. schools. Part 3, "A Century of Victims," has two subdivisions: "Adult Victims" and "Child Victims."

Entries are brief, with most taking up less than half a page. Cross-references help link the three parts. A list of references including Internet sources and an index of names conclude the volume.

Despite its subject matter, the volume generally manages to avoid sensationalism. The preface states that it is suitable for academic study in disciplines such as criminal justice and criminology. It would also appeal to public library true-crime buffs. Information on some of the same crimes can be found in The Encyclopedia of Modern Murder, 1962–1982 (Putnam, 1985) and World Encyclopedia of Twentieth Century Murder (Paragon House, 1992), but these titles are not as current.

Encyclopedia of Crime and Justice. 4v. 2d ed. Ed. by Joshua Dressler. 2002. 1,780p. bibliogs. glossary. indexes. Macmillan, $475 (0-02-865319-X). 364.

The second edition of this encyclopedia was worth the wait of nearly 20 years. Often, the publication of a new edition of a subject encyclopedia merely means the addition of a paragraph or two to the end of existing essays and perhaps a few original essays to address new concepts. This second edition reads like a new work. Nearly all the essays have been completely rewritten by different contributors; some old topics were discarded or reclassified; and new essays addressing topics like Hate crimes, Human Immunodeficiency Virus, Popular culture, and Stalking have been added.

The signed essays are written by respected scholars in the fields of law, sociology, and criminal justice and range in length from 800 to 12,000 words. All include a list of related entries and a bibliography, which typically cites both classical works and contemporary literature. Most essays also include a new feature that researchers will find quite useful: a list of leading cases. The essays are scholarly and authoritative yet easy to read and accessible to laypersons. The essay on Accomplices, for example, uses a question-and-answer format that greatly simplifies this complex legal concept. When relevant, tables, sidebars, and figures are included to graphically present information and statistical data. Three entries on careers in criminal justice are a welcome surprise.

Although the focus is primarily on the U.S., there are essays on comparative criminal law and enforcement in various societies, crime in developing countries, criminal law reform in Europe and England, comparative criminal procedure, and international criminal law. Many essays, including Abortion, Euthanasia and assisted suicide, Homosexuality and crime, and Terrorism, take an international perspective. A glossary, "Legal Index" (a table of cases and an index of other cited legal documents), and general index complete the set.

There is some overlap with West's Encyclopedia of American Law (West, 1998), but entries in Encyclopedia of Crime and Justice are generally more extensive and place more emphasis on theory and research. Recommended for high-school, college and university, and public libraries, this set will be in high demand by "issues" researchers as well as by researchers in the fields of law and criminal justice.

Education, Commerce, Custom

Encyclopedia of American Education. 3v. 2d ed. By Harlow G. Unger. 2001. appendixes. bibliogs. illus. index. Facts On File, $225 (0-8160-4344-2). 370.

Education in the U.S. has changed significantly since 1996 when the first edition of this volume was published, so it is no surprise that Facts On File updated it. The surprise rests in the number of entries that did not change. The work still includes about 2,500 entries in about 200 subject areas. Topics range from history to current issues, from leading figures and movements to legislation and Supreme Court cases, from administration to adolescence. About 50 new articles deal with distance learning and other emerging trends. Approximately 500 articles have been updated. Some statistics were revised (although the number of California State University campuses was not updated). Library has some very current information, while Children's literature is severely out of date.

Entries range in length from a couple of sentences to several pages. Length does not necessarily correlate with current importance; for instance, Missionary education movements is longer than Minority education, and Military education is longer than Migrant education. The humanities are covered more extensively than the sciences. Individual colleges and historical aspects of education outweigh research and reform (e.g., there is no index listing for statistics, and ethnography is missing entirely). Literacies are under-represented; computer literacy is included but media, visual, and information literacies are excluded. There is no mention of young adult literature, which continues to be a controversial and important topic. Except for those appended to new entries, lists of references contain few current titles.

Several appendixes follow the entries: a sketchy chronology of significant educational benchmarks (none for the 1980s), a list of significant U. S. Supreme Court decisions in education, a list of education majors and degrees, and a topical bibliography of generally older resources.

Despite some gaps this set covers much ground and is useful for many libraries, but should not be considered the definitive source or the only purchase in this area. Given the limited amount of updating, libraries may choose not to replace the previous edition.

World Education Encyclopedia: A Survey of Educational Systems Worldwide. 3v. 2d ed. Ed. by Rebecca Marlow-Ferguson. 2002. 1,747p. appendixes. bibliogs. index. maps. Gale, $395 (0-7876-5577-5). 370.

Gale and editor Marlow-Ferguson have done a good job in revising the World Education Encyclopedia (WEE), published in 1988 by Facts On File. The introduction notes that the title has been "reconceptualized" with 100 percent revision. New contributors have been recruited; the majority are faculty from U.S. colleges and universities. The glossaries at the end of each country article have been eliminated but the bibliographies remain, with current titles and some Web sites. A flaw of the first edition has been corrected—entries are now arranged in a single alphabet rather than in three groups depending on the amount of information available about each country.

More than 225 countries are included, among them "new" countries of the former Soviet Union and territories and departments such as Guadeloupe, Puerto Rico, and Saint Helena. The country essays can be as short as a page or as long as 12 pages for China, Greece, New Zealand, Uganda, the U.S., and others. There is a basic structure for the essays. They begin with the history of the country followed by the constitutional and legal foundations of the education system; an overview of the educational system; and sections on preprimary, primary, secondary, and higher education; administration, finance, and educational research; the profession of teaching; and a summary. The authors are objective in their writing, and the editor provides consistency in style. Tables, graphs, and pie charts from current publications of the World Bank, UNESCO, and UNICEF accompany some of the articles. These graphics do not identify the country to which they refer so it is only by checking the original source that one can be sure they appear in the correct entry.

There are two appendixes. One ranks countries by public expenditures on education, literacy rate by sex, number of teachers, etc. Appendix 2 has regional maps of the countries of the world. The index is useful in helping to compare different attributes by country—academic year, grading, life skills training, and so on.

A similar title, International Encyclopedia of Education (2d ed., Pergamon, 1994), covers education topics as well as countries but is now out-of-date. WEE is a current subject encyclopedia and a necessary purchase for academic and large public libraries that support a strong education program.

In an Influential Fashion: An Encyclopedia of Nineteenth-and Twentieth-Century Fashion Designers and Retailers Who Transformed Dress. By Ann T. Kellogg and others. 2002. 371p. appendixes. bibliog. glossary. illus. index. Greenwood, $49.95 (0-313-31220-6). 391.

Entrants in this book were chosen not for their artistic merit alone but because their influence on fashion is reflective of societal, political, or economic change. The focus is primarily on the U.S. Examples range from Coco Chanel, Calvin Klein, and Vera Wang to FUBU, the Gap, and Nike. Each entry contains basic biographical information about the designer or founding information about the company, describes signature styles, and outlines the career or company history. When appropriate, the entry summarizes licensing agreements and influential marketing innovations and defines the entrants' significance within fashion. Each entry is from one to two pages long and is completed by a short list of readings. Where available, Web site addresses are also included. The black-and-white illustrations were created specifically for this book.

The glossary following the entries is only slightly more than one page and could have been expanded. Appendixes include a chart of designers listed alphabetically showing the time periods in which they were active, a list of designers and retailers broken down by country and by specialty, a list of colleges with fashion design programs, and a list of museums with costume collections. This is followed by a short list of professional organizations and a selective bibliography of less than three pages.

This book offers good general coverage of the topic and is recommended for high-school, public, and academic libraries. Some recent comparable volumes with more complete coverage are *Contemporary Fashion* (St. James, 1995), which contains hundreds of black-and-white photos plus much more complete bibliographies; *The Fashion Book* (Phaidon, 1998), which includes excellent color photos with brief biographies; and *Fashion: The Century of the Designer, 1900–1999* (Konemann, 2000), which includes exquisite color photos and an extensive glossary of terminology. Any of these titles should make the current book supplementary.

The Christmas Encyclopedia. By William D. Crump. 2001. 346p. bibliog. illus. index. McFarland, $55 (0-7864-1034-5). 394.2663.

This work contains a wealth of information about the Christmas holiday, from its inception around A.D. 350 to the present day. The entire Christmas season from Advent through Epiphany is covered in more than 340 entries. Both religious and secular observances; Santa Claus and other mythical beings who bring gifts; Christmas symbols (*Christmas tree*, *Poinsettia*, *Yule log*); sacred and popular carols and music; and Christmas customs in the U.S. and around the world are well covered in detailed articles. Many countries that celebrate the holiday extensively have their own articles (*France*, *Czech Republic*, *Mexico*); others have a subsection under regional groupings like *Africa* and *Asia and the South Pacific*. There are also many articles on Christmas as portrayed in the popular media—literary works, motion pictures, and television specials. Examples of entries include A *Charlie Brown Christmas*, *Christmas seals*, *Christmas stamps*, *Eggnog*, *Hanukkah*, *Kwanza*, *Miracle on 34th Street*, *New Year's Day*, *Salvation Army*, and *Winter solstice*. *See* references, an index, and a list of references are well done. There are many interesting historical illustrations in black and white.

Other recent Christmas titles are *Encyclopedia of Christmas* (Omnigraphics, 2000) and *The World Encyclopedia of Christmas* (McClelland & Stewart, 2000). The former has 186 entries; the latter has more than 1,000 entries and a section of color plates, though it suffers somewhat from the lack of an index. It seems a library can never have too many Christmas books around holiday time, so public libraries, in particular, that already own one of the other titles should consider adding *The Christmas Encyclopedia*. With its festive subject, extensive information, and exuberant spirit, the book would be an asset to any collection.

Encyclopedia of Easter, Carnival, and Lent. By Tanya Gulevich. 2002. 729p. bibliog. illus. index. Omnigraphics, $48 (0-7808-0432-5). 394.2667.

This reference consists of 154 entries, arranged alphabetically, that address Easter-related folk customs, religious observances, history, legends, folklore, and symbols. The intent, according to the introduction, is to provide not exhaustive coverage but a solid introduction. The author manages to do just that through a series of engaging and sometimes in-depth essays that run between one paragraph and several pages. Topics range from celebrations that precede that 40-day period of Lent, such as Mardi Gras and Pancake Day, to the Easter bunny and the stations of the cross.

There is an emphasis on Christian beliefs as professed by the Roman Catholic, Protestant, and Orthodox religions. Other observations are discussed, including Passover and Shavuot (Jewish), Hilaria and Floralia (ancient Rome), No Ruz (Persian New Year), Beltane (Celtic), and May Day. Twenty nations have specific entries, and additional local information is provided through articles on customs such as Easter eggs and Carnival that trace the historical development and culture-specific interpretations of these traditions around the world. Entries end with further reading selections and Web sites. A bibliography of all referenced sources and a detailed index complete the volume. The black-and-white illustrations are not an enhancement.

The only reference work devoted exclusively to Easter currently in print, this is an entertaining and solid introduction that will be useful for both report writing and ready reference. Recommended for public, high-school, and academic collections.

Encyclopedia of Folk Heroes. By Graham Seal. 2001. 347p. bibliog. illus. indexes. ABC-CLIO, $85 (1-57607-216-9); E-book, $95 (1-57607-718-7). 398.

Seal (of the Curtin University of Technology in Perth, Australia) has put together an interesting if sporadic collection of folk heroes. He refers to it as a "representative collection of legendary, historical, and magical heroes from many of the world's extensive folklores." South and Central America receive very little coverage. Polynesia and Melanesia are barely covered. Europe, North America, China, Japan, and select parts of Africa are covered, as are both settler and Aboriginal Australia.

After a long introduction that surveys both the nature of the folk hero and the author's criteria for inclusion and exclusion, the work itself is in alphabetical order. There are liberal *see* references between variant forms of names. Entries range from a paragraph to several two-columned pages (e.g., *Culture heroes*; *James, Jesse*; *Snow White*). Each entry has a list of related entries and a list of references and further reading. Black-and-white illustrations are scattered throughout the text.

Folk heroes are those "who have received celebration in one or more forms of folkloric expression and practice—in folktales, folk songs, folk customs, folk speech, and the other informal genres of everyday life." They include real people whose lives were large enough to have a fantastic component to them, like Davy Crockett, or whose deaths made publicity machines crank out stories about them, like Ned Kelly. Outlaws, tricksters, heroes and heroines of fairy tales and story cycles, numbskulls, and monsters are included. There are some puzzling assertions. In the *Heroes of struggle* entry, Helen Gurley Brown is identified as an "occupational" hero from American labor lore, along with Joe Hill.

Following the entries are an "Index of Heroic Types," a "Country/Culture Index," and a "Chronology of Folk Heroes" as well as a general index. There is an extensive bibliography besides the references given at the end of each entry.

Although many of the same topics are covered in other reference books on folklore, *Encyclopedia of Folk Heroes* includes a number of figures not easily found elsewhere. Larger public and academic libraries with folklore collections may find it useful.

Encyclopedia of Urban Legends. Ed. by Jan Harold Brunvand. 2001. 525p. bibliogs. illus. index. ABC-CLIO, $75 (1-57607-076-X); e-book, $100 (1-57607-532-X). 398.2.

Although other titles on urban legends are entertaining, the approach here is also scholarly and reflects the author's academic background. He defines urban legends as "all those bizarre, whimsical, 99 percent apocryphal, yet believable stories" of modern oral tradition.

Among the nearly 500 entries are specific legends ("The Blind Date," "The Poison Dress," "Snakes in Playland"), along with common legend topics, categories, and themes (*Fast food*, *Celebrities*, *Jumping to conclusions*). Other entries deal with terms and concepts related to the study of urban legends (*Motif*, *Ostension*). Coverage focuses on the U.S. but also extends to Canada, England, and other English-speaking countries and to countries, such as Romania, in which published urban-legend collections are available. Most entries end with references to books and journals, and many include *see also* references. At the end of the volume is a selected bibliography including collections of American folklore and legends.

Legends are entered under their conventional names, but few readers will be familiar with the conventions, and there are many variations. *See* references point from alternate to standard titles (*Mall slashers* SEE "The Slasher under the Car"). The index also helps in locating appropriate entry headings (*contact lenses* SEE "The Unlucky Contact Lenses," "The Welded Contacts"). However, there is no index entry for *tickets* to send the reader to "*Take My Tickets, Please*." More detailed keyword indexing would improve access.

Libraries will find that this volume fills a gap between traditional folklore and stories of popular culture. It should be popular at the junior-high-school level and up. Schools will want to be aware that there are a few sex stories.

The Mythical West: An Encyclopedia of Legend, Lore, and Popular Culture. Ed. by Richard W. Slatta. 2001. 400p. bibliogs. illus. index. ABC-CLIO, $75 (1-57607-151-0). 398.

Slatta (a professor of history at North Carolina State University) and his contributors have combed histories, documents, films, and the Internet for legendary images, events, people, and places associated with the American West. The goal is "to identify, describe, and analyze many myths of the Old West and the New so that readers can distinguish them from historical fact."

Topics treated include *Alamo*, *Barbecue*, *Billy the Kid*, *Cowboy poetry*, *Ghost towns*, *Hispanics in Western lore*, *Lewis and Clark expedition*, *Television*, and *Route 66*. Articles range from short paragraphs to several pages. Most list sources, including Web sites, for further reference, with more comprehensive listings following the A–Z entries. The writing style is generally breezy.

Slatta notes in his preface that, besides considering whether a subject was mythical or mythologized, he based his selection of topics on how many Internet sites covered them. He also chose not to duplicate coverage available in other ABC-CLIO titles. This may explain why there is no entry for Larry McMurtry, although the article on his son, singer-songwriter James McMurtry, takes up more than two pages. Only Louis L'Amour and Elmer Kelton among contemporary Western writers have their own articles. There are some other surprising omissions. Wild Bill Hickock has no main entry but is discussed in the entry *Dead Man's Hand*. There are no entries for the Colt .45 or the Winchester.

This volume would be an interesting but not essential purchase for academic and large public libraries with western, folklore, or media collections. The emphasis on mythical aspects makes it a complement to *The New Encyclopedia of the American West* (Yale, 1998), with which it shares some topics.

Language

The Facts On File Dictionary of Foreign Words and Phrases. By Martin H. Manser. 2002. 414p. index. Facts On File, $45 (0-8160-4458-9). 422.

As the English language ceaselessly absorbs and assimilates more and more elements of other languages, Manser has reason to quote Emerson's observation that English is indeed "the sea which receives tributaries from every region under heaven." In this volume he presents more than 4,000 examples, from *Abacus* to *Zombie*. Information regarding grammar and usage accompanies each entry, and in many entries examples are included to lessen the possibility of misuse. Etymological information is provided as well. All of the entries are indexed, individually and by language, and variant spellings are cross-referenced.

Manser's pronunciation system offers good approximations of foreign sounds. A two-page guide in the introduction is simple and readily understood, for example, Manser's pronunciation of *mutatis mutandis*: "myootahtas myootandas," with an underline indicating the accented syllable in the second word (that accent being dominant in the phrase) but no accent indicated in the other word, a practice consistent throughout. Many entries include variant pronunciations, but Latin words beginning with *v* are all represented with a vee sound, as in *ad verbum*, rendered as "ad verbam," following the ecclesiastical method, without acknowledging the acceptability of the classical pronunciation—which renders the first syllable of "verbum" as "wer." A small matter.

Designed to meet the needs and expectations of a general readership, Manser's book should be a strong contender in its class.

British English A to Zed. Rev. ed. By Norman W. Schur. Rev. by Eugene Ehrlich. 2001. 430p. appendix. index. Facts On File, $45 (0-8160-4238-1); paper, $18.95 (0-8160-4239-X). 423.

In an effort to unravel the differences between British and American English, Schur published his first guide, entitled *British Self-Taught: With Comments in American*, in 1973. When a revised edition appeared in 1980, the title was changed to *English English*, and the 1987 revision was published as *British English A to Zed*. This latest edition has been revised by Ehrlich, coeditor of the *Oxford American Dictionary*.

The approximately 5,000 Briticisms covered in this dictionary include words and phrases that Americans generally do not use at all (for example, *dabs*, meaning fingerprints) as well as terms used in both the U.S. and Britain but that have different meanings (such as *bomb*, which in Britain means a smash hit, but in America indicates just the opposite). Entries indicate the American equivalent for each Briticism and usually provide additional explanation. Valuable supplemental material appears in two appendixes, the first of which outlines the basic differences between British and American English regarding syntax, pronunciation, punctuation, and spelling. The second appendix provides a means of identifying terms in specific areas, including currency, finance, weights and measures, and cricket. An index to American equivalents completes the volume. Ehrlich has put his stamp on the dictionary by condensing and rewriting significant portions of the work. He has dropped a large number of terms and has significantly shortened many of the remaining entries by deleting illustrative examples and editorial commentary. In addition, Ehrlich has added a handful of new terms, including *finger* (shot of booze), *ruby wedding* (fortieth wedding anniversary), and *scrotty* (crummy).

British English A to Zed continues to be a useful source for public and academic libraries. Because this revision treats relatively few new terms, it is not an essential purchase for libraries that own the 1987 revision or its 1991 paperback reprint.

First School Dictionary. By Jock Grapham and Marie Lister. 2001. 184p. illus. Barron's, $13.95 (0-7641-5434-6). 423.

Junior Dictionary. By Evelyn Goldsmith. 2001. 272p. illus. Barron's, $16.95 (0-7641-5435-4). 423.

These are two entries in the Barron's Dictionaries for Children series. Both offer clear definitions often accompanied by colorful illustrations or photographs. The dictionaries reflect the sophistication and needs of the intended age group. *First School Dictionary*, designated for ages five and up, has larger print, fewer definitions, and cartoonlike illustrations. The guide words at the top of each page are highlighted in a yellow box. An alphabet line runs down the outer edge of each page, with the appropriate initial letter of the alphabet highlighted to help find definitions. Plurals and tenses are provided along with a definitions. To enhance the definition, a sample sentence might be provided.

Intended for children ages six and up, *Junior Dictionary* uses a smaller print size. There are more words defined and more sophisticated illustrations, including a greater number of photographs. In addition to definitions and spellings, the part of speech is provided, as are irregular forms of words, some pronunciations for homographs, and labels such as "formal," "informal," or "trademark."

Each book ends with supplemental pages that provide additional information in a visual format. Like the definitions, these pages reflect the intended audiences. For example, although both dictionaries have a page showing parts of the body, the child used as a model is younger in *First Dictionary* than in *Junior Dictionary*. The pages in *First School Dictionary* are illustrated by larger pictures, while the pages in *Junior Dictionary* include such features as grammar hints and vocabulary builders.

Smaller and more basic than other dictionaries serving the same age groups, these offerings might be considered as supplemental purchases by school and public libraries.

Microsoft Encarta College Dictionary. Ed. by Anne Soukhanov. 2001. 1,678p. illus. St. Martin's, $24.95 (0-312-28087-4). 423.

Those few users of this dictionary who venture into its prefatory matter might conclude that English lexicography and its traditions of more than two centuries require a makeover. The apparent reason is that college students lack familiarity with the language, its usage, and those features (e.g., homophones) that make English so devilish. The foreword explains what sort of problems the dictionary's College Usage Advisory Board (a group of 80 lexicographers and English professors) identified as worthy of special attention. These include common usage problems (addressed in 630 usage notes), words misspelled because they are misheard, and those pesky homophones. This dictionary offers new features intended to address the problems.

One feature called "Spellchecks" occurs 400 times. A typical example is the Spellcheck for *horse*, which directs the confused speller to *hoarse*. Its companion in the entry *hoarse* warns "your spellchecker will not catch this error." The dictionary's other special features include entry words as common misspellings along with their correct counterparts; the "Quick Facts" feature on "70 key concepts" as well as science topics; "Literary Links;" and the presence of a lightning-bolt icon before entry terms to signify those derived from "high technology." Literary Links "reveal interesting, sometimes surprising literary associations of selected words." These associations resemble the results one gets from keyword searches on Internet search engines. For example, a thumbnail summary of Joseph Conrad's *Heart of Darkness* is the subject of a Literary Link following the entry on *heart*. Such oddities distract from the dictionary's main purposes.

More to the heart of the matter is the light the dictionary sheds on usage. The usage notes on issues such as when and how to use an apostrophe, the difference between *lose* and *loose*, and when to use *should* and when to use *would* can help a student avoid common pitfalls. (The absence of a usage note differentiating the verbs *lie* and *lay* is an unfortunate omission.) As for the dictionary entries themselves, new words are relative to the larger *Encarta World English Dictionary* (1999). Many come from the field of technology as well as from the fields of science and medicine. Otherwise, the word stock of the two is very similar, perhaps even identical. The entries differ in depth and length; in some cases, the originals have shed some of their detail, and the number of photographic illustrations and drawings has been trimmed. Definitions are clear and succinct. Entries also provide pronunciation (using a proprietary system of symbols); identify a word's part of speech; and in many cases provide a very brief etymology. Integrated into the alphabetical presentation of the English lexicon are entries on people, places, and events. This sort of information can become dated quickly, but its presence is unquestionably a convenience for the target audience.

If this dictionary truly could remedy the written language problems the Advisory Board identified, it would be a "must" purchase. It does offer a contemporary approach in some of its selection of senses of words and in its definitions. However, cluttered with features of dubious value, it does not displace standard collegiate dictionaries.

The New Oxford American Dictionary. Ed. by Elizabeth J. Jewell and Frank Abate. 2001. 2,023p. illus. maps. Oxford, $55 (0-19-511227-X); CD-ROM, $21 (0-19-515061-9); book and CD-ROM, $65 (0-19-515060-0). 423.

The *New Oxford American Dictionary* (NOAD) may be competition for the *American Heritage Dictionary* (4th ed., 2000). Both of these dictionaries are a cross between a desk and an unabridged dictionary. They each have about 2,000 pages and more than 100,000 definitions.

The words in NOAD are taken from the 200-million-word databank of the North American Reading Program of Oxford University Press and the files of the *Oxford English Dictionary*. The entries are structured around "core" senses. *Core* is defined as "the one that represents the most literal use that the word has in ordinary modern American usage," which may not necessarily be the oldest or most frequent use. Core senses appear first in each definition, with related subsenses grouped under the core. For example, *label* is defined first as "a small piece of paper, fabric, plastic, or similar material attached to an object and giving information about it," with various other meanings (e.g., "the name or trademark of a fashion company"; "a classifying phrase or thing applied to a person or thing") listed as subsenses.

The definitions are clear and descriptive but still provide technical information when necessary. Some words are used in a sentence to illustrate meaning, although NOAD does not use quotations as the *American Heritage Dictionary* does. Pronunciation is given, but the pronunciation key is found only in the introduction. Following the tradition of the OED, many entries include word origins. Labels ("dated," "humorous," "offensive," "vulgar slang," etc.) indicate in what context a word should be used. As is now common in dictionaries, there are 5,000 place-names (*Dan River, Eiffel Tower*), 4,000 biographical entries (*Lenin, Vladimir* and *Lennon, John*, both with black-and-white photographs), and 3,000 proper names (*Blue Law State, Organization of American States*). There are line drawings of some items (*dumbbell, gazebo*) and simple maps of countries. Also included are highlighted boxes of usage (*Hispanic, mental*) and some encyclopedic information, usually a paragraph in length (*Bronze Age, Paraguay*). Current terms include *cybersex* (but not *cybercafe*), *dot-com, downsize*, HTML, and SUV. A ready-reference section at the end of the volume has an odd assortment of items—usage and punctuation guides, the Constitution, weights and measures, heat index and windchill temperatures, selected proverbs, and members of the Baseball, Basketball, Pro Football, and Rock and Roll Halls of Fame.

This dictionary shouldn't be confused with other dictionaries that Oxford has published recently—*The Oxford American Desk Dictionary* (1998), *The Oxford American Dictionary of Current English* (1999), *The Oxford American Dictionary and Language Guide* (1999), or *The Oxford Dictionary of American Usage and Style* (2000). To choose between NOAD and the fourth edition of the *American Heritage Dictionary* is difficult. The *American Heritage Dictionary* is aesthetically more pleasing, with color photos and maps in the margin. But NOAD, with the OED database behind it, provides a well-researched and current source of definitions of U.S. English and is $10 cheaper. For all high-school, academic, and public libraries.

Encyclopedia of Literary Translation into English. 2v. Ed. by Olive Classe. 2000. 1,714p. bibliogs. indexes. Fitzroy Dearborn, $285 (1-884964-36-2). 428.

"A rose is a rose is a rose"—unless, of course, it is a rose (or even some other flower) in another language. That oversimplifies but also typifies the problem facing translators striving to remain faithful to the spirit of the original while at the same time presenting its particulars with accuracy. This very specialized encyclopedia's 600 articles probe that problem as played out in translations from significant languages into English and in the translations of works of individual authors whose creations have been translated into English.

Nearly every reader of a literary work translated into English reads with the disadvantage of not being able to judge the fidelity of the translation. The encyclopedia helps those dependent upon translations to make that assessment. Its articles on Georges Bernanos, Cicero, Gustave Flaubert, Homer, Czeslaw Milosz, Aleksandr Pushkin, Shiga Naoya, Jules Verne, and other authors follow a pattern consisting of brief biography, a bibliography of works translated into English, a signed essay, and a bibliography of additional items for "further reading." The essays identify the challenges specific works and authors pose for translators and the quality of the work of the translators who have taken these on. For example, the essay on Homer analyzes the strengths and weaknesses of translations by Chapman, Dryden, Pope, A. T. Murray, Richard Lattimore, Robert Fitzgerald, and others. Just as knowledge of the body of critical literature on a poem, a play, or a novel can add depth to a reader's experience, these essays assessing translations can also add depth to understanding. In the case of works translated multiple times, they can also help readers select the best translation or at least the translation most congenial to their tastes.

Other types of articles cover the work of significant translators (John Dryden, Ezra Pound) or theorists (Matthew Arnold), major topics (*Deconstruction and literary translation, Gender and gender politics in literary translation, Improving on the original*), and various languages. Articles on Arabic, Czech, modern Greek, Hungarian, Norwegian, Russian, etc., describe the ease or difficulty with which English and the other language mesh through literary translation and the challenges inherent in conveying into English meaning originally expressed in the other language. All articles also conclude with unannotated reading lists. The volume closes with title, translator, and general indexes.

Mona Baker's *The Routledge Encyclopedia of Translation Studies* (Routledge, 1998) explores many of the topical areas and examines translation traditions in various languages. However, it does not specifically address the issues involved in translations into English. *Encyclopedia of Literary Translation into English* complements Baker's work and will meet the needs of advanced students of world literature.

Science

Science Reference Center. 2001. Marshall Cavendish, pricing from $595. [http://www.marshallcavendish.com].

Created in partnership with EBSCO, *Science Reference Center* is the online version of three print titles: *Encyclopedia of Earth and Physical Sciences* (1998), *Encyclopedia of Life Sciences* (1996), and *Encyclopedia of Technology and Applied Sciences* (2000). Each title constitutes a separate database, and libraries many subscribe to one, two, or (for $995) all three. Currently, there is no searching across databases. Overall, *Science Reference Center* contains 1,200 articles, more than 7,500 magazine and newspaper articles, 650 images, and links to 350 Web sites.

Searching is by category (such as Botany, Chemistry, or Energy and Resources) and subcategory, keyword, person, and article title. Terms, including Boolean operators, may also be entered in a search box. Among added features are links to Web sites and a note-taking function. A "For Educators" page offers lesson plans and other teacher resources, and a "For Students" page provides links to Web resources. Articles are nicely displayed with all of the sidebars and some of the images found in the print sets. The user can select the article text, citation, sidebars, images, or any combination of these four to print, save, or e-mail. A Related Resources link leads to additional material, which may include magazine articles, newspaper articles, and more images.

Several factors diminish the user-friendly aspects of the databases. Search terms are not highlighted in the text of the articles. The two-step print/save/e-mail feature offers flexibility, but a shortcut for those who want to print (or save or e-mail) everything instead of indicating choices would be helpful. There is no access to Web links from within articles but only via the Weblinks tab, which opens a menu of 14 broad categories under which sites are grouped. It should be noted that Person Search simply links to every occurrence of a person's name, because the three encyclopedias do not contain biographical articles.

The print counterparts of the encyclopedias included in *Science Reference Center* all have as their intended audience students in grades seven and higher and are excellent reference resources for this age group. Compared to the print sets, the electronic versions offer the flexibility of online searching and a rich collection of magazine article; however, there are far fewer illustrations. Links to Web sites are limited. *Science Reference Center* is recommended for public libraries and high schools that do not already own the print sets and have adequate budgets to acquire access for more than one workstation.

UXL Encyclopedia of Science. 10v. 2d ed. Ed. by Ron Nagel. 2002. 2,048p. bibliog. illus. index. maps. UXL, $350 (0-7876-5432-9). 503.

With more than 600 entries—approximately 50 new and 100 updated—this latest edition of a title first published in 1998 provides information on topics in the study of physical, earth, and life sciences as well as the fields of technology, engineering, mathematics, environmental science, and psychology. Each volume begins with a cumulative table of contents and an alphabetical list of entries categorized by their scientific fields and ends with a listing of books, periodicals, and Web sites and a set index.

Entries vary in length from 250 to 2,500 words. Longer articles are divided by subheadings, adding to clarity. As is common format for UXL publications, extensive cross-referencing directs users to related articles, and sidebars define "Words to Know." Most of the photographs and technical diagrams are in color, a definite improvement over the previous edition's all black-and-white illustrations. Among the new entries are DVD *technology* and *Internet*.

It difficult to find fault with this clearly written resource that uses simple, nontechnical terms to explain scientific concepts at a basic level. Its A–Z format distinguishes it from other multivolume science sets for a similar age group, such as *The New Book of Popular Science* (Grolier, 2000) and *The World Book Encyclopedia of Science* (World Book, 2001), which have a topical arrangement. Visually appealing and user-friendly, UXL *Encyclopedia of Science* is sure to find success with beginning researchers and is recommended for middle-school and junior-high-school students and the libraries that serve them.

Visual Science Encyclopedia. 12v. By Brian Knapp. 2002. illus. index. Grolier, $279 (0-7172-5595-6). 503.

Intended for elementary-and middle-school students, this set consists of thematic volumes such as "Weather," "Elements," "Light and Sound," "Water," "Plants," "Earth and Space," "Computers and the Internet," among others (but no volumes on the human body or on animals). As the title implies, there is an abundance of full-color photographs and diagrams. Within volumes, entries are in an A–Z arrangement, with cross-references to other terms highlighted in boldface. In general, entries are one-or two-sentence definitions of terms, although some topics (*Eye, eyesight*; *Lava*; *Petroleum*) are treated in greater detail. Because of the brevity of most entries, some may argue this set is more a dictionary than an encyclopedia.

Each volume stands alone, with neither a cumulative set index nor cross-references to topics in other volumes. The volume on weather presents a discussion of El Nino along with maps and an illustration. In the volume on water, El Nino is briefly defined in relationship to ocean currents. The two articles do not present the same information—one claims El Nino occurs "about every four years," while the other states it "happens about once every five years."

This is a useful resource for students seeking quick definitions and clear illustrations that help explain terms, but it is weakened by the lack of integration among volumes.

The Nature Yearbook of Science and Technology. Ed. by Declan Butler. 2001. 2,124p. Palgrave, $75 (0-312-23842-8). 505.

This new reference is intended to be an annual, like the publisher's *Statesman's Yearbook*. The text includes articles; facts and figures on science research, top science institutes, and the world's leading scientists; and information on funding, education, annual prizes, and the commercial exploitation of science and technology.

The volume begins with a week-by-week chronology of events for the year. The articles, written by top scientific and political figures and *Nature's* network of correspondents, are specially commissioned and focus on topical issues, such as the sequencing of the human genome, the challenge of fighting lethal diseases in developing countries, and efforts to curb biological, chemical, and nuclear weapons. Scientists will find the sections on international organizations and large scientific facilities useful.

The largest section is the "Country Guide," in which research information is organized by country, with state-by-state coverage for the U.S. For each country there is information about the current government, international relations, economic performance, and government divisions; national agencies (learned societies, regulatory bodies, museums, advisory committees, research institutes, and nongovernmental organizations, etc.); and diplomatic representatives related to science and technology. Contact information, including Web sites and e-mail addresses, is provided for all agencies. Especially for longer entries, making one's way through the "Country Guide" can be a challenge. Guide words at the tops of pages would help, as would a clearer differentiation between one section within an entry and another. The book concludes with notable obituaries, innovative ideas from the "Daedalus" column from *Nature*, and appendixes. There is no index.

This is a useful resource that fills a gap for researchers who want to stay up-to-date on the current major players and trends in the fast-paced field of science.

Groundbreaking Scientific Experiments, Inventions, and Discoveries of the 17th Century. By Michael Windelspecht. 2002. 270p. appendix. bibliogs. glossary. illus. Greenwood, $65 (0-313-31501-9). 509.032.

The scientific method, first widely used in the seventeenth century, created a worldview based less upon observation and belief and more upon experimentation and proof. This established a link between science and technological advancement, forming a foundation for our modern world. This source, the first in the new Groundbreaking Scientific Experiments, Inventions and Discoveries through the Ages series, describes key inventions and discoveries at the beginning of the scientific revolution. The author is a biologist from Appalachian State University. In the preface, series editor Robert E. Krebs states that the audience is middle-school and senior-high-school students, college-level nonscience majors, and adult readers interested in scientific history, but the more appropriate audience is advanced high-school students, college-level nonscience majors, and adult readers. College science majors would find the entries useful but may want more detailed information.

Entries cover concepts in astronomy, biology, geology, chemistry, mathematics, and physical sciences and inventions of tools—such as the telescope or barometer—that helped scientists measure and test their hypotheses. Developments in the seventeenth century are discussed in context, including their origins, usually from ancient Greek science, and in light of modern theories. Cross-references are represented within entries by all capital letters. There is a glossary at the end of the work, and glossary terms are highlighted the first time they are used in an entry. Bibliographies are included, and a complete list of bibliographic references is found at the end of the book.

The history of science is a hot area for publishers of reference books. The *Encyclopedia of the Scientific Revolution: From Copernicus to Newton* (Garland, 2000) and *The Scientific Revolution: An Encyclopedia* (ABC-CLIO, 2001) are two recent titles that come to mind. Comparing the coverage of Galileo illustrates how these encyclopedias complement one another. Because the new Greenwood title is conceptually arranged, there is no entry for Galileo, but there are about five pages on heliocentrism, with bibliographical references, including a translation of Galileo's most significant work. The *Encyclopedia of the Scientific Revolution* has about seven pages on Galileo and nine citations in the bibliography, including a translation of his seminal work. For a less-scholarly audience, *The Scientific Revolution* has three pages on Galileo, with three references in the bibliography.

Newton said, "If I have seen further, it is by standing on the shoulders of giants." *Groundbreaking Scientific Experiments, Inventions, and Discoveries of the 17th Century* documents the work of those giants. Recommended for academic and public libraries.

International Women in Science: A Biographical Dictionary to 1950. Ed. by Catharine M.C. Haines with Helen M. Stevens. 2001. 383p. bibliogs. illus. index. ABC-CLIO, $75 (1-57607-090-5). 509.2.

The focus here is on British women, although the book does include women from Europe, South Africa, China, Japan, Australia, India, and New Zealand. It covers the time period from around 1600 to the present (i.e., those who began their careers in the 1950s). As with other dictionaries of women scientists, *scientist* is broadly defined, encompassing archaeologists, home economists, and scientific illustrators as well as chemists, engineers, and physicians. American women are not included unless they spent a majority of their careers in Great Britain. ABC-CLIO published a complementary volume, *American Women in Science: Colonial Times to 1950*, in 1994.

The 400 or so entries are in alphabetical order by surname and include birth names and nicknames, followed by the woman's area(s) of expertise. Birth and death dates and details of education, employment, and marital status are outlined before the main part of the entry. Fewer than half of the entries include a portrait. The entries average three to five paragraphs, with several taking a page or more. They explain, in as much depth as is appropriate for a dictionary, the work and significance of the woman profiled. The bibliographies attached to each entry reflect extensive use of primary materials. A list of "Women by Profession" facilitates access to the dictionary's content.

Some of the recognizable names included are Charlotte Auerbach, Edith Bulbring, Marie Curie, and Janet Vaughan. One particularly interesting entry is for James Miranda Steuart Barry, 1795–1865, who went to medical school disguised as a man and became a respected military physician. After her death her gender was revealed, and she was stripped of all her military honors.

There are a number of other biographical resources on international women scientists, including *The Biographical Dictionary of Women in Science: Pioneering Lives from Ancient Times to the Mid-Twentieth Century* (Routledge, 2000), which profiles approximately 2,500 women; and *Notable Women Scientists* (Gale, 1999), which covers 485. Even with fewer entries, *International Women in Science* includes a number of women absent from these titles, among them ornithologist Phyllis Barclay-Smith (1903–1980), the first woman to be named a Member of the Order of the British Empire for work in conservation; Lilian Lindsay (1871–1960), the first British woman to be licensed as a dentist; and mathematician Elizabeth Stephansen (1872-1961), the first Norwegian woman to obtain a doctorate. *International Women in Science* is recommended for high-school, public, and academic libraries, although its British emphasis may make it a secondary purchase.

Makers of Science. 5v. Ed. by Derek Gjertsen and Michael Allaby. 2002. glossary. illus. index. Oxford, $140 (0-19-521680-6). 509.2.

A slightly different approach to ordinary biographical information on scientists, this set incorporates the political and social setting as well as the scientific achievements of each scientist. Volumes are arranged chronologically, beginning with Aristotle and ending with Stephen Hawking. In between are biographies of more than 40 European and U.S. scientists "whose discoveries were crucial to the development of science," ranging in length from 8 to 16 pages. The authors, who have written several popular works on science for Oxford and other publishers, know how to keep readers interested. Included in each chapter are sidebars about practical applications of a discovery or other individuals who developed related theories or built on earlier work. For example, the chapter on Fritz Haber includes features on chemical warfare and the history of explosives; the chapter on J. Robert Oppenheimer includes a section on Communism and a short piece on Edward Teller; and the chapter on Edwin Hubble has sidebars on Henrietta Leavitt, George Ellery Hale, and Fred Hoyle as well as on the Hubble Space Telescope.

Scientific principles are clearly explained, often with diagrams. Intriguing personal stories are also woven in—Michael Faraday turned down a knighthood, Richard Leakey left high school at age 17, Alan Turing was questioned by police for homosexuality, Marie Curie became a governess to help support her older sister's medical studies. Photos, quotations, and *see* references provide many appealing hooks and links. Two parallel time lines at the end of each chapter offer scientific and political and cultural context. At the end of the set are an extensive index, a glossary, brief biographies of many other scientists, and suggestions for further reading.

Middle-and high-school students will enjoy using this for reports (and may willingly page through other articles). Science teachers will love the connections made between different inventors' works and how science is relevant to our life today. Recommended as an attractive supplement to other, more comprehensive science biography resources.

The Scientific Revolution: An Encyclopedia. By William E. Burns. 2001. 387p. bibliogs. illus. index. ABC-CLIO, $85 (0-87436-875-8). 509.4.

This encyclopedia covers the advances in science during the fifteenth and sixteenth centuries. Many of us are familiar with the ideas of Copernicus, Descartes, and Galileo, but here we are also introduced to the lesser-known ideas and scientists of the movement known as the Scientific Revolution.

More than 200 entries of one or two pages discuss topics including *Atomism*, *Blood transfusions*, *Humanism*, *Navigation*, *Physics*, *Telescopes*, and *Witchcraft and demonology*. Also discussed are individuals such as Maria Cunitz, who simplified Kepler's theories for working astronomers; and Andreas Vesalius, whose anatomical charts revolutionized the study of the human body. Numerous *see also* references are provided, as are bibliographic citations to works for further research. An assortment of beautiful black-and-white prints and photographs complements the entries. An extensive bibliography adds great value, but the list of Web resources is a token one, listing just seven sites.

A comparable title is *Encyclopedia of the Scientific Revolution: From Copernicus to Newton* (Garland, 2000), which has almost twice the number of entries. Topics that are covered in both encyclopedias are often treated at greater length and in more detail in the Garland volume, and supported by more extensive and scholarly bibliographies. *The Scientific Revolution* is generally more accessible, and has the added bonus of entries on several women not found in the Garland offering. It is recommended for high-school, undergraduate, and large public libraries.

Mathematics. 4v. Ed. by Barry Max Brandenberger Jr. 2002. glossary. illus. index. Macmillan, $375 (0-02-865561-3). 510.

"Like the crest of a peacock so is mathematics at the head
of all knowledge." —Anonymous

This quote helps demonstrate the content, scope, and nature of this encyclopedia. The rich content covers the gamut from *Abacus* to *Zero*. Coverage is given to figures in mathematical history and development such as Galileo, Grace Hopper, and Pythagoras. Careers that rely on mathematics, like air traffic controller, insurance agent, radio disc jockey, and stonemason, have one-half to one-page articles describing how mathematics and a knowledge of it are essential to the profession. Standard mathematical and arithmetical topics are covered as well. The numerous contributors include college and university professors, K–12 teachers, and curriculum specialists.

This work is designed to give users a view of how mathematics functions "in everyday life, as well as its role as a tool for measurement, data analysis, and technological development." The "broader look at mathematics" means that articles are written as simply as possible, and topics one would not ordinarily think of being in a work entitled *Mathematics* (for example, *Cooking, measurement of*; *IMAX technology*; *Quilting*; *Television ratings*) are included.

Because this encyclopedia takes a refreshing, cross-disciplinary approach, it is hard to compare it to existing standard mathematics encyclopedias such as *The Prentice-Hall Encyclopedia of Mathematics* (Prentice-Hall, 1982) or *The VNR Concise Encyclopedia of Mathematics* (2d ed., Van Nostrand Reinhold, 1989), where most pages are full of "pure" mathematical explanation and symbols. Here, articles are arranged alphabetically, and headings, subheadings, and nicely spaced text make the reader more comfortable than seeing a mass of symbols and very little text. Terms are defined in the margins, and in many cases, the bibliography at the end of an article contains Internet resources as well as books.

This work is an excellent complement to the handbook variety of mathematics encyclopedia. It meets its goal of presenting mathematics in a realistic, practical manner and is recommended for school and public libraries. The Library of Congress has assigned to it the subheading of Juvenile Literature, but this should not deter universities from considering it a great addition to an undergraduate collection where many works on this subject do not exist.

Science

The Cambridge Encyclopedia of the Sun. By Kenneth R. Lang. 2001. 280p. appendixes. bibliog. glossary. illus. index. Cambridge, $49.95 (0-521-78093-4). 523.7.

The purpose of this volume is to provide a thorough, up-to-date reference on all aspects of our home star, from basic physical data to detailed concepts. Written by an astronomer and award-winning author of numerous books and articles, the work is intended for both the specialist and the interested layperson. It is written in a clear style with a minimum of equations. Focus boxes provide added information without interrupting the flow of the narrative. Tables of fundamental data complement the text.

Each of the nine chapters addresses a different theme. These themes include physical properties, the magnetic solar atmosphere, solar winds and explosions, solar observations, and the Sun-Earth connection. The volume is well illustrated with figures and photographs in both color and black and white. A 35-page glossary provides definitions of terms and acronyms as well as information on telescopes, satellites, and instruments. A short annotated bibliography and an unannotated directory of Web sites are appended. Indexing is crucial in an encyclopedia that is thematically arranged; fortunately, the index that concludes the volume is quite detailed.

Most astronomy-related reference books provide some basic information on the Sun. This encyclopedia is particularly suited to academic and special libraries with a need for more comprehensive information.

The Great Atlas of the Stars. By Serge Brunier. 2002. 112p. glossary. illus. index. maps. Firefly, $59.95 (1-55209-643-2). 523.8.

A journalist and astrophotographer teamed up to create this stunning photographic guide to 30 of the most prominent and beautiful constellations visible in the Northern Hemisphere. Written for a general audience, the atlas includes familiar constellations such as the Big Dipper, Orion, Pegasus, Cassiopeia, Sagittarius, and Leo.

The strength of the atlas is in the quantity and quality of the photographs. The telescope transforms what appears to the naked eye to be a grouping of a few bright stars into a world of nebulas, star clusters, red giants, and distant galaxies. The large format of the book allows for some magnificent color double-page photographs of celestial objects such as the Milky Way, Orion Nebula, and Andromeda Galaxy. (Because of its large size and soft cover, the atlas needs to be shelved on a flat surface.)

Information provided on each constellation includes its history and features, the main stars or interesting objects, the minimum requirements for viewing, a map, and, most importantly, a full-page detailed color photograph of the constellation and the surrounding area. An unusual and useful feature is the use of transparencies that overlay the photographs and identify the main stars and other celestial objects. Sidebars provide brief, well-written narratives on topics ranging from the big bang theory to supernovas. An index and glossary are included.

Though not as comprehensive as the more scientific *Cambridge Atlas of Astronomy* (1994), this volume is recommended for academic, public, and high-school libraries that need a guide to the night sky.

Physics Matters! 10v. By John O. E. Clark. 2001. bibliog. glossaries. illus. index. Grolier, $309 (0-7172-5509-3). 530.

Remember when you didn't take physics in high school because you thought you weren't smart enough to "get it"? Here is a reference source that aims to make this complex topic accessible to an even younger audience, grades five through ten.

The set consists of 10 volumes covering broad subjects such as "Matter," "Heat," "Sound," and "Electric Current." The dozen or so more-discreet topics within each volume are treated in two to six pages. Half of the page space is text, and the rest is devoted to photographs, illustrations, and captions that explain the text more fully. There may also be biographical sidebars that briefly profile important scientists. The narrative is very clear, avoiding the use of complicated terminology. Scientific terms are defined in the text when they are first used, and there is a glossary of terms unique to each volume. Each volume also includes a set index and at least six volume-specific "student projects" that reference relevant topics discussed in the main text.

This is an excellent set for every school and public library. Though written for the middle-school level, it will be appreciated by a wide range of physics-challenged readers. The illustrations and color photographs are striking and help the user understand how the concepts discussed in the text apply to life situations. The projects are simple, and most won't require adult supervision, though adults will have as much fun with them as kids will.

Encyclopedia of the Atomic Age. Ed. by Rodney P. Carlisle. 2001. 400p. bibliog. illus. index. maps. Facts On File, $70 (0-8160-4029-X). 539.7.

In more than 500 alphabetically arranged main entries averaging less than one page in length, this volume aims to give students and general readers a guide to the "Atomic Age" (1938–1961), with some coverage of important events and persons before and after the target date range. Emphasis is placed on important personalities, political decisions, terminology, controversies, and applications of nuclear power. Examples of entries include E*isenhower, Dwight David*; *German atomic bomb project*; *Low-level waste*; *Potsdam Conference*; and *Tritium*. Many entries explain the status and history of nuclear power in individual countries and identify emerging nuclear powers. Illustrations include captioned black-and-white photographs, maps, and charts. Entries have cross-references and many include suggested reading lists of a few books. Other features are an informative introductory essay, a list of scientific and technical abbreviations, a list of acronyms, a chronology, a bibliography, and a thorough index.

The inclusion of maps and numerous photographs gives this volume an advantage over *Historical Encyclopedia of Atomic Energy* (Greenwood, 2000). *Historical Encyclopedia* extends coverage to the present and has longer suggested reading lists, bibliography, and chronology. Its bibliography is arranged by source type while that of *Encyclopedia of the Atomic Age* is a simple list. *Encyclopedia of the Atomic Age* is the more scholarly of the two, having entries written by authorities in the field. The entries on scientific and technical terms include more technical detail than those in *Historical Encyclopedia of Atomic Energy*.

Encyclopedia of the Atomic Age is easy to use, with entries that are clearly written and understandable for the general reader. It covers the topic thoroughly and is a convenient, one-stop companion for the study of the topic. Recommended for public and academic libraries.

Nature's Building Blocks: An A–Z Guide to the Elements. By John Emsley. 2001. 538p. appendix. bibliog. Oxford, $29.95 (0-19-850341-5). 546.

Written by the author of *The Elements* (3d ed., Oxford, 1999), a data book on chemical elements created for scientists, this work is aimed at a general audience. All of the elements are covered, from actinium to zirconium to an element thought to exist but not yet synthesized (element 119). The alphabetically arranged entries range in length from two (*Actinium*) to nine pages (*Hydrogen*). Elements of atomic number 101 and above are discussed in a single entry for the transfermium elements.

Following brief information on the element's name and pronunciation, each entry is arranged into several sections addressing specific uses or roles. For example, "Food Element" treats the importance of the element in the human diet, and "Element of History" deals with the element's discovery. Also covered are medical, economic, environmental, and chemical aspects. There is even an "Element of Surprise," which highlights some interesting facts. Here and in occasional sidebars we learn that Mozart may have been accidentally poisoned by antimony, cobalt was once used to make invisible ink, silver can be used to sterilize water, mercury was once used to treat syphilis, and Napoleon may have been poisoned by arsenic from the wallpaper at his home on St. Helena.

There are many sources of accurate information on the chemical elements. A distinguishing feature of this work is the inclusion of unusual facts that should appeal to the general reader with little science background. It is recommended for special, public, and academic libraries.

Encyclopedia of Prehistory. By David Lambert and the Diagram Group. 2002. 400p. bibliog. illus. index. maps. Facts On File, $60.50 (0-8160-4547-X). 550.

Although its purpose is to "provide a concise, up-to-date key to the processes that forged our planet, and to the vast array of prehistoric animals, plants, and other organisms" that appeared and vanished, this volume also includes plenty of information about modern plants, animals, and geographic features. Typical Diagram Group charts and illustrations help tie old and new together.

Arrangement is in four sections ("The Evolving Earth," "Evolving Life," "Dinosaurs," and "The First Humans") that offer a chronological presentation. Within these sections, chapters are divided into one-or two-page spreads that address topics such as "How Lakes Form," "Jawless Fishes," "How Primates Began," and "Neanderthal Toolkits." The two-color drawings, charts, and diagrams are well labeled and very good for showing landforms, body parts, and relationships between modern and ancient organisms.

Current evolution and dinosaur theories are presented, often with "probably" and "may have" as qualifiers in the text. The chapter on "Dinosaur Life" states that "much of what we say and show is not proven fact, just plausibly inferred from careful scientific study and research." Specific sources aren't cited, but there are a few references provided at the end of the volume. Also listed are world museums and scientists, although neither listing is detailed or comprehensive. Younger students may the material is challenging reading. An example is this statement on chelonians: "They might be anapsids evolved from pareiasaurs, but molecular studies place them near crocodiles as reptiles that lost their diapsids' skull holes."

With some direction from librarians, users will find this work tremendously valuable, especially for the diagrams and charts. Drawings showing how land is shaped by ice, the difference between the monocot and dicot types of flowering plants, the evolution of the horse, and the like fill page after page. Keeping in mind the reading level, the fact that one-fifth of the pages deal with the ever-popular dinosaurs, and that there's nothing quite comparable, many school and public libraries will want to add this title.

Exploring Earth and Space Science. Ed. by Peter Mavrikis. 11v. 2002. 880p. glossaries. illus. indexes. maps. Marshall Cavendish, $329.95 (0-7614-7219-3). 550.

Another set of attractive but slender science encyclopedias from this publisher. Ten volumes contain only 800 pages of alphabetically arranged topics, and the eleventh volume is an index plus assorted science data. An editorial board of U.S. and British professors has put together an inviting collection of articles, from *Acid and base* to *X ray*, ranging in length from one to four pages. Entries explain major concepts and people involved in the fields of chemistry, earth science, physics, space science, and environment. There are color photos, diagrams, and charts illustrating most concepts, plus "Highlights" boxes to emphasize basic facts. "Look Closer" features provide a little more detail for difficult concepts, and "Check These Out" are links to other related articles.

The set is appropriate for upper-elementary-and middle-school students. High-school students could probably use the concepts but may find the set's appearance too juvenile. Writing is usually clear, and many terms are defined in context (with a short glossary in each volume and a longer one in volume 11). Pronunciation guidance can be inconsistent; pronunciation for *Pangaea*, for example, is given in some articles but not others. Some terminology ("coefficient of static friction," "supertwist nematic LCD") may be confusing. Volume 1 lists articles thematically, so a user sees headings for all of the chemistry or physics articles at once. The last volume is an assortment of lists and concepts ("Places to Go," "Things to Do," "Science Time Line," "The Atomic World"). "Things to Do" lists additional resources, such as books, magazines, and Internet resources; some readers may question the fact that only five magazines and 14 Web sites are included.

Other titles that cover some but not all of the same territory include DK *Space Encyclopedia* (DK, 1999), which has limitations as a research tool because of its very brief text; and *Earth Science for Students* (Macmillan, 1999), which is designed for older students. *Exploring Earth and Space Science* may be useful in school and public libraries where brief, clear, current information is needed.

The Oxford Companion to the Earth. Ed. by Paul L. Hancock and Brian J. Skinner. 2001. 1,174p. appendixes. bibliogs. illus. index. maps. Oxford, $75 (0-19-854039-6). 550.

A "Note to the Reader" states that "A Companion is a special type of reference book," and this one is that on several levels. It is applicable to many libraries and users: a large library's ready-reference shelf, a small library's need to have an economical overview of a discipline in which it has few holdings, and the collections of earth scientists, engineers, and other professionals.

More than 900 entries signed by some 200 scientists cover climatology, geology, geophysics, oceanography, paleontology, and other earth sciences. Although language is somewhat technical, care has been taken to make concepts accessible. Definitions are carefully incorporated into explanations. Graphic analogies and word images are used to explain phenomena. For example, *Folds and folding* uses the analogy of flexing a telephone book to explain flexural slip. Line drawings, black-and-white photographs, charts, and tables occur throughout the volume. There are also 16 pages of color plates. Many of the entries have several suggestions for further reading. Appendixes include geological time scales; data on planets in the solar system; the periodic table; and scientific units and notation, conversion tables, and abbreviations. The volume concludes with a thematic list of entries and an extensive index. The endpapers have eight paleographic maps of Earth showing the movement and configuration of landmasses from the late Proterozoic to modern times.

Synthesizing, single-volume reference resources such as this one are valuable because they provide discipline-specific overviews of information in conditions of exponential information growth. This volume is a good value for its price and is recommended to public and academic libraries.

Atlas of the Evolving Earth. 3v. By Richard T. J. Moody and others. 2001. 432p. glossary. illus. index. maps. Macmillan, $175 (0-02-865387-4). 551.7.

Written at a level accessible to high-school students, this atlas provides a comprehensive survey of the development of Earth and its life-forms from about four billion years ago to the present. The atlas is divided into six chapters that cover the origin and nature of Earth and the beginnings of life and the early Paleozoic, late Paleozoic, Mesozoic, Tertiary, and Quaternary ages. These chapters are subdivided according to geological era. For example, part 5, "The Tertiary," is divided into "The Paleogene" and "The Neogene." Each consists of 20 or more pages of general discussion, followed by one or two two-page features. "The Paleogene" has features on "The Evolution of Mammals" and "The Evolution of Carnivores." Geological and biological developments of each era are presented by means of well-written text, maps, time lines, illustrations, and photographs. Sidebars describe important events and concepts.

The 400 full-color illustrations, photographs, and maps in this atlas are outstanding and should stimulate the interest of the students. A 12-page glossary provides succinct definitions of important terms. A useful feature is the inclusion of the index and glossary for the whole set in each volume.

This set pulls together key concepts on the development of Earth and presents them in a very attractive, interesting manner. It is recommended for high-school and public libraries.

Encyclopedia of Weather and Climate. 2v. By Michael Allaby. 2002. 672p. appendixes. bibliog. illus. index. maps. Facts On File, $150 (0-8160-4071-0). 551.6.

What is the Gaia hypothesis? Who was Cleveland Abbe? Where does the *zonda* blow? With the growing interest in climate changes, weather, and the scientific methods of evaluating these phenomena, there has been a need for a basic reference that is accessible. This book stands out because it is an easy-to-understand, well-put-together text.

Allaby, a British writer of the sciences, covers approximately 3,000 words and phrases in meteorology and climatology. Length of entries varies from a few lines to more than a page for some topics. Among the longest are those for individuals who contributed to the study of weather, including Daniel Bernoulli, Edmund Halley, and John Tyndall. Cross-references are plenty and useful. Under *Cloud classification*, for example, 32 other terms, such as *Accessory cloud*, *Cirrus*, and *Stratus*, are cross-referenced. Those students seeking further information can use the pertinent Web sites that are provided at the ends of some entries. Numerous line drawings and graphs help explain concepts such as the Cromwell Current and the hydrological cycle. Appendixes provide chronologies of weather-related disasters and discoveries.

The Facts On File Dictionary of Weather and Climate (2001) is an equally useful volume with a similar design but with just 2,000 entries. Smaller libraries may opt for this less expensive title, but larger high-school, public, and academic libraries will definitely want the two-volume set. It is designed for an older audience than UXL's *Complete Weather Resource* (1997), *Macmillan Encyclopedia of Weather* [RBB S 15 01], and Grolier's *Weather Watch* (2000) but is less scholarly than Oxford's *Encyclopedia of Weather and Climate* (1997).

The Macmillan Encyclopedia of Weather. Ed. by Paul Stein. 2001. 295p. bibliog. glossary. illus. index. Macmillan, $125 (0-02-865473-0). 551.5.

Edited by the senior meteorologist at the Weather Channel, this title is designed to acquaint readers in grades six through the adult level with important concepts in the field of meteorology. From A*cid rain* to *Zonal flow*, 150 entries are arranged alphabetically and vary in length from two or three paragraphs to almost 10 pages for *Hurricanes* and *Tornadoes*. Most entries are devoted to meteorological terms (*Alberta Clipper*, *Hygrometer*, *Wind chill*), but a handful of individuals, such as Theodore Fujita (he developed the Fujita scale for classifying tornadoes, although his entry neglects to mention this), are also included. The text is readable and does not overwhelm the reader with technical jargon. Each entry concludes with cross-references to other appropriate entries.

The illustrations are superior. The photographs are often dramatic, capturing weather phenomenon such as lightning strikes or cloud formations. Charts and satellite images help demonstrate points in the entries. Reference aids include a glossary with very brief definitions of terms, a bibliography of books published within the last five years, recent periodicals and Web sites, and an index. The index indicates main entries in bold type but does not list illustrations or charts.

This book will be useful for student reports as well as for browsing. UXL's *The Complete Weather Source* (1997) covers some of the same topics in more depth, using a textbook rather than a dictionary approach; and Grolier's colorful 12-volume *Weather Watch* (2000) examines the topic month-by-month; both are aimed at a slightly younger audience. The Macmillan volume is recommended for school and public libraries needing an accessible reference source on the topic.

Biology. 4v. Ed. by Richard Robinson. 2002. bibliogs. glossary. illus. index. Macmillan, $375 (0-02-865551-6). 570.

Part of the Macmillan Science Library series, *Biology* serves students from middle school to the undergraduate level. It provides 432 signed entries on a broad range of topics pertaining to biology, including basic concepts (*Antibody*, *Genetic code*, *Nervous systems*, *Wetlands*); history of the science (*Crick, Francis*; *History of medicine*); related fields (*Agronomist*, *Emergency medical technician*); and issues (*Environmental health*, *Genetic control and development*) as well as topics of interest to young adults, such as smoking, birth control, alcohol, and STDs. Emphasis is on molecular genetics, human physiology, and biodiversity. The articles range in length from a few paragraphs to a few pages. They appear in alphabetical order, and each concludes with *see also* references as well as suggestions for further reading, including Web sites.

Helpful reference tools appear in the front matter of each volume, among them a geologic timescale, a metric conversion table, and diagrams of a typical plant and animal cell. Some 550 words appear in bold type in the text and are defined in the page margins as well as in a glossary. Each of the volumes contains a topic outline and index, and a cumulative index is found in volume 4.

The eye-pleasing layout features many colorful photographs and diagrams that will appeal to casual browsers, and the articles contain more than enough information to meet the needs of students. This informative set is highly recommended and would be a useful addition to a middle-or high-school library as well as a public library.

The Encyclopedia of Life Sciences. [Internet database]. 2001. Nature Publishing, pricing from $1,500 [http://www.els.net]. (Last accessed September 6, 2001).

Nature Publishing Group, which is responsible for the British science journal *Nature*, has joined with Macmillan Online Publishing to produce this Web site, the electronic counterpart of the 20-volume *Encyclopedia of the Life Sciences*, available in November 2001. The encyclopedia covers core subjects including biochemistry, ecology, evolution, genetics, microbiology, plant science, and virology. The online version will include more information, all color illustrations (in the print set only the section of plates in each volume is in color), and multimedia, in addition to being updated more frequently.

This is an incredible reference source with an estimated 30,000 internal links and up to 180,000 index entries. Intended for use by undergraduate and graduate students in the life sciences, scientists, researchers, and librarians, the encyclopedia contains approximately 3,000 specially commissioned, original, peer-reviewed articles written by more than 5,000 contributing scientists and accompanied by 6,000 illustrations The articles are identified as belonging to one of three types. "Introductory" articles are intended for undergraduates and nonspecialists, examples being *Acquired Immune Deficiency Syndrome* (AIDS), *Death and dying*, and *Paleoclimatology*. Among other "Introductory" articles are biographies, a feature not always found in large science encyclopedias. "Secondary" articles are appropriate for advanced undergraduates, graduates, and researchers. The third article type, "Special Essay," covers hot topics and controversial issues. Some examples we found are *Ageing and the brain* and *Scopes Trial and fundamentalism in the United States*. If there is an easy way to access lists of articles grouped under the three types, we did not find it. The encyclopedia's British origins are evident in some spellings (e.g., *paediatric*).

A number of features are available on the home page. The user can read selected daily news stories, access the glossary and links page, and set up and use work groups. What's New provides information on new and forthcoming content and research highlights. Explore ELS introduces the encyclopedia to students and general readers. A Quick Search box is available for simple searches. The more complex Standard and Advanced options enable the user to search by category (Title, Author, Keywords, Free Text, Illustration) and by article type (Any, Introductory, Secondary, or Special Essay) and to combine search terms. Content can also be browsed by article title or by subject. The A–Z Article Browse can be limited by subject area. The Subject Browse is hierarchical. There is also a Contributor Browse, although this option does not seem to be available from the home page. A Reference search limits searches to references and further reading lists.

Results are ranked by relevance but may also be sorted alphabetically by title or author. Citations include author's name and a brief summary, with icons that indicate article type or lead to related articles. Article displays include lists of content and relevant keywords, as well as buttons that link to graphic material, information on how to cite, and PDF versions for downloading. There are also links to related articles, primary literature, and scientific Web sites. The cross-referencing and links are extremely valuable.

The publisher indicates that the online content will be updated monthly and that at least 20 percent of the online content will be updated each year. Despite some sluggishness and a few minor difficulties (we could not access Help, for example), this site is an ambitious collection of information that will be extremely useful to its users. We have not seen the print set, but because it is priced at more than $4,000, the online version should prove to be an economical alternative. The publisher is offering a bundled price for libraries that purchase both.

Dinosaur Encyclopedia. By David Lambert and others. 2001. 376p. glossary. illus. index. DK, $29.95 (0-7894-7935-4). 567.9.

Though designed for ages eight and up, this resource, published in conjunction with the American Museum of Natural History, offers information for fossil hunters and dinosaur fans of all ages. The title is somewhat misleading because the volume covers other prehistoric animals besides dinosaurs.

Arrangement is based on cladistics to make it "easier to understand how different groups of animals evolved from common ancestors." Chapters cover "Fish and Invertebrates," "Amphibians and Reptiles," "Dinosaurs and Birds," and "Mammals and Their Ancestors." Within these chapters are numerous two-page spreads treating more-specific topics, such as *Jawless fish*, *Plated dinosaurs*, and *Early carnivores*. Each spread includes a fact box, a time line for quick identification of the period covered, numerous annotated illustrations, and a paragraph of basic information about the topic. Also included are two-page "realistic restorations" of various prehistoric animals in their natural habitats.

Additional information can also be found in the encyclopedia's reference section. Among the features in this section are a pronunciation guide, a list of famous fossil sites, an explanation of paleontology terms and concepts, a description of fossil-hunting techniques, and short biographies of nearly 100 scientists and paleontologists past and present. Listings of dinosaur displays around the world and dinosaur information on the Internet are useful for those wanting even more information.

A characteristic DK publication, this encyclopedia is attractive and easy to navigate. Dinosaur fans will be drawn to the illustrations and photographs. Public and school libraries will be well served by this title. It makes a good, inexpensive, single-volume complement to more in-depth examinations, such as *Dinosaurs of the World* (Marshall Cavendish, 1999).

World of Genetics. 2v. Ed. by K. Lee Lerner and Brenda Wilmoth Lerner. 2002. 826p. bibliog. illus. index. Gale, $150 (0-7876-4958-9). 576.5.

Featuring simple language geared toward the student, this resource provides information on concepts, theories, and individuals in the field of genetics. It is a part of a series that includes *World of Biology* (1999) and *World of Chemistry* (2000).

The introduction provides a brief but thorough introduction to the history of genetics. Approximately 800 entries are alphabetically arranged from *Adenosine deaminase* (ADA) *deficiency* and *Altman, Sidney* (American molecular biologist) to *Zamecnik, Paul Charles* (American physician and geneticist) and *Zygote*. Articles focus on the impact of genetics on history, ethics, and society. The unsigned articles range in length from a few paragraphs to three pages. Within an article text cross-references are indicated in bold type and each article also concludes with an additional list of cross-references. For the most part the cross-referencing is adequate, although there are a few omissions. For example in the entry for James Watson there is a cross-reference to James Crick, while there is no cross-reference to Watson in the article on Crick. Black-and-white photographs, graphs, and charts are included throughout. The set concludes with a bibliography that includes Web sites, a chronology from prehistory to 2001, and an index.

Researchers looking for information on genetic disorders would be better served by referring to the *Gale Encyclopedia of Genetic Disorders* [RBB Mr 1 02]. Also, while students and the general public will appreciate having all of this easy-to-read information in one collection, much of the biographical data is available in other Gale resources including *Notable Twentieth-Century Scientists* (1995). Unlike the *Encyclopedia of Genetics* (Salem, 1999), there are no lists of suggested readings at the end of each entry for students who require more information. However, the coverage in the Gale volumes is more extensive, with nearly four times the entries. Recommended for college and high-school libraries, and any public library that has a large science collection.

★**World Atlas of Coral Reefs.** By Mark D. Spalding and others. 2001. 424p. bibliog. illus. index. maps. University of California, $45 (0-520-23255-0). 577.7890223.

This unique atlas, written by a team of experts with support from a variety of organizations, summarizes our present knowledge of the geographic distribution and conservation status of coral reefs. It should be of interest to anyone seeking definitive information on one of the most beautiful, biologically diverse ecosystems on the planet.

The outstanding color maps, based on coral reef mapping from the United Nations Environment Programme World Conservation Monitoring Centre, depict major natural features as well as human factors, such as settlements and dive centers. Two hundred color photographs illustrate reefs and reef organisms. Eighty-five photographs of coral reefs taken by NASA astronauts from space provide another perspective.

The atlas is divided into four parts. Part 1 contains general information on coral reefs, such as their diversity and biology and threats to their existence. Also found here is information on reef mapping techniques. Sidebars highlight such topics as the aquarium trade, coral diseases, and astronaut photography of reefs. The other three parts of the volume are arranged geographically and provide a world tour of reefs in "three broad realms": the Atlantic and Eastern Pacific, the Indian Ocean and Southeast Asia, and the Pacific. These parts are divided into chapters (e.g., "Northern Caribbean," "Middle Eastern Seas") accompanied by regional maps. The chapters are subdivided into smaller sections ("Florida and the U.S. Gulf of Mexico," "Northern Red Sea: Egypt, Israel, Jordan"), each with an overview, a map, and data tables. Maps here are more detailed than the regional maps and show the location of rivers, forests, mangroves (important because of their close association with reefs), protected areas, and major population centers, as well as the distribution of coral reefs. One type of data table lists protected areas with coral reefs, along with their designation (e.g., national park, World Heritage site), abbreviation, IUCN (International Union for the Conservation of Nature and Natural Resources) management category, size in square kilometers, and year of designation. The other provides statistical data on human population, reef status and threats, and biodiversity of reef areas. Each chapter ends with a bibliography of scholarly publications and a list of map sources.

Though the text is not overly technical, the atlas requires some work on the part of the reader. The map keys are listed just once, and additional help in interpreting the maps and data tables is buried in the "Technical Notes" section at the end of the volume. There is no glossary to define terms like *hermatypic*. These factors along with the specialized nature of the topic and the scholarly treatment may limit use. However, with its beautiful photographs, excellent maps, and authoritative text, *World Atlas of Coral Reefs* is highly recommended for academic and large public libraries. Because it is so reasonably priced, high-school libraries may also want to consider it.

Encyclopedia of Rainforests. By Diane Jukofsky. 2001. 384p. illus. index. Greenwood, $79.50 (1-57356-259-9). 578.734.

On a topic that often calls forth large, lush books, here is a tightly produced volume teeming with short descriptions, definitions, and facts. Some entries are dictionary-like in their brevity, and others are up to a page long. The volume is divided into five main parts along with a preface and introductory essay accompanied by two maps and a table of the changes in the world's tropical rain forests. The introductory essay is exactly what it should be—an introduction to tropical rain forest locations, occupants, and ecology along with a statement of their value.

The first part, "Tropical Forest Wildlife," is arranged alphabetically by animal class, order, family, and species, while the second part, "Tropical Forest Plants," includes descriptions of 261 plant families and species. "People and Tropical Forests" has brief descriptions of indigenous groups living in rain forests and biographical information on 54 naturalists, explorers, scientists, and activists important to rain forest conservation. "Saving Tropical Rainforests" has 27 entries on issues related to deforestation, from *Agriculture* to *Wildlife research management*.

The last part, "Rainforest Resources," offers more than 50 pages of reference publications, periodicals, videos, and postal and e-mail addresses for government agencies and organizations. The reference publications are grouped to match the organization of the rest of the volume and include URLs if the information is available electronically. The book's organization makes the detailed index imperative. It is only by using the index that one can locate animals and plants by their common names, because they are listed by their scientific names in the text. With a few exceptions, illustrations are confined to a 16-page section of color plates.

The major value of this book is that it collects and organizes some of the significant rain forest species, people, and resources in one volume and then points the way to finding more information. It should be considered by academic and large public libraries. For school libraries, Marshall Cavendish's lavishly illustrated 11-volume *Rain Forests of the World* [RBB Ap 15 02] will have more appeal.

Rain Forests of the World. 11v. 2002. 670p. bibliog. glossary. illus. indexes. maps. Marshall Cavendish, $329.95 (0-7614-7254-1). 578.734.

Rain forests, both tropical and temperate, are home to a vast array of plants, animals, people, and microorganisms. This set presents readers in grades four through eight with information about these topics as well as the issues affecting rain forests, including conservation, deforestation, and tourism.

Approximately 210 entries are arranged alphabetically and range in length from one to six pages. Each entry is color coded into one of five categories: "Rain Forest Types and Characteristics" (*Australia*, *Forest Floor*, *North America*); "Peoples of the Rain Forest" (*Makah people*, *Resettlement*); "Animals" (*Amphibian*, *Owl*); "Plants, Algae, and Microorganisms" (*Bacteria*, *Leaf*, *Rattan*); and "General Topics" (*Clear-cutting*, *Humidity*, *Symbiosis*). Entries longer than one page include a "Key Facts" box accenting points of interest concerning the topic. Many also have "In Focus" boxes providing more detailed information about one particular aspect of the topic. Entries are further enhanced by maps, illustrations, and vivid color photographs, and each ends with a list of related topic headings.

Volume 1 contains an introduction to rain forests and several key terms, as well as a reader's guide and table of contents to the entire set. Every volume has its own table of contents as well as a glossary of terms mentioned in the text and an index. The final volume contains a cumulative glossary and index as well as topic-specific indexes for categories such as birds, mammals, places, and scientific names. Listings of Internet sites, books, organizations, and museums to contact for further research are provided.

This comprehensive encyclopedia is easily accessible and provides a nice introduction to topics not easily found in other sources. An excellent purchase for school and public libraries.

Animal Sciences. 4v. Ed. by Allan B. Cobb. 2002. bibliogs. glossary. illus. index. Macmillan, $375 (0-02-865556-7). 590.3.

This encyclopedia set, part of the Macmillan Science Library series, is designed to accommodate middle-school students through college undergraduates. The work contains approximately 300 signed entries on a variety of topics relating to animal science, including animal development, functions, behavior, ecology, and evolution. The connection between animals and humans is also explored in entries such as *Animal testing*, *Apiculture*, and *Domestic animals*. Also included are biographies of noted scientists who have made "significant contributions" to the field (for example, Henry Walter Bates, Rachel Carson, Gregor Mendel) as well as introductions to career opportunities in the related disciplines. Articles appear in alphabetical order and range in length from several paragraphs to several pages. All are accompanied by *see also* references and further reading suggestions (including Web sites).

Each volume begins with a complete table of contents, a geological time scale, five-and six-kingdom classification comparisons, a phylogenetic tree of life, and a chart of measurements, abbreviations, and conversions. Each concludes with a topic outline, an index (volume 4 contains a cumulative index), and a 600-plus-word glossary.

Articles are clear and well written, and the appealing layout includes many colorful photographs, diagrams, and sidebars. Words highlighted in the text are defined in page margins (in addition to the glossary). This set contains sufficient information to serve the needs of a variety of student users and will appeal to the casual browser as well. Attractive and informative, it is highly recommended and would serve junior-or senior-high-school, general undergraduate, and public libraries well.

Encyclopedia of the World's Zoos. 3v. Ed. by Catharine E. Bell. 2001. 2,000p. appendix. bibliogs. illus. index. Fitzroy Dearborn, $295 (1-57958-174-9). 590.73.

The title is somewhat misleading, as this set is more than just an encyclopedia of zoos. It also covers zoo inhabitants, individuals prominent in zoo administration, and organizations that are directly related to zoos. Of the more than 400 separate entries, 146 represent the most important zoos of the world. Space, time, and project manageability dictated which zoos would be included. Aquariums are not included. There are 90 entries for individual animals and groups of animals. Remaining entries cover such subjects as individuals, legislation that impacts zoos, associations, facilities and exhibits, conservation programs, and a sampling of various institutional structures and jobs within the modern zoo.

A profile of each of the zoos gives detailed information about the facility, its history, location, inhabitants, and educational and research functions. At the end of each zoo entry are such data as address, founding date, number of animals, and attendance, plus, in most instances, the full list of each zoo's directors, with their years of tenures. In many cases, the URL for a Web site is also provided. Each of the entries for animals provides information on natural history and biology, exhibit and collection history, and conservation programs and partnerships.

There are numerous black-and-white photographs of the animals and various depictions of the zoos. Most of these are clear. The lack of color illustrations is a disappointment, as is the fact that some of the historical pictures of the zoos do not have the dates. Most of the entries have a further reading list that includes key resources dating to the late 1990s. There is a comprehensive index in the third volume.

The text is very readable and would be useful to students and the general public. This is a recommended set for public and undergraduate libraries.

International Wildlife Encyclopedia. 22v. 3d ed. 2002. 3,168p. bibliog. glossary. illus. indexes. Marshall Cavendish, $499.95(0-7614-7266-5). 590.

Written by experts, this updated and revised edition of the *International Wildlife Encyclopedia* is aimed at students and general readers. All forms of world wildlife are covered—insects, fish, amphibians, reptiles, birds, and mammals. Although most of the entries deal with individual species, "guidepost" articles, new to this edition, discuss animals such as apes or owls as a group. "Fact file" boxes, color-coded according to whether an animal is a mammal, reptile, and so on, provide a summary of the important characteristics of the animal or group of animals; in addition, a color range map is usually included.

Eye-catching color photographs illustrate each entry and should serve to entice the reader to learn more about the animal. Examples of photographs include an archerfish spitting a stream of water at a spider, a flying squirrel gliding through the air, a close-up of the head of a housefly, and a clouded leopard camouflaged in the forest. The 1,200 well-written articles, ranging from about two to four pages in length, are arranged in alphabetical order by the animal's most common English name. Cross-references help pull related material together; for example, the guidepost article *Owls* is cross-referenced to entries on particular owl species, such as the barn owl and the snowy owl. Also helpful is the comprehensive general index in the last volume of the set. In addition to the general index, there are separate indexes to animal behaviors, places, scientific names, and common names. A glossary and bibliography as well as listings of Internet resources, resources for younger readers, wildlife refuges, and wildlife conservation organizations are provided in the last volume.

This encyclopedia provides a good introduction to the wildlife of the world. The combination of familiar and uncommon species, extensive color illustrations, and informative text should provide material for many school reports. It is particularly recommended for school and public libraries.

Magill's Encyclopedia of Science: Animal Life. 4v. 2d ed. Ed. by Carl W. Hoagstrom. 2002. 1,820p. bibliogs. glossary. illus. index. Salem, $435 (1-58765-019-3). 590.

This encyclopedia set is an update and expansion of the 1991 *Magill's Survey of Science: Life Science* and its 1998 supplement. The scope of the work has been refocused from general life science to a discussion of nonhumans from the kingdom *Animalia*, with an emphasis on animals in nature. Entries on domestic animals also cover their wild relatives (dogs, wolves, and coyotes are discussed under one heading). This edition contains 385 signed entries ranging in length from two to eight pages and is arranged alphabetically. All classifications of the animal kingdom are discussed except humans (although early humans are treated in an evolutionary context). Additional topics cover anatomy (*Muscles in invertebrates*, *Noses*); behavior (*Migration*, *Nocturnal animals*); ecology (*Adaptations and their mechanisms*, *Endangered species*); evolution (*Mutations*, *Phylogeny*); fields of study (*Marine biology*, *Paleontology*); geography and habitats (*Lakes and rivers*, *Savannas*); physiology (*Metamorphosis*, *Osmoregulation*); reproduction and development (*Courtship*, *Offspring care*); and scientific methods (*Breeding programs*, *Veterinary medicine*).

Each entry begins with information on the categories of animal science and fields of study under which the topic falls and a listing of principal terms with brief definitions. Every essay ends with *see also* references and an annotated bibliography for further reference. (Those entries reused from *Magill's Survey of Science* have been updated with recent sources.) Species overviews include fact boxes with classification, habitat, life span, and geographic distribution information. Several biographical entries are included as 500-word sidebars within entries. Disappointing black-and-white photographs accompany some entries. Several are unclear, including the one accompanying *Whale sharks*, where it is difficult to distinguish the shark's outline.

A complete alphabetical list of contents appears in the back of all four volumes, as does a category list. Volume 1 includes a listing of contributors and their affiliations, and volume 4 contains a plethora of highly useful supplementary matter. Examples are a classification table, an evolutionary time line, and a list of 51 scientists, past and present, with brief biographical sketches. A geographical list of animals breaks species down into areas, both land and water. A wonderful animal terminology index lists the male, female, young, and group name of all animal types. Major journals and scientific organizations are also listed with contact information and Web sites, if applicable.

A number of reference works offer A–Z coverage of individual animals but without the more comprehensive animal science perspective. This useful set geared to high-school and undergraduate students would serve junior-or senior-high-school, general undergraduate, and public libraries well.

Medicine, Health, Technology, Management

The Gale Encyclopedia of Cancer: A Guide to Cancer and Its Treatments. 2v. Ed. by Ellen Thackery. 2002. 1,239p. appendixes. illus. index. Gale, $275 (0-7876-5609-7). 616.99.

Every year more than one million people in the U.S. learn that they have cancer. This diagnosis is no longer an automatic death sentence. Research has provided improved diagnostic and treatment methods that lead to cures in many cases. Understanding that cancer is in fact a generic name for many different diseases and learning how it occurs and spreads will help patients make decisions about treatment.

This encyclopedia, compiled by physicians, nurses, pharmacists, and medical writers, provides detailed information about the various kinds of cancer (*Acute myelocytic leukemia, Ovarian cancer*); diagnostic procedures (*Biopsy, Upper GI series*); drugs (*Capecitabine, Marijuana*); treatments (*Colectomy, Bone marrow transplantation*); and scientific concepts (*Cancer biology, Chromosome rearrangements*). The signed, alphabetical entries range in length from one paragraph to several pages. The longer articles have shaded boxes with definitions of key terms and questions to ask the doctor. They also have resource lists. More than 200 illustrations, photographs, and charts augment the text. A set of anatomical diagrams highlighting the organ systems appears in the front of each volume. Three appendixes provide lists of National Cancer Institute–designated Comprehensive Cancer Centers, national support groups, and government agencies and research groups.

Because this encyclopedia focuses on cancer, it provides more detailed information about specific cancers and their treatments, including alternative and complementary therapies, than the *The Gale Encyclopedia of Medicine* (Gale, 2001). Some of the articles on procedures (for example, angiography) are taken from that title. *The Gale Encyclopedia of Cancer* has more color photographs and scanning electron micrographs. It also has information about rare cancers, like choriocarcinoma, that do not appear in most lay cancer resources.

This set emphasizes scientific and clinical information. It does not address practical considerations and quality-of-life issues in detail. *Informed Decisions: The Complete Guide to Cancer Diagnosis, Treatment, and Recovery* (American Cancer Society, 2001) does this, along with providing current basic clinical and scientific information at a fraction of the cost. But consumer health collections and large public libraries with sufficient funds and the need for a comprehensive lay cancer source will want to consider the Gale set.

The Gale Encyclopedia of Nursing and Allied Health. 5v. Ed. by Kristine Krapp. 2002. 2,762p. appendix. illus. index. Gale, $850 (0-7876-4934-1). 610.73.

This new encyclopedia from Gale covers a wide range of subjects related to nursing and the allied health professions. The 850 signed alphabetical entries deal with diseases and disorders (*Alcoholism, Movement disorders*); tests and procedures (*Barium enema, Lithotripsy*); equipment and tools (*Heart-lung machines, Stethoscope*); human biology and body systems (*Cardiovascular system, Cell division*); nursing and allied health professions (*Biomedical engineering, Nurse midwifery*); and current health issues (*Americans with Disabilities Act, Managed care plans*).

The entries are one to six pages long. They include definitions and descriptions along with basic material related to the subject (diagnosis and treatment of diseases, maintenance of equipment, and required education for careers). Definitions of key terms appear in shaded boxes, and black-and-white illustrations augment the text. Resource lists appear at the ends of the articles. An appendix lists allied health and nursing organizations.

Although there is a great deal of useful material here, all of it is readily available in other sources that libraries may own. General medical encyclopedias such as *The Gale Encyclopedia of Medicine* (2d ed., Gale, 2001), the *Encyclopedia of Careers and Vocational Guidance* (11th ed., Ferguson, 2000), *The Encyclopedia of Associations* (Gale, annual), and the *Lippincott Manual of Nursing Practice* (7th ed., Lippincott, 2001) cover much of this subject matter. This high-priced, redundant source is not a necessary purchase.

Magill's Medical Guide. 3v. 2d rev. ed. Ed. by Tracy Irons-Georges. 2002. 2,576p. bibliogs. glossary. illus. index. Salem, $325 (1-58765-003-7). 610.

Magill's Medical Guide has come a long way since it was first published in 1995. At that time, it was marketed for school and public libraries. The current edition still targets that population but goes further in providing a comprehensive general encyclopedia of medical information for all users. Although there are numerous encyclopedias for the professional, and numerous consumer guides that offer brief information, this edition of *Magill's Medical Guide* bridges the gap between the highly technical and the very general.

The 883 entries, written by 265 professionals, cover the major diseases and disorders that affect the human body. This edition contains 39 newly commissioned essays, including *Irritable bowel syndrome* (IBS), *Post-traumatic stress disorder*, and *Trachoma*; completely rewritten essays on topics that have new information, including *Acquired Immunodeficiency Syndrome* (AIDS), *Alzheimer's disease*, and *Creutzfeldt-Jakob disease and mad cow disease*; and expanded informative articles on such topics as *Clinical trials, Club drugs, Gulf War syndrome, Internet medicine*, and *Stem cell research*. In addition, 101 entries were taken from two other Magill publications—*Children's Health* (1999) and *Aging* (2000).

The essays continue to be divided into three types—100-to 350-word brief definitions, 1,000-word medium-length essays, and 2,500-to 3,500-word full essays. Each entry indicates the type of article, the anatomy or bodily system affected, the specialties involved, and a brief definition. The medium-length and full essays include a list of key terms with definitions. Updated bibliographies are provided, with all citations for the full essays containing short annotations.

Magill's Medical Guide is a well-designed encyclopedia with a pleasing layout. It should stand up to heavy use with no difficulty. Aids to making the best use of this guide—including an alphabetical list of contents, entries by specialties and related fields, and entries by anatomy or system affected—are included in each volume. In addition, volume 3 includes a glossary of medical terms, an appendix detailing the training and duties of various health-care providers, a list of medical journals, a general bibliography, a Web site directory, a resources list, and a very comprehensive subject index.

Another resource for the same nonspecialist audience is *The Gale Encyclopedia of Medicine* (2d ed., 2001), with 1,500 entries. Despite its smaller size, *Magill* has entries not found in Gale, such as a series of articles that relate to human anatomy. *Magill's Medical Guide* has become an excellent general medical encyclopedia that is recommended for high-school, public, and academic libraries. It deserves a place on the shelf beside the more technical dictionaries and encyclopedias in medicine.

The Oxford Companion to the Body. Ed. by Colin Blakemore and Sheila Jennett. 2002. 753p. illus. index. Oxford, $65 (0-19-852403-X). 612.
The Oxford Illustrated Companion to Medicine. 3d ed. Ed. by Stephen Lock and others. 2001. 891p. illus. indexes. Oxford, $75 (0-19-262950-6). 610.

Developed by Oxford University Press with the support of the Physiological Society, *The Oxford Companion to the Body* strives to bring "the wonders and excitement of the science of physiology to a broad audience." In addition to science, it includes cultural, historical, and religious perspectives.

The approximately 1,000 alphabetically arranged entries range from short definitions to longer entries that that include contributors' names and recommended readings. Many scholars, mostly from the U.S. and UK, including historians and physiologists, contributed to this guide. Although anatomical systems and physiological functions make up the bulk of the entries, examples of the broad scope of coverage include *Furniture and the body, Hinduism and the body, Lifespan, Mermaid*, and *Tattooing*. Also included are some biographies of noted physicians. There are a few color plates, and plates of the human body follow the index. This is neither a medical guide nor a medical dictionary; rather, it is a summary of the art and science of our bodies.

In the preface of *The Oxford Companion to the Body*, the reader is referred to *The Oxford Illustrated Companion to Medicine* "for more specific reference to medicine in all its aspects." The third edition is very different in arrangement and writing from the second, *The Oxford Medical Companion* (1995). More than 500 articles cover the major diseases and medical specialities, national medical systems, history of medicine, and how medicine intersects with such topics as art. Examples include *Abuse of old people; Cardiology; Cholera; Evidence-based medicine; Holocaust; Japan; Music;* and *Sleep*. The reading level is fairly high, with a strong dose of medical terminology thrown in.

The arrangement is generally alphabetical. Text is supplemented with photos and charts as well as margin notes, most of which are biographical. The numerous sidebars mean that readers will often have to rely upon the topic, disease, people, and general indexes and the extensive cross-references to locate specific information. Bibliographies are not included. In both this volume and in *The Oxford Companion to the Body*, the emphasis in many of the entries is British though the scope is international.

Because it complements standard medical dictionaries, academic, medical, and large public libraries may want to add *The Oxford Illustrated Companion to Medicine* to their collections. Libraries that own the second edition will want to update. Suitable for a wider audience, *The Oxford Companion to the Body* is recommended for academic, medical, and large public libraries.

Encyclopedia of Women's Health Issues. By Kathlyn Gay. 2002. 300p. bibliogs. illus. index. Oryx, $69.95 (1-57356-303-X). 613.

From *Abortion* to *Working women*, Gay's encyclopedia offers some 200 alphabetical entries on contemporary issues that directly impact the health of women who reside in the U.S. and, to a lesser extent, Canada.

The issues presented involve a diverse group of women: African Americans, Latinas, Native Americans, Asians, lesbians, the middle-aged, the elderly, and youngsters. Concise biographies, such as those of Mary Ware Dennett, Maggie Kuhn, and Antonia Novello, outline some of the controversies in the history of women's health. It was Dennett, for example, rather than the much more familiar Margaret Sanger, who was the first person to establish a birth control organization in the U.S.

Informative discussions, clearly written, fill the volume. For example, millions of Americans, primarily females but also males, have been trespassed against through sexual abuse, and entries such as *Child sexual abuse*, *Rape and sexual assault*, and *Sexual harassment* provide related information. Contemporary ethics color the struggle to define the term *person* as evidenced in the entries *Abortion*, *Center for Reproductive Law and Policy*, and *Pregnancy*. Discussions of the price women pay for being outside weight norms may be found in the entries *Dieting and diet drugs*, *Eating disorders*, *Obesity*, and *Weight discrimination*, among others.

Cross-references, charts, graphs, and black-and-white pictures are used where appropriate, and following each entry is a very useful "Further Reading" guide that includes books, periodicals and Web sites. In addition, the encyclopedia provides an extensive bibliography, a selected list of Web sites, and addresses of relevant organizations. A listing of the U.S. Department of Health and Human Services agencies and offices with women's health initiatives and a well-thought-out index round out the volume.

The book's approach is evenhanded, and the reading level should be comfortable for both general adult and teen audiences. With its emphasis on social rather than medical aspects of women's health, it will be a wonderful tool for those moments that every reference librarian faces when an angst-driven student approaches 30 minutes before closing, gasping, "I have a (health/science/current events) report due tomorrow! Help me find something good!"

The Complementary and Alternative Medicine Information Source Book. Ed. by Alan M. Rees. 2001. 229p. bibliog. index. Oryx, $49.95 (1-57356-388-9). 615.5.

Intended as a supplement to Rees' *Consumer Health Information Source Book* [RBB My 1 00], this text provides a thorough listing of resources pertaining to alternative medicine. The topics range from acupuncture to herbal medicine, from reflexology to ayurvedic medicine, all presented in a nonjudgmental manner. The book is divided into 12 sections, beginning with a discussion of Complementary and Alternative Medicine (CAM) terminology and background. Among the sections that follow are a list of contact information for several hundred CAM associations and individual sections rating magazines and newsletters, pamphlet materials, professional literature, CD-ROMs, sources on the Internet, and books. Rees rates the resources based on a list of criteria including authority, credibility, comprehensiveness, readability, ease of use, and identification of further sources of information. There are 350 books rated, and most are current, having been published in the last three years. The "best" sources from all of the formats are compiled in Section 2.

Rees' text is more current and covers more resources and a wider variety of formats than other works, including *Alternative Medicine Resource Guide* (Scarecrow, 1997). This publication is a useful guide both for librarians building a collection and for patrons looking for CAM materials.

The Encyclopedia of Drugs and Alcohol. By Greg Roza. 2001. 199p. bibliogs. illus. index. Franklin Watts, $39 (0-531-11899-1). 615.

For grades six and up, *The Encyclopedia of Drugs and Alcohol* covers more than 250 commonly used and abused legal and illegal drugs—prescription, over-the-counter, and recreational. The origin, history, effects, and uses of drugs are discussed in the concise A–Z format characteristic of encyclopedias. In addition, entries such as *Binge drinking*, *Birth defects*, *Hazing*, and *Sudden sniffing death* describe various dangerous conditions associated with drug abuse. Drug-related terms (*Bong*, *Freebase*, *Homegrown*) are identified.

In each entry, numerous terms are italicized. These are apparently intended to refer the reader to related topics, but in many cases (e.g., *drug recovery*, *freebase cocaine*, *injected*, *psychologically*) they do not match entry headings, which may be confusing. More helpful *see also* references appear in the margins. There are occasional black-and-white photographs, along with several time lines and timetables. Following the entries is a section called "Where to Go for Help," which provides addresses and telephone numbers for such organizations as Al-Anon/Alateen and National Clearinghouse for Alcohol and Drug Information, a wonderful resource for health instructors. Also listed are a handful of hotlines and 12 Web sites, including *prescriptionabuse.org*, *streetdrugs.org*, and *WebMD*. Less useful is the bibliography of just seven titles, including one published in 1972 and two published in the 1980s.

The author states in the introduction that the driving premise behind this source is to assist the youth of the U.S. to make informed decisions about drugs and thus reduce the problems of teenage abuse and misuse. However, the dull-looking design will not catch the eye of the teen or promote casual browsing. Because this is a relatively inexpensive purchase and does present current information and statistics, public and school libraries might consider adding it to their collections to serve as a starting point for curriculum-related assignments.

The Cornell Illustrated Encyclopedia of Health. Ed. by Antonio M. Gotto Jr. 2002. 1,312p. appendix. illus. index. LifeLine, $45 (0-89526-186-3). 616.

General health guides abound. They may take different approaches to their subject, but the one thing they all have in common is size. Most are well over 1,000 pages and weigh as much as 10 pounds!

This newest entry in the well-populated field of home health guides checks in at 1,312 pages. It covers 40 areas of medicine and 3,600 health issues and has 1,200 color illustrations. The alphabetical entries run from a paragraph to several pages in length. Entry headings appear in bold blue type followed by a brief (usually a sentence) definition. Below this the expanded explanation appears. Color-coded boxes cover such things as medical alerts, symptoms, and medical precautions. Resource boxes direct readers to relevant books, Web sites, and organizations; unfortunately, the print in these boxes is very small, giving the appearance of one reference when in fact there are usually several. Illustrations too are small and appear in the margins of the pages, precluding any detail. Entries are cross-referenced to articles that give anatomical or background information as well as related articles. Terms in the index are color coded for easy access to main entries.

The encyclopedia covers terms related to physical and mental health. Some rare disorders and specialized areas of medicine (*Aviation medicine*) are included, as are organizations (AMA) and alternative medical therapies. Emergency medical procedures and first aid are covered in an extensive appendix.

If the article on Parkinson's disease is an example, some entries may raise questions and concerns. The article erroneously states that hand tremor is the first sign of the disease and in discussing possible causes makes an overly generalized statement about use of recreational drugs such as ecstasy and marijuana.

Both the *Mayo Clinic Family Health Book* (2d ed., Morrow, 1996) and the *Johns Hopkins Family Health Book* (HarperCollins, 1999) offer more in-depth coverage of medical topics. In addition they contain sections on medication and elder care as well as full-page medical illustrations. Either of these titles would better fill the need for a comprehensive consumer-health resource.

The Encyclopedia of Depression. 2d ed. By Roberta Roesch. 2001. 278p. appendixes. bibliogs. index. Facts On File, $60.50 (0-8160-4047-8). 616.85.

This title, a revision of the 1991 edition, asks the question, "What's new in depression?" One of the most obvious changes is that some famous personalities who suffer from depression have been replaced. Mozart remains, but Abbie Hoffman is out and Tipper Gore is in. Other new subjects include alternative therapies, new treatments, an online self-test for depression, and the potential benefits of the Human Genome Project. Other than that, not much seems to be new. Some articles have been revised and statistics updated, but most entries are the same as in the earlier edition. This includes references and the bibliography, where most titles date from the mid-1980s. Some of these will be difficult to locate.

The format follows that of other Facts On File Library of Health and

Living titles. Entries range from a short paragraph to essay length. The scope of the book is broad, covering all aspects of depression. Psychological and medical terms coexist with popular terms such as B*aby blues* and B*lahs*. Tests, medications, measurement tools, research, and biological and psychological elements related to depression are covered.

There are cross-references to related articles. Terms that are mentioned in an entry and are also entry headings are in capital letters. Neither of these finding tools is used consistently. There is no cross-reference, for example, from the mention of barbiturates in the entry *Depressants* to the entry B*arbiturates*. The entry *Types of depression* states that there are "various forms and types" but does not list them and does not provide cross-references to entries for B*ipolar affective disorder*, *Dysthymia*, etc.

Six appendixes complete the encyclopedia. Among these are a list of psychiatric drugs, a resource list, and several World Health Organization studies, one of which dates from 1984. Although it was a landmark study, the time lapse weakens its usefulness. The volume concludes with an index.

Serious students and researchers will need more authoritative resources such as *Encyclopedia of Psychology* [RBB Ag 00] or Raymond J. Corsini's *Encyclopedia of Psychology and Behavioral Science* (Wiley, 2000). For the layperson who needs only a definition, this title will suffice.

The Encyclopedia of Fertility and Infertility. By Carol Turkington and Michael M. Alper. 2001. 308p. appendixes. bibliog. glossary. index. Facts On File, $71.50 (0-8160-4154-7). 616.6.

In the past, infertility was not discussed publicly. It was accepted as a condition that could not be corrected. That changed in 1978, when Louise Brown, the first "test tube" baby, was born. Now, new fertility drugs and medical procedures are in the news almost daily.

This A–Z encyclopedia is designed to give basic definitions of the many terms associated with fertility and infertility. Intended for the layperson, the 600 entries range in length from a sentence to several paragraphs.

Entries cover causes, symptoms, and treatments, as well as physical conditions (*Diabetes*, *Endometriosis*) that can affect conception. Medical tests are explained, and procedures are described. Coverage includes the latest research and treatments, such as ganirelix acetate and ultrasound egg retrieval. A useful feature is the indication within an entry that a procedure has been replaced by a newer one. Controversial matters such as gender selection and multifetal reduction are discussed in entries that examine not only physical aspects but also ethical considerations.

Supplemental information includes a topical list of organizations covering specific disorders, sperm banks, and adoption resources. Also provided are lists of hotlines and newsletters, advice on selecting a fertility specialist, and a state-by-state directory of infertility clinics.

The encyclopedia is an ideal quick reference guide and a good starting point for health-information consumers looking for information about a complicated and ever-changing area of medicine. Recommended for public libraries.

The Encyclopedia of Mental Health. 2d ed. By Ada P. Kahn and Jan Fawcett. 2001. 468p. bibliog. index. Facts On File, $71.50 (0-8160-4062-1). 616.89.

This is an updated version of a volume originally published in 1993. As in the first edition, there are more than 1,000 alphabetized entries. Coverage includes symptoms, disorders, treatment descriptions, pharmacology, theories, and contributors to the field of mental health. An extensive bibliography offers hundreds of avenues for further reading on topics ranging from AIDS to yoga. Contact information for helpful organizations is contained in the "Resources" section.

Many entries provide bibliographic references. Most also include cross-references, some of which clarify inappropriate or commonly misunderstood terms, such as S*plit personality*. In addition to specialist terminology, common contemporary words and phraseology abound—examples are B*ullies*, *Change of life*, *Jet lag*, and *Light therapy*. Many entries are new, among them C*limate and mental health*, *Holistic medicine*, *Managed care*, *Post-traumatic stress disorder* (PTSD), *Reflexolog*, and *Viagra* (sildenafil).

Considering that the audience is general readers as well as medical professionals, some entries are curiously missing from the index, for example, *therapist*. The array of professionals available to treat mental illness can be daunting. Under the entry *Psychotherapies*, it is possible to find a very brief discussion of professional differences, but that may not allay confusion for the consumer. Another term that is missing is *rage*, as applied to the condition "road rage." The exclusion of Carl Jung as a discrete entry also is noted.

Despite its limitations, *The Encyclopedia of Mental Health* is a very useful resource and should be considered for purchase in public, high-school, and academic libraries, especially those that do not own the earlier edition. It is less scholarly than the three-volume *Encyclopedia of Mental Health* published by Academic Press in 1998.

The Encyclopedia of Sleep and Sleep Disorders. 2d ed. By Michael J. Thorpy and Jan Yager. 2001. 341p. appendixes. bibliog. index. Facts On File, $66 (0-8160-4089-3). 616.8.

This encyclopedia defines more than 800 terms related to sleep and sleep disorders. Scientific, medical, and commonly recognized terms (*Bedtime*, *Naps*, *Snoring*) are included. Entries range in length from a sentence to several pages and cover a broad spectrum, from best ways to handle bedtime issues with children to how specific diseases impact sleep. There are short entries for significant personalities in the field and entries on the development of sleep disorder medicine, research, and treatment.

Introductory essays on the history of sleep and humans and the relationship of psychology to sleep and associated disorders provide a good background for anyone interested in the subject. Cross-references and the use of small caps to indicate a separate entry make the volume easy to use. The list of associations and organizations is international in scope, and there is an extensive state-by-state directory of American Academy of Sleep Medicine (AASM) sleep centers and laboratories. Complete contact information, including contact names and Web addresses, is provided. Other appendixes cover classification of sleep disorders.

This is the second edition of a work first published in 1990. It has been updated and revised to "reflect the current science and understanding of sleep disorders." There is new information on the advances in the understanding of the pathophysiology of sleep and wakefulness as well as new diagnostic tools and treatment procedures. Revised articles reflect current information in the areas of sleep apnea, insomnia, and narcolepsy. Resource lists and the bibliography have been updated, although only seven titles in the bibliography were published after 1990.

There is enough important new information to warrant considering this edition. The encyclopedia will be useful to upper-level students, especially those in health programs. Public, academic, and medical libraries will certainly want to include it in their collections.

The Gale Encyclopedia of Genetic Disorders. 2v. Ed. by Stacey L. Blachford. 2002. 1,345p. bibliogs. illus. glossary. index. Gale, $275 (0-7876-5612-7). 616.

Current research has heightened interest in genetics. This new encyclopedia compiled by genetic counselors, physicians, and medical writers explains genetic and congenital disorders in lay language. The 400 alphabetically arranged signed entries cover genetic disorders (*Down syndrome*, *Sickle cell disease*), congenital disorders (*Cleft lip and palate*, *Patent ductus arteriosus*), scientific concepts and research (*Chromosome*, *Human Genome Project*), and clinical tests and specialties (*Amniocentesis*, *Genetic counseling*). There are also articles about conditions such as prion diseases, which have a genetic component but can be transmitted between unrelated individuals, and Accutane embryopathy, a combination of birth defects that occurs when a pregnant woman takes the drug Accutane.

The entries are from one to four pages long. They include a definition of the subject, a description of the disorder, genetic profile, demographics, signs and symptoms, diagnosis, treatment and management, and prognosis. Color boxes have definitions of key terms. The articles also have resource lists. Over 200 illustrations, including color photographs and pedigree charts, supplement the text. A symbol guide for the pedigree charts, gene maps, a glossary, a list of organizations, and an index complete the work. There are ample cross-references within the articles.

Although some articles, such as *Tay-Sachs disease*, are virtually unchanged from the first edition of *The Gale Encyclopedia of Medicine* (1999), most of the entries are new or major revisions. The broad scope of the encyclopedia, which covers both common (*Asthma*) and rare (*Simpson-Golabi-Behmel syndrome*) disorders, makes it a very useful resource. The second edition of the Encyclopedia of Genetic Disorders and Birth Defects (Facts On File, 2000) has a nice history of human genetics, but its entries on the disorders are quite short. The Genetic Disorders Sourcebook (2d ed., Omnigraphics, 2000) and the Congenital Disorders Sourcebook (2d ed., Omnigraphics, 2000) cover only the more common disorders.

Families affected by genetic or congenital disorders and students writing reports will find accurate, current information in The Gale Encyclopedia of Genetic Disorders. Public libraries and consumer health collections will find it well worth the price.

Weapons and Warfare. 2v. Ed. by John Powell. 2002. 748p. appendixes. bibliogs. glossary. illus. index. maps. Salem, $185 (1-58765-000-2). 623.4.

Weapons and Warfare strives to achieve an overview of all weapons and their use in warfare from ancient to modern times. Volume 1 covers the period of ancient times to 1500, and volume 2 continues coverage of weapons and strategies up through modern times. Each of the volumes is arranged with the same scheme. Discussions of major weapon groups are followed by sections that survey historical periods and are further divided by geographic region. The total number of topics covered in the two volumes exceeds 100, ranging from 2,000 to 7,000 words.

All weapons-oriented essays are organized into sections that discuss the development and use of each type of weapon. The sections treating regions of the world survey such topics as military organization, strategy, and tactics. The concluding section, "Warfare in the Global Age," includes an essay on terrorism and antiterrorism since 1990, with a very good summary of information current up to the bombing of the USS Cole in October 2000. In addition to the main essays on the weaponry and the context of warfare, volume 1 includes a section entitled "Research Tools" offering brief biographies of significant military theorists, an essay on "Geography and Military Development," a general time line, and an extensive glossary. A bibliography of books and articles is appended to each topical essay. Illustrations appear throughout, and these, as well as maps and time lines, are listed at the beginning of each volume, which makes locating these features very easy. A categorized list of essays is repeated in both volumes. Appendixes, located in volume 2, include an annotated bibliography as well as a listing of Web sites. A complete index to the two volumes is also found in volume 2.

Weapons and Warfare is aimed at college and high-school students, but the set is very accessible for the general audience. The publisher notes that Weapons and Warfare may be used as a supplement to their other volumes on warfare, which include Magill's Guide to Military History [RBB S 1 01] and World Conflicts and Confrontations (2000). The newest title also stands alone and would be a welcome addition to a high-school, public, or academic library's military engineering collection.

The Cambridge Dictionary of Space Technology. By Mark Williamson. 2001. 464p. illus. Cambridge, $39.95 (0-521-66077-7). 629.4.

Written by a space technology consultant, this dictionary is intended for both the specialist and interested layperson. Emphasis is on defining words or phrases rather than providing background information. The approximately 2,300 alphabetically arranged entries are concise and well written, averaging from one sentence to a paragraph in length.

All aspects of space technology are covered. There are terms applying to spacecraft technology (aerobraking, heat sink), communications (background noise, decryption), propulsion (apogee engine, pyrotechnic valve), manned and unmanned spaceflight (Apollo, cosmonaut, Mars Pathfinder), space centers and organizations (Cape Canaveral, Intersputnik), and more. There are no biographies of individuals important to space technology, such as astronauts, physicists, or engineers.

Numerous cross-references guide the user from one entry to another. A few black-and-white line drawings and photographs supplement the text. A "Classified List of Dictionary Entries" groups entries under general headings. There are no references or bibliography. Because there is very little white space between entries and both entry headings and cross-references are printed in the same typeface, it can be hard to distinguish where one entry ends and another begins.

The Cambridge Dictionary of Space Technology is a revised and expanded edition of a dictionary first published by the Institute of Physics Publishing in 1990. It is particularly recommended for special or academic libraries. Because of the Cambridge title's design and fairly technical language, public and high-school libraries might do better with Facts On File's Dictionary of Space Technology (1999).

Distinguished African Americans in Aviation and Space Science. By Betty Kaplan Gubert and others. 2002. 336p. bibliogs. illus. index. Oryx, $59.95 (1-53756-246-7). 629.13.

Every year Black History Month brings the onslaught of requests for biographies of civil rights leaders. Library shelves are quickly depleted, and customers are disappointed when all the material on Martin Luther King Jr., Rosa Parks, and Harriet Tubman is gone. The accomplishments of these figures are indeed significant, but what a shame that so many other lesser-known African Americans who faced similar obstacles with courage and determination go unknown.

In this title, the third in the Distinguished African Americans Series, the biographies of 80 men and 20 women are recorded. The lives cover 80 years of the twentieth century. There is Eugene Bullard, born in 1895, who flew for the French in World War I, and astronaut Robert Curbeam, born in 1962. The women, too, span the century, from Bessie Coleman, the first black woman to earn a pilot's license, to Apprille Ericsson-Jackson, a NASA aerospace engineer born in 1963.

The stories of their lives have been culled from articles, interviews and research. These sources lend a lively "in-the-moment" tone to the narrative and bring the accomplishments of the biographees into sharp focus.

Each entry gives basic biographical information in the form of a brief summary paragraph highlighting the significance of the person's accomplishments. The essay-length biography discusses childhood, education, and career. A list of sources follows each entry, and a bibliography is included at the end of the book. Some entries are accompanied by photographs. The Internet offers numerous links to African American aviation pioneer sites, and it is hoped that these will be included when the book is updated.

Public and school libraries should not hesitate to add this title to their collections and to suggest to young customers that as important as the civil rights figures are, there are other African Americans who have made history.

Encyclopedia of Flight. 3v. Ed. by Tracy Irons-Georges. 2002. 899p. bibliogs. glossary. illus. indexes. maps. Salem, $325 (1-58765-046-0). 629.13.

This set presents an impressively broad range of information on more than 300 scientific and historical topics related to the field of aviation. Attention is given to all categories and types of civil and military aircraft, principles of aerodynamics, and mechanical and technical aspects of flying. Besides conventional topics one would associate with a resource devoted to flight and aviation, some unexpected entries, guaranteed to pique the reader, include Animal flight, Baggage handling and regulations, Bermuda Triangle, Paper airplanes, "Vomit Comet," Whirly-Girls, and Wing-walking. Relevant biographies of pioneers in aviation and profiles of major airlines are incorporated. Information is current through September 2001.

Alphabetically arranged entries—varying in length from several paragraphs to several pages—begin with a brief definition of the topic and its significance to aviation, with dates supplied when applicable. All entries are signed and accompanied by annotated bibliographies and cross-references. Each volume has a list of topics found in that particular volume and two set indexes, one alphabetical and one that groups entries by category. Volume 3 contains a plethora of supplemental information, including a bibliography; a list of Web sites; directories of North American flight schools, training centers, and museums; and lists of international airports, air carriers, and airplane types. Two time lines record events in aviation history and air disasters from 1785 to 2001.

This comprehensive reference source would be a valuable addition to public and academic libraries. High schools might consider it, depending on their curricular needs and budgetary restraints.

Annuals and Biennials. By Roger Phillips and Martyn Rix. 2002. 288p. illus. index. Firefly, paper, $24.95 (1-55297-566-5). 635.9.
Perennials. By Roger Phillips and Martyn Rix. 2002. 480p. bibliog. glossary. illus. index. Firefly, $49.95 (1-55209-641-6); paper, $34.95 (1-55209-639-4). 635.9.

Although these outstanding horticultural works are just appearing in Canada and the U.S., both were published previously in Great Britain—Annuals and Biennials in 1999 and Perennials in 1991 as the two-volume set, Early Perennials and Late Perennials.

Perennials includes about 2,500 plants commonly found in temperate zone gardens but hardy enough to withstand winters without shelter.

Alpine, rock garden, and desert plants and succulents have been omitted. The approximately 1,000 annuals, biennials, and short-lived perennials found in A*nnuals and* B*iennials* reside primarily in temperate to tropical zones throughout the world. The decidedly British tone and references to the Royal Horticultural Society in no way alter the universal scope or content of each title. Both have similar formats, with small type and large, clear photographic layouts. In A*nnuals and* B*iennials* plants are grouped by families, while in P*erennials* they are grouped by families within each season or flowering time (spring, early summer, midsummer, late summer and autumn).

That these books are geared for the more sophisticated gardener is evidenced by the practice of listing all plants by their Latin scientific names (genus and habitat) with occasional use of common names. Country of origin, natural habitat, physical characteristics, and leaf and petal measurements (in metrics) are given for every entry. Photographs have scientific labels. Sketchy but adequate propagation information appears. Horticultural associations, specific gardens to visit, hardiness zone charts, a glossary, a bibliography, and an index complete each book.

Though novices seeking detailed planting and care instructions need more basic guides, experienced horticulturalists will welcome these volumes. Where the earlier British editions are owned, these new ones need not be purchased. Otherwise, they will be an important addition, especially where detailed scientific flora encyclopedias are needed.

★**Encyclopedia of Gardens:** History and Design. 3v. Ed. by Candice A. Shoemaker. 2001. 1,545p. bibliogs. illus. index. Fitzroy Dearborn, $385 (1-57958-173-0). 635.03.

Produced under the auspices of the Chicago Botanic Garden and edited by the former director of the school there, this comprehensive resource provides information on garden history and design. The contributors, the majority of whom are from the U.S. and Great Britain, fulfill the aim of the work, which is to describe and provide analysis of garden-related individuals, places, and topics.

The entries are alphabetically arranged and vary in length from a page to more than 10 pages for the entry U*nited States*. Depending on whether the entry deals with an individual, a place, or a topic, it includes an essay, a biography, a list of works, a chronology, and a bibliography. Examples of individuals who are covered include Joseph Addison, whose writings in T*he Spectator* had an influence on English garden design; Swedish naturalist Carl Linnaeus; and the Olmsteads, father and son landscape architects who made their mark in cities across the U.S. Because garden design is also a profession of women, there are entries for Jocelyn Brown of Australia, Sylvia Crowe of England, and Ellen Shipman of the U.S., to name a few. The editor notes that the volume is Eurocentric, so there are entries for many European countries and cities while other areas of the world are covered in survey articles. However, Japan and China do have separate entries. Examples of topics covered include B*otanical illustration*, L*andscape architecture*, M*odernism*, O*rnamental plant*, P*ests and diseases*, W*ildflower*, and W*eed*.

There is a general bibliography after the list of entries and advisors in the beginning of volume 1. Volumes 2 and 3 also have the list of entries. Notes on and affiliations of the contributors follow the index in volume 3. Access to some of the individuals or places that do not have their own entries is provided through the index. Longwood Gardens in Pennsylvania, for example, does not have an entry but can be found in the index. Seamus Heaney is in the index because a poem written by him is in the poetry entry. Black-and-white photographs and drawings that are interspersed throughout the text are also noted in the index. A number of somewhat fuzzy color plates are inserted in each volume. The encyclopedia is current, with a mention of HGTV in the J*ournalism* entry and a photograph of the FDR Memorial in Washington, D.C., in the U*nited States* article.

This is certainly a definitive source for garden design and history and is appropriate for academic and large public libraries. The recently reissued T*he Oxford Companion to Gardens* (2001) could be a substitute for libraries that cannot afford this three-volume work.

Storey's Horse Lover's Encyclopedia: An English and Western A-to-Z Guide. Ed. by Deborah Burns. 2001. 471p. illus. index. Storey, $37.50 (1-58017-336-5); paper, $24.95 (1-58017-317-9). 636.1.

Written in layman's language, this encyclopedia's A–Z entries offer insight into all aspects of English and Western horsemanship. The editor has done an excellent job of covering equine health issues, care,

riding, tack, and horse breeds. The history and evolution of the horse are discussed, as are such topics as stable design and how to load a horse into a trailer. Fact boxes and numerous line drawings provide useful supplemental information. Short topic-specific glossaries define, for instance, racing terms. There are also useful charts, illustrations of plants poisonous to horses, and stepbystep drawings of how to braid a tail and tie various knots. The horse trivia and horserelated quotations add an interesting and entertaining dimension to the book.

A resource list includes general and breed-specific organizations as well as academic programs with a specialty in equine science. Cross-references lead the reader to related articles. Terms within an article that have a main entry are in bold type. The general index is thorough and uses italics to indicate illustrations and bold type to indicate charts. There is even a separate index to the quotations that appear throughout the book.

One must look elsewhere, such as T*he Horse Encyclopedia* (Firefly, 1998), for color photographs of breeds. T*he Horse Dictionary* (McFarland, 1995) has more terms, and both the I*nternational Encyclopedia of Horse Breeds* (Univ. of Oklahoma, 1995) and T*he Encyclopedia of Horses and Ponies* (Macmillan/Howell, 1995) cover more breeds. Still, S*torey's Horse Lover's Encyclopedia* has a lot going for it. The broad scope and userfriendly design make this a good choice for public libraries of all sizes.

Junior Worldmark Encyclopedia of Foods and Recipes of the World. 4v. Ed. by Karen Hanson. 2002. bibliogs. glossary. illus. index. maps. UXL, $160 (0-7876-5423-X). 641.3.

This approach to world cultures through food could have been a major breakthrough for its intended middle-school audience. It has many of the right ingredients, especially its established Junior Worldmark format, where alphabetized country entries are divided into standard subsections covering geography; history; foods (including those of different culture groups); religious and holiday celebrations; mealtime customs; politics, economics, and nutrition; and both print and Web-based resources for further study.

The 70 articles cover nations and culture groups worldwide and offer more than 700 recipes for both traditional and modern dishes. Introductory material addresses basic safety and health issues, defines cooking terminology and procedures, and lists ingredients, with suggestions on how to locate more exotic goods. Unfortunately, the set has several drawbacks. The most noticeable is the lack of color photographs or graphic enhancement. Murky black-and-white pictures accompany the recipes, creating tableaus that are particularly unappetizing. The photos are so grainy that even shots meant to instruct or demonstrate are useless. The recipes themselves are serviceable but unexciting.

Although there is useful information here about food and dietary customs, it is difficult to discern the practical application for the recipes. Are the volumes meant to be used as cookbooks, because middle-school curriculum often rotates students through electives, including foods preparation classes? Are they meant for the social studies classroom, where cooking facilities are rare? If the majority of students will be preparing the dishes at home, as seems likely, wouldn't a loose-leaf binder with easily reproducible pages have made more sense? Considering the intended audience, other user-friendly enhancements, such as consecutive numbering throughout all four volumes instead of a cumbersome volume-page system, would also have been preferable.

This resource could have been a visually enticing, innovative introduction to different cultures and ethnic groups. Perhaps the publishers will consider serving up something a bit more palatable in future editions.

The New Complete Book of Herbs, Spices, and Condiments: A Nutritional, Medical, and Culinary Guide. 2d ed. By Carol Ann Rinzler. 2001. 422p. appendixes. bibliog. illus. index. Facts On File, $49.95 (0-8160-4152-0); paper, $19.95 (0-8160-4153-9). 641.3.

This new edition of a title first published in 1990 pulls together an unusual group of ingestible substances to explain how they affect the human body. Along with popular healing herbs and food supplements such as e*chinacea* and St. J*ohn's wort*, entries summarize the good and bad effects of such substances as *allspice, coffee, lemon, salsa,* and *soy sauce*. The text concludes with an appendix of herbs, like foxglove, that are used in commercial drugs and a listing of such toxic plants as blue flag and wormwood.

Arrangement is alphabetical by the names used in T*he Complete German Commission E Monographs, Therapeutic Guide to Herbal Medicine*. Each entry provides a summary chart of vital information on the plant or condiment, followed by a profile of the substance as food or drink, a description of the effects on the body, and recommended safe uses. The text offers succinct commentary on the practical worth of each substance—for example, spearmint and chives as insect repellents, sesame as cooking oil, turmeric as a cheap substitute for saffron. Most helpful is information for pregnant and nursing women. The index groups entries under such headings as *appetite stimulants*, *fabric dyes*, and *protein sources*.

The 34 postage-stamp-sized line drawings of such familiar plants as parsley and basil do little to particularize the plants as they appear in nature or to introduce less familiar entries, such as buchu and celandine. Omitted from the text and index are corn starch, a common remedy for prickly heat, and arthritis, one of the most pervasive focuses of alternative healing methods from ancient times to the present.

Other books, such as *The Complete Book of Herbs* (Dorling Kindersley, 1988) and the old faithful handbook *Magic and Medicine of Plants* (Reader's Digest, 1986), are enhanced by color illustrations, history, peripheral commentary, and folklore. Though not as appealing, Rinzler's book is beautifully organized, suitably priced, and more current. Libraries that found the first edition useful will want this update.

For Appearance' Sake: The Historical Encyclopedia of Good Looks, Beauty, and Grooming. By Victoria Sherrow. 2001. 299p. bibliog. illus. index. Oryx, $67.50 (1-57356-204-1). 646.7.

An unusual resource, this overview of cosmetics, treatments, beautiful people, organizations, and social issues concerning appearance zeros in on a definite reference need for the professional, school, college, and public library but falls short of mastering the subject. The work presents a cornucopia of 203 topics as essential as Elizabeth Arden, Mary Kay Ash, and Estee Lauder and as arcane as facial patching, Nefertiti, and Wodaabe, a nomadic group that lives in Niger and gives a great deal of attention to how they look. For anyone anticipating nonstop frivolity, photos of an X ray of bound feet, eye-lift surgery, a South African children's beauty pageant, a beaded coif of a Kenyan woman, and the notorious Draize test on rabbits should broaden expectations.

The author skimmed over much of the field, incorporating Turkish baths, tattoos, Yardley of London, and models Twiggy and Cindy Crawford along with data on color additives, critics of the cosmetics industry, and Madame C. J. Walker, America's first black female millionaire. Notably absent are male fashion-plate Oscar Wilde and numerous Native American contributions. Generous cross-referencing and lists of additional books, periodicals, and Web sites point the way to a fuller study for classroom research as well as personal concerns regarding topics such as hair loss. A "Guide to Selected Topics" lists entries under several broad categories such as "Companies" and "Social Issues." Useful to the researcher is a 16-page bibliography amassing a broad span of resources, including a sprinkling of up-to-the-minute writings on bulimia, makeup, wrinkles, plastic surgery, allergies, and Latino standards of beauty. Indexing is adequate.

The text exhibits a straightforward, nonacademic style but fails at examples and in-depth commentary (for instance, *Suntan* fails to mention any risks associated with tanning booths; *Teeth* fails to name the specific chemicals that are "applied daily for a certain number of days" as current tooth-whitening treatments). Some illustrations, such as a cheesecake shot of Betty Grable's legs, sharpened teeth of a Sarawakan woman, and a late-nineteenth-century Japanese barbershop, are wisely chosen, but a half-page each is wasted on nail painting and Avon products. More damaging to quality are insufficient commentaries on topics such as feminism and the personal appearance messages that provoke binge dieting and anorexia.

Despite these weaknesses, the book should be popular in high-school and public library collections. It provides numerous interesting tidbits of information and covers a topic of perennial interest.

Fine Arts, Decorative Arts, Music

The Artist's Illustrated Encyclopedia. By Phil Metzger. 2001. 512p. bibliog. illus. North Light, $29.99 (1-58180-023-1). 702.

Metzger explains in his introduction that this book is intended to define terms, techniques, and materials but not explain how to use them. His goal is achieved with a dictionary arrangement of definitions supplemented with many illustrations and cross-references. The definitions are limited to how the word applies to art. Emphasis is on contemporary usage, although older usages are sometimes indicated. Where there has been some confusion (as in *Watercolor*), it is noted. Most terms are familiar, but when pronunciation is not obvious, a simple phonetic guide is provided.

Definitions are easy to understand. Although most entries consist of only a few sentences, some, such as *Design*, are longer and more detailed. Cross-references refer the user to related entries. Some brand-name products (*Colour Shapers*, *Liquin*) are defined. Many entries (such as *Air eraser* and *Printing press*) have a picture of the object being defined or small reproductions of artworks that demonstrate the results of using a technique or material. As one might expect in a resource intended for artists, the reproduction quality is superb. Entries are supplemented by occasional boxed information, some brief (e.g., in the entry *Hardboard*, the description of how Masonite came to be developed) and some lengthy, such as the seven-page table of art movements. A bibliography lists books and magazines but no Web sites.

This book will be useful for beginning art students who need to understand the specialized vocabulary of artists. Recommended for public libraries.

Schirmer Encyclopedia of Art. 4v. By Ann Landi. 2002. illus. index. Schirmer, $345 (0-02-865414-5). 703.

Author Landi writes that this introductory work responds to increased interest in the visual arts and in visual culture in general. The set is accessible in an A–Z format and is appropriate for students in middle school through high school, as well as general readers. There are 300 biographies of artists and 100 topical articles that cover eras (*Greek art*, *Mayan art*); movements (*Cubism*, *Surrealism*); and genres (*Photography*, *Stained glass*). Information is supplemented with many interesting sidebar articles. Art terms (*plein air*, *triptych*, *ziggurat*) are defined in the margins of pages where they are used. Cross-references, volume indexes, and a cumulative index make use of the set easy. Color reproductions of artworks are good. The especially strong bibliography of suggested resources, including Web sites, is subdivided by subject.

The set reflects new thinking about art, for example, the amplification of art formerly termed "primitive" and the inclusion of artists and schools outside the Western mainstream. An attempt is made to place art in its historical context, with descriptions of the political, religious, and cultural climate—the article on Mary Cassatt, to take one example, emphasizes restraints on women's freedom that she faced.

This attractive set is recommended for high-school and public libraries. For a similar audience, Oxford's six-volume *Encyclopedia of Artists: From Andrea Del Sarto to Zurburan* [RBB My 1 01] concentrates on Western art, covering 222 artists as well as movements and styles.

A to Z of American Women in the Visual Arts. By Carol Kort and Liz Sonneborn. 2002. 258p. bibliogs. illus. index. Facts On File, $44 (0-8160-4397-3). 704.

The publication in the A to Z of Women series profiles 130 American women artists who work in a variety of visual mediums, among them painting, sculpture, printmaking, graphic arts, photography, architecture, and quilting. Coverage ranges from colonial times to the present and includes a representative collection of artists from different geographical, cultural, and socioeconomic backgrounds.

Each entry is between one and three pages long and begins with a paragraph assessing the artist's impact, then continues with biographical information, including influences on the artist and the evolution of her style. The text also includes descriptions of significant exhibits and assessments by contemporary critics. Each entry concludes with an average of three to five references. Fifty-five of the entries contain a picture of the artist.

"Recommended Sources on American Women in the Visual Arts" follows the last entry and includes periodicals and Web sites as well as books. There are also lists of the artists sorted by medium, artistic style, and year of birth. The volume concludes with a comprehensive index.

The main defect of this book is that there are no pictures of works unless they happen to appear in the artists' photographs. A reader can only try to imagine from the description what the art being discussed looks like or use the book as a jumping-off point to another resource that does include images. Other than that drawback, this is a well-written reference tool that gives a good deal of information in a relatively short space. Fifty-nine of the women in this book are also covered in Delia Gaze's *Dictionary of Women Artists* (Fitzroy Dearborn, 1997), and 39 are in Laurie Collier Hillstrom and Kevin Hillstrom's *Contemporary Women Artists* (St. James, 1999). Libraries that have comprehensive collections on art and artists will probably not need to supplement their holdings with this work. However, high-school, public, and academic libraries that wish to expand their coverage of American women artists in the visual arts will find this a useful addition.

Masters of Traditional Arts. 2v. Ed. by Alan Govenar. 2001. 1010p. bibliog. illus. index. ABC-CLIO, $185 (1-57607-240-1). 704.

The National Endowment for the Arts began the National Heritage Fellowship program in 1982 to recognize outstanding individual artists and different cultural styles. Nominated by the American public and selected by a panel of folklorists, ethnomusicologists, artists, and cultural specialists, fellows are chosen for their contributions to folk arts, mainly music, dance, crafts, and spoken-word traditions.

This set surveys the first 20 years of the National Heritage program by providing information about the lives and careers of the fellowship recipients. More than 250 artists profiled A–Z by name include accordionists, beadworkers, blues guitarists, hula masters, metalsmiths, quilters, saddle makers, santos carvers, singers, and storytellers. A photograph of the recipient and such basic information as craft, ethnic identification, and the artist's place and date of birth introduce individual entries. The entries themselves are short, usually a page or two, and are descriptive and biographical rather than analytical. Except for examples which appear in some artists' portraits, there are no photographs of artworks. Much of the entry material came from the program books created by the staff of the folk and traditional arts program of the NEA. The set includes a selected bibliography, discography, and filmography; a resource list; and a useful index. The index helps the reader locate entries by art form or ethnic heritage.

As an overview of the National Heritage Fellowship program's many folk and traditional art forms, this set will be of particular interest to libraries and teachers specializing in American folklore, cultural arts, and traditions. This set will complement the coverage of the *Museum of American Folk Art Encyclopedia of Twentieth-Century American Folk Art and Artists* (Abbeville, 1990).

Artists: From Michelangelo to Maya Lin. Vols. 3 and 4. By Judy Galens and Mark Swartz. 2002. 737p. bibliogs. glossary. illus. index. UXL, $90 (0-7876-5363-2). 709.

This set both updates and expands the first two volumes, published in 1995, which contain entries on 62 architects, designers, illustrators, painters, and photographers from the Renaissance to the present day. Of the 60 entries in the new volumes, 10 are updated and 50 are new. Among the artists who have been added are Sandro Botticelli, Julia Margaret Cameron, Edgar Degas, Yoko Ono, Norman Rockwell, Jan Vermeer, and Grant Wood.

As is typical with UXL titles, coverage is representative rather than comprehensive. Although the choices of who is profiled and who is overlooked may be questionable, the entries are well written, with sidebars labeled "Masterworks" listing each individual's important works. Entries average seven pages in length, and a brief bibliography of both print and Web sites appears at the end of each. A picture is provided for most artists, often a self-portrait. All artwork is reproduced in black and white; it is unfortunate that no color plates are included.

Problems begin with the subtitle, which implies a chronological arrangement of artists, yet in the text, they appear alphabetically. Several artists that predate Michelangelo are covered. The fact that these two books are labeled volumes 3 and 4 is also confusing because they are not integrated with volumes 1 and 2. This fragmentation between the two sets requires users to refer to the general index or the index of "Artists by Field and Media" in volumes 3 and 4 to locate information scattered throughout the four books.

If additional volumes are being prepared, the publisher might want to consider reissuing all the volumes into a more cohesive work that will be easier for students to use. Most libraries can pass on purchasing this set unless they already possess volumes 1 and 2. For the same young adult audience, Oxford's *Encyclopedia of Artists* [RBB My 1 01] covers 223 individuals in entries that are shorter and less detailed but do offer color reproductions of artwork.

The Oxford Companion to Western Art. By Hugh Brigstocke. 2001. 820p. bibliogs. illus. index. Oxford, $75 (0-19-866203-3). 709.

Intended primarily as "a stimulating point of departure," this successor to Harold Osborne's *Oxford Companion to Art* (1970) features more than 2,600 entries ranging from a few sentences to a few pages on subjects including artists, art terms and techniques, movements and schools, museums, the arts of selected countries, and the art of different places as objects of patronage and collecting. The great majority of entries were newly commissioned to some 160 contributors, while a small number of articles from *The Oxford Companion to Art* have been retained.

Leaving coverage of architecture and non-Western art for other volumes, Brigstocke has focused on Western painting, sculpture, and graphic arts. Significant living artists "whose careers have already taken shape" are included. Many entries are accompanied by a short bibliography. Asterisks within each entry refer readers to separate articles, and cross-references are found between entries. Wherever possible, the present location of works of art is indicated. Several sections of color plates reflect the themes of "the human form and the face, as interpreted from antiquity to the present day." There is an index of artists and other people not given main entries but mentioned in other articles; unfortunately, there is no indexing to the articles on the arts of different countries.

Coverage is selective but balanced. Only three New York City museums (Frick, Metropolitan, and Museum of Modern Art) are given separate entries, but the article *New York: Patronage and collecting* gives nods to a few others as well as to many historically important galleries. The article on Mexican art, while acknowledging the importance of the muralist movement and mentioning many other twentieth-century Mexican artists, does not name the "Three Great" muralists Orozco, Rivera, or Siqueiros; each artist, however, has a main entry. A small number of errors were noted; the most serious was the entry for the Smithsonian Institution, whose heading reads *Washington, Smithsonian Institute* and whose founder is twice identified as "James Smithsonian" (should be "Smithson").

The Oxford Companion to Western Art is highly recommended for academic, public, and high-school libraries. Because *The Oxford Companion to Art* covers architecture and non-Western art, it should be retained.

Encyclopedia of Architectural and Engineering Feats. By Donald Langmead and Christine Garnaut. 2001. 372p. bibliogs. glossary. illus. index. ABC-CLIO, $99 (1-57607-112-X); E-book, $110 (1-57607-569-9). 721.

History is full of great buildings and structures. Each age and society has harnessed existing technologies and developed new ones to meet the human imperative to build.

The *Encyclopedia of Architectural and Engineering Feats* presents information about 200 significant structures from antiquity to the present. Items selected for inclusion are not necessarily the largest, but the authors state in the preface that they "have sought to identify those achievements that demonstrate discovery, creativity and innovation." Architecturally significant structures such as cathedrals, dams, train stations, and ancient stone works are included. The data presented are very up to date, including an entry on the building and destruction of the World Trade Center.

Entries contain a page or two describing the historical context, architectural elements, materials used, significance, and, where relevant, recent uses and preservation schemes, followed by a brief list of further readings. Approximately half of the entries are accompanied by black-and-white photos. There are some inconsistencies with cross-references. For example, the entry for Hagia Sofia in Istanbul, Turkey, refers the reader to an entry on the Sultan Ahmet Mosque in the same city. However, the entry on the Sultan Ahmet Mosque refers the reader to the Dome of the Rock in Jerusalem and the Masjed-e-Shah (Royal Mosque) in Isfahan, Iran, but not to Hagia Sofia.

This source is well suited to engineering and architectural students but will also appeal to general readers who may want information about worldwide structures. Emphasizing "biggest," "tallest," and so forth, *The Reference Guide to Famous Engineering Landmarks of the World* (Oryx, 1997) covers many more structures, though entries are generally shorter. The *Encyclopedia of Architectural and Engineering Feats* will be very useful in the reference collection and is highly recommended for engineering and architecture collections.

Fine Arts, Decorative Arts, Music

The Illustrator in America, 1860–2000. By Walt Reed. 2001. 452p. bibliog. illus. index. Watson-Guptill, $50 (0-8230-2523-3). 741.6.

This is the third edition of this standard art reference work, and coverage has been expanded and enhanced. The first edition (1964) covered 1900 to 1960; the second (1984) covered a century, 1880 to 1980. This version goes back to the Civil War and continues into the twenty-first century. The basic format remains the same. The history of American illustration is outlined decade by decade through a series of biographical essays on noteworthy artists accompanied by representative illustrations. The essays range in length from a couple of paragraphs to a couple of pages. The author packs a great deal of information into the brief entries: training, influences, life circumstances, career highlights, notable works, and lasting contributions or influences to the field. The illustrations have been well chosen and are crisply reproduced in a full-color process. One innovation in this latest offering is that now all of the reproductions are in color. As a result, almost all artists are represented by works new to this edition.

Entries chronicle the achievements of more than 450 artists, among them printmakers Currier and Ives; caricaturist Al Hirschfeld; Kewpie creator Rose O'Neill; graphic novelist Art Spiegelman; book illustrator Chris Van Allsberg; and Alberto Vargas, known for his pinup girls. A time line provides an overview of major artistic influences. A selected bibliography of print sources and an index of artists complete the work. There are no sources cited for individual entries because, as explained in the introduction, "the information is an amalgam from many sources," including questionnaires, reference works, and periodicals.

This new edition will be welcomed by collections that support an art curriculum. Those libraries that own the first two editions will want to update because of the expanded chronological coverage, the use of color throughout, the introduction of new art reproductions, and the addition of new artists to every decade. The vivid illustrations and historical arrangement make for delightful browsing. Recommended for secondary, academic, and public libraries.

Terror Television: American Series, 1970–1999. By John Kenneth Muir. 2001. 685p. appendixes. bibliog. index. McFarland, $75(0-7864-0890-1). 741.45.

With the popularity of *The X-Files* and horror movies, producing a reference work on television series featuring terror is a timely effort. Not only do genre aficionados want to compare productions, but social anthropologists and the mass media may find this information revealing.

Muir writes reference works on television regularly for McFarland. This volume has the same format as his other television series works and shows his thorough research and expertise. He begins his coverage with *Rod Serling's Night Gallery*, which debuted in 1970, because the program "was the first prime-time, color network TV series devoted exclusively to macabre tales." Muir also notes that special effects and sophisticated makeup reached a higher level with the opening of *Planet of the Apes* in 1968. Coverage is limited to "live" productions aimed at adult audiences, so cartoon series are not treated.

The volume is divided into three parts: the series themselves (comprising about 85 percent of the work), series similar to the genre, and a number of appendixes providing the author's own classifications of terror elements. An adequate index refers to key people and titles.

In part 1, each of the 40 series is arranged chronologically and allocated from 3 pages (for a show that lasted only a couple of episodes) to more than 40 pages (for *The X-Files*); entries average about 20 pages. Each entry begins with a few quotes from critics, then explains the series format, traces the program's history, provides a critical commentary reflecting the author's personal point of view, and finishes with a listing of each episode (writer, director, airdate, guest cast, and short plot summary). History and critique overlap somewhat because the author tends to editorialize about each series' rise and fall. The reader can tell that Muir is well versed in his subject, but a greater variety of opinions would have been welcomed; in general, he waxes enthusiastic about most efforts. The tone is factual yet personal and clearly shows the author's perspective (e.g., "The first complaint came from the moral watchdogs, those despicable people who make a living telling other viewers what they should or should not watch.")

Part 2 briefly covers other television series that touch upon terror. Most are grouped under "Anthologies" such as *The Outer Limits*. Among other groupings are "'Man-on-the-Run' Series" (*Nowhere Man*) and "Horror Lite" (*The Munsters Today*). This section is rather limited.

Part 3 is, frankly, fun. Muir lists his favorite (*The X-Files* being the natural pick) and his least favorite terror series. Probably the most insightful appendix is a list of 50 common concepts in terror TV (*astral projection*, *dreams*, *vampires*, etc.), with a list of illustrative episodes. Another appendix lists "sups" (supporting actors) who appear in several series. The usual McFarland reference format holds: two columns, no illustrations, dense text.

Coverage is sound, and the author's dedication to the genre is sincere and informed. For larger collections with a readership in this area, the volume provides useful information.

The Oxford Companion to J. M. W. Turner. Ed. by Evelyn Joll and others. 2001. 478p. bibliog. illus. Oxford, $95 (0-19-860025-9). 759.2.

What could be more British than an Oxford Companion to J. M. W. Turner? This solid handbook is as densely packed with articles about Turner's art and life as a proper plum pudding is stuffed with raisins. Turner (1775–1851), considered the greatest British painter, was a prolific artist and a private person. Page after double-columned page discusses nearly every aspect of Turner's work, from media and techniques to working practices, exhibited and unexhibited watercolors and oils, subject matter, and more. Turner's life, too, is examined in articles on his family, travels, interests, friends, and so on. Many of the signed entries are actually essays rather than brief paragraphs, and that is what makes this book useful for more than just quick reference.

All the alphabetically arranged entries are connected by a thorough system of cross-references. There is also a classified contents list at the front of the book that sets out the topics addressed in a well-organized array. What would an art reference book be without illustrations? The center of this work serves up 32 full-color plates reproducing some of Turner's finest watercolors and oils. A sizable bibliography with entries representing work by more than a few of the editors and contributors is appended, as is a list of public collections with works by Turner (with galleries and museums cross-referenced to the A–Z entries).

There is one other noteworthy feature: a chronology in which events in Turner's life; developments in painting, architecture, music and literature; and other events in Britain and abroad are listed side by side. A quick look at the chronology shows that Turner's career flourished in the same time period as the Romantic movement that engendered Wordsworth, Byron, and Blake as well as revolution on both sides of the Atlantic. The singular subject of this book makes it most appropriate for fine arts and large reference collections; however, any collection serving anglophiles and art lovers should also considering adding it.

Photographers and Filmmakers. 2001. 452p. bibliog. glossary. illus. index. Macmillan, $80 (0-02-865635-0). 770.

This latest offering from the Macmillan Profiles series considers 125 film animators, movie directors, photographers, and video artists. Aimed at middle-and high-school students, the collection features alphabetically arranged articles incorporating sidebars, inserts, time lines, pull quotes, definitions, and a glossary. An international roster of artists represents a variety of specializations that chronicle technical developments. Subjects range from Joseph-Nicephore Niepce, who launched his photographic experiments in 1793, to Japanese animator Hayao Miyazaki, of Princess Mononoke fame. Also included are Annie Leibovitz, who began her involvement with *Rolling Stone* in 1970, and Carrie Mae Weems, whose photo documentaries are currently on display in the Museum of Modern Art. Numerous American film directors are represented, as are such international luminaries as Jane Campion, Akira Kurosawa, and Satyajit Ray.

As in other Profiles, some of the entries (32 out of 125) have been adapted from other sources. This process has resulted in occasional unevenness. The entry on Woody Allen, taken from 100 *Years of American Film* (Macmillan, 1999), consists of little more than a chronological listing of his films sandwiched in between brief introductory and concluding paragraphs. Entries written specifically for this publication, such as the piece on Diane Arbus, tend to be more reflective.

Overall the articles are accessible and insightful. Boxed inserts complement the text (information on Ed Wood accompanies the article on Tim Burton; the Sundance Film Festival is mentioned in conjunction with the Coen Brothers, etc.). The "Additional Resources" section lists general film and photography sources including books, periodical articles, video recordings, and Web sites, as well as bibliographies specific to each artist.

Of special interest to collections that support a film curriculum, this

Music Since 1900. 6th ed. Ed. by Laura Kuhn. 2001. 1174p. glossary. index. Schirmer, $175 (0-02-864787-4). 780.

For the latest edition of *Music Since* 1900, editor Laura Kuhn has taken over the reins from eminent musicologist Nicolas Slonimsky, who died in 1995, just a year after the fifth edition of this work was published. The book is now in a larger format, which allows more content to fit into fewer pages. As with earlier editions, the main text is called the "Descriptive Chronology," with events such as deaths, performances and productions of importance (usually debuts of new works), music-publishing milestones, and more, arranged by date. New to this edition are more than 1,500 entries from January 1, 1992 (the first performance of a Jonathan Lloyd composition), through December 14, 2000 (the start of a three-day festival celebrating Messiaen).

Each entry notes relevant data (e.g., performer or composer name, title and type of work, place of performance, cause and place of performer's or composer's death, festival program listings) in a single sentence. The scope is international, with a primary focus on music in the classical realm. Although there are inevitable omissions (e.g., guitarist and composer Celedonio Romero's death in 1996), the breadth of coverage is impressive, and the opinionated writing makes for interesting browsing. The entire, lengthy text of the 1985 Senate hearing on record labeling, including the testimony of the late Frank Zappa, has been added to the "Letters and Documents" section. A "Dictionary of Terms" yields a few surprises along with more serious stuff, such as a little essay on a sleep disorder that notes "symphony concerts are notoriously conducive to narcolepsy." A detailed index to proper names and musical terms is included.

Libraries with older editions will want this update.

American Musical Traditions. 5v. Ed. by Jeff Todd Titon and Bob Carlin. 2001. 1,064p. bibliogs. glossary. illus. index. Schirmer, $450 (0-02-864624-X). 781.62.

Imagine that you have the entire Smithsonian Folkways Recordings collection in the jukebox and further imagine that sitting around you in the pub are the people who wrote the liner notes, all in a talkative mood, explaining the history, context, and instruments as you listen to the music. A*merican Musical Traditions* may be the closest you will get to that experience.

This is not a traditional A–Z encyclopedia of music but rather a collection of more than 100 essays that was conceived to "reflect recent research by folklorists and ethnomusicologists on the one hand, and the holdings of the Smithsonian Institution's Center for Folklore and Cultural Heritage on the other." These essays are not aimed only at the music scholar but at all who would like to enjoy a deeper understanding of U.S. musical heritage. The Folkways catalog number is included in selected essays, allowing the reader to access samples of the music on the Smithsonian's Web site.

Native American music is the subject of volume 1, with volume 2 covering African American music, volume 3 the music of the British Isles, volume 4 European American music, and volume 5 Latino American and Asian American music. The editors have "selected representative communities and musical genres to give an idea of the range of traditional music in the United States." Essays titled "Caribbean Percussion Traditions in Miami"; "Diwali in Seattle: The Joyous Traditions Continue"; and "The Gandy Dancer Speaks: Voices from Southern Black Railroad Gangs" give an idea of the set's coverage. The opening introduction is repeated in each volume, as are the table of contents and the indexes to all five volumes. At the beginning of each essay is a short biographical paragraph about the author. At the end of each essay are a bibliography and occasionally a discography and videography. There is an additional bibliography at the end of each volume. Throughout the text, some words are in bold type, with definitions provided in a glossary at the end of each volume for words in that volume. Colorful maps and historic photographs add to the richness of the set.

This work is not for an audience looking for two pages on Celtic music, but it is for libraries with strong music collections or that want to provide a source of unique information for traditional or folk musicians in their communities. Though there is overlap with the more scholarly and comprehensive "United States and Canada" volume of *The Garland Encyclopedia of World Music* (1994), *American Musical Traditions* treats some topics in greater detail, and students may find it more accessible. Just be sure to have an Internet connection nearby with headphones so that users can listen to the Folkways samples.

★**The New Grove Dictionary of Jazz.** 3v. 2d ed. Ed. by Barry Kernfeld. 2002. 1,159p. appendixes. bibliogs. illus. Grove's, $550 (1-56159-284-6). 781.65.

The second edition of *The New Grove Dictionary of Jazz* is finally here. Originally published in 1988 by Grove as a two-volume set (and reprinted in 1994 by St. Martin's Press in a more economical single volume), this revision encompasses three volumes. Although some reviewers quibbled over the exclusion of their pet journeyman jazz musicians in the first edition, everyone recognized the publication as the reigning authority in the world of jazz scholarship. With the new edition, the work supersedes itself as a landmark. Included are more than 2,700 new entries (1,500 of them biographical) and revisions to most preexisting entries.

The signed entries, written by jazz scholars worldwide, vary in length from a paragraph to several pages. The organization and scope are the same as in the previous edition: entries are arranged alphabetically and cover individual musicians, bands, concepts, styles, terms, instruments, record labels or companies, and institutions. Each entry ends with chronological lists of selected recordings (where applicable), a bibliography of selected books and articles, and, for the first time, Internet sites. New to this edition are lists of selected jazz films or videos in which artist(s) can be seen either performing or being interviewed. In the back of volume 3 there is a cumulative bibliography, "more than twice the size it was previously," listing reference and general books, discographies, and periodicals. A new calendar of jazz births and deaths is also appended. There is still no index, but there are cross-references throughout. A small number of black-and-white photographs has been added.

The New Grove Dictionary of Jazz is now the most up-to-date source for information on contemporary jazz musicians, outshining its closest competitor, *The Oxford Companion to Jazz* (Oxford, 2000). The latter only mentions selected contemporary musicians in its topical survey essays. Although the Oxford book offers surprisingly broad coverage of jazz outside of the U.S., *New Grove* offers expanded coverage of other countries and regions, particularly Japan, South Africa, and the Caribbean. There are updated lists of the major jazz festivals and jazz venues worldwide (with their own internal indexes) and an updated section on worldwide library and archive collections related to jazz. Newly added topics include *Dance*, *Poetry*, and *Women*, and styles resulting in the intersection of jazz with other genres, such as *Acid jazz* and *Smooth jazz*. A new section, "Cultural Meanings of Jazz in Film," was added to *Films*. The new biographies are mostly of musicians who have become prominent during the 1980s and 1990s, along with a few, such as Peggy Lee, excluded from the last edition. Some of the new musician entries include drummer Brian Blade, violinist Regina Carter, free jazz sax players Paul Dunmall and Jemeel Moondoc, eclectic band leader Ken Vandermark, and pianist Kenny Werner, to name just a few. Readers will be hard-pressed to think of excluded artists this time around.

The revised edition of *The New Grove Dictionary of Jazz* reaches new heights in jazz scholarship. The price tag is steep, but this set is essential for libraries with patrons studying jazz. Recommended for all libraries with serious music collections and jazz enthusiasts.

American Song: The Complete Companion to Tin Pan Alley Song. Vols. 3 and 4. Ed. Ken Bloom. 2001. 2,023p. indexes. Schirmer, $210 (0-02-865478-1). 782.1.

In the first two volumes of *American Song* (Schirmer, 1996), Bloom covered the musical theater. More than 4,800 shows (e.g., *Oklahoma*!) were arranged alphabetically by title, with information about song titles and writing, production, and cast credits. Volume 2 indexed those entries. Here he covers the people and popular songs of Tin Pan Alley in the broadest sense of that term, for the time period from 1880 to the late twentieth century.

Following a short introduction in volume 3, entries for 164 composers and lyricists (e.g., *Dorothy Fields*, *Henry Mancini*, *Johnny Mercer*) are arranged alphabetically by last name. A brief paragraph provides such facts as birthplace, dates of birth and death, education, career directions, names of collaborators, and "standard" songs—those that are best known. To save needless repetition of credits, there is often a note preceding the song section for those writers who were regular collaborators. For instance, the entry for Lorenz Hart notes: "all music by Richard Rodgers and lyrics by Lorenz Hart unless indicated otherwise." Chronological listings of song titles are divided into separate categories for pop songs and show songs (including stage and film productions). Collaborators' names, if any, are noted next to the song or show title.

Volume 4 contains three indexes. Writers who did not get their own entries but are listed alongside credits in volume 3 are listed in the collaborator index. The song index lists every title alphabetically, with a reference to the writer's name and year the song was written. According to the introduction, more than 54,000 song titles (not counting different songs with the same name) are included. The chronological index, arranged by year, lists every song title for that year in alphabetical order, with a reference to the songwriter.

Although *American Song* is the most comprehensive source for data on songs from the musical theater and Tin Pan Alley, it does not cover many other popular music genres, such as jazz, swing, R & B, country, rock, and folk. Libraries should have Lissauer's *Encyclopedia of Popular Music in America: 1888 to the Present* (Paragon, 1991) on hand to answer questions about any of the 19,000 most popular songs it includes from all these genres. Bloom's *American Song*, with its massive quantities of data within a more limited scope, is a major reference work that will be a standard in any music collection. Libraries with the first two volumes will certainly want to complete their set.

Performing Arts, Recreation

Acting: An International Encyclopedia. By Beth Osnes. 2001. 439p. bibliog. illus. index. ABC-CLIO, $85 (0-87436-795-6); E-book, $95 (1-57607-804-3). 791.

Broad in both geographical and temporal scope, this volume's definition of *acting* includes all forms of public performance rather than the more accepted definition of interpreting written text before an audience. Osnes, a theatrical scholar and practitioner, has gathered a wealth of information from a wide variety of sources.

The 370-plus cross-referenced entries are alphabetically arranged. Each concludes with a list of references, which are repeated in the 32-page bibliography at the end of the book. There is no introduction that could have provided the rationale for the inclusion or exclusion of subjects. Entries cover actors (the Barrymores, Sarah Bernhardt, Marlon Brando, John Wayne); playwrights (Jean Cocteau, Athol Fugard, Sophocles); acting companies (*Abbey Theatre, Group Theater*); conventions and devices (*Clown, Deus ex machina*); movements (*Romanticism, Symbolism*); and dramatic forms (*Kabuki, Spaghetti Western, Vaudeville*). Many entries relate the history of performance in a specific country or region. Puppet theater, the circus, and film and television performance are all included. Most of the coverage is up-to-date, but the entry on Whoopi Goldberg stops at 1992, and Kenneth Branagh's latest listed work is a 1993 film.

Overall, this is not the first source of information about the men and women who appear on stage, but it is a very good source for the context of what they do. Recommended for larger libraries, especially those with active theater collections or that serve theater communities.

A to Z of American Women in the Performing Arts. By Liz Sonneborn. 2002. 264p. bibliogs. illus. index. Facts On File, $44 (0-8160-4398-1). 791.

Facts On File's compendium of biographies of 150 American female performers packs a wealth of data into compact form. Pleasingly presented in clean typeface and illustrated with a sprinkling of photos, the book is easy to use. Choice of entries is multicultural and multinational, including Latina dancer Rita Moreno, Osage ballerina Maria Tallchief, Canadian singer and actress Eva Tanguay, and Chinese American actress Anna May Wong. The selection of entries rightly includes foreign-born women like Ingrid Bergman, Audrey Hepburn, and Elizabeth Taylor who anchored their careers in the U.S. The book considers performing arts broadly, even reaching out to rodeo for famed Wild West shooter Annie Oakley.

The writing style is simple, yet thorough. Introducing each entry are alternate names (e.g., Frances Anne Butler for Fanny Kemble), birth and death dates, and talents (e.g., Moms Mabley is described as "Comic, Actress"). Entries conclude with suggested biographies and periodical interviews and articles as well as recommended recorded performances, such as the video version of *Sophie's Choice*, a screen vehicle for Meryl Streep. Rounding out the text are a two-page list of sources, most composed after 1990; a list of entries by metier; a separate list of entries by birth date, ranging from 1800 to 1969; and a meticulous index by name and subject.

Overall, the balance tilts toward actresses. The author omits some memorable stars, notably orchestral conductor Sarah Caldwell, pioneer TV comics Imogene Coca and Harriet Nelson, lead Mouseketeer Annette Funicello, ballerina Gelsey Kirkland, top USO performer Martha Raye, and Metropolitan Opera stars Rise Stevens and Kathleen Battle, two of many opera greats passed over in favor of popular personalities rather than major talents.

Despite these omissions, the book is an engaging text well suited to junior-high, high-school, and public libraries.

Celebrities in Los Angeles Cemeteries: A Directory. By Allan R. Ellenberger. 2001. 256p. appendixes. bibliog. index. McFarland, $35 (0-7864-0983-5). 791.43.
Resting Places: The Burial Sites of Over 7,000 Famous Persons. By Scott Wilson. 2001. 440p. bibliog. index. McFarland, $85 (0-7864-1014-0). 920.02.

Here are two easy-to-use volumes, prepared to facilitate the search for a famous person's final resting place.

Celebrities in Los Angeles Cemeteries, which concentrates on people in film, is arranged alphabetically by cemetery, from Beth Olam Cemetery of Hollywood to Woodlawn Cemetery, and then by person. Entries include birth and death dates, cause of death if known, headline of the obituary, and location of grave, as well as other details. The volume concludes with several appendixes, including "Miscellaneous and Unusual Grave Sites" and "Sea Burials, Cremations and Donations to Science."

Resting Places covers more than 7,000 persons from political, military, and cultural history, including the notorious and scandalous. Emphasis is on "persons in the arts who are situated on the West and East coasts of the United States and in England and France," but one also finds entries for Eldridge Cleaver, Pocahontas, Richard III, Babe Ruth, Joseph Valachi, and Antonio Vivaldi. Arrangement is alphabetical by person's name, and in many instances entries provide one or two paragraphs of biography. Each entry ends with the place of interment (including grave lot number) or information on how the remains were dispersed. In some cases there are details about grave inscriptions, legends, and regular visitors, such as the unknown person who marks Edgar Allan Poe's birthday by leaving a flower and a bottle of wine at his grave. The volume concludes with a bibliography of resources and an index that interfiles persons and place-names and refers the reader to the numbered entries.

These volumes complement each other. They are not necessary purchases but make for interesting reading and might be useful additions to the trivia collection. A good online source is [http://www.findagrave.com].

The Encyclopedia of Alfred Hitchcock: From Blondes to *Vertigo*. By Tom Leitch. 2002. 416p. bibliog. illus. Facts On File, $60 (0-8160-4386-6); paper, $19.95 (0-8160-4387-6). 791.43.
The Encyclopedia of Stanley Kubrick: From *Day of the Fight* to *Eyes Wide Shut*. By Gene D. Phillips and Rodney Hill. 2002. 424p. bibliog. illus. Facts On File, $60 (0-8160-4388-4); paper, $19.95 (0-8160-4389-2). 791.43.

Facts On File's Great Filmmakers set includes individual volumes on three major directors (Hitchcock, Kubrick, and Orson Welles) as well as the two-volume *Encyclopedia of Filmmakers* (p.2008). Entries in the two volumes reviewed here are arranged alphabetically and cover films and screenplays (e.g., *A Clockwork Orange, North by Northwest*); themes and motifs (*Blondes, Eating and drinking, Film noir, Science fiction*); people (*Lombard, Carole; Hecht, Ben; Kubrick, Christiane; Sellers, Peter*); process (*Suspense vs. surprise, Long takes, Steadicam*); and other important topics (*MacGuffin, HAL-9000*).

Biographical entries in the Kubrick volume focus on the subject's importance and influence on Kubrick's life or works and are especially informative and interesting to read. Those for Hitchcock are generally shorter and more numerous, seemingly covering everyone who ever appeared in or worked on his productions. Both books also include entries for prominent biographers and critics. Each film analysis discusses its significance in the director's oeuvre as well as describing the plot, characters, acting, production details, critical response, and other notable data. Although both books have general bibliographies, reference lists for articles (often extensive) are found only in the volume on

Kubrick. A surprising omission in both titles is a straight filmography, with works in chronological order, though this may be gleaned from the biographical narratives for each director. Cross-references are noted in the text by capitalized words. Attractive black-and-white photos accompany many of the major articles.

Because Hitchcock and Kubrick are among the best, most popular, and most-studied film directors, these authoritative books will get a lot of use in both public and academic libraries.

The Encyclopedia of Filmmakers. 2v. By John C. Tibbetts and James M. Welsh. 2002. 776p. bibliogs. illus. index. Facts On File, $125 (0-8160-4384-1). 791.43.

The title of this new set is a bit misleading, because "filmmaker" is limited in scope to "director." The set contains more than 350 entries on individual directors, arranged alphabetically by surname and generally ranging in length from one to four pages. The geographic and artistic range is expansive; the set attempts to embody a "representative selection of international 20th-century movie directors from across all film genres." Entries are written by film scholars, and the editors and contributors appear to have made selections based on personal preferences as to who they feel is significant.

Each entry gives brief biographical and critical commentary on the director, explaining his or her entry into the film industry, followed by a discussion of key films and major themes. The entry concludes with a list of "Other Films" not discussed in the essay and references from books and periodicals for further reading. More than 80 black-and-white photographs and drawings accompany the material. The encyclopedia concludes with a list of contributors and affiliations, a selected general bibliography, and an index.

As with any project of this nature, complaints are bound to surface over exclusions or inequitable coverage of the directors who are included. This encyclopedia does a laudable job of trying to include cinematic regions that are often neglected, for example, providing an entry on Brazilian director Mario Peixoto and discussion of his classic *Limite* and an entry on the African filmmaker Ousmane Sembene. However, at times the amount of coverage allotted to certain directors seems arbitrary. Established director George Cukor gets less written about him than contemporary indie Allison Anders. And sometimes important films are glossed over—Russian director Tarkovsky's *Solaris* is mentioned only in passing while his *Andrei Rublyov* gets an entire page devoted to it. More consistent in its coverage of directors is the similar-minded volume two of the *International Dictionary of Films and Filmmakers* (St. James, 2000), which also lists more comprehensive bibliographies and has a more erudite tone. Also comparable in aim is *World Film Directors* (H. W. Wilson, 1987–1988), which features longer essays but, despite its title, favors English-speaking countries heavily.

Providing a survey of important directors encompassing a wide range of geographical territory, *The Encyclopedia of Filmmakers* is recommended for public and academic libraries. It complements the *International Dictionary of Films and Filmmakers* and *World Film Directors* with some unique content amid the overlap. Because coverage is uneven, libraries already owning the other titles may not feel the need to add to their holdings.

The Encyclopedia of Science Fiction Movies: From 1897 to the Present. By C. J. Henderson. 2001. 512p. appendixes. bibliog. illus. index. Facts On File, $75 (0-8160-4043-5); paper, $24.95 (0-8160-4567-4). 791.43.

One wonders if the world is in need of yet another science fiction encyclopedia, be it covering film, television, or literature. Yet it is hard to fault this offering from Facts On File. In spite of some rather dubious additions to make the work appeal to the science fiction market (an off-putting introduction by *Star Trek*'s William Shatner and an interview with Frank Herbert discussing the first movie adaptation of *Dune*), it provides a basic overview of the science fiction movie genre.

The main part consists of alphabetically arranged entries for more than 1,300 theatrical-release science fiction movies. Some basic credits are included, as well as the availability of the title on video, DVD, or laser disc. Then follows a synopsis and the author's opinions of the movie's watchability, validity as science fiction, and overall contribution to the genre. There is no standard length, with some entries earning two or three columns depending on their importance. The author, a film critic, makes no apologies for the fact that the opinions are his and his alone.

The work tries to include "as many movies as possible." It opens with an entry on the horrendous *Abbott and Costello Go to Mars* (1953) and closes with Z.P.G. (for zero population growth) (1971). In between are some of the gems of the genre, including *Enemy from Space* (*Quatermass II*) (1957), *Metropolis* (1926), and *This Island Earth* (1954).

The entries are followed by four appendixes, one a useful list of literature adapted to the screen and another of science fiction at the Oscars. The other two, the aforementioned interview and a chart explaining the language created for *Quest for Fire*, add nothing. The book is a worthy addition to science fiction reference, but libraries with tight budgets might want to assess if their collections are already complete enough before purchasing.

The Espionage Filmography: United States Releases, 1898 through 1999. By Paul Mavis. 2001. 462p. bibliog. illus. index. McFarland, paper, $65 (0-7864-0861-8). 791.43.

This volume includes "films that deal with undercover agents of any government, including . . . FBI and CIA agents, postal inspectors, army and Department of Treasury investigators, and other special government agents." Mavis, a freelance writer, begins with an introduction that discusses the power of escapism, the history of spy films, and the reasons they attract an audience. He states, "When a genre character . . . not only makes manifest our secret desires of power and fluidity, but also manages to transcend, subvert and conquer the rules and formalities of our little lives, well, that's why we still have spies up on the screen today."

The 1,760 entries are listed in alphabetical order by film title. Each entry includes the year of release, running time, alternate titles, cast and crew members, and a brief synopsis. Entries conclude with comments from Mavis—statements about the film as a whole (such as "Forgettable" [*Operation Lovebirds*] or "A real find late at night" [*Firestarter*]) as well as commentary on acting, directing, and audience reception upon release. The length of this commentary can range from one or two sentences to one-third of a page. Occasionally, quotes from film reviews are also included. There are more than 60 black-and-white images with accompanying captions interspersed throughout the filmography; these include movie posters and stills.

The author provides a two-page bibliography of works consulted in his research. Two alphabetical indexes provide referencing by film entry number—one lists names of cast members; the other lists crew. The filmography would benefit from a chronological list.

Similar in scope and content to *The Great Spy Pictures* (Scarecrow, 1974) and *The Great Spy Pictures II* (Scarecrow, 1986) but much more up-to-date, *The Espionage Filmography*, although priced a bit high, is recommended for comprehensive academic collections and performing arts or film libraries.

Filmography of American History. By Grant Tracey. 2002. 352p. appendixes. bibliogs. indexes. Greenwood, $55 (0-313-31300-8). 791.43.

This guide to more than 200 films that explore "the relationship between American history and American film" contains 14 chapters that progress from "America before the Civil War" to "Watergate, Political Cynicism, and Hope, 1972–Present." Other landmark events that Tracey uses to provide frames of reference include western expansion, immigration, the two World Wars, civil rights, the cold war, Vietnam, and the counterculture movement of the 1960s. There are appendixes listing multicultural films and woman-centered films as well as a general index and a title index. Focusing on social history rather than selecting only those films that depict historical events, the author includes works such as *It Happened One Night*, *Blackboard Jungle*, *The Hustler*, *The Godfather*, and *Traffic*.

Films are arranged in alphabetical order within each chapter. Each entry provides setting, director, screenplay authors, director of photography, cast, credits, year of production, distributor, running time, and Motion Picture Association of America ratings. Sources for further reading include book chapters, popular and scholarly periodical articles, and Internet sites. Annotations offer a brief plot summary, sometimes interspersed with film dialogue. PBS documentaries such as *Baseball*, *The Way West*, and *The Civil War* are included "in an attempt to correct some of the distortions of Hollywood films." Many chapters pair similar films together and address them as a "double bill." Additional films are listed at the end of each chapter.

There are some glaring errors in the book that should have been caught before publication. For example, in the annotation for *Boys Don't Cry*, one of the characters is referred to as "Tim" instead of his actual character name "Tom." In the entry for *Dead Man Walking*, the rapist and murderer played by Sean Penn is described as being "on death row in Angola, Los Angeles" when it should be Angola, Louisiana. However, the book is a worthwhile purchase for libraries with extensive film collections.

The Great Radio Audience Participation Shows: Seventeen Programs from the 1940s and 1950s. By Jim Cox. 2001. 264p. appendix. bibliog. illus. index. McFarland, $45 (0-7864-1071-X). 791.44.

Old radio shows were wonderful, and who is left to remember them? Cox is a fan who appreciates the historical impact of the radio and the intimacy the hosts had with their listeners, an intimacy that is rare in television. He defines audience participation shows as those "on which there were frequent exchanges between a host (or other figures) and a live, on-premise audience."

Cox focuses on 17 archetypal programs, including "Art Linkletter's House Party," "Arthur Godfrey's Talent Scouts," "Truth or Consequences," "Queen for a Day," and "You Bet Your Life." The entries, which are four to ten pages long and appear in alphabetical order by program name, begin with a description of the premise followed by lists of on-air and production staff, sponsors, ratings, and broadcast dates and times. Cox then discusses the backgrounds of the hosts, the development of the shows, the history of the shows on radio and television, and the impact the shows and their hosts had on society. The analysis of the programs is informative and deep. The entries are interesting to read, with some fun facts about the history of radio in general, sponsorship, the interactions of the personalities, and the scandals that sometimes occurred. A few photographs are included.

The appendix lists additional audience participation shows with brief descriptions, networks, and years of broadcast. The volume wraps up with a bibliography and an index.

As fun as this book is, it may not be that helpful to the reference desk except in libraries with comprehensive radio collections. It seems better to put it in the circulating collection so patrons can take it home and savor the memories.

Hi There, Boys and Girls! America's Local Children's TV Programs. By Tim Hollis. 2001. 361p. bibliog. illus. index. Univ. of Mississippi, $50 (1-57806-395-7); paper, $25 (1-57806-396-5). 791.45.

Local children's programming had its roots in radio, where it consisted mainly of storytelling by "uncle" hosts. When TV stations started broadcasting old Westerns and syndicated cartoons, the "host" pattern reemerged. Other genres arose: TV "school" settings, puppets, birthday parties. *Romper Room* and *Bozo the Clown* were strong franchised children's programs produced locally. Children's programs are not well researched, so this reference work is an initial effort in this area of popular culture.

The author sets the scene in his 20-page history, discussing local programming from its beginnings through the early 1970s. The remainder of the volume is arranged alphabetically by state, and within each state, by city. Each station's history of children's programming is related in a conversational style. The vast majority of content deals with the personalities of the program hosts, including the local beginnings of national figures such as Captain Kangaroo, Shari Lewis, and Mr. Rogers. The length of each city's entry ranges from a quarter page to more than a dozen pages (Chicago, Los Angeles, New York). About 20 percent of the pages include a black-and-white photo (sometimes a page away from the related text). An end-volume bibliography lists the interviews, print, video, and Internet sources Hollis used to gather his facts.

Partly because of a lack of adequate information, coverage is spotty. Spokane, Washington, is not covered well: no hosts (such as Cap'n Sid) identified, some stations that included children's programming (such as KXLY) not noted, no mention of Spokane's strong German-language programs for children (which also featured children), no mention of a popular children's talent show. Indeed, a major limitation of the work is the almost total lack of mention of children's talent variety shows.

This work is a good start on the topic but is limited in scope. For large collections that specialize in television or popular culture.

Performers' Television Credits, 1948–2000. 3v. By David Inman. 2001. 3,109p. McFarland, $255 (0-7864-1041-8). 791.45.

Considering the vast number of television programs that have been aired, one can imagine the difficulty of ferreting out the broadcasting history of television performers. This reference work tries to do just that.

Inman's database reflects 15 years of compiling data from periodicals, the Internet, program producers and syndicates, and other sources. He begins with 1948 and concludes with the 1999–2000 season. Coverage includes "persons appearing on dramatic and comedy programs, made-for-TV movies and miniseries, game and quiz shows, performance-oriented talk shows and variety shows"; but not sporting events, news shows, and other programs "with very little performance activity."

Performers are listed under their most popular name and are generally crossreferenced from a less-well-known name (*Cupito, Suzanne* SEE *Morgan Brittany*). In some cases, famous duos are crossreferenced (although Cher is not connected with Sonny Bono). Highprofilers such as Ken Berry, Jimmy Durante, and Connie Stevens are here, but one also finds performers usually associated with the theater (e.g., Theodore Bikel and Lillian Gish) and "live" entertainment (e.g., Don Ho and Beverly Sills), some of whom are sometimes surprisingly prolific in their television appearances. The volume shows the importance and ubiquity of character actors, who are often overlooked in other volumes, such as Joel Brooks, Mitzi Hoag, and Vaughn Taylor, whose credits take up a whole page.

Entries are arranged alphabetically, and range from two lines (one appearance in one show) to a page and a half for personalities such as Steve Allen and Milton Berle. Each entry typically includes vital dates, birthplace, general type, or best-known character. Regular appearances are listed first, followed by guest appearances. Each category is arranged chronologically and includes the series name, episode, network, and year. Emmy Awards are noted, and sometimes a brief editorial comment concludes the entry.

This work does not capture every single performance (Mel Arrighi and Dennis McNiven are two oversights), but the editor has done a thorough job—exhausting, if not exhaustive. Researchers should welcome having so much data pulled together in a single set. For large collections where comprehensive information on television and performer history is needed.

The Wallflower Critical Guide to Contemporary North American Directors. Ed. by Yoram Allon and others. 2001. 560p. index. Columbia Univ., $65 (1-903364-10-8); paper, $25 (1-903364-09-4). 791.

This, the first of a planned three-part Wallflower Critical Guides to Contemporary Directors series, profiles more than 500 film directors actively working within the American and Canadian film industries. (Other volumes will cover British and European and world cinema directors.) The focus is on directors of fiction feature films released in the last decade. Along with expected luminaries, such as Steven Spielberg and Woody Allen, and such indie giants as Quentin Tarantino and the Coen Brothers, many entries are devoted to lesser-known or first-time directors. Harmony Korine, Doug Liman, and Audrey Wells, for example, are not covered in any other directory.

Entries are arranged alphabetically by director and range in length from a few paragraphs to a few pages. Each consists of a brief biographical profile, filmography, and a signed essay discussing each film's critical and commercial reception and synthesizing recurring themes and styles, where applicable. Inclusion is not limited to successful directors, and the contributors are not shy about criticizing films they dislike. All entries are written by film critics, journalists, industry practitioners, or film scholars. The writing is lucid, and the information is remarkably current; entries often cite upcoming films currently in production. Minor errors, such as the attribution of a role in Curtis Hanson's *Wonder Boys* to Reese Witherspoon rather than Katie Holmes, are scarce. The volume concludes with an index of film titles.

This directory offers unique content. The *St. James Film Directors Encyclopedia* (Visible Ink, 1998) has a similar format but is international in scope and only covers successful mainstream or independent directors. The *International Dictionary of Films and Filmmakers* (4th ed., St. James, 2000) is also worldwide, and although it offers individual bibliographies and at times surprises by including directors such as Todd Solondz or Whit Stillman, it cannot compete with the *Wallflower Guide* for coverage of modern U.S. and Canada.

Inevitably, the guide leaves out a few directors: the prominent Mike Nichols is missing, for example, and the lesser-known Noah Baumbach, Mo Ogrodnik, and Susan Skoog are not here. The editors hope to cover more films and directors in updates every two years. This unparalleled directory should be purchased for film students, researchers, and enthusiasts in academic and public libraries.

Solo Performers: An International Registry, 1770–2000. By John Cairney. 2001. 218p. bibliog. illus. index. McFarland, paper, $49.95 (0-7864-1022-1). 792.

Solo theater involves an actor or actress who uses a prepared or improvised text, assumes a character or performs in his or her own person, and holds the audience's attention for the evening. This volume combines essays on the evolution of this form of theater, followed by a registry of performers. Author Cairney was himself a solo performer between 1965 and 1988. His registry has grown to more than 1,000 names and forms the core of the book.

The essays provide a history of solo theater from its beginning in the eighteenth century. The registry is arranged alphabetically by name of performer and is confined to persons with evening-length shows, or presentations lasting not less than an hour. Most entries are quite brief, consisting only of the name of the performer, the name of the one-person show, and the place (frequently the Edinburgh Festival) and year the show was performed. Some entries, such as those for Charles Dickens, Barry Humphries (also known as Dame Edna), and Anthony Aston (c. 1680–1750), "the Founding Father of the Theatrical Solo," go on for several pages and provide considerably more detail. Dates of birth are provided only for those performers who are deceased. Though the emphasis is British, the U.S. audience will recognize such names as Henry Fonda, Hal Holbrook, and James Whitmore. Entries may be accompanied by photographs, theater posters, or sketches. The volume concludes with a bibliography and an index.

This volume could best be used in libraries (academic or public) that support a strong performing arts curriculum.

Gambling in America: An Encyclopedia of History, Issues and Society. By William N. Thompson. 2001. 509p. appendixes. bibliogs. glossary. illus. index. ABC-CLIO, $85 (1-57607-159-6). 795.

Written by a University of Nevada, Las Vegas, professor and gambling scholar, *Gambling in America* examines the "people, places, events, laws and policies, and concepts concerning gambling as well as gambling equipment." The focus is on gambling in the Western Hemisphere.

Nearly 200 entries are arranged in alphabetical order and vary from a paragraph to several pages in length. Most are written by Thompson, but others are signed or coauthored by contributors with financial, legal, and academic backgrounds. Each state has its own entry, as do most Latin American countries and Canadian provinces. Not surprisingly, there are separate entries for Las Vegas and Reno. Entries for notable figures in gambling (Sheldon Adelson, Benjamin "Bugsy" Siegel, Steve Wynn) and brief entries for different games of chance are also included. Running more than 20 pages in length, the entry on horse racing serves as an excellent overview of the sport. Other entries deal with the culture, economics, and legality of gambling. In addition to the main entries, the book contains a chronology, a glossary of gambling terms, an annotated list of relevant court cases, and a bibliography for further reading. The index is lengthy and indexes the black-and-white photographs present in many entries as well as the text.

For a well-rounded collection, librarians will want to combine *Gambling in America* with the *Encyclopedia of Gambling* (Facts On File, 1990). The latter presents a more detailed look at individual games of chance and gives a more global view. Thompson has "striven for objectivity" in presenting this controversial industry and has achieved it. The entries are well written, accessible, and generally without bias. *Gambling in America* is highly recommended for all libraries with a popular culture, current issues, or sociology collection.

Baseball Players' Best Seasons. By Michael S. Jones. 2001. 292p. index. McFarland, $45 (0-7864-1086-8). 796.357.

Baseball's Best Careers. By Michael S. Jones. 2001. 378p. appendix. index. McFarland, $45 (0-7864-1087-6). 796.357.

Baseball fans live and breathe statistics when discussing (and arguing) about favorite players. But how to compare players from different time periods when there are significant differences in the way the game was played? Jones strives to make such comparisons using the base statistical numbers that are available throughout the history of baseball and applying a "sabremetric" formula (*sabr* refers to the Society for American Baseball Research) also used in John Thorn and Pete Palmer's *Total Baseball* (Total Sports, 2001) and *The New Bill James Historical Baseball Abstract* (Free, 1985).

Best Careers rates and ranks the greatest players by position based on their entire career performance. Statistical tables are arranged by major league teams (even if a player switched teams, overall career performance is listed under his "primary" team) and then by position. Each table ranks players by rate of success (or short-term performances) and by volume of success (or long-term performances). In addition, rankings are compiled for the top 25 team players from 1900 to the present. Following the chapters on major league teams are sections on expansion teams and nineteenth-century players. An appendix shows American League, National League, and overall greatest career rankings for each position. The *Best Seasons* has the same arrangement, except that it ranks greatest player seasons instead of analyzing results over entire careers.

The books fit well together as companions, and if either is considered, both should be purchased. Suitable for midsize to large libraries.

The Baseball Timeline. 2d ed. By Burt Solomon. 2001. 1,216p. bibliog. illus. index. DK, $50 (0-7894-7132-9). 796.357.

Major League Baseball Transactions, 1946. By Robert J. Levy. 2001. 327p. appendix. bibliog. index. tables. McFarland, paper, $39.95 (0-7864-0947-9). 796.357.

This Day in Yankees History. By Ronald L. Meinstereifel. 2001. 231p. bibliog. index. McFarland, paper, $29.95 (0-7864-1002-7). 796.357.

Three unique baseball books offer much to baseball enthusiasts but little in the way of substance for most reference collections.

This Day in Yankees History presents all things New York Yankees in a day-by-day format covering the club from its move from Baltimore in 1903 to the 2000 World Series. Essential information such as significant games, memorable moments, player births and deaths, and statistical milestones are described in concise but informed narratives. *The Baseball Timeline* is also a day-by-day historical account, with the focus here on the most prominent events in baseball for each year. The reader can browse baseball history and read astute yet brief entries regarding all of baseball's essential players, teams, and events. This work could be enjoyed for its photography alone as it offers hundreds of color photographs, many page-sized. In addition to the photos and entries, each year's coverage features newsworthy and cultural happenings and has several sidebars containing trivia, rules, and other fun facts. Each year concludes with a "Best of" list that highlights the season's top performers.

Major League Baseball Transactions, 1946 presents a complete picture of baseball just after World War II came to a close, a time of tremendous change and readjustment for baseball as players returned from military service. The product of extensive research, the book begins with a day-by-day account of the season. Starting with the waning days of fall 1945, the author describes the player transactions, military discharges, and business of baseball that took place during that off-season. Then, when the season begins, in April 1946, the reader is treated to a review of all the major events. Those interested in the history of professional baseball are sure to appreciate how the author not only details these events but also puts them in context. For instance, when describing player transactions, Levy frequently notes how players performed for their new club and how careers eventually turned out. After the day-by-day accounts conclude with the World Series, the book turns to facts and figures. A section called "The Grids" outlines daily player use for all 633 players who played in the majors during 1946, and the "Annotated Team Rosters" provides number of games, positions, and applicable transaction or injury information for each player.

Fans of baseball history are likely to enjoy these books by reading them cover to cover. Reference collections extensively catering to baseball or professional sports history should consider all three. Other libraries may find one or more of these titles appropriate for circulation.

The Best of Baseball: The 20th Century's Greatest Players Ranked By Position. By Warren N. Wilbert. 2001. 320p. appendixes. bibliog. illus. index. McFarland, paper, $45 (0-7864-0930-4). 796.357.

The Best of Baseball incorporates the rotisserie league–inspired field of baseball statistics known as sabermetrics to rank the best players of the 1900s at each position. The sabermetric system dynamically indicates players' strengths relative to their chronological peers instead of using traditional statistical measures such as home runs, batting average, and RBIs. One-to three-page biographical summaries including quotes from baseball legends, plus statistical tables, are included on each player selected. Numerous black-and-white pictures showcase the selected players. As evidenced by the recent reorganization of the National Baseball Hall of Fame selection committee makeup, and the changes to Hall of Fame entry requirements, ranking baseball players is far from a scientific process. However, Wilbert's book successfully applies scientific analysis to the inherently unscientific process.

As recreational reading, this text excels because of the informative tone and smooth writing style. It also provides excellent biographical and career information on players who are often subjects of research in secondary and undergraduate libraries. Useful complementary titles are *Baseball Players' Best Seasons* and *Baseball's Best Careers* [both RBB F 15 02], which use a similar system to rank players by season and by position but do not have biographical profiles.

The Encyclopedia of American Soccer History. Ed. by Roger Allaway and others. 2001. 496p. appendixes. bibliog. Scarecrow, $65 (0-8108-3980-6). 796.334.

Long before the arrival of Brazilian superstar Pele, soccer was an American pastime. The sport got its American start in the mid-1800s and has seen an increase in popularity over the last quarter-century. This reference book, volume 20 in the publisher's American Sports History Series, covers the history of soccer in America through 1999.

More than 400 alphabetically arranged entries range in length from one paragraph to several pages (on topics such as *College soccer*) and encompass a variety of people, leagues, other countries, and events. There are entries for 200 individuals (players, coaches, referees, and administrators) who have contributed to the game in America. For teams and leagues with frequent name changes the authors list the most common or last used name and guide readers to this entry heading with cross-referenced notes.

An appendix of statistics and records is included and arranged by league or championship. This appendix is sometimes difficult to decipher but useful for those obscure soccer stats such as the leading goal scorer in the American Soccer League for the 1921–1922 season. The appendix of memorable games is a listing of the 51 games "most worthy of being remembered" as defined by the authors.

This book would have benefited from the inclusion of a glossary of soccer terms and a good editor to minimize the frequent grammatical mistakes. It is also unfortunate that the publication of this title preceded the 2001 start of the women's professional soccer league, making it already out of date.

For soccer enthusiasts looking for an in-depth history of the sport in America, definitions of terms and rules, historical pictures, and individual player statistics through 1979, *The American Encyclopedia of Soccer* (Everest House, 1980) is arranged more appropriately for browsing. *The Encyclopedia of American Soccer History* is a comprehensive survey of American soccer history and is valuable for its statistics and player biographies, especially those from the 20 years since the publication of the Everest House title. Public libraries where soccer books are popular would be well served by this title.

Martial Arts of the World: An Encyclopedia. 2v. Ed. by Thomas A. Green. 2001. 894p. bibliogs. illus. index. ABC-CLIO, $185 (1-57607-150-2). 796.8.

This is a look at many unique fighting styles from around the world, encompassing not only judo and karate but also archery, dueling, stick fighting, and wrestling, among others. Topics were selected based on the following premise: "Martial arts are considered to be systems that blend the physical components of combat with strategy, philosophy, tradition or other features that distinguish them from pure physical reaction."

There are 96 articles of at least three pages each, written by academics and practitioners alike. Some entries cover specific styles, such as *aikido*, *capoeira*, and *wing chun*, and include history of the style, significant individuals, major components of the style, and most common levels of achievement. Other entries discuss a wide range of related topics: *Chivalry*; *Medicine, traditional Chinese*; *Swordsmanship, European medieval*; *Wrestling and grappling: India*. All entries are signed and provide cross-references and sometimes extensive bibliographies. At the end of volume 2 are a chronological history of significant events in martial arts from around 30,000 years ago to 1993 and a general bibliography listing books, theses, magazine articles, and Web sites. A detailed index rounds out the set.

The level of scholarship is high and the information is thorough. While giving a nod to martial arts in popular culture, the volumes provide a much more comprehensive approach to fighting styles than is offered by looking at films and professional wrestling. At the same time, this is not a "how-to-guide." Photographs are informative and illustrative but not instructional as to techniques.

Although the price will make this resource out of reach for some, libraries serving martial art students who are serious about their chosen styles will need to add it to their collections.

Literature

Brewer's Dictionary of Modern Phrase and Fable. By Adrian Room. 2001. 773p. Cassell; dist. by Sterling, $39.95 (0-304-35381-7). 803.

In this work, Room, editor of the sixteenth edition of *Brewer's Dictionary of Phrase and Fable* [RBB O 15 00], focuses not only on phrases and terms that have come into the English language during the past 100 years but also on other aspects of modern society. The result is an eclectic mixture of entries that includes colloquialisms, idioms, catchphrases, slang expressions, acronyms, trade names, organizations, events, fictional characters, and titles of films, plays, novels, television programs, and works of art.

Approximately 8,000 entries are alphabetically arranged. Standard entries, which range in length from several lines to a column, treat such diverse topics as *Falun Gong*, *Inspector Morse*, *Jaws of Life*, *My Fair Lady*, *Never a dull moment*, *Pooper scooper*, and *URL*. In addition, the volume features a variety of theme entries, including *Advertising slogans of the 20th century*, *First lines of novels*, and *Rock group names*, which often extend to multiple pages. Accompanying many entries are illustrative quotations, most often garnered from British newspapers and periodicals. The work's British origins are evident in other ways as well. For instance, the entry for *What's My Line?* contains no mention of the U.S. version of the game show. Inevitably, one questions some of the editor's choices. *Garfield* and *Starsky and Hutch* are here, but where are *The Far Side* and *Hill Street Blues*?

Though at first glance this work would appear to be a revision of *Brewer's Dictionary of Twentieth Century Phrase and Fable* (Houghton, 1992), its scope is much broader, and about three-fourths of its entries were not in the earlier dictionary. There is some duplication between this volume and the sixteenth edition of *Brewer's Dictionary of Phrase and Fable*; however, the overlap is not significant enough to be of concern.

In spite of its British slant and its somewhat erratic selectivity, this entertaining compendium serves as a valuable record of twentieth-century words, expressions, and cultural allusions. It will be a useful addition to high-school, public, and academic libraries.

The Continuum Encyclopedia of Children's Literature. Ed. by Bernice E. Cullinan and Diane G. Person. 2001. 864p. bibliogs. illus. index. Continuum, $150 (0-8264-1271-8). 809.

Cullinan, past president of the International Reading Association and the Reading Hall of Fame and author of the acclaimed *Literature and the Child* (now in its fifth edition), and librarian and children's literature authority Person have accomplished the daunting task of putting together a complete reference source for children's literature. *The Continuum Encyclopedia of Children's Literature* is a valuable tool in the growing bibliography of secondary material on a genre that has gained a high level of academic as well as popular interest.

The encyclopedia surveys 150 years in the history of children's literature. Though coverage is global, emphasis is on English-speaking countries and works appearing in English translation. More than 150 contributors from librarianship, academia, publishing, writing, and illustration provided 1,200 biocritical entries and almost 100 topical articles that survey genres (*Adventure stories*, *Easy-to-read books*, *Fairy tales*), themes and trends (*Death and dying in children's literature*, *Multicultural literature*), and history (*British literature*, *Caldecott Medal*). Individuals who are treated were chosen "based on an evaluation of an author or illustrator's significant contribution to the field regardless of the amount of work written or published" and range from Hans Christian Andersen, Arthur Rackham, and Jules Verne to Kevin Henkes, Walter Dean Myers, and J. K. Rowling. Samples of illustrations and photographs of 130 authors and illustrators are included. The work is alphabetically arranged, and each entry includes a bibliography. In the case of authors or illustrators, a list of awards and further works is also included. All entries are well written and highlight the authors' or illustrators' lives and most-acclaimed works. Entries on genres discuss the genre's history, significance, and examples. The index lists only individuals and will not help researchers seeking out references to *Booklist*, *Charlotte's Web*, or *Harry Potter*.

This work would be useful for parents and teachers as well as scholars, librarians, and writers. It is well researched, well written, and easy to use. The *Oxford Companion to Children's Literature* (1984) has entries for titles and characters as well as authors, illustrators, and literary types but is not as up to date. *International Companion Encyclopedia of Children's Literature* (Routledge, 1996) has far fewer entries and a British focus. *The Continuum Encyclopedia of Children's Literature* is recommended for all libraries with holdings in children's literature.

Gothic Writers: A Critical and Bibliographical Guide. Ed. by Douglass H. Thomson and others. 2001. 516p. bibliogs. indexes. Greenwood, $95 (0-313-30500-5). 809.

As the field of Gothic studies has mushroomed in the last few decades, so, too, has the academic debate about the meaning of the term. Though they do not provide their own definition, the editors of this volume have chosen "to reflect the repercussions of the broader application of the adjective 'Gothic' currently used to describe many works and writers not previously associated with horror literature." They cover not only familiar eighteenth-century horror writers such as Ann Radcliff and Horace Walpole, but also Margaret Atwood, Stephen King, D. H. Lawrence, Herman Melville, and Joyce Carol Oates, as well as several non-Western writers.

Each of the 52 author entries and 2 thematic entries contains a list of principal Gothic works as well as modern reprints and editions, followed by a critical essay examining Gothic themes. At the end of each entry, the researcher finds an annotated bibliography of scholarly works. The volume concludes with a time line of Gothic authors and works (1762–2000). Following the time line is a general bibliography of critical resources, including eight Web sites. There are two indexes, one of authors and titles and one of editors, compilers, and translators.

Many of the authors found here are discussed in other resources, such as *St. James Guide to Horror, Ghost, and Gothic Writers* (Gale, 1998), but no other work treats them in the context of current Gothic studies. Recommended for academic and large public libraries.

MagillOnAuthors. [Internet database]. 2001. Salem, pricing from $750 (1-58765-139-4). [http://www.salempress.com]. (Last accessed February 20, 2002).

While *MagillOnLiterature* primarily covers the well-known *Masterplots* series, *MagillOnAuthors* (MOA) consists of the *Critical Survey* line of Salem Press literary reference sources focusing on drama, long fiction, mystery and detective fiction, poetry, and short fiction. Additionally, four titles from outside the Critical Survey line are incorporated within MOA: *Magill's Choice: 100 Masters of Mystery and Detective Fiction*; *Magill's Choice: Notable Poets*; *Magill's Choice: Shakespeare*; and *World Philosophers and Their Works*. Altogether, MOA includes more than 2,100 writers. Updates occur quarterly.

MOA employs the EBSCOhost interface. Searchers can choose between two browsable indexes, Author or Movement, and three types of search screens: Basic Search, Guided Search, or Expert Search. Whereas Basic Search presents a single text-entry box, Guided Search provides four text-entry boxes with accompanying field limit options (e.g., Record Title) joined by a choice of Boolean operators. The Expert Search lists a selectable history of previous searches and enables users familiar with EBSCOhost's search syntax to construct sophisticated search statements. Users should be aware that, when searching multiple databases via EBSCOhost, some search options change. For example, when searching MOA and *MagillOnLiterature* simultaneously, the browsable indexes (Author and Movement) are no longer available.

In many cases, users seeking information on a writer will probably ignore MOA's Expert and Guided Search screens and rely instead on typing the name of a writer in the text box located on the Basic Search screen. In most cases, this search strategy works fine if the user is searching MOA only. For other types of searches, for example, "I need to write about a Native American writer," the Limit Your Search options will come in handy. These options accompany all three search screens and include Gender, Cultural Identity (e.g., Native American), National Identity (e.g., China), Genre (e.g., Drama), Record Type (Author Profile, Philosopher Profile, Overview Essay), and Images Available. Expand Your Search options enable searching for related words and searching within the full text.

Articles are signed and average 3,000 words (10,000 for overview essays). Biographical essays provide date and place of birth, a list of principal publications, life history, and an annotated bibliography. Articles extracted from a *Critical Survey* title also include analysis of selected works. Hypertext links and more than 400 images are interspersed among the articles. The article on Jack Kerouac yields 11 printed pages and includes 17 links to related topics, such as entries on Allen Ginsberg, the beat movement, and Thomas Wolfe. Articles can be printed, downloaded, and e-mailed.

Gale's *Literature Resource Center* covers a larger number of writers—a total of 122,000, with 2,500 of them treated in-depth. It is also more expensive. MOA would make a fine addition to libraries serving high-school and lower undergraduate students, especially where the print counterparts have been well used. Libraries subscribing to *MagillOnLiterature* should consider acquiring MOA; Salem offers both as a discounted package starting at $1,400 (single site). *MagillOnAuthors* is recommended for college, public, and high-school school libraries.

Masterplots 2: Poetry Series. 8v. Rev. ed. Ed. by Philip K. Jason. 2002. 4,462p. bibliog. indexes. Salem, $475 (1-58765-037-1). 809.1.

This set supersedes the six-volume *Masterplots 2: Poetry Series* (1992) and the three-volume *Masterplots 2: Poetry Series Supplement* (1998). It contains 1,385 signed entries written by scholars on individual poems, arranged alphabetically by poem title and ranging in length from three to five pages apiece. Each entry begins with the author's name and life span, the type of poem, and the date the poem was originally published. For foreign-language poems, the original date and title are given along with the name and date of the English translation. Following this introduction is a plot summary section called "The Poem" followed by a section on "Forms and Devices," which examines poetic devices such as meter, rhyme, point of view, symbolism, or language choice. Finally, each entry concludes with a section on "Themes and Meanings," which analyzes the main focus of the poem and provides a context in which to place the work.

As in the old editions, there is a bibliography at the back of the last volume (now updated) with general and specific author sources; title and author indexes; a "Type of Poem" index; and a list of contributing reviewers and their affiliations. In addition, two new reader aids have been added to the revised edition: a geographical and ethnic index and a glossary of terms. The majority of poems included are English language, but there are also a significant number of foreign-language poems. As with other Masterplots series, the poem analysis is general, yet insightful, and can aid the befuddled poem interpreter tremendously in understanding the basic import of a poem.

Libraries owning the original and supplemental volumes may be hesitant to update because there are only 271 entirely new entries. This means that only about 20 percent of the content is entirely new (although 29 new poets do make an appearance in this edition). No poems analyzed in *Masterplots, Revised Second Edition* (Salem, 1996) are duplicated here, but the handful of poems from that series are indexed in the back of volume 8. Examples of new poems explicated in this edition include classics like Elizabeth Bishop's "Filling Station" and "Sestina" and Robert Frost's "Out, Out—" and "The Gift Outright" as well as contemporary poems such as Adrienne Rich's "Living in Sin" and "Trying to Talk with a Man" and N. Scott Momaday's "Earth and I Gave You Turquoise."

This edition, like all of the Masterplots series, is written in readable language best suited for high-school and undergraduate students. Poem analysis this foundational at the individual title level is difficult to come by; series like Gale's Poetry Criticism tend to survey an author's entire repertoire and thus be too expansive, and *The Encyclopedia of American Poetry: The Twentieth Century* (Fitzroy Dearborn, 2001) [RBB Fe 1 02] only analyzes selected "landmark" poems specific to time and place. Recommended for public, school, and academic collections that can afford it.

Who's Who of Twentieth-Century Novelists. By Tim Woods. 2001. 374p. appendix. Routledge, $29.95 (0-415-16506-7). 809.3.

With the goal of extending "the focus of literary importance" and including "those areas, countries, and languages which have hitherto remained forgotten or marginalized in a predominantly Anglocentric selection of the world's 'best' writers," Woods has compiled entries on approximately 1,000 novelists. Entrants include English-speaking writers (John Dos Passos, Louise Erdrich, Iris Murdoch) and writers whose work has been translated into English, has influenced English-language fiction, and been in print for the past 10 years (Naguib Mahfuz, Augusto Roa Bastos, Christa Wolf). Also covered are major writers of popular and genre fiction, such as Arthur C. Clarke, Michael Crichton, and P. D. James. Emphasis is on the post–World War II period, although some earlier writers are included.

Entries range from a few sentences to just over a page for James Joyce and provide biographical data and a summary of major works and themes. Sources are sometimes listed. An appendix lists winners of the Booker Prize, the Pulitzer Prize for fiction, and the Nobel Prize in literature.

Woods is to be commended for his efforts to offer a diverse list of authors, and it is useful to consider familiar English-language writers within a global context. Because so many of the authors can also be found in sources such as the Wilson World Authors series and the Gale Contemporary Authors and Contemporary Literary Criticism series, this guide is a supplemental purchase.

★**The Companion to Southern Literature:** Themes, Genres, Places, People, Movements, and Motifs. Ed. by Joseph M. Flora and Lucinda H. MacKethan. 2002. 1,054p. bibliog. index. Louisiana State Univ., $59.95 (0-8071-2692-6). 810.9.

In the 1980s and 1990s, Flora coedited a four-volume series on southern writers published by Greenwood Press. Now he has teamed with a fellow English professor to compile this sourcebook that explores the multifaceted aspects of the "southern experience as it is depicted in literature." Focusing on common threads that run through southern writing and set it apart from the literature of other regions, the more than 500 alphabetical entries cover a wide range of topics, including themes, genres, customs, locales, stereotypes, historical events and entities, places and regions, colleges and universities, and periodicals and other publications. Although the editors stress that this is not a biographical volume, they do include a limited number of entries on individuals, covering 12 major southern authors (such as Faulkner and Welty) and an eclectic assortment of 29 other figures (e.g., Harriet Beecher Stowe, Abraham Lincoln, Elvis Presley) whose works or lives are inextricably linked with southern literature.

Written primarily by scholars representing a wide range of academic institutions, the entries are signed, and most conclude with cross-references to related articles and a brief list of bibliographic references. Treatment ranges from the lighthearted and folksy approach in shorter entries such as *Grits*, *Sears Catalog*, and *Yellow-dog Democrat* to the scholarly, more serious tone of longer articles like *Art and artists*, *Conservatism*, and *Slave narrative*. Some of the longest articles (4 to 10 pages) are those that explore the literary history of each southern state. Although it is disquieting to see an entry for "*Nigger*," the scholarly and reasoned article provides a valuable overview of the history of the term and its usage by both black and white authors. Facilitating access to the entries are a subject guide near the beginning of the volume that groups article titles by broad categories, such as "Customs, Rituals and Icons," "Literature by Period," and "Religion," and a detailed index that is invaluable for locating references to individual authors.

Superior in quality and scope to *Encyclopedia of Southern Literature* (ABC-CLIO, 1997), this volume serves as a greatly expanded and updated extension to the "Literature" section of the *Encyclopedia of Southern Culture*, edited by Charles Reagan Wilson and William R. Ferris (University of North Carolina, 1989). Well-written, meticulously edited, and thoughtfully organized, *The Companion to Southern Literature* is an excellent resource for anyone who is studying or reading southern literature. It is highly recommended for high-school, public, and academic libraries.

Dictionary of Midwestern Literature: Volume One: The Authors. Ed. by Philip A. Greasley. 2001. 666p. bibliogs. illus. index. Indiana Univ., $59.95 (0-253-33609-0). 810.9.

A project of the Society for the Study of Midwestern Literature headquartered at Michigan State University, this first volume of a projected three-volume series provides information on the lives and writings of close to 400 midwestern authors. The introductory material defines a 12-state region (Ohio, Michigan, Indiana, Illinois, Wisconsin, Minnesota, Iowa, Missouri, Kansas, Nebraska and the Dakotas) and includes a discussion of midwestern literature and thought. The scope is broad and encompasses journalists, poets, critics, writers of fiction, and playwrights representing a diversity of race, ethnicity, and gender as well as intellectual focus. Criteria for inclusion specify a significant connection between author and the Midwest reflected in writings, a body of writings dealing with life and people of the region, and literary products of quality and significance. The usual authors associated with the midwestern experience—Sherwood Anderson, Willa Cather—are included, as are modern writers such as Jane Smiley and children's author Patricia Polacco.

The individual author entries (signed by more than 100 contributors identified in an appended list) include basic biographical information, descriptions of the author's literary significance, a list of most-significant publications, and suggestions for further reading. The best-known authors are of course included in numerous reference works; one can find sufficient and more expansive discussions of Hamlin Garland or Gwendolyn Brooks in many places. However, quite a few lesser-known figures are included here, both emerging authors and forgotten names who have expressed the midwestern experience in their work. An appendix provides information on the recipients of the MidAmerica Award, an annual award by the Society for the Study of Midwestern Literature to recognize scholars and critics who have made contributions to study of midwestern literature. A detailed index is an aid using this reference work, but it would have been very useful to include indexes by ethnicity, geography, and genre as well.

Volume 2 of this project will provide coverage of nonauthor topics such as sites, movements, influences, themes, and genres. The third volume is to be a literary history of the region. Although it seems that each volume can be used alone, the entire set will provide a unique coverage of the body of literature that communicates the experience, values, and images of the U.S. heartland. Academic and larger libraries in the Midwest will find the most use for these volumes.

Merriam-Webster's Dictionary of American Writers. 2001. 560p. bibliog. illus. Merriam-Webster, $24.95 (0-87779-022-1). 810.9.

Designed for the average reader as a companion volume to C-SPAN's 38-part series *American Writers: A Journey through History*, this alphabetically arranged dictionary treats the 400-year literary history of the U.S., from the time of the earliest European colonists to the eve of the twenty-first century. Entries are arranged into three sections: "Authors," "Literary Works," and "Groups, Movements, and Periodicals."

The first section, by far the largest, with more than 1,000 entries, covers a wide range of authors, including novelists, poets, dramatists, historians, diarists, essayists, journalists, philosophers, and even screenwriters. Entries, generally a paragraph or two in length, contain biographical information and a listing of important works, some cross-referenced to entries in the "Literary Works" section. Twentieth-century authors predominate, but writers from other time periods are well represented. America's pluralism is reflected, although several omissions were noted, among them Denise Chavez, Michael Dorris, and David Henry Hwang.

Although fewer in number, the 500 entries of the "Literary Works" section are no less significant. They provide a brief publishing history, summary, and discussion of important poems, plays, novels, essays, autobiographies, short stories, and historical works. Coverage is thorough, except for the last category, which could have been enriched by the inclusion of the *Declaration of Independence* and *Gettysburg Address*. Excluded presumably because they are not considered literary works per se, their absence is surprising considering their routine appearance in many literary anthologies.

In "Groups, Movements, and Periodicals," readers can explore the evolving nature of the American tradition in 75 entries as varied as the *Hartford wits*, *Kenyon Review*, and *Transcendentalism*.

Overall, this resource has much to recommend it—clarity, ease of use, fine organization, and sound information, not to mention 150 black-and-white photographs. There are numerous other reference books covering the same topics, but generally in one alphabetical sequence; this volume's three-part arrangement offers a different approach. Although neither exhaustive nor definitive, it would make a nice addition to high-school, public, and academic libraries needing an affordable, accessible one-volume guide.

Encyclopedia of American Poetry: The Twentieth Century. Ed. by Eric L. Haralson. 2001. 846p. bibliogs. indexes. Fitzroy Dearborn, $125 (1-57958-240-0). 811.

Its predecessor, *The Encyclopedia of American Poetry: The Nineteenth Century* (Fitzroy Dearborn, 1998), served as a companion to the anthology *American Poetry: The Nineteenth Century* (Library of America, 1993), but this encyclopedia is not directly tied to *American Poetry: The Twentieth Century* (Library of America, 2000). It is a self-contained encyclopedia intended to "translate... a broad selection of poems" and make the reader "consider all that poetry has 'made happen'" in America during the twentieth century.

The volume features more than 400 entries written by academic contributors on individual poets, landmark poems, and major topics. The poet entries are usually 1,000 to 2,000 words long and offer critical treatment of the poet's career and major achievements along with a capsule biography. Choices for inclusion usually correspond to the canon. Poets who fail to get their own entry, like C. K. Williams or Ai, are often mentioned in another entry under the style or movement they are affiliated with; disappointing exceptions include Native American poet Sherman Alexie and blues poet Sherley Anne Williams, who are not represented at all. Approximately one-third of the poet entries include subentries for one or more landmark poems. The "major topics" entries are longer (around 3,000 words) and include periods or movements (*Black Arts movement*, *Dada*), verse traditions (often ethnic, such as *Asian American poetry*), and styles and themes (*Confessional poetry*, *War and antiwar poetry*). All entries in the encyclopedia include a "Further Reading" list of between five and ten books or journal articles. Additional reader aids include cross-references, a poem title index, and a thorough general index.

The closest encyclopedia in scope is *The Oxford Companion to Twentieth-Century Poetry in English* (Oxford, 1994), which includes entries on poets as well as genres, movements, and other topics. However, the Oxford entries are much shorter, and the concentration is divided among British and American authors. *Contemporary Poets* (St. James, 2001) offers similar biocritical coverage of American poets in one volume but has fewer suggested readings and also includes British writers.

The encyclopedia is written in sophisticated yet readable language best appreciated by undergraduates and above. Most of the information, especially poet and poem analyses, can be found in more detail in multivolume sources such as Gale's various literary criticism series (or the corresponding electronic *Literature Resource Center*), but this is a valuable tool for the student interested in twentieth-century American poetry as a whole and offers yet another "expert" voice speaking on the popular poets and poems of the period. Recommended for academic and large public libraries.

American Naturalistic and Realistic Novelists: A Biographical Dictionary. By E. C. Applegate. 2002. 425p. bibliogs. index. Greenwood, $95 (0-313-31572-8). 813.009.

According to the introduction, naturalism and realism arose as literary movements in the U.S. during the nineteenth century. Realistic writers such as Theodore Dreiser, Joyce Carol Oates, and Edith Wharton "attempt to depict accurately the world, or at least part of it, in which they live." Naturalism is closely related to realism, except that writers "focus on the poor or the unfortunate primarily to gain the reader's sympathy and understanding." Writers of naturalism include Stephen Crane, James T. Farrell, and Frank Norris. Some 125 writers, many of whom fall into both categories, are discussed in this volume. Chronologically, coverage begins with Caroline Kirkland (1801–1864), who wrote about frontier life, and extends to contemporary authors such as Larry Heinemann and Toni Morrison.

Entries are arranged alphabetically by author and vary in length from two to seven pages. Information includes birth and, when appropriate, death dates and a brief summary of the writer's life and works. These readable summaries are more descriptive than analytical, though they do generally provide some insight into the writer's relationship to realistic or naturalistic traditions. Each entry concludes with a list of the writer's representative works and some secondary references. Following the entries are a selected bibliography and an index listing all authors mentioned within the dictionary as part of an entry or as a reference.

Many of these writers are covered in greater detail in resources such as Scribner's American Writers series. *American Realists and Naturalists* (1982), volume 12 of Gale's Dictionary of Literary Biography series, covers 42 turn-of-the-century writers, most of them born in the 1870s. With its specific context and wide range, *American Naturalistic and Realistic Novelists* is a useful supplemental tool for academic or high-school libraries that support courses on these authors.

Dictionary of American Children's Fiction, 1995–1999: Books of Recognized Merit. By Alethea K. Helbig and Agnes Regan Perkins. 2002. 614p. index. Greenwood, $95 (0-313-30389-4). 813.

Latest in a series of books that cover American children's fiction beginning in 1859, this one treats 245 books published from 1995 to 1999. The previous volumes were well received by reviewers, and this one continues the legacy of being a potential source for studying the changing fashions of realistic children's fiction over the last 140 years.

The A–Z entries cover titles that have won awards or been cited on "best books" lists during the five-year period, as well as authors (192 of them), characters, and some settings. Picture books are not included. Book synopses run from one to two pages and often offer critical analysis. Author entries contain brief biographical facts. There is an appendix listing fiction awards and recipients, which would be improved by giving the years in which awards were received. The extensive, detailed index is an excellent resource for locating fiction about a wide range of specific topics, characters, authors, and genres.

The authors plan five-year updates to the series, which comprises *Dictionary of American Children's Fiction, 1858–1959* (1985), *Dictionary of American Children's Fiction, 1960–1984* (1986), *Dictionary of American Children's Fiction, 1985–1989* (1993), and *Dictionary of American Children's Fiction, 1990–1994* (1996) in addition to the volume reviewed here. All are in print, valuable as a social history of children's fiction, and recommended for academic and large public libraries.

William Faulkner A to Z: The Essential Reference to His Life and Work. By A. Nicholas Fargnoli and Michael Golay. 2002. 327p. appendixes. bibliog. illus. Facts On File, $65 (0-8160-3860-0); paper, $17.95 (0-8160-4159-8). 813.

From *Abe*, a character in *Sartoris*, to *Zsettlani*, a term used to identify a group of soldiers in *A Fable*, this volume provides both the literary scholar and the general reader with more than 1,500 cross-referenced, alphabetically arranged entries. Each entry varies in length from a few sentences, like *Sol* (another *Sartoris* character), to three or more pages for *The Unvanquished*, a novel in the Yoknapatawpha County cycle. Entries encompass a wide range of topics relating to Faulkner's life and work. They include titles, places (historical and fictional), events, ideas, and characters from his writings. Biographical entries cover friends, family, Faulkner biographer Joseph Blotner, and writers such as Ernest Hemingway—whom Faulkner did not hold in high regard.

Following the entries, one finds five extensive appendixes: a chronology of works and adaptations; a list of resources such as library holdings, bibliographies, and conferences; family trees for the Faulkners as well as for fictional families like the Compsons; Faulkner's appendix to *The Sound and the Fury*; and a time line of Faulkner's life.

A William Faulkner Encyclopedia (Greenwood, 1999) covers some similar as well as some unique topics but, with 400 entries, does not offer the same level of specificity. The most recent addition to the Facts On File Literary A to Z series provides a wealth of information in just one volume and is recommended for public, academic, and high-school libraries where Faulkner is studied at length.

The Cambridge Guide to Children's Books in English. By Victor Watson. 2001. 814p. illus. Cambridge, $50 (0-521-55064-5). 820.9.

This encyclopedic resource contains more than 2,500 entries on children's literature of the English-speaking world, not only Britain "from pre-Norman times to the present" and the U.S. but also Australia, Canada, India, Ireland, New Zealand, and South Africa. The book has a British slant, with Briticisms and British spelling. Entries cover titles, authors, illustrators, and terms. Also treated are series (*Babar series*, *Little House series*), genres (*Classical mythology*, *Pantomimes*, *Picturebooks*), and other related subjects (*Horn Book Magazine*; *Rollins, Charlemae*). Longer articles, some many pages in length, cover subjects such as *Animals in fiction*, *Gay and lesbian fiction for children and young adults*, and *Television for children*.

Articles are alphabetically arranged, signed, and cross-referenced. In addition to factual information, articles on authors and titles include critical analysis. Information appears to be current through 2000. The dense text is occasionally broken by black-and-white book illustrations. The appendix of selected literary prizes is quite extensive, focusing on awards from the U.S., Australia, Canada, Great Britain, Ireland, and New Zealand. Each winning author or title that has a separate entry in the encyclopedia portion of the volume is indicated with capital letters.

This title joins the growing ranks of reference sources on children's literature. *The Oxford Companion to Children's Literature* (1984) treats characters as well as authors, titles, and so on but does not deal with current trends. *The Continuum Encyclopedia of Children's Literature* [RBB S 15 01] has a more global reach but spans just 150 years. Its 1,300 entries do not cover individual titles but do have bibliographic references, which the Cambridge title lacks. *International Companion Encyclopedia of Children's Literature* (Routledge, 1996), also global in coverage, has 80 essays arranged in thematic sections.

Geared to the adult researcher interested in children's literature in English, *The Cambridge Guide to Children's Books in English* will be useful in the public or academic library setting.

Encyclopedia of Life Writing: Autobiographical and Biographical Forms. Ed. by Margaretta Jolly. 2001. 1,090p. bibliogs. index. Fitzroy Dearborn, $150 (1-57958-232-X). 820.9492.

The *Encyclopedia of Life Writing* purports to be the first substantial reference work in English to "provide a map of the field across discipline and region." "Life writing" is defined by the editor as something that "encompasses the writing of one's own or another's life," meaning standard autobiography and biography as well as letters, diaries, and memoirs. Other formats that aid in the telling of life stories are also included, in entries such as *Film*, *Photography*, and *Testimony*.

More than 600 alphabetically arranged entries are written by scholars in various disciplines. The aim is to provide an overview of central genres or themes and shed light on the significance of important individual writers and works in the field of life writing, all across an international and historical perspective. There are a complete alphabetical list of entries in the front of the encyclopedia as well as a thematic list that is classified according to chronological, regional, and subject divisions. Other reader aides include *see* and *see also* references, notes on the contributors and advisors, and a comprehensive index.

Each entry contains a descriptive and critical essay with a "Further Reading" list of anywhere from a few to more than 60 books and journal articles. Entries on people also have a brief biographical sketch and a list of selected writings related to life writing. Where possible, English translations of foreign writings are given, and in cases where no English language translation is available, literal translations of titles are usually given in brackets. More autobiographers are featured than biographers to keep the focus on the form and skill of the writing rather than the fame of the life in question. Most seminal individuals in the field appear to be covered, although it is surprising that Jacobean diarist Lady Anne Clifford does not rate a main entry.

Some libraries on a tight budget may not feel the need for this resource since so much of the content is biographical, and most disciplines are already teeming with biographical dictionaries. However, this scholarly source does offer a unique perspective because it focuses on a person's contribution to life writing, to the exclusion of his or her other accomplishments. Recommended for academic libraries and large public libraries.

World Literature and Its Times: British and Irish Literature and Its Times: Celtic Migrations to the Reform Bill (Beginnings–1830s). Volume 3. By Joyce Moss and Lorraine Valestuk. 2001. 549p. bibliogs. illus. index. Gale, $110 (0-7876-3728-9). 820.9.

World Literature and Its Times: British and Irish Literature and Its Times: The Victorian Era to the Present (1837–). Volume 4. By Joyce Moss. 2001. 579p. bibliogs. illus. index. Gale, $110 (0-7876-3729-7). 820.9.

This series of literary criticism from Gale takes a wholly unique approach—it analyzes works from a historical, political, and social perspective rather than a strictly literary view. The projected 12-volume series is arranged geographically, with volumes 3 and 4 covering British and Irish Literature from their beginnings to the present day. Previous volumes have covered African and Latin American literature. Each volume profiles 50 works including fiction, nonfiction, poetry, drama, and essays. A team of experts from both high schools and universities selected the works, while scholars in English literature and history reviewed the essays for accuracy. The essays were written by Ph.D. candidates and associate professors at universities both in the U.S. and abroad.

In each of the volumes under review, a time line presents historical events in Britain and Ireland during the period, with the related literary works listed at the time of their publication. These chronologies are quite extensive and help place the works in their historical framework. Volume 3 includes works by Charlotte Bronte, Charles Darwin, Charles Dickens, T. S. Eliot, Bram Stoker, Alfred Tennyson, and more. Among the writers covered in volume 4 are Seamus Heaney, Kazuo Ishiguro, Iris Murdoch, Salman Rushdie, Muriel Spark, and Tom Stoppard. Arranged alphabetically by title and written in a style that is accessible for high-school students and above, each entry generally follows a standard format, with background information on the author; a discussion of the events at the time in which the literary work is set; a synopsis of the work, with discussion of its historical, social, and political themes; a summary of events at the time the work was written; and a short bibliography of related books. All terms and events are well explained and related to the piece of literature. The represented works tend to be each author's best known or most often studied by students. They are also the works that fit the themes being discussed in the volume. Although Charles Dickens' novels cover many topics, *Great Expectations* is discussed because it illustrates the themes of political reform and the treatment of convicts.

Masterplots: 1801 Plot Stories and Critical Evaluations of the World's Finest Literature (Salem, 1996) gives plot summaries of many of the same works, but it does not analyze the works in historical context. The various other literary series by Gale concentrate on criticism of either works or authors. The World Literature and Its Times series tries to show students the connections between the political and social climate of the times and how the authors used the themes of the day in their works. By emphasizing the context of literature, it offers a unique perspective and a fresh approach and will be a valuable set in larger school, public, and academic libraries.

★**The Oxford Companion to Shakespeare.** Ed. by Michael Dobson and Stanley Wells. 2001. 529p. bibliogs. illus. maps. Oxford, $45 (0-19-811735-3). 822.3.

It is difficult to think of a topic that is not touched upon in this new handbook designed "to inform readers about Shakespeare's works, times, lives, and afterlives." As one might expect, there are entries for the plays and sonnets, sources and themes, and significant people and places in Shakespeare's life, as well as for aspects of interpretation and performance over the years. What one might not expect are entries that throw light onto obscure details (*Mulberry tree*; *Performance times, lengths*; *Shakespeare Society of China*; *Trapdoors*), as well as those for topics that at first glance seem only remotely relevant (*Ceramics*; *Melville, Herman*; *Romania*; *Tobacco*).

Among the more than 3,000 signed entries are brief identifications of every character and in-depth treatments of each play. Articles on plays are several pages long and provide background information on text and sources, followed by plot summaries and discussions of artistic features, stage history, and screen presentations. Other entries cover biographical details, literary and cultural context, publishing history, literary terms, criticism, and scholarship. Particular emphasis is placed on theatrical history, from the productions of Shakespeare's time to *Royal Shakespeare Company*, *Silent films*, and *Television*. Notable players, from Thomas Betterton (1635–1710), "the greatest actor of the Restoration period," to Kenneth Branagh, Judi Dench, and Ian McKellen are included. Also represented are countries and regions, among them *Arab world*, *Japan*, and *Scandinavia*. Most entries are quite short, but broader topics, such as *Music*, *Nineteenth-century Shakespearian production*, and *Trade, travel, and colonialism*, are given at least a page. Many entries conclude with a brief list of resources. A detailed "Thematic Listing of Entries" helps compensate for the paucity of cross-references. Among other supplemental aids are a chronology and a bibliographic essay noting introductory treatments and standard reference works.

Coeditor Wells also edited (with Gary Taylor) the modern-spelling edition of Oxford's *Complete Works* (1986) upon which the companion is based. In their introduction, Wells and Dobson admit to "some small bias" toward theaters in London and Stratford-upon-Avon. North American readers may take issue with the short shrift given to the Stratford Festival in Stratford, Ontario, and its "Hollywood-like emphasis on costumes, props, and gimmicks." The entry *United States of America* talks about the Classics Illustrated comic-book versions of the plays and notes Shakespearian elements in television series such as *Gilligan's Island*, but does not mention the Chicago Shakespeare Theater, the Oregon Shakespeare Festival, or any of the many other serious American enterprises devoted to Shakespeare's work. Some entries, such as *Cultural materialism*, will baffle nonspecialists. A few entry headings are arcane (movies are discussed under *Shakespeare on sound film*), and the lack of indexing means that information can be hard to retrieve. But its embrace of all things Shakespearian makes this volume a necessity for academic and public libraries. High-school libraries should also consider it, although high-schoolers may find Scribner's *Shakespeare's World and Work* [RBB S 1 01] more accessible.

World Literature and Its Times, v.5: Spanish and Portuguese Literatures and Their Times (The Iberian Peninsula). By Joyce Moss. 2002. 558p. illus. index. Gale, $115 (0-7876-3730-0). 860.

This is the fifth of a projected 12-volume series from Gale that examines world literature from a historical, rather than strictly literary, perspective. Previous volumes highlighted African (2000), Latin American (1999), and British and Irish [RBB D 15 01] literature. The premise of the series is that literature offers clues to the history of its people and leads to insight on their perspectives, emotions, and actions.

Volume 5 features 51 signed entries averaging 10 pages in length, authored by scholars from universities in the U.S. and beyond. Each entry focuses on a particular title culled from Spanish and Portuguese literature. Examples include *Don Quixote* by Miguel de Cervantes Saavedra, *The House of Bernarda Alba* by Federico Garcia Lorca, *The Interior Castle* by Saint Teresa of Avila, and *The Quest* by Pio Baroja. Criteria for inclusion ask that the work be frequently studied, tied to pivotal events in history, and have enduring appeal. Works must be originally written either in Portuguese or Castilian (the standard form of Spanish) and translated into English; the literature of small nations such as Catalonia, the Basque provinces, or Galicia has been excluded. There is an inclusive time line at the beginning of the book presenting historical events in Spain and Portugal, with the related literary works listed beside them to encourage comparison. Entries are arranged alphabetically by title of the work, but there are also separate author, title, and general indexes to provide alternate methods of access.

The amalgamation of history and literature that the World Literature and Its Times series offers its readers is unique and invaluable to those not expert in world history. The content in this particular volume is especially unparalleled because most of these authors are excluded from Gale's other literary criticism series. Small overlaps of author coverage occur in *Modern Spanish and Portuguese Literatures* (Continuum, 1988), which features criticism from works in the twentieth century, and the *Dictionary of the Literature of the Iberian Peninsula* (Greenwood, 1993). However, neither of these focuses on the events and attitudes of the historical period, placed in the context of a specific work.

This volume is indispensable for schools with foreign literature classes in Spanish or Portuguese due to the paucity of English-language foreign literature guides. One could quibble over the works chosen for scrutiny, but what is included is well covered. Recommended for high-school, public, and academic libraries.

Geography, Biography

The Encyclopedia of World History. 6th ed. Ed. by Peter N. Stearns. 2001. 1243p. appendixes. index. maps. Houghton Mifflin, $59.95 (0-395-65237-5). 902.

Stearns is provost and professor of history at George Mason University and editor of *Encyclopedia of European Social History* [RBB My 15 01], among other works. His present effort is a major revision of a classic reference book edited by William Langer that has been around since 1883. The monograph was last published in 1972, so it was in substantial need of revision. This task has taken Stearns and a panel of prominent scholars 10 years to complete.

This book is intended for students, scholars, and amateur historians. It contains more than 20,000 entries covering prehistory through the year 2000. Examples of the currency of this work are the coverage on the 2000 presidential elections and the attack on the USS *Cole*. Coverage of Western European history has been reduced to make way for additional material on Africa, South Asia, Latin America, and the Middle East. In addition, coverage of traditional historical fields like national histories has been updated, and new historical fields such as women's history, social and cultural history, technology, and international government have been added.

Content is divided into broad time periods, from "Prehistoric" to "Contemporary." Each section starts off with a global survey. This is followed by regional divisions within which individual countries or cultures are treated. By and large, information for each region and country is presented chronologically, although there are also some narrative overviews. The extensive table of contents and index are essential tools for finding one's way. Appropriately placed throughout the text are 57 black-and-white maps and 66 genealogy tables of monarchies. The volume comes with a CD-ROM version that installs easily and is very user-friendly. Maps on the CD-ROM are in color, unlike those in the book.

Other recent single-volume world history reference tools are Facts On File's *Encyclopedia of World History* (2000) and Oxford's *Encyclopedia of World History* (1998). Both are arranged in A–Z format, and because of its largely chronological organization, the latest *Encyclopedia of World History* complements rather than competes with them. It would be a useful reference for high-school, public, and academic libraries.

Natural Disasters. Rev. ed. By Lee Davis. 2002. 420p. bibliog. illus. index. Facts On File, $60 (0-8160-4338-8). 904.

This work documents natural disasters through recorded history. The disasters are grouped by 12 types, among them "Avalanches and Landslides," "Famines and Droughts," "Plagues and Epidemics," and "Volcanic Eruptions and Natural Explosions." Each section provides a time line and a listing of the "worst" events of that particular type of disaster. Within sections, arrangement is chronological. The entry for each disaster begins with a brief summary of the causes, casualties, and unique traits of that particular event. For example, in January to June 1783, "Twenty thousand people—one-third of the population of Iceland—were killed by the monumental, multiple eruptions of Laki, a 15-mile-long series of 100 craters and vents near Lakagigar."

Most entries run about one-half to one page and sometimes include quotes from those who experienced the disasters in person. This edition adds disasters occurring since the 1992 edition was released, such as the Kobe earthquake in Japan in 1995; Hurricane Gilbert, which struck the Caribbean in 1997; and flooding in Southeast Asia from July to October 2000. Numerous black-and-white photos, an extensive bibliography, a listing of Web sites, and an excellent index round out the text. The author's straightforward, informative writing style makes this book easily readable by secondary school and college students. Libraries owning the first edition will want to update.

Warfare and Armed Conflicts: A Statistical Reference to Casualty and Other Figures, 1500–2000. 2d ed. By Micheal Clodfelter. 2002. 856p. bibliog. index. McFarland, $195 (0-7864-1204-6). 904.

Clodfelter is the author of three books on military history and has also written this reference on military casualties, which was originally published in 1992. It has now been significantly revised and updated. Coverage has been expanded from the original dates of 1680 to 1992 to 1500 to 2000. The number of conflicts covered has increased from 820 to approximately 932. The bibliography has been expanded from approximately 268 citations to about 482. A random comparison of the original text of the two volumes shows cosmetic rewording. There are no photographs or illustrations in either edition, although both contain appropriately placed tables in the text.

This reference covers land, naval, and air conflicts ranging from wars to local riots, such as the Haymarket Riot. Entries are grouped by century and by region, then arranged chronologically. They vary from a paragraph for Ute War to many pages for major conflicts, such as the Vietnam War. All entries provide a historical description with statistical information on the conflict given in the text. Significant conflicts have a list of all major battles and casualties at the end of the entry. Assisting users is a large index listing conflicts, battles, ships, weapons, and persons. A check of the index noted a few omissions (e.g., M-16).

In some cases the bibliography cites older editions of references that have had statistical information updated in more recent editions, for example, Boatner's *Civil War Dictionary* (McKay), which was revised in 1988. Also, some well-known references on casualty figures for particular conflicts have not been cited. An example is *The Toll of Independence: Engagements and Battle Casualties of the American Revolution* (Univ. of Chicago, 1974), by Howard Peckham, the standard reference for casualties of the American Revolution. In addition, there are no citations to sources of information used within the text, and this is a serious shortcoming for scholars.

Warfare and Armed Conflicts, although not quite as far-reaching as some in its treatment of ancient history, has more overall coverage of conflicts and excels in modern coverage. It remains a useful statistical resource on warfare that should be considered for the reference collection by academic and large public libraries.

Encyclopedia of Western Atlantic Shipwrecks and Sunken Treasures. By Victoria Sandz and Robert F. Marx. 2001. 240p. illus. index. McFarland, $75 (0-7864-1018-3). 909.

Written by a U.S. Coast Guard officer with the assistance of a noted shipwreck author, this volume's emphasis is on "sunken treasure." Part 1 is a dictionary of shipwreck terms, specifically as they apply to commercial salvage. Photographs and illustrations accompany the text, but some photographs do not give the reader enough information. Part 2 is a catalog of shipwrecks in the western Atlantic, arranged geographically and then alphabetically by the name of the ship. Perhaps because it is a center for underwater treasure hunting, Florida has its own chapter rather than being included under the U.S. Each entry includes the ship's name, nationality, type, and function, along with the location and a generally brief description of the wreck. Because of the difficulties of converting older monetary values to the current monetary system, the value of treasure is described as in the original documentation. An extensive index indicates each page where a wreck is mentioned and also lists dictionary entries.

One wreck not listed is *Morrow Castle*, lost off the coast of New Jersey in the 1930s. The wreck of *Andrea Doria* in 1956 is listed under New Jersey even though, as the entry notes, it sank off the coast of Massachusetts. No mention is made of the role of *Ile de France* in the dramatic rescue by the *Andrea Doria*'s passengers and crew. At the beginning of the U.S. section, the Abandoned Shipwreck Act of 1987 is discussed but not the controversial salvage of *DeBraak* off the Delaware coast that spurred the legislation. The entry on *DeBraak* also does not mention the controversy.

This source covers more lesser-known shipwrecks, specifically in Caribbean waters, than *Shipwrecks: An Encyclopedia of the World's Worst Disasters at Sea* (Facts On File, 2000). A more scholarly source of information is the *Encyclopedia of Underwater and Maritime Archaeology* (Yale, 1998). Marine archaeologists may find this source useful, but it has a focus on commercial salvage. Recommended for libraries serving patrons with an interest in diving, marine archaeology, and sunken treasures.

Facts about the Twentieth Century. By George Ochoa and Melinda Corey. 2001. 1,004p. bibliog. index. Wilson, $95 (0-8242-0960-5). 909.82.

Part of Wilson's Facts About series, this volume "combining the features of a chronology, encyclopedia, and almanac" is aimed at a general audience. Four main chapters cover the "who, what, where, and when" of the years 1900–1999.

Chapter one, "Chronology of the Century," is a year-by-year time line of world events from 1900 to 1999. Entries for each year are divided into seven topic headings (e.g., "Arts and Entertainment," "Politics"), and items are further categorized by country. Supplemental lists include Nobel Prize winners from 1901 to 1999 and a chart of the years and locations of the Olympic games.

Chapter two, "Events and Ideas of the Century," is an alphabetical (*Abdication crisis* to *Zionism*) survey that briefly defines more than "300 selected events, movements, trends, and concepts that defined the century." Chapter three, "Who: People A–Z," offers 900 short biographies of noteworthy individuals. Birth and death dates are provided, as are nationality and profession or occupation, followed by a brief summary of the individual's accomplishments. Chapter four, "Nations of the World," contains the "where" of the twentieth century. More than 190 countries are treated in brief histories that range from two paragraphs (St. Lucia) to more than four pages (U.S.). Each entry includes a chronology of leaders, geographical location, official name (if applicable), capital, area in square miles, population, languages, type of government, religions, monetary unit (pre-Euro), and main exports.

Additional features include tables, a "Historical Gazetteer," a bibliography, and an index. The gazetteer "shows at a glance how the world of 1900 was transformed into the world of 2000." Name changes of countries or territories are noted, as are unions of countries and their gain or loss of independence.

Facts about the Twentieth Century is a compact, browsable work with extensive coverage and an appropriate addition to most library collections.

Medieval World. 10v. Ed. by Sally MacEachern. 2001. bibliog. glossary. illus. index. maps. Grolier, $345 (0-7172-5520-4). 909.

This work is designed to introduce important people, places, events, concepts, and customs of the medieval period to middle-and high-school students. In arrangement and design, the set is very similar to Grolier's 10-volume *Ancient Civilizations* (2000).

Some 226 articles are arranged alphabetically, beginning with *Abelard* and ending with *Writing*. Entries vary in length from a single page for most individuals to four pages for most countries to six or seven pages for major topics such as *Cathedrals*, *Education*, and *Jews and Judaism*. A full-color illustration appears on every page. Bulleted *see also* references accompany each article, and sidebars provide expanded information. Maps show the location of empires, states, and cities as they were in the Middle Ages but use modern place-names for the sake of clarity. Each volume ends with the same reference tools: a brief glossary, a time line, a bibliography of both books and Web sites, and a set index. The writing is clear and easy to follow.

Although the emphasis is upon European history, there are plenty of entries and sidebars concerning Asia and Africa, and the rise and influence of Islam is covered thoroughly. Some minor editorial decisions are puzzling. *Astronomy* has a four-page article, but there is no entry for astrology. The subject can be found by using the index, in articles on *Magic and superstition*, *Medicine*, and *Science and mathematics*, but this does not reflect the importance of astrology during the period. Another omission is the contribution of women to the monastic movement. Although it is true that more men entered monasteries than women, it is unfortunate that only the Poor Clares receive mention, within the entry *Women*.

For a similar audience, Scribner's *The Middle Ages: An Encyclopedia for Students* (1996) has 700 entries. UXL's *Middle Ages Reference Library* [RBB Ap 1 01] combines broad narrative overviews with a selection of biographies and primary material. *Medieval World* is the only set that uses full color throughout. It is an attractive and helpful reference source that will provide information on a variety of subjects related to this complex historical period.

The New York Times Twentieth Century in Review: The Cold War. 2v. Ed. by Francis J. Gavin. 2001. 964p. illus. indexes. Fitzroy Dearborn, $150 (1-57958-321-0). 909.2.

The New York Times Twentieth Century in Review: The Gay Rights Movement. Ed. by Vincent J. Samar. 2001. 590p. illus. indexes. Fitzroy Dearborn, $85 (1-57958-225-7). 305.9.

These are the first volumes in a series that will consist of some 50 titles on issues and events that defined the past century and continue to be relevant today.

Content consists of articles from the *New York Times*. *The Cold War* is arranged in two volumes covering from 1918 to 1963 and 1964 to 1992 and nine parts. Part 4, "The Eisenhower Period," to take one example, reprints almost 60 articles, beginning with a January 16, 1953, report on President Truman's official farewell and ending with a July 16, 1958, report on Eisenhower's dispatch of marines to Lebanon. Included among the articles are some opinion columns, book reviews, and full-text documents such as Eisenhower's farewell address.

The Gay Rights Movement is arranged in nine parts that reflect the concerns of gay men and lesbians (e.g., "The Impact of AIDS," "Redefining the Family") and then chronologically within these sections, from 1927 to 2000. The volume includes a number of reviews of books, films, and plays; many opinion columns; photos; and several long articles, such as a March 28, 1971, report on the Daughters of Belitis.

The articles in both works, including the headlines and subheadlines, have been electronically reformatted for ease in reading. The Subject Index and Byline Index in each work are extensive and accurate.

Although encyclopedias and compilations of journal articles are available on both subjects, the value of these sources will be the longer view and changing perspectives they provide. Students may depend on online sources for information on recent events, but these print resources will be useful for retrospective newspaper research at the high-school and college levels.

Pan-African Chronology III: A Comprehensive Reference to the Black Quest for Freedom in Africa, the Americas, Europe and Asia, 1914–1929. By Everett Jenkins Jr. 2001. 628p. bibliog. index. McFarland, $75 (0-7864-0835-9). 909.

This is the third volume in a work that seeks to capture the African experience throughout the world. The first volume, published in 1996, covers the years from 1400 to 1865, and the second, published in 1998, covers 1865 to 1915. The author, an attorney, also compiled *The Muslim Diaspora*, volumes 1 (McFarland, 1999) and 2 (McFarland, 2000).

A nicely written introduction is followed by three sections: "1914–1918," "1919–1924," and "1925–1929." The sections are divided by year, and within each year events are listed first under U.S., followed by other geographic groupings, and ending with additional listings related to key figures (W. E. B. Du Bois, Marcus Garvey) and "Related Historical

Events." For the U.S., there are several subdivisions such as "The Civil Rights Movement" and "The Performing Arts."

The listings consist of brief bulleted items, often accompanied by a paragraph or several pages of explication. For example, for 1924, under the heading "The United States: Notable Births," one finds more than two pages on the life and writings of James Baldwin. The reader is struck by the large number of long entries on early African American baseball players, as well as the detailed information on battles in Africa during World War I. The year-by-year approach means that information on an individual such as Colonel Charles Young, the highest-ranking African American officer in World War I, is scattered throughout the volume, but the index is a help in pulling everything together.

There are many excellent resources on African American history, heritage, and biography, although not in the same chronological arrangement. This work's value lies in its broad perspective, looking at the African experience on all continents during the time period. However, the format is less than user-friendly. Although the years are clearly noted in running heads, other divisions are less easy to distinguish, making it easy for the reader to get lost. Recommended for libraries that already have the previous volumes or are seeking an inclusive collection in the subject area.

Columbia Gazetteer of the World Online. [Internet database]. Ed. by Saul B. Cohen. 2001. Columbia, $645; $495 for K–12 and for libraries that own a print copy. (Last accessed September 8, 2001).

Columbia University Press, following a trend among reference book publishers, introduces an online version of its 1998 definitive English-language gazetteer, *The Columbia Gazetteer of the World*. Annual subscribers to the new *Columbia Gazetteer of the World Online* (CGWO) will access the same 165,000 entries. Periodic updates are promised.

CGWO users can choose from three search options: PlaceName Search, Type of Place Search, and Word Search. Users can also choose between a text version and a frames version of CGWO: the frames version "is designed to provide a rich, graphic interface"; the text version is designed for those with older browsers or "needing a more accessible interface." In both the text and frames versions, search screens are concise, uncluttered, and easy to use. Access to online help, information about the gazetteer and its editor, and other options are located at the top of the screen. The PlaceName Search screen consists of a single text-entry box with an accompanying Go button. Typing in a place-name and pressing the Go button results in an alphabetical list of placenames arranged in a fourcolumn format consisting of PlaceName, Type of Place, Country, and Political Division (such as province or state). In the text-only version, results are displayed vertically. A PlaceName search for *Salem* finds 35 Salems, including cities, towns, villages, and two nuclear power plants. Clicking once on an entry reveals the full record.

Word Search enables fulltext searching of all entries. Results are listed alphabetically by place-name. Search tips such as enclosing phrases in quotes are helpfully listed next to the text-entry box. Type of Place Search permits four search combinations: Type of Place, Other Criteria, Continent, and Country. Essential popdown boxes facilitate selection. Clicking the arrow next to Type of Place reveals more than 160 choices, including *bridge, cave, island, state, town,* and *volcano*. Some types are similar, for example, *mountain* and *mountain peak*. Users can choose to search up to three place types simultaneously. Clicking on the arrow next to Other Criteria presents seven variables: Area, Length, Width, Depth, Elevation, Capacity, and Population. After selecting one variable, a criterion can then be modified by Is Less Than, Is Greater Than, or Is Equal To, followed by a number. Users can choose to search five Other Criteria at the same time. Continent and Country are the final options. The various search options mean that a user could create, for example, a list of cities with more than 100,000 in population located in South Korea. Hyperlinks are sparse. Frame users who wish to print will need to click once in the appropriate frame before printing (or click on the Text-Only Version link at the top of the page).

Online competitors are limited. The U.S. Geological Survey's Geographic Names Information System [http://geonames.usgs.gov/gnishome.html] and its international cousin, GEOnet Names Server [http://164.214.2.59/gns/html/index.html], hosted by the National Imagery and Mapping Agency, although free and broad in scope, provide limited amounts of information. The free Web site World Gazetteer [http://www.gazetteer.de/], maintained by Stefan Helders, focuses on large cities. Therefore, scope is limited compared to CGWO.

The advantages of the online version are the host of search options and the periodic updates. However, some libraries may settle for a printed copy situated on a nearby reference shelf. Suitable for academic and large public and school libraries.

The Encyclopedia of Women's Travel and Exploration. By Patricia D. Netzley. 2001. 259p. bibliog. illus. index. Oryx, $65 (1-57356-238-6). 910.

Women travelers and explorers have been largely ignored in favor of their male counterparts. Few histories record that Sir Samuel White Baker, explorer of Lake Albert in Africa, was accompanied by his wife, Florence. Although women's role in travel and exploration has received more attention recently, an encyclopedic treatment is long overdue.

This volume covers women explorers, tourists, mountain climbers, writers, geographers, anthropologists, archaeologists, missionaries, and more. Although the 315 entries are primarily biographical, there are also entries for continents, travel guides, clothing, transportation, and other travel-related topics. A number of black-and-white illustrations and further reading lists add value. The work concludes with a bibliography of 80 volumes and 40 Web sites and an index with main entries in bold type.

Entries vary in length from several paragraphs to several pages. A typical entry is the half-page article on Alexine Tinne (1835–1869), the Dutch explorer who searched for the source of the Nile and collected botanical specimens until she was killed trying to be the first European woman to cross the Sahara desert. More general entries, such as *Disguises* and *Pirates*, cover two or three pages. There are a few inconsistencies and omissions. For example, the picture caption and article on Mary Bosanquet (1918–1969), who rode a horse across Canada in the 1930s, give contradictory information. Although early figures such as St. Helena and Margery Kempe are included, Eleanor of Aquitaine's famous trip to Jerusalem with the Crusaders is not.

A work such as this saves a number of important women from obscurity. Comparable titles include *Women into the Unknown: A Sourcebook on Women Explorers and Travelers* (Greenwood, 1989), which treats just 42 women, and *Wayward Women: A Guide to Women Travelers* (Oxford, 1990), which covers 400 women, mostly British, whose travel accounts were published in book form. *The Encyclopedia of Women's Travel and Exploration* is more comprehensive and is recommended for school, public, and academic libraries.

Encyclopedia of World Geography. 24v. 2d ed. Ed. by Peter Haggett. 2002. 3,456p. glossary. illus. indexes. maps. Marshall Cavendish, $459.95 (0-7614-7289-4). 910.

An update of the original 1994 set, this edition has many positives and a few detractions.

The set is aimed for school and public libraries, though undergraduates may also find the material a useful starting point in research. It is a well-written, easily understandable resource. The first 23 volumes cover specific areas of the world, beginning with the U.S. in volumes 1 and 2 and ending with Australasia, the Pacific Islands, and Antarctica in volume 23. Entries include variously detailed information about the countries and territories in each region, followed by sections on the physical geography, nature habitats, animal life, plant life, agriculture, industry, economy, peoples and culture, cities, government, and environmental issues. Each page contains photographs, maps, or other helpful illustrations to graphically present the information. These are a welcome addition and contribute a great deal to the text. Sidebars include data boxes that contain information for each country and thematic topic and have been revised to reflect data from 1999 and 2000. These data boxes are useful for quick reference. Volume 24 is an index volume that contains a subject index, 13 thematic indexes, and a glossary, as well as credits and an updated bibliography of further reading for each volume.

There are some examples of poor editing in the set. Although the articles are well written by numerous academics from around the world, some sidebar articles do not match facts with each other. Two different meanings for *Zimbabwe* are given in separate sidebars, without an explanation that there is scholarly disagreement about the two meanings. Many believe that *Zimbabwe* is a contraction of the Shona phrase *dzimba dza mabwe*, "houses of stone." Others feel the word more likely derives from *dzimba woye*, "venerated houses," a term usually reserved for chiefs' houses or graves. In volume 10, the text on one page states that Portugal is made up of 22 districts; on another page, only 18 districts are mentioned. Portugal is actually made up of 18 districts on the mainland and 4 districts that comprise the Azores and Madeira autonomous regions. The set is heavily weighted toward European and American audiences, with eight volumes covering Europe and three covering the U.S. and Canada. The whole continent of South America is covered in one volume, as are Australia and Oceania. France takes up an entire volume, whereas Cuba gets three columns.

Even given these drawbacks, this set is worthy of consideration. It is more extensive in scope and coverage than Salem's *World Geography* [RBB O 15 01] and is written for a wider audience. It presents a range of data consistently, colorfully, and informatively. Recommended for school, public, and undergraduate libraries.

Rivers of the World: A Social, Geographical, and Environmental Sourcebook. By James R. Penn. 2001. 357p. bibliog. glossary. illus. index. maps. ABC-CLIO, $85 (1-57607-042-5); E-book, $95 (1-57607-579-6). 910.

This compelling look at the important rivers of the world provides both timely environmental information and historical data to highlight the impact of rivers on the economies and cultures of the communities that surround them. There are about 200 river entries, ranging in length from several paragraphs to several pages. All of the major rivers are covered—the Amazon, Mississippi, Nile, Wei, and others—and enough are included from outside North America to give the book a comprehensive global feel. The entries are arranged alphabetically, with cross-references to help locate rivers with variant spellings.

Each entry begins with information on the source of the river, its length, major tributaries, and outlet. The entries feature geographical information but, much like a river, often gently meander into historical and environmental discussions. Curious readers will be rewarded whether they choose to browse entries or look for specific information about a particular river. As is the case with the author's earlier work, the *Encyclopedia of Geographical Features in World History: Europe and the Americas* (ABC-CLIO, 1997), many entries end with a suggestion or two for further reading. Some of these suggested readings are very current, but many public and school libraries will not have these citations, as they are somewhat esoteric.

Although there is a general index, a subject index would allow readers to tie together rivers with related histories. It might have been nice to have an index that brought together rivers dealing with the Napoleonic Wars, for example, especially when the book is filled with so much interesting detail. A country/continent location index to the rivers would also have greatly increased the book's value for student assignments.

Many public, academic, and school libraries will want to have this book, as there are few river encyclopedias with this depth of coverage. It is reasonably priced and accessible.

World Geography. 8v. Ed. by Ray Sumner. 2001. 2,304p. appendixes. bibliog. glossary. illus. maps. index. Salem, $480 (0-89356-024-3). 910.

World Geography presents the topic in accord with the national K–12 geographic standards, "Geography for Life." Volume 1 covers "Basic Geographic Concepts and World Overview." Volumes 2 to 7 focus on the major world regions. Volume 8 contains a glossary, set index, a bibliography, and appendixes, which consist of tables and listings of various ordinal data (lakes, mountains, population, etc.) similar to tables found in almanacs.

The 236 entries in volumes 2 to 7 are written by 175 contributors. Entries are organized in sections entitled "Regions," "Physical Geography," "Biogeography and Natural Resources," "Human Geography," and "Economic Geography." Each of these volumes also includes a gazetteer containing terms and location names found in the respective volume and an index. Of 1,300 photos throughout the set, 800 are full color, placed in one of four 16-page plates sets per volume. Icons in text margins refer readers to photos and maps located in the plates, although numbering the photos in the plates would have been helpful.

Entries are current and provide a good mix of additional references to both scholarly monographs and popular articles (e.g., *National Geographic*). Also listed are a few carefully selected and annotated Web resources. Much useful, current, and interesting information is found in some 500 sidebars scattered throughout the text. Indexing is generally very good, although photo references are indistinguishable from text entries. Rarely, facts on the more obscure areas of the world are somewhat dated and misstated. For instance, Micronesia comprises more than 2,000 islands, not the 25 stated in the entry on the Pacific Islands. The discussion of Melanesian prehistory uses a term, *Negrito*, that is no longer in scientific use.

This work is appropriate for the middle-and high-school levels. It would work well both as a classroom reference set and in the school or public library reference collection. Although many scholarly works are referenced in the entries and the bibliography, the text generally lacks sufficient depth to be of use in any but the most introductory college-level courses.

DK Concise Atlas of the World. Ed. by Andrew Heritage. 2001. 350p. index. maps. Dorling Kindersley, $29.95 (0-7894-8002-6). 912.

For this new concise atlas, Dorling Kindersley has used as a basis their DK *World Atlas* that was first published in 1997 with a revised second edition in 1998. The concise version is slightly smaller in size, with about the same number of place-names in the index. It does contain more pages than the larger edition. As with many DK books, each page is filled with maps, photographs, charts, tables, and text. The main maps cover about 75 percent of each page and include most cities, rivers, mountains, and so forth.

Maps for the solar system and the world as a whole are first in the volume. Coverage of the continents follows, beginning with North America and ending with Australasia and Oceania. (The classic arrangement of many atlases begins with Europe and ends with South America.) In addition to the continent maps, there are 75 regional maps. Europe has 15 regional maps; Asia has 18. Some of the information accompanying the regional maps is not very useful. There are graphs for urban/rural population and statistics for miles of roads, railways, and rivers. Presumably this information is the average for states or countries on the page, but this is not clear. Brief almanac-type information (ethnic mix, literacy rate, and so on) for individual countries follows the maps. A brief glossary precedes the index. The index entries do not include longitude, latitude, or population but do indicate by a symbol if the entry is something other than a city.

Though not a first choice among atlases, this is a good bet for libraries needing an inexpensive supplemental source.

World Atlas of the Oceans: More Than 200 Maps and Charts of the Ocean Floor. Ed. by Manfred Leier. 2001. 264p. illus. index. maps. Firefly, $50 (1-55209-585-1). 912.

Oceans and seas cover most of our planet, almost 71 percent. It is not surprising, then, to find that an atlas of the world's oceans would contain a wealth of information. This work begins with several sections about oceans in general, including relief maps as well as chapters on "How the Oceans Were Formed" and "The Ocean as a Habitat and Commercial Area." The section that follows contains bathymetric charts documenting the levels of individual oceans and basins.

The General Bathymetric Chart of the Oceans (GEBCO) contained in this atlas is the result of a collaborative effort among the world's major seafaring nations. Until now, it was available only in a small edition published in the 1980s by the Canadian Hydrographic Organization and known only to specialists. In the atlas, the GEBCO charts are juxtaposed with highly detailed relief maps drawn for the National Geographic Society during the 1960s and 1970s. Readers will find that the bathymetric charts, which follow U.N. naming conventions, generally list water names in English and land names in national spellings. This is unlike place-names found on the relief maps, which are in English, but the publisher does alert users to this in an introductory note.

The habitats and commerce section is extensive and covers many fascinating topics such as ocean currents and tides, hurricane formation, sea life, sea trade, oil and mineral deposits, and canals and ports. There is new information on sunken ships and treasure and shipwrecks of the twentieth century. Each topic warrants a two-page spread with photographs, maps, tables, or all of the above. Some of this information may be hard to access, because only place-names are included in the index.

The photographs in this volume are stunning. Relief maps and satellite images provide detailed information, and the definition and color of maps and charts increase their ease of use. This oversize work is large (each two-page spread is 14 inches by 20 inches) and heavy, and the binding is less than desirable. For the price, it would be a useful and up-to-date addition to a public or academic library's reference collection.

County Name Origins of the United States. By Michael A. Beatty. 2001. 671p. bibliogs. index. McFarland, $150 (0-7864-1025-6). 917.3.

Pursuing a private interest for more than 20 years, Beatty researched historical association archives and university library resources around the U.S., gathering details on the origins of the names of counties in 48 states and the names of parishes in Louisiana. (The fiftieth state, Alaska, which does not have corresponding governing divisions, was omitted.) His dedication has resulted not only in the documentation of the name origins but also the accumulation of an abundance of historical, geographical, and societal information reflecting the development and progress of this nation over the last 400 years.

The volume is organized alphabetically by state. A total of 3,069 entries are numbered consecutively throughout the volume, with each state heading giving the number of counties for its state. Entries include the date of the county's creation (where known) and a description of how or why the name was selected. In some cases, no specific reason was identified for the selection of a name, and Beatty has provided any background information he was able to locate that may have contributed to the choice. A list of references, in some cases extensive, follows the entries for each state. Additionally, there is a separate bibliography.

Entries range in length from a single paragraph for *Choctaw County*, in Oklahoma (named for the Choctaw Indians), to a page and a half for *Lewis and Clark County*, in Montana. This entry includes a short history of the political events leading up to and including the Lewis and Clark expedition and brief biographies of some of the members of the expedition. Another typical entry is for Carbon County, Pennsylvania, the name of which refers to the large deposits of anthracite coal, which led to the formation of the Lehigh Coal & Navigation Company in 1818. Some names reflect historical events, such as *James City County*, in Virginia, site of the first English settlement in 1607, or links to other parts of the world, such as *Medina County*, in Ohio, which refers to the holy city of Medina in Saudi Arabia. Famous people, such as former presidents and generals, are featured, frequently in more than one state.

A straightforward index provides not only easy access to the information but also an overview of the wealth and diversity of the information contained in the county entries. The names of the counties are followed by the abbreviations for their states and the numbers of the individual entries. Other references are followed by the number of the entry or entries, as in the case of *Houston, Samuel*, with 21 listings.

Containing a unique collection of historical and geographical details of American history and expansion, this volume will be of interest to serious researchers and browsers alike and is recommended for public and academic libraries.

Biography Reference Bank. [Internet database]. Wilson, pricing from $2,595. [http://hwwilsonweb.com]. (Last accessed September 12, 2001).

Biography Reference Bank (BRB) is actually a compilation of two Wilson databases—*Biography Index Plus* and *Wilson Biographies Plus Illustrated*. *Biography Index Plus* consists of citations to approximately 2,500 books of individual and collective biography and citations from the 3,000 journals indexed in the Wilson databases. More than 1,450 journals include full-text content. Adding *Wilson Biographies Plus Illustrated* fattens BRB with more than 28,000 photographs and the full text from more than 100 Wilson biographical reference resources, including all volumes from the publisher's well-known and trusted *Current Biography*. BRB also has material licensed from ABC-CLIO, Fitzroy Dearborn, and others. Coverage is international and includes both the living and the dead for a combined total of more than 195,000 individuals—and growing.

Users can choose from three search screens—Browse, Search, and SearchPlus. All three search screens load fast. In Browse, a pop-down box enables the user to select from 27 various indexes. The Subject of Biography index is the default.

When utilizing the second type of search, simply titled Search, users type in their terms and then select from the following: Words Anywhere, Subject, Title, or Author. Subject is the default. A subject search for Buster Keaton (word order and case do not matter when searching by subject) retrieves 20 records. Results from *Wilson Biographies Plus Illustrated* are listed first, followed by results from *Biography Index Plus*. Clicking on the citation for one of the full-text entries displays a hefty 15-page article from *World Film Directors, Volume 1* (Wilson, 1987). A picture is included as are links to More Information and More Images. Results can be e-mailed (without pictures), printed, or saved to a disk.

The third type of search screen, SearchPlus, provides several advanced search features. Two text boxes linked together by selectable Boolean operators (AND, OR, NOT) offer intuitive advanced searching. Limit features include Date of Birth, Profession/Genre, Place of Origin, Gender, and Ethnic Background. The Profession/Genre category is extensive. A pop-down menu offers choices from from more than 1,000 professions.

Those considering BRB should also review the Gale product *Biography Resource Center*, which combines 80 Gale Group biographical resources with more than 250 full-text periodicals. While *Biography Resource Center* covers more individuals, *Biography Reference Bank* pulls content from more resources—in particular, many more periodical titles—and is highly recommended for academic and public libraries.

Ahead of Their Time: A Biographical Dictionary of Risk-Taking Women. By Joyce Duncan. 2002. 312p. appendixes. bibliogs. illus. index. Greenwood, $55 (0-313-31660-0). 920.72.

This selective dictionary describes the lives of 75 women from the eighteenth through the twentieth centuries who have "broken traditional bounds and ventured into uncharted territory" on land, at sea, or in the air. The alphabetical entries are introduced with dates of birth and, where appropriate, dates of death; country of origin; field of endeavor; and, in many instances, a photograph. Narratives of two to four pages are accompanied by short bibliographies. The volume concludes with several appendixes: "Vignettes of Other Women" about whom little is known, followed by lists of women grouped by category (e.g., "Aviators," "Iditarod Champion") and by nationality.

The women include mountaineers, explorers, aviators, anthropologists, archaeologists, environmentalists, naturalists, sailors, and adventurers. One finds such well-known names as anthropologist Ruth Benedict, aviator Amelia Earhart, and astronaut Mae Jemison; but there also are entries for Ruth Nichols, heiress turned aviator; Marianne North, nineteenth-century conservationist; and Alexandrine Tinne, Dutch explorer of the Middle East. Though subjects are predominantly from the U.S. or England, there are some representatives from other parts of the world (Valentina Nikolayev and Junko Tabei, for example).

This easy-to-use, highly readable dictionary is suitable for high-school, public, and undergraduate collections, although libraries that own other titles such as *Encyclopedia of Women in Aviation and Space Technology* (ABC-CLIO, 1998) and *Encyclopedia of Women's Travel and Exploration* (Oryx, 2001) may find it an optional purchase.

The American Scene: Lives. 12v. 2001. 1,536p. illus. indexes. Grolier, $329 (0-7172-9572-9). 920.073.

This biography resource, a companion to *American Scene: Events* (1999), is designed for students "at all grade levels." The entries are arranged alphabetically by the subject's last name and cover more than 1,300 significant and well-known Americans. Each individual, from Hank Aaron to Florenz Ziegfeld, is treated in a one-page spread. The set covers a diverse range of people, including many women and minorities, from Margaret Wise Brown to Orville Redenbacher and from Yo-Yo Ma to Tiger Woods.

The entries are color coded, and each has an icon to indicate one of six different categories: "America at War," "Notable People," "Arts and Entertainment," "Discoveries and Inventions," "Important Events," and "Life in America." At the top of each page is a fact box that provides the key information in the person's life (such as birth and death data) or facts about the event that made the person famous and a map that shows where each person was born or lived or where a major event occurred. On the edge of each page, a time line indicates the period in which the subject made his or her most important contribution. A quarter of the page consists of an illustration of the subject, along with a caption explaining the picture. Each individual's life is described in two or three short paragraphs. A special fact of interest is included in a "Did you know" section at the end of each entry. The set index, which appears at the end of each volume, helps readers locate biographies by ethnic group, religion, place, and topic.

Although this set is nicely arranged and has an appealing layout, it is weak on content. Each entry provides only a brief summary, lacking any in-depth information or resources for further reading. Considering all the other biographical reference sets available, this one is an additional purchase only.

Ancient Egyptians: People of the Pyramids. By Rosalie F. Baker and Charles F. Baker. 2001. 189p. appendixes. bibliogs. glossary. illus. index. maps. Oxford, $40 (0-19-512221-6). 920.032.

This collection of profiles of 28 famous Egyptians, mostly kings and queens, is a solid addition to the Oxford Profiles series, designed for students ages 10 and up. Some nonroyals, like Imhotep, architect and physician to King Djoser and creator of the first pyramid tomb, and Ahmose, who distinguished himself as a soldier under several kings in the New Kingdom period, are included. Some women are profiled, including queens Hatshepsut and Nefertiti.

The book is in five parts, each covering a particular historical period, with four-to-five-page biographies of individuals prominent during the time. Quotations from various tomb inscriptions and other Egyptian writings enhance the biographies. At the end of each part is a section of capsule biographies called "More Ancient Egyptians to Remember." There are three appendixes. One explains the five names of each ruler; another lists foreign rulers of Egypt, including Libyans, Persians, Greeks, and Romans. The last appendix, a time line of events in Egypt, would have been more helpful if it included events in other parts of the world for comparison. Other aids are a glossary and a bibliography in which books recommended for younger readers are marked with an asterisk. The bibliography includes a list of Web sites.

Ancient Egyptians will be very helpful for the "ancient Egypt assignment." The text is readable and should be accessible to most students. At the high-school level, its biographical focus makes it a good complement to works like Rosemary David's *Handbook to Life in Ancient Egypt* (Facts On File, 1998). Suitable for school and public libraries.

Making It in America. Ed. by Elliott Robert Barkan. 2001. 448p. glossary. index. ABC-CLIO, $75 (1-57607-098-0). 920.073.

This source provides short (500 to 530 word), signed biographies of approximately 400 "models of eminent Americans" from all ethnic backgrounds, including Madeleine Albright, Ingrid Bergman, Jacob Riis, Martina Navratilova, I. M. Pei, Tecumseh, and Oprah Winfrey. The author's aim was to assemble a representative group of people "who illustrate the opportunities America has provided those able to overcome the obstacles (and motivated enough) to take advantage of these opportunities." The subjects represent 90 different ethnic groups from all periods of American history and include indigenous peoples, immigrants, the children of immigrants, and, for some groups, third-or later-generation Americans. Eleven broad categories of occupations are represented. In addition to the care the editor took to balance the different ethnic groups and historical time periods, he was careful to include 100 women.

Entries are arranged alphabetically. Each begins with the subject's full name, birth date (and death date), occupation(s) or spheres of influence, and ethnicity, and ends with a bibliography of references. The text succinctly places the biographee in historical context, outlines major accomplishments, and describes obstacles he or she has overcome. All the entries are chatty and interesting to read. Lists of individuals by occupation and by ethnicity facilitate access.

Because short, easily accessible biographies of many of these people are difficult to find, this volume will be a welcome addition to collections in high-school, junior-college, college, and public libraries that seek to improve access to multicultural materials. Although there is a great deal of reference material on American biography and on specific ethnic groups, and many of the individuals covered here can also be found in numerous other sources, there really is no other one-volume work that provides this kind of broad coverage.

Native American Women: A Biographical Dictionary. 2d ed. Ed. by Gretchen M. Bataille and Laurie Lisa. 2001. 384p. appendixes. bibliogs. index. Routledge, $85 (0-415-93020-0). 920.72.

This second edition of *Native American Women* is much enlarged over the first edition, published by Garland in 1993. As always with works by Bataille, who has been writing about native Americans for nearly 25 years, great attention has been paid to detail, and the list of contributors is a veritable who's who of persons working in the field of Native American studies.

The volume contains A–Z biographies of more than 270 women with diverse roles within their cultures, from fur trader Sally Ainse (c. 1728–1823) to lawyer Melody McCoy (1960–) and from traditional medicine practitioner Coocoochee (early 1740s–post 1800) to tribal leader Wilma Mankiller (1945–). Entries are generally less than a page in length and conclude with bibliographical references. The volume has four valuable appendixes: "Primary Areas of Specialization," "Decades of Birth," "State/Province of Birth," and "Tribal Affiliation." The index is a little slim and does not include many of the names and organizations mentioned within the entries. Less than one tenth of the entries have illustrations. The bibliography has citations for several new items published since 1993.

Overall, this volume is exceptional. It offers more than twice the entries of Liz Sonneborn's *A to Z of Native American Women* (Facts On File, 1998), although Sonneborn's entries are generally longer and include more illustrations. Recommended for academic libraries as well as public and high-school libraries that need a new resource in this area.

Who's Who in the Roman World. By John Hazel. 2001. 372p. appendixes. bibliogs. glossary. maps. Routledge, $29.95 (0-415-22410-1). 920.037.

Who's Who in the Roman World covers the period from the fifth century B.C.E. to A.D. 364. Approximately 1,500 entries give crisp biographical sketches on significant personages "from all walks of Roman life," including both the famous and the lesser known. The author, a former university professor and subject expert, writes a straightforward prose that, though lacking in drama, is clear and concise.

The alphabetical organization aids in locating entries, though the Roman naming conventions (admirably explained in the opening "Note on Roman Names") are such that the reader must sometimes skim through a particular cognominal list (e.g., *Claudius*) before finding the entry sought. Generally speaking, chronological order is followed where there is more than one person with exactly the same name. Exceptions to this are made in the case of a few emperors with long, detailed entries, who are placed first in the section. Weighting is entirely appropriate, with more column inches dedicated to those who cut a greater historical swath. The cross-referencing is superb, with *see* items printed in small capitals within the text of entries. A number in brackets following a name is included when it is necessary to indicate a particular subentry under a cognomen. Brief bibliographies are appended to articles on major figures where suitable works exist. A glossary of 65 terms serves to extend and clarify the entries. Three appendixes—a general chronological table of Roman history from B.C.E. 509 to A.D. 364; a list of Roman emperors; and maps of Italy in the Age of Augustus, the Roman Empire in A.D. 211, and the center of Rome circa A.D. 200—serve to enhance the information in the articles.

A serviceable work for college and university students, this title is a good companion to the author's *Who's Who in the Greek World* (2000).

History

History Resource Center: The Modern World. [Internet database]. 2001. Gale, pricing from $6,495. (Last accessed September 5, 2001).

This new database in Gale's shelf of electronic reference works covers the period from 1900 to the present. It draws on 1,300 Primary Source Microfilm documents, articles from 102 journals, and 18 reference titles from Gale, Macmillan, St. James Press, and Scribner, among them *Encyclopedia of the Holocaust* (Macmillan, 1990), *Historic World Leaders* (Gale, 1994), and *Worldmark Encyclopedia of Nations* (17th ed., Gale, 2001). Content can be searched by person or subject as well as by keyword. An advanced search allows the user to combine terms and to search by full-text, keyword, subject, person, title or headline, source, or author. One feature, a useful Student Research Guide, introduces the user to methods of choosing, analyzing, and citing materials from primary and secondary sources. A Faculty Guide presents an index to the program's primary documents as well as topical essays to facilitate classroom discussion for the advanced-placement high-school level and up. Other features include a Dictionary, a limited Chronology, a Digital Forum, and a News Digest, which allows the user to search *Keesing's Contemporary Archive*, 1931–1945.

On the surface, the database promises speed and quality for student research. The search engine assembles sources attractively on the page, summarizes offerings succinctly and clearly, and requires few intermediate clicks for navigation. We tried a number of basic searches and found results ranging from two full-text journal articles and one journal citation for *illicit drugs* to 20 reference book entries, 28 full-text articles, 2 primary documents, and 2 images for *Persian Gulf*. The user researching *home economics* can move quickly to a substantial article from *Encyclopedia of European Social History* [RBB My 15 01] that concludes with 42 bibliographic citations. However, this search also reveals the uneven coverage of the database, because it results in only three total reference material hits (two entries from Gale's *Encyclopedia of World Biography* [2d ed., 1998] and the *Encyclopedia of European Social History* article) along with an assortment of full-text journal articles. Some topics, such as *human rights* and *Israel*, yield substantial results, but relatively limited offerings accrue around *atomic bomb*, *Depression*, and *Eleanor Roosevelt*, to cite a few examples.

Overall, this database is colorful, quick, easy to master, and engaging for adult or student use. However, like many other databases that assemble content from a disparate collection of resources, its assortment of materials can be hit and miss, and researchers expecting comprehensive coverage of a topic will generally be disappointed. No doubt the treatment of many topics will become fuller as the database grows.

Encyclopedia of Archaeology: History and Discoveries. 3v. Ed. by Tim Murray. 2001. 1,500p. bibliog. glossary. illus. index. ABC-CLIO, $275 (1-57607-198-7). 930.1.

In 1999, ABC-CLIO published the two-volume *Encyclopedia of Archaeology: The Great Archaeologists*, which took a biographical approach to the field. This next installment of the *Encyclopedia of Archaeology* takes a more standard topical approach, with entries covering the history of archaeology in specific countries or regions as well as "the histories of significant sites, debates, techniques, methods and issues that are central to the global practice of the discipline." Examples include *Abydos*, *Babylonian civilization*, *Dating*, *Chaco Canyon*, *Industrial archaeology*, *Iran*, *Sweden*, and *Terracotta warriors*. There are also entries for individuals (Thomas Jefferson) who did not appear in the earlier volumes and a few (Howard Carter) who did.

The signed entries are arranged alphabetically and vary in length from a paragraph to more than 30 pages for *Island Southeast Asia*. Most are accompanied by cross-references and bibliographies, which in some cases are quite extensive. A comprehensive table of contents is repeated in all three volumes, and volume 3 also offers a glossary and a well-done index. It is unfortunate that there is no indexing that refers the reader to *The Great Archaeologists*, although there are references to those volumes in some of the bibliographies. The lack of guide words makes it difficult to navigate through the pages, especially because some of the entries are so long.

The national and regional surveys are the most valuable aspect of this resource. Titles such as *Encyclopedia of the Archaeology of Ancient Egypt* (Routledge, 1999) and *Archaeology of Ancient Mexico and Central America* [RBB Mr 1 01] offer more depth, but entries here on Egypt, Mexico, and Maya civilization, to name a few, provide useful synthesis for the general reader. Libraries that purchased *The Great Archaeologists* will certainly want to add *History and Discoveries* to their collections.

Encyclopedia of the Ancient World. 3v. Ed. by Thomas J. Sienkewicz. 2002. 1,275p. bibliog. glossary. illus. indexes. maps. Salem, $325 (0-89356-038-3). 930.

This set goes well beyond what most readers consider the ancient world, encompassing not only Greece and Rome but also "the civilizations, cultures, traditions, monuments and artifacts, significant wars and battles, and important personages of the rest of the world: Europe (outside Greece and Rome), Africa, the Americas, Asia, and Oceania." The time span is from prehistory to approximately 700 C.E. Editor Sienkewicz oversaw 359 contributors who are primarily affiliated with American academic institutions.

The set opens with 26 overviews ("Death and Burial," "Religion and Ritual"), then continues with 1,169 alphabetically arranged entries. There are also 25 maps, 25 sidebars (such as "Emperors of the Gupta Dynasty, c. 320–550 C.E."), and about 300 illustrations. The set concludes with numerous useful appendixes: a time line (arranged by region with general events, not necessarily tied to specific articles); a glossary; "Geographical Guide to the Ancient World" (a list of entries divided into 22 geographical areas); "Chronological List of Entries"; Web sites (active as of June 2001); bibliography (divided by broad subject area); "Categorized List of Entries" (arranged by 40 categories); "Personages Index"; and subject index. It is worth noting that the bibliography is "intended primarily for the general reader, advanced high-school student, and college undergraduate," with all entries in English.

Although the work is intended for the general reader, terms are occasionally used that imply some general knowledge of the subject. The section on Roman art in the overview "Art and Architecture: Europe and the Mediterranean Region," for example, refers to the "intersecting groin vault" as a variant of the round arch but with no supporting illustration. The entry *Ba Twa* opens with mention of their being "regarded as one of the major surviving autochthonic groups in Central and South Africa." The majority of entries are eminently readable, however, if somewhat brief. Once past the 26 overviews, articles tend to be in the 200-to 400-word range with some exceptions, such as articles on Egypt, Greece, and Rome. Other longer entries include *Babylonia* (approximately 2,000 words), *China* (2,700 words), and *Persia* (1,600 words).

Entries begin with significant date, locale, related civilization, and significance for topical entries; and birth/death dates, related civilization, and major role/position for biographical entries. All entries conclude with a list of additional, up-to-date resources and a list of cross-references.

What makes this work unique is the number of entry headings unlikely to be found in other reference sources for the same audience—*Maroboduus*, a Germanic military and political leader; *Marpole phase*, a climax of Northwest Coast prehistoric culture; *Mulanshi*, a Chinese ballad; and *Muwatallis*, a Hittite statesman, are typical of the set's wide range. Although the brevity of many articles may be disconcerting to some, the encyclopedia provides extremely useful background information for names and events that students may run across while reading other works. An eye-pleasing and, at $325, a budget-pleasing resource for public, smaller academic, and larger secondary school libraries that otherwise would not invest in works on the ancient world.

Ancient History: An Online Encyclopedia. [Internet database]. Facts On File, pricing from $300 (0-8160-4695-6). [www.factsonfile.com]. (Last accessed February 20, 2002).

Facts On File has scored a winner with this addition to its suite of online offerings. The database combines the full text of 10 of the publisher's print sources, such as *Biographical Dictionary of Ancient Greek and Roman Women* (1998), *Encyclopedia of African History and Culture: Volume I: Ancient Africa* (2001), and *The Encyclopedia of Ancient Mesoamerica* (1996), with more than 300 illustrations, more than 100 maps and charts, 200 historical documents, and 15 Web links.

Content can be searched by word or phrase or browsed at several levels. At the broadest level, the researcher can choose Subject Entries, Biographies, Historical Documents, Gallery, Maps and Charts, or Timeline and then limit each of these by Civilization (Africa, Egypt, Greece, Rome, or Mesoamerica, with an option to select the entire ancient world). The next level varies. Biographies can be searched by Era, Topic, or Activity, which refers to the type of activity the biographees engaged in (for instance, "Educators and Scholars"). Historical Documents can be searched by Era, Topic, and Type (essay, letter, treatise, etc.). Navigation and custom searches pose no problems, even to beginners at online research. The attractive arrangement of each entry clearly identifies subject, source, commentary, related subjects, and suggested readings. There are also links to related entries. The Help feature summarizes in readable language the elements of the database and how each functions.

One outstanding feature is the Era search, which can be applied across the entire ancient world as well as within each of the five civilizations. This search pulls together the entries related to particular spans of years. For example, under the earliest era, which begins in prehistory, one can find entries on the importance of Australopithecus to human evolution, the contributions of the Leakey family to anthropological fieldwork, and the difference between an alphabet and hieroglyphs. A major strength of the database is its range of coverage, which reaches into the dark corners of ancient civilizations to pull out details that deserve scrutiny, for example, the difficult concept of Monophysitism, the construction and use of *chinampas* to grow corn, and links between the quetzal and Quetzalcoatl.

Weaknesses are few, but worth consideration, especially for school and public reference librarians. Because they are drawn from a variety of sources, entries vary in quality. Some are much too short (e.g., *Felicitas*, *Lost wax process*, and *Catacombs*). A few (for example, *Coins, origin of*) offer more related readings than definition or summary. A few entries fail to identify phrases. There are just two mentions of the Popul Vuh, neither one explaining that it is the Quechuan scripture. Other entries leave untranslated difficult terms (e.g., *patera* in the entry on the Roman deity Salus and *pomerium* and *primi pili* in *Mercury, temple of*). A glossary to which terms could be hyperlinked would be a helpful addition.

Overall, despite some faults, *Ancient History: An Online Encyclopedia* has much to offer the school and public library for grades 7 to 12 and for general readers seeking to increase their knowledge of early times. The publisher plans semiannual updates.

History

Ancient Rome. By Don Nardo. 2002. 324p. illus. index. maps. Greenhaven, $74.95 (0-7377-0551-5). 937.

Greek and Roman Mythology. By Don Nardo. 2002. 304p. illus. index. Greenhaven, $74.95 (0-7377-0719-4). 398.2.

These are two entries in the Greenhaven Press Encyclopedia Of series, which is intended to help students with research. The arrangement of both books is curious. Rather than being dictionary style, the topics are broken up into chapters ("Prominent People," "Government and Law," "Major and Minor Gods"), and the topics within each chapter are listed alphabetically. The table of contents lists all the entries in each chapter. An index provides additional access points. Many entries have *see* references, and if the entries to which the reader is being referred occur in another chapter, chapter numbers are provided.

Both books are sturdy and well designed. They will lay flat for copying, and most of the illustrations (photographs, line drawings, and woodcuts) should copy well. Maps accompany some entries, but a series of maps in the front matter supplemented by smaller maps of battles and so forth would have been useful. The writing should be accessible to advanced-placement middle-school students and above.

Articles in both works range from a few lines to a few double-column pages. The volume on Rome includes a chronology and a list of emperors that ends with Romulus Augustulus, the last Western Roman Emperor. The mythology volume includes a chapter covering 12 major myth cycles, which should be helpful to students with mythology assignments. Also useful is a chart showing relationships between characters in classical mythology. Both books have bibliographies with works that can be found in most medium-sized to large public libraries.

These volumes would be suited to school libraries and to public libraries serving middle-and high-school students. Libraries owning titles like *Ancient Greece and Rome: An Encyclopedia for Students* (Scribner, 1998) and *Encyclopedia of Greco-Roman Mythology* (ABC-CLIO, 1998) may want to pass on the Greenhaven titles unless such material is heavily used.

Daily Life in the Middle Ages. By Paul B. Newman. 2001. 301p. appendix. bibliog. illus. index. McFarland, $38.50 (0-7864-0897-9). 940.1.

Written in a style that is accessible to junior-high-school students and up, this book shows that life during the Middle Ages was neither as dark nor as primitive as novels, movies, or earlier historians have depicted it. In seven long chapters, the author, a lecturer on medieval history, analyzes "Eating and Cooking," "Building and Housing," "Clothing and Dressing," "Cleaning," "Relaxing and Playing," "Fighting," and "Healing." Each of these topics is broken down into its major components, with numerous aspects of daily life treated under each of the headings. "Clothing and Dressing," for instance, starts with a discussion of the sources for reconstructing what people wore, followed by sections on fabrics, clothing, fashions, and accessories. The section on fashions, to take one example, has subsections for tunics and doublets, capes and cloaks, and other items of apparel. Black-and-white drawings and photographs are used throughout. Though the book synthesizes a wealth of material from all over Europe, Newman rarely discusses the differences in daily life in the various countries of Europe, painting a general picture instead.

Daily Life in the Middle Ages is similar to Jeffrey Singman's *Daily Life in Chaucer's England* (Greenwood, 1995), which also divides the subject into topics such as clothing and accessories, arms and armor, food and drink, and entertainment. However, Singman's book focuses only on life in England, and each chapter is shorter and less detailed. Singman discusses bread in one paragraph, while Newman takes two pages to talk about not only bread but every grain that was used in bread.

Because of its greater detail and modest price, this is an excellent resource for school and public libraries that need accessible secondary sources for students doing papers on the Middle Ages. Even if libraries have *Daily Life in Chaucer's England*, they will want to add *Daily Life in the Middle Ages* to their collections.

★ **The Encyclopedia of Jewish Life before and during the Holocaust.** Ed. By Shmuel Spector and Geoffrey Wigoder. 3v. 2001. 1,769p. bibliog. glossary. illus. indexes. New York Univ., $395 (0-8147-9378-9). 940.

The Holocaust was a calculated effort to wipe out all traces of an ancient culture. The Nazis not only tried to destroy the Jewish people but they also wanted to obliterate any memory of them, whether in the form of books, works of art, schools, synagogues, or businesses. Fortunately, they did not succeed. In fact, the Nazis' meticulous documentation of their efforts helped create a record of what they tried to annihilate. Survivors provided testimony, too. In 1953, the Israeli Parliament passed the Yad Vashem Remembrance Authority Law to perpetuate the memory of all that the Nazis destroyed. The resulting museum, memorial, archives, and research center, located in a country settled in large part by survivors, takes its name from Isaiah 56:5: "I will give them in My House and within My walls a monument (*yad*) and a name (*vashem*)." As part of their mission, the scholars working there produced a 38-volume Hebrew-language encyclopedia of Jewish communities. This three-volume English-language work is a condensation of that source.

Jewish life is communal. Study, worship, charity, and family require a group. The encyclopedia chronicles the people, habits, and customs of more than 6,500 Jewish communities that were thriving in the early part of the twentieth century. Their precise locations are based on documents from recently opened archives. The alphabetical entries are arranged by community name transcribed as it is in the language of its country without diacritical marks. Russian names are transliterated using the standard English-language system. Hebrew personal names are transliterated rather than translated. The country locations provided are from September 1939, with added information about their present location after border changes; for example, "Bobrka, Lwow dist., Poland, today Ukraine." For parts of Germany annexed by Poland, both the Polish and German names are given: "Gdansk (Ger. Danzig)."

Entries range in length from a few sentences for small villages to several pages for large communities such as Vilna and Warsaw. They include information about how long Jews lived there, what kind of work they did, the communal facilities that they maintained (synagogues, schools, ritual baths, etc.), attacks on the community throughout history, how many Jews lived there when the Nazis arrived, and how many were deported and killed by them. In this condensed edition, the pre–World War I material has been abridged so that the editors could emphasize the interwar and Holocaust periods. Statistical tables and the source lists at the end of articles have been eliminated.

A glossary, selected bibliography, chronological table of Jewish communities from the fourth century B.C.E. to 1989, and a series of maps showing Jewish communities, concentration camps, death camps, and mass murder sites appear at the end of volume 3. There are two indexes, one of communities and one of persons. The "Index of Communities" includes those communities with main entries, those mentioned in the text without main entries, and variant spellings and additional names. There are cross-references in the index, but not in the text. There are no main entries for people, but the "Index of Persons" refers users to the articles where their names appear.

The encyclopedia has beautiful archival black-and-white photographs portraying daily life in the cities and towns discussed in the text—shopkeepers, students, athletes, and political activists go about their daily business. There is also a pictorial supplement, "In Memoriam," at the end of volume 3, documenting what happened to these vibrant communities that existed throughout Europe and North Africa.

The Encyclopedia of Jewish Life before and during the Holocaust is an outstanding tribute to the vanished communities as well as a valuable document. It shows users how old and respected communities such as that of Tunis, dating from the tenth century B.C.E., and Vilna, from the fifteenth century A.D., were systematically destroyed. By preserving their memory, the editors have created a valuable resource for students, scholars, genealogists, and anyone interested in modern history. They have given the dead a monument and a name.

History of World War I. 3v. 2002. 976p. bibliog. glossary. illus. indexes. maps. Marshall Cavendish, $279.95 (0-7614-7231-2). 940.3.

Aimed at an audience from sixth grade up, this set is divided into three volumes: *War and Response, 1914–1916*; *Victory and Defeat, 1917–1918*; and *Home Fronts/Technologies of War*. The volumes are organized into from 15 to 17 chapters covering major topics, and the information is presented in a narrative style rather than in discrete entries. Chapter titles include "The Western Front, 1914–1915," "Neutrals and Supporters," "The War at Sea, 1917," "Germany's Last Attacks," "France at War," and "Armor and Transport." The indexes give good access to more specific subjects. Each of the three volumes includes illustrations on the majority of pages, and there are many maps and charts to complement the text. The writing style and vocabulary are accessible to the intended audience.

Volume 3 concludes with a glossary; a topical list of books and Web sites for additional research; a time line; indexes to personalities, places, and battles and campaigns; and a general set index.

Sources with similar subject coverage, such as *The European Powers in the First World War: An Encyclopedia* (Garland, 1996) and *The United States in the First World War: An Encyclopedia* (Garland, 1995), offer the user short entries arranged alphabetically but are more research oriented. The visual appeal of *History of World War I* will certainly make it attractive to younger readers, especially in libraries that do not already own *The Grolier Library of World War I* (1997). Recommended for school and public libraries.

The Holocaust Encyclopedia. Ed. by Walter Laqueur. 2001. 765p. illus. index. maps. Yale, $60 (0-300-08432-3). 940.5318.

Although this resource, the work of more than 100 contributors, concentrates on the Nazi persecution of the Jews, there are articles on other persecuted groups, such as Gypsies and Jehovah's Witnesses. Preceding the entries is a day-by-day chronology beginning with January 1933 and continuing until May 8, 1945. The alphabetical encyclopedia entries vary greatly in length. Most biographies are very brief, some exceptions being those for Anne Frank, Adolf Hitler, and Raoul Wallenberg. Even figures such as Joseph Goebbels, Hermann Goring, and Adolf Eichmann warrant only a paragraph (Eichmann's trial, however, receives greater coverage in a separate entry). Longer signed articles, many several pages in length, cover places (concentration camps, German occupied countries, etc.), concepts (*Literature, Rescue, Restitution*), events, policies, and groups (*Polish Jewry, Refugees, Righteous among the Nations*).

Black-and-white illustrations consist mostly of captioned photographs but also include documents, maps, and posters. Limited cross-references direct readers to related articles, The inclusion of *see* references would have made the content more accessible; for example, researchers looking for an entry on the U.S. might not think to look under *American policy*. Instead of a traditional bibliography, there is a "Bibliographical Essay" written by the director of the Yad Vashem Library, discussing the vast amount of Holocaust literature, including Web sites. Minimal bibliographic information embedded in the essay makes it difficult to use for collection development.

The analysis of events is what sets this title apart, and in many instances serious researchers will find a satisfying depth of information. Recommended for public and academic libraries needing an up-to-date, single-volume reference on the topic.

World Eras: European Renaissance and Reformation. Volume 1: 1350–1600. Ed. by Norman J. Wilson. 2001. 522p. bibliog. glossary. illus. index. Gale, $95 (0-7876-1706-7). 940.2.

Designed primarily for high-school students and general users, this resource, modeled after the American Decades series, is comprised of 10 chapters. The first two, focusing on world events and geography, respectively, provide users a global perspective and context for the culture and time period in question. Remaining chapters treat other cultural elements, including art, communication, transportation, exploration, social classes, economy, politics, law, military, recreation, family, religion, philosophy, science, technology, and health. Each chapter is subdivided into five types of material: chronological, overview, topical, biographical, and documentary. These first two divisions provide readers a visual time line and brief overview of the area presented. The topical entries that follow these sections convey even more specialized, detailed information. In the "Arts" chapter, for example, readers will find *Princely courts and patronage, Sacred art, Sculpture,* and *Woodcuts,* just to name a few. The final two subdivisions in each chapter contain information on significant individuals and annotated checklists of documentary material that served as the principal sources for the material in this work.

This volume, in addition to its fine organization, structure, and arrangement, is equally impressive for its inclusive, well-written content. In choosing material, the editor and compilers endeavored to cover a diverse group of men and women—both well known and lesser known—from a variety of countries, backgrounds, professions, and socioeconomic levels. This choice of material is complemented by balanced, well-articulated prose. Entries are concise, but thorough, straightforward, and highly understandable, all of which should make this work very popular with high-school and undergraduate students. Material is further enhanced by 150 illustrations, maps, diagrams, and drawings, not to mention sidebars that contain interesting tidbits of knowledge.

This valuable reference tool is highly recommended and would greatly enhance not only high-school libraries but public and smaller academic libraries as well.

British Political Leaders: A Biographical Dictionary. Ed. by Keith Laybourn. 2001. 363p. bibliogs. illus. ABC-CLIO, $85 (1-57607-043-3); e-book, $95 (1-57607-570-2). 941.

This volume offers serious Anglophiles 198 entries covering the British leaders who filled "the top four offices of state and the post of secretary of state for the colonies between 1730 and the present," the four top offices being prime minister, chancellor of the exchequer, foreign secretary, and home secretary. Arrangement of entries is alphabetical, either by name or by title depending on how the individual was best known. For example, Benjamin Disraeli is listed under his given name, not as the Earl of Beaconsfield. In cases where official titles have evolved over the centuries, the editors have, for the sake of consistency, used the modern title. Thus, all prime ministers are listed as such, even though the post was once referred to as First Lord of the Treasury.

Entries range in length from just under half of a page for Richard Ryder, home secretary from 1809 to 1812, to almost five pages for Tony Blair. Each individually signed biography concludes with a list of the main sources used in its preparation. For general background information, especially regarding lesser-known figures, the editors relied on *The Dictionary of National Biography* and *Dod's Parliamentary Companion,* among other standard British biography reference sources. A comprehensive bibliography appears at the end of the book. Also provided is a "Chronological List of Leaders by Cabinet Office." A small number of black-and-white illustrations accompanies the text.

The volume does an admirable job of pulling together concise biographies of Great Britain's leaders since the early decade of the sixteenth century and presenting them in straightforward prose. It will be a welcome addition to the reference collections of libraries serving researchers with deep interest in British history, politics, and government. However, libraries that do not see heavy traffic in this area may find that sources such as general encyclopedias will serve well enough.

Collins Encyclopedia of Scotland. Rev. ed. Ed. by John Keay and Julia Keay. 2001. 1,102p. appendix. illus. index. maps. HarperCollins UK; dist. by Trafalgar Square, $75 (0-00-710353-0). 941.1003.

Here is a revised version of the 1994 encyclopedia covering all things Scottish. There are more than 4,000 A–Z entries, with more than 100 illustrations, on the places, people, and events of ancient and modern Scotland. A list of more than 100 contributors is included at the beginning, but all entries are unsigned. The lengthy index is helpful, as are extensive cross-references within each entry. Appendixes include the lineage of the Presbyterian Churches of Scotland and royal genealogy.

Coverage of people includes such well-known figures as poet Robert Burns, physician Alexander Fleming, artist Charles McKenzie, and King Robert I ("The Bruce"). Among the places that are treated are major and minor cities, ranging from Aberdeen to Melrose; castles and cathedrals, such as Edinburgh Castle and Iona Cathedral; and other significant locations, such as Loch Ness and Inchmahome Priory on the Lake of Menteith, where Queen Mary was sent at the age of four in 1547 for her safety. Major events include *Glencoe, Massacre of; Potato famine;* and *Lockerbie air crash.* Also covered are such general topics as *Football* and *Shipbuilding and marine engineering.*

According to the editors, there are 100 new entries (*Dolly the Sheep* and *Scottish Parliament* being notable examples), and revisions have been made to 1,000 more. Many entries (for example, *Oil and gas*) have not been updated since the first edition.

The selection of entries is puzzling at times. For example, there are long discussions of *Fish farming, Fishing* (angling), and *Fishing industry* but, except for a few scattered entries, such as *Haggis* and *Oatmeal,* nothing related to cooking or food. Overall, however, this volume provides a thorough examination of Scotland and Scottish life. Recommended for all libraries where there is an interest in the topic, especially those that do not have the first edition.

Encyclopedia of the Wars of the Roses. By John Wagner. 2001. 350p. appendixes. bibliogs. illus. index. ABC-CLIO, $75 (1-85109-358-3). 942.04.

Alphabetically arranged and targeted for students and other nonspecialists, this 281-entry encyclopedia comprises primarily terms, places, individuals (130 of the entries are biographical), and events pertaining to the Wars of the Roses, with entries as varied as *Artillery; Hungerford,*

Sir Thomas; London; and St. Albans, Battle of. The scope is quite impressive, covering not only the conflicts in question but also areas and issues beyond, including Brittany, Ireland, and Hundred Years War. Entries average 500 words in length and are noteworthy for their clarity and accessibility, the latter improved by Wagner's skill in contextualizing content. Strengthened by cross-references and followed by lists of recommended titles for further reading, entries are thorough and well balanced. One entry heading is conspicuously absent—Rose, which readers may wish to consult to learn more about the emblems of the contending Lancaster and York families. Although this information is provided in several entries, including Badges and Wars of the Roses, Naming of, its location may not be readily apparent to readers who do not turn to the index for help.

This minor criticism aside, the encyclopedia has much to recommend it, including a detailed chronology, fine illustrations, a map of important battle sites, genealogical charts, an extensive bibliography, selected Web sites, and special features, such as the table of dynastic affiliations, which allows readers to look up noblemen and instantly see the house to which they owed allegiance. With such value-added features, fine content, and high usability, this reference book would be a welcome addition to academic and large public libraries.

Nazi-Deutsch/Nazi German: An English Lexicon of the Language of the Third Reich. By Robert Michael and Karin Doerr. 2002. 480p. appendix. bibliog. Greenwood, $79.95 (0-313-32106-X). 943.086.

An important and unique addition to the literature of Nazi Germany, this lexicon serves as a dictionary of the terminology and specialized vocabulary of Nazi ideology. It covers hundreds of propaganda slogans, military terms, abbreviations and acronyms, euphemisms, and code names. It also defines ranks and offices in the Nazi Party, the German Reich government, and the armed forces. An appendix includes lists of concentration camps, Nazi songs, the Nazi Party Program, the Hitler oaths, and examples of Nazi material included in children's textbooks.

Each entry includes the Nazi-German term, its abbreviation if applicable, the literal English translation, and the definition of the term within its Third Reich context. Cross-references help draw related terms together.

Familiar, if disturbing, terms such as "Juden raus!" (Jews out) and Blut und Boden (blood and soil) illustrate the aggressive and chauvinistic nature of Nazi German, while terms such as "Arbeit macht frei" (work will set you free)—a slogan placed at Auschwitz and other death camps—illustrate the ironic and euphemistic qualities that often made Nazi German a kind of doublespeak.

Although most definitions are brief, some, such as Endlosung der Judenfrage (the "Final Solution of the Jewish question"), contain a more detailed description of how and when the term was used. There are also illuminating and scholarly essays by the authors that detail "The Tradition of Anti-Jewish Language" and "Nazi-Deutsch: An Ideological Language of Exclusion, Domination, and Annihilation."

Because this work provides great detail, it adds a dimension not completely covered in The Penguin Dictionary of the Third Reich (Penguin, 1997) or Dictionary of the Holocaust: Biography, Geography, and Terminology (Greenwood, 1997). This compilation will be a strong research tool for academic, public, and high-school libraries, especially those with students or scholars studying Nazi Germany, the Holocaust, or World War II.

The Regions of Italy: A Reference Guide to History and Culture. By Roy Domenico. 2001. 465p. bibliog. glossary. illus. index. maps. Greenwood, $60 (0-313-30733-4). 945.

Domenico, a history professor at the University of Scranton, illustrates the importance of the 20 regions of Italy by devoting a chapter to each of them. Beginning with Abruzzo and ending with Veneto, he provides statistics and general information, including a line map of the region and another map placing it in the country as a whole. This is followed by a few pages describing the economy, history, politics, and cuisine, with a representative recipe.

Because Italian regions are divided into provinces, the author continues with the history and culture of each province and then mentions important communes (towns or cities) within the province. Significant buildings, especially cathedrals and churches, and famous people of a city are highlighted. Each chapter ends with a selective bibliography. Several pages of black-and-white photographs are placed in the middle of the volume. An index, a chronology, a bibliography, and a small and simple glossary complete the volume.

This is an obvious labor of love by an academician. With a scholarly tone, it is an appropriate purchase for either the reference or circulating collections of academic libraries.

Russia and Eastern Europe: A Bibliographic Guide to English-Language Publications, 1992–1999. By Helen F. Sullivan and Robert H. Burger. 2001. 537p. index. Libraries Unlimited, $90 (1-56308-736-7). 947.

This is the latest in a series of volumes covering the English-language monographic literature about Russian and Eastern Europe back to 1900. The authors, both with the Slavic and East European Library at the University of Illinois at Urbana-Champaign, are also responsible for two volumes covering 1986 to the early 1990s. They describe the works listed in this volume as a "representative selection." Items were chosen from titles reviewed in Slavic Review (a highly selective source) and titles listed in the OCLC WorldCat database. Excluded are items under 50 pages, routine government publications, serials, juvenile literature, local genealogies, museum guidebooks, music, dissertations and theses, and nonbook media.

Following a chapter on general works, the main arrangement is by country or region. By far the largest section is devoted to Russia, and within this large topic, works are listed by discipline, such as education and culture, history, military affairs, and sociology. Most of these broad areas are further subdivided by format, time, or topic. For example, the section on the economy includes subsections for statistics, economic history, perestroika, major issues (e.g., unemployment, privatization), and major economic sectors (e.g., agriculture, industry, finance). Chapters on other countries are considerably shorter, and topical divisions vary according to the nature of the material that is listed.

Numbered entries are arranged alphabetically by author or title. Citations contain all the standard information except for ISBNs and are followed by descriptive annotations, which in some cases consist of quotations from the work itself. Illustrations, maps, bibliographies, and indexes are noted. The volume concludes with a name (i.e., author) index and a subject index. The biggest weakness of the subject index is a lack of cross-references. The arrangement of index entries can be problematic as well, with *agriculture and state* preceding *agriculture*.

All libraries with interest in Russia and Eastern Europe will want this bibliography, especially if they have the earlier volumes.

Korean War: Almanac and Primary Sources. By Sonia G. Benson. 2002. 313p. glossary. illus. index. maps. UXL, $49 (0-7876-5691-7). 951.904.
Korean War: Biographies. By Sonia G. Benson. 2002. 268p. glossary. illus. index. UXL, $49 (0-7876-5692-5). 951.904.

This addition to UXL's Reference Library series, aimed at supporting the middle-and high-school history curriculum, is made up of two volumes: *Almanac and Primary Sources* and *Biographies*. Consistent with the series, the layout provides uncrowded pages with boxed information clearly delineated in gray-toned areas. There are approximately 140 black-and-white photographs and maps complementing the text. Both volumes provide a time line and a "Words to Know" section. Web-site suggestions are current through mid-2001.

The *Almanac and Primary Sources* volume has 13 chapters in the "Almanac" section and 12 documents in the "Primary Sources" section. The 13 chapters provide an overview of the war, its causes, major battles, and the peace process. The 12 documents include excerpts from speeches, memoirs, oral histories, reports, and government documents including the "Bridge at No Gun Ri: Survivors' Petition," Mao Zedong's "Nuclear Weapons Are Paper Tigers," and Harry S. Truman's "President's Address: Korean War Dismissal of General Douglas MacArthur." For each document, important background information is provided, and the document's impact on its author and audience is explored. A glossary in the margin defines terms, people, and ideas.

The *Biographies* volume profiles 25 people who played pivotal roles in the Korean War, including generals such as Mark W. Clark and Douglas MacArthur and leaders such as Kim Il Sung, Mao, Truman, and Syngman Rhee. Arranged alphabetically, each entry offers a black-and-white portrait, birth and death dates and places, occupation, brief summary of the early years, emphasis on the person's work and involvement in the Korean War, and a short "Where to Learn More" list of resources.

These two volumes provide students, teachers, and the general public with an excellent starting point for researching the events and people of the Korean War. Like other titles in the series, its selective coverage and wealth of background and context make it a good choice for the designated age group. Older students will want to consult Spencer C.

Tucker's *Encyclopedia of the Korean War: A Political, Social, and Military History* (ABC-CLIO, 2000), which is the most complete treatment in a single source.

Encyclopedia of Contemporary Japanese Culture. Ed. by Sandra Buckley. 2002. 634p. index. Routledge, $140 (0-415-14344-6). 952.04.

A fascinating culture balancing traditional and modern elements, a history of intense American-Japanese relations dating back to Commodore Perry, and, despite a downturn well into its second decade, being one of the world's top economic powers are more than enough reasons to welcome an encyclopedia of contemporary Japanese culture. Editor Buckley, who has written several hundred of the more than 750 signed articles, has combined with Routledge, a leading publisher of studies on contemporary Japan, to produce a valuable addition to library reference collections.

More than 100 contributors, largely affiliated with American, Japanese, Australian, and Canadian universities, provide entries on topics ranging from important personalities, cities and districts, organizations, and industries to *Arranged marriages*, *Baseball*, *Dialects*, *Foreign food*, *Installation art*, *Manga* (comic books), *Mobile telephones*, *Peace and anti-nuclear movements*, *Sex tourism*, *Textbook controversies*, and *Zen*. Some of the more surprising entries for Westerners only marginally familiar with Japan include *Bedridden patients*, *Beer*, *Brazilian Japanese*, *Christmas*, *Coffee*, *Pickles*, and *Whiskey*.

Articles range in length from a paragraph to several pages, and each is followed by a list for further reading. There are *see also* references at the end of many articles, cross-references between articles, and boldfaced words within articles to indicate topics with main entries. Articles cover the period from 1945 through the end of the century, adding historical perspective where necessary. *Romaji* (romanized transliteration of Japanese) is used throughout, and Japanese names are given in Japanese order (i.e., family name first). The complete absence of illustrations may deter browsers.

Two recommended encyclopedias that take in the whole scope of Japanese history and culture are the profusely illustrated *Cambridge Encyclopedia of Japan* (Cambridge, 1993) and Boye Lafayette De Mente's lightly illustrated *Japan Encyclopedia* (Passport, 1995). Neither is as up-to-date nor has the depth of post-1945 focus as *Encyclopedia of Contemporary Japanese Culture*, which is recommended for larger public and academic libraries.

Kodansha Encyclopedia of Japan. [Internet database]. Macmillan Online, pricing from $450 for public and academic libraries, $300 for school libraries. [http://www.ency-japan.com]. (Last accessed February 22, 2002).

Building upon *Japan: An Illustrated Encyclopedia* (Kodansha, 1993) and its predecessor, the nine-volume *Kodansha Encyclopedia of Japan* (Kodansha, 1983), the online *Kodansha Encyclopedia of Japan*, with 11,203 entries and some two million words, is at least as comprehensive as its predecessors and far more up-to-date. Nearly all of the 11,000 articles appearing in *Japan: An Illustrated Encyclopedia*, thousands in updated form, also appear here. In addition, there are 150 new articles reflecting "people, companies, events, trends, etc." that have figured importantly in the last decade. An international group of some 1,400 scholars, primarily from Japan and the U.S., have contributed articles ranging from 50 to more than 4,000 words. According to the publisher, there are 1,119 portraits, 651 other photographs and illustrations, 47 prefectural maps, more than 4,000 titles for cross-reference, and 698 URLs.

The small photographic portraits are easy to locate, as portraits can be browsed A–Z; but we were unable to locate either prefectural maps or URLs. There is a map of Japan showing where each prefecture is located and allowing the user to access articles relevant to a chosen prefecture. *Japan: An Illustrated Encyclopedia*, with some 4,000 color illustrations, is superior in this regard; it also provides the titles of entries in both English and kanji characters, whereas the online version provides titles in English and romaji (or transliteration of the Japanese sounds into roman characters). In fact, Chinese (kanji) and Japanese (kana) characters do not appear at all in the text of the online encyclopedia; this fault is most apparent in the articles related to the Japanese language.

Navigation is simple. From the home page, one may search, browse, or access help, the foreword, or the introduction. There are options for full-text, Boolean, topic, and image searches. A–Z article, contributor, and portrait lists can be browsed. Full-text searches produce a ranked list of articles and their first few sentences, with the search term in red. Selecting one of these produces the full article, with hyperlinked terms underlined and in blue, as well as options to link to related articles and, far less frequently, to related images. For best results, Internet Explorer 6 and a screen resolution of at least 800 by 600 are recommended.

Kodansha Encyclopedia of Japan is highly recommended for academic and large public libraries as well as any institution where current, accurate information on all aspects of Japan is a necessity. Though many articles are annoyingly brief, this work is unsurpassed for scope and currency. For illustrations, hold on to *Japan: An Illustrated Encyclopedia*.

Africa: An Encyclopedia for Students. 4v. Ed. by John Middleton. 2002. illus. index. maps. Scribner, $375 (0-684-80650-9). 960.

The highly regarded *Encyclopedia of Africa South of the Sahara* was published by Scribner in 1997. The editor, John Middleton, has now produced an abbreviated version, appropriate for high-school and undergraduate students and adults. The original included 896 articles. This new version has about 450 entries in just under 1,000 pages. Topics include countries, regions, geographic features, cultural groups, personalities, and general subjects, such as *Body adornment and clothing*, *Oral tradition*, and *Writing systems*.

The preface indicates that many of the original articles have been adapted and updated and that a substantial amount of new information has been added on North Africa. In an effort to make the resource user-friendly, time lines, sidebars, and definitions now appear in margins next to related text; and individual country entries include quick reference fact boxes. Each volume has an eight-page color photo-essay: "People and Culture" in the first volume, followed by "The Land and Its History," "Art and Architecture," and "Daily Life" in subsequent volumes. Additional black-and-white photographs and more than 50 maps are also offered.

Despite these enhancements, the work retains a scholarly mien. Although articles range from a few paragraphs to several pages, dense blocks of text with an encyclopedic style of writing may prove daunting to younger researchers. Subjects are covered in depth and include discussions on adult topics such as female circumcision and various cultural attitudes toward homosexuality.

Comparable in scope and level to Willie F. Page's *Encyclopedia of African History and Culture* [RBB Ja 1 & 15 02], this offering will be more accessible to researchers because of its straight alphabetical arrangement (*African History and Culture* is arranged chronologically and then alphabetically). *Africa: An Encyclopedia for Students* should be seriously considered by high-school, undergraduate, and public library collections that do not own the parent set.

Encyclopedia of African History and Culture. 3v. By Willie F. Page. 2001. bibliogs. glossary. illus. index. maps. Facts On File, $247.50 (0-8160-4472-4). 960.

African history from the earliest stages to 1850 is the focus of this set intended for students and general readers. The author is emeritus professor of Africana Studies at Brooklyn College and former director of the Africana Research Center.

Overall arrangement is chronological. Volume 1, "Ancient Africa," covers prehistory to 500 C.E.; volume 2, "African Kingdoms," covers 500 to 1500; and volume 3, "From Conquest to Colonization," covers 1500 to 1850. Within each volume, arrangement is alphabetical. Entries range in length from a paragraph to several pages and treat a wide variety of topics, including places (*Ghana empire*, *Mozambique*, *Timbuktu*), geographical features and wildlife (*Ethiopian highlands*, *Lualaba River*, *Giraffe*), people and groups of people (*Imhotep*, *Bantu*, *Craftspeople*, *Hunter-gatherers*), commodities (*Bananas*, *Cloth*, *Gold*), practices (*Child rearing*, *Farming techniques*, *Initiation rites*), and more. There are also broad entries such as *Art*, *Climate*, and *Towns and cities*. Some entries conclude with lists of further readings. Occasional sidebars and illustrations break up the text. Readers are aided by a glossary, a time line, and a set index that are repeated in every volume. Another useful tool is an alphabetical list of all entry headings and the volume or volumes in which they appear. We counted more than 1,350 headings, but because many headings occur in more than one volume, the total number of encyclopedia entries is considerably more.

Although the chronological approach provides a useful historical perspective, it also creates challenges for the reader. Some topics, such as *Ancestor worship*, *Body adornment*, and *Family structure*, are addressed only in volume 1 although they also have relevance for volumes 2 and 3.

Coverage of other topics can be disjointed, because the reader must check in each volume for entries on *Egypt*, to take one example. Fortunately, the index and extensive cross-references do a good job of referring readers to content in all three volumes.

Although we have seen many reference sources related to African American culture and history, Africa is not as well represented. This is a problem that the editors of *Africana: The Encyclopedia of the African and African American Experience* (Perseus, 1999) tried to address, and for smaller collections *Africana* may suffice. *Encyclopedia of Africa South of the Sahara* (Scribner, 1997) is more scholarly and covers a wide range of contemporary as well as historical topics. *Encyclopedia of African History and Culture* fills a gap in the reference collection and is recommended for high-school, public, and academic libraries that need to expand their coverage of Africa.

★ Encyclopedia of American Indian Contributions to the World:
15,000 Years of Inventions and Innovations. By Emory Dean Keoke and Kay Marie Porterfield. 2001. 384p. appendixes. bibliog. glossary. illus. index. maps. Facts On File, $65 (0-8160-4052-4). 970.

More than 450 inventions and innovations that can be traced to indigenous peoples of North, Middle, and South America are described in this wonderful encyclopedia. Criteria for selection are that the item or concept must have originated in the Americas, it must have been used by the indigenous people, and it must have been adopted in some way by other cultures. Some of the innovations may have been independently developed in other parts of the world (geometry, for example, was developed in ancient China, Greece, and the Middle East as well as in the Americas) but still fit all three criteria. The period of time covered is 25,000 B.C. to the twentieth century. Among the entries are *Adobe, Agriculture, Appaloosa horse breed, Chocolate, Cigars, Diabetes medication, Freeze-drying, Hydraulics, Trousers, Urban planning,* and *Zoned biodiversity*. Readers will find much of the content revealing. The authors note that the Moche "invented the electrochemical production of electricity" although they used it only for electroplating, a process they developed "more than a thousand years" before the Europeans, who generally get the credit. The Aztec medical system was far more comprehensive than anything available in Europe at the time of contact.

The entries are in alphabetical order. Most are anywhere from one paragraph to a column in length, though some (*Stonemasonry techniques, Pharmacology, Road systems*) cover a page or more. Each entry includes the date and area of origination and has a short bibliography of secondary resources at the end. The cross-references appear in capital letters within an entry or as *see also* references at the end. The introduction has cross-references in it as well. Some of the entries include black-and-white illustrations or photographs. The only critical item missing from most entries is a pronunciation guide.

The end matter includes two appendixes: "Tribes Organized by Culture Area" and a selection of maps. These are followed by a glossary (of mostly medical terms used in many entries but again with no pronunciation guides), a chronology, and a bibliography (with a few Internet sites). There are several indexes: "Entries by Tribe, Group, or Linguistic Group"; "Entries by Geographical Culture Area"; a subject index; and a general index.

This is a well-written book with fascinating information and wonderful pictures. It should be in every public, school, and academic library for its depth of research and amazing wealth of knowledge.

Encyclopedia of Contemporary Latin and Caribbean Cultures. 3v. Ed. by Daniel Balderston and others. 2000. 1,754p. bibliogs. index. Routledge, $399 (0-415-13188-X). 972.9003.

Reference sources on Latin America and the Caribbean that are accessible to general readers and students are not easy to find. This set presents more than 4,000 entries that document "social, political and cultural developments . . . from the 1920s to the present day."

Except for an initial series of articles that survey each decade, the work is in straight dictionary format. Articles range in length from a short paragraph to several two-columned pages. All articles are signed, and many have some suggested readings, some of which may be available in a large public library. Each country has its own entry. Also covered are topics in food and drink (*Cacao, Eating out, Maize*), cultural institutions and phenomena (*Beauty pageants, Libraries, Pan American Union*), intellectual life (*Chemistry, Historiography*), performing arts (*Alonso, Alicia; Carnival; Teatro Libre*), and sport (*Clemente, Roberto; Tennis*). Popular culture is as richly represented as are high culture and political and historical matters. Significant movies, plays, and television programs have a place, as do musical forms. Items in bold type within entries have their own articles elsewhere in the text. There are no illustrations or maps, an omission in a work that might be used by general readers whose geographical knowledge may be shaky. A "Thematic Entry List" groups articles by countries, from Antigua to Virgin Islands, and categories, from "Architecture" to "Writers." This is supplemented by a more expansive general index.

With its emphasis on contemporary culture, the set complements *Encyclopedia of Latin American History and Culture* (Scribner, 1996). For ready-reference and introductory information, it should be considered by larger public libraries, community college libraries, and academic libraries with introductory courses on Latin America.

Handbook to Life in the Ancient Maya World. By Lynn V. Foster. 2002. 402p. bibliogs. illus. index. maps. Facts On File, $50 (0-8160-4148-2). 972.81.

This useful new source for readers interested in the Maya is arranged in 12 readable chapters covering topics such as archaeology, geography, government, cosmology, architecture, astronomy, and daily life. These chapters are subdivided into sections that are usually several pages in length; examples are "Agriculture," "Other Food Production," "Craft Production," and "Trade" in the chapter "Economy, Industry, and Trade." The subdivisions are in turn divided into smaller sections that each address a specific topic, such as "Soil Conservation and Intensive Cultivation or "Salt Production." An extensive index gives access to all of the topical subdivisions, and there are cross-references within the essays. Each chapter includes a reading list. The volume also includes a chronological chart of Maya history, an extensive bibliography, black-and-white illustrations and photographs, and maps.

The Oxford Encyclopedia of Mesoamerican Cultures: The Civilizations of Mexico and Central America (Oxford, 2001) [RBB S 1 01] and *Archaeology of Ancient Mexico and Central America: An Encyclopedia* (Garland, 2001) [RBB Mr 1 01] each covers a wider scope of geography and cultures and is organized alphabetically instead of thematically. If forced to choose only one reference source on ancient Mesoamerican cultures, *Archaeology of Ancient Mexico and Central America: An Encyclopedia* provides the best balance of comprehensive coverage and relatively low price ($150). The *Handbook* would be a useful addition to public and academic library collections that need more extensive coverage of the Maya.

★ The Oxford Encyclopedia of Mesoamerican Cultures: The Civilizations of Mexico and Central America. 3v. Ed. by David Carrasco. 2001. 1,424p. illus. index. maps. Oxford, $395 (0-19-510815-9). 972.01.

In his preface, Carrasco, professor of History of Religions and director of the Raphael and Fletcher Lee Moses Mesoamerican Archive at Princeton University, explains why the time is right for a major reference work on Mesoamerican cultures. Significant archaeological excavations, linguistic breakthroughs (in particular the decipherment of the Maya code), and advances in the study of the postcolonial and modern periods have generated a great deal of new knowledge in recent years, and this multidisciplinary work organizes and interprets that knowledge.

In basic terms, the area covered by the encyclopedia encompasses "the southern two thirds of mainland Mexico, as well as Guatemala, Belize, El Salvador, and parts of Honduras, Nicaragua, and Costa Rica." But *Mesoamerica* is more a cultural concept than a geographical entity, shaped by two major transformations in the history of the Western Hemisphere: the evolution of urbanized cultures and the encounter between Europe, Africa, and the Americas. The encyclopedia reflects these roots and continuing influences by considering not just the pre-Hispanic and colonial eras but the modern period as well. Coverage begins with the Olmecs (extant around 1200–500 B.C.E.), "the first Mesoamerican society to create stone monuments," and extends through the twentieth century.

More than 300 scholars contributed 617 articles, which are alphabetically arranged. Length ranges from 500 words for some biographies (*Cuauhtemoc; Kahlo, Frida*) to 7,000 words for broad topics such as *Anthropology*. The bibliographies attached to each entry include titles in Spanish as well as English and are often annotated. Cross-references aid navigation, as do a "Synoptic Outline of Contents" and a very detailed index. The "Synoptic Outline of Contents" groups entries under conceptual categories such as "Written and Oral Sources" and "Economy and Subsistence," identifying both the principal articles (*Conquest nar-*

ratives, Agriculture) and more specific entries (*Popol Vuh, Maize*) related to each concept. The "Directory of Contributors" that precedes the index itemizes not only the credentials of each contributor but also the particular entries for which he or she is responsible. The black-and-white photographs scattered throughout the text tend to be fuzzy.

Entries cover cultures (*Mayac, Toltec*), people (*Cortes, Fernando; Zapata, Emiliano*), and sites (*Copan, Tenochtitlan*). Readers will also find discussions related to economic, political, social, and religious organization (*Fishing, Gender roles, Slavery,* Jesuits); practices and beliefs (*Ballgame, Creation myths, Curing and healing*); and artistic expression (*Baroque, Feathers and featherwork*). In addition, there is coverage of developments in the field of Mesoamerican studies, treated in entries such as E*pigraphy* and *Periodical literature and reference works* and in biographies of several archaeologists and scholars. The editorial decision "to emphasize the long history of Mesoamerica" is apparent throughout. The lengthy *Art and Architecture* begins with the sculpture and urban architecture of the pre-Hispanic period and ends with a discussion of how ancient themes and styles are incorporated into late-twentieth-century work. Similarly, *Cuisine* begins with a description of the Aztec diet and ends by noting the influence of American food on present-day Mexican eating habits. However, some entries, such as *Maize*, give only a cursory nod to developments after around 1500.

Prior to publication of this work, the most important source on Mesoamerican culture was the 16-volume H*andbook of Middle American Indians* (Austin), which was published from 1964 to 1976 and to which Carrasco acknowledges a debt. T*he Oxford Encyclopedia of Mesoamerican Cultures* both builds upon and updates that resource and is highly recommended for all academic and large public libraries. Other libraries serving readers with a strong interest in these cultures may also want to consider it.

★**America the Beautiful.** [Internet database]. 2001. Grolier, pricing from $209 in combination with other Grolier databases. [http://www.go.grolier.com]. (Last accessed December 12, 2001).

Grolier's latest addition to its excellent online offerings of reference materials is the venerable state series found in most K–12 and public libraries. Although *America the Beautiful* (ATB) online statistics are impressive—1,000 articles; 2,700 photographs; 400 maps, many of them interactive; 1,000 Internet links; 550 profiles; 115 games and puzzles; 60 time lines; and 400 places to visit—it is the site's user-friendliness, clean look, and well-planned arrangement that will draw users.

Libraries already subscribing to Grolier databases have two ways to search for information because a customized splash screen provides a means for searching all the subscriptions at the same time. The results are then posted with the Grolier source noted. Noting the source is a boon to librarians and teachers trying to match students with grade- and reading-level-appropriate resources. A search for *California* across all of Grolier's online databases identified 108 documents in a matter of seconds. The second search strategy is, obviously, just to search ATB itself. Given the wealth of information in ATB, this search strategy can lead to many fascinating hours of learning.

The main part of the clean-looking home page is a clickable map of the 50 states, offering a colorful display without affecting readability. The top of the page features a collage of American images and a place to enter a term for searching. Immediately under this banner are tabs for specific searches: U.S. Topics, Timelines, Profiles, Games, and Almanac. At the bottom right of the home page are buttons for Puerto Rico and U.S. Territories; on the left, for About, Help (which makes an excellent "cheat sheet" to post near research stations), and Teacher Resources. The banner, tabs, and buttons (except those for Puerto Rico and U.S. Territories) remain in position on all pages.

The U.S. Topics tab allows searches by Cities, Famous Places, Native Americans (that is, Native American tribes), Natural Wonders, and Presidents. Time lines can be searched by U.S. History, Science and Technology, Arts and Entertainment, Written Word, and World History. In addition, any two state time lines can be compared. Profiles, an alphabetical list by person of the biographies in the database, range from *Aaron, Henry* to *Zitkala-Sa*. Games include puzzles and quizzes on topics such as state capitols. Almanac is a cornucopia of economic, geographic, and political facts and figures: the number of farms in each state, notable U.S. bridges, state symbols, data on U.S. dependent areas such as Howland Island, and more.

Each state entry is organized into sections: Introduction, Fast Facts, History, Geography, Economy, Culture, Government, Cities, Spotlights, and Profiles. Spotlights focuses on anywhere from 3 (for Iowa) to more than 40 (for New York) notable places or historic events, and Profiles offers biographies, generally numbering around 10. A geopolitical map that enlarges in a separate window shows smaller cities as well as major ones, along with Indian reservations and other locations. Links to pre-screened Web sites and options to print or e-mail the data are offered. Other features provide links to a state-specific time line (which shows state events in relation to events in the U.S. as a whole), a word search puzzle and state history quiz, and resources for teachers. A multimedia button leads to a list of available maps, illustrations, and audiovisual resources.

The various tabs and menus make information easy to access, but those who want to design their own ride through the database can enter terms in the Search box for a full-text tour, or use the simple Advanced Search feature. Advanced Search allows the user to combine two or three terms and to limit searches to article titles only.

This well-designed database does an excellent job of bringing ATB to the online world. Students and patrons of all ages will enjoy using it to research U.S. history and geography. Highly recommended for school and public libraries.

The American Civil War: Letters and Diaries. [Internet database]. Alexander Street, pricing from $1,000. [http://www.alexanderstreet.com/]. (Last accessed February 22, 2002).
North American Women's Letters and Diaries, Colonial–1950. [Internet database]. Alexander Street, pricing from $1,000. [http://www.alexanderstreet.com/]. (Last accessed February 22, 2002).

These two databases offer unique perspectives by focusing "on the personal and the immediate" as revealed in diaries and letters.

The American Civil War: Letters and Diaries (CWLD) pulls together more than 400 sources containing diaries, letters, and memoirs—approximately 1,000 published and previously unpublished items. To be included, a document must have been written between 1855 and 1875 and must be contemporaneous with events it describes. Letters must be of a personal nature. Memoirs must describe events that took place during the war years. Bibliographies such as *The American Civil War: A Handbook of Literature and Research* (Greenwood, 1996) and *American Diaries: An Annotated Bibliography of Published American Diaries and Journals* (Gale, 1983) were used to select the texts.

Content was browsable by Author, Sources, Months, Places, Battles, Personal Events (from "Absence of Parent" to "Wounded") and Day-by-Day, a chronological outline based on T*he Civil War Day-by-Day* (Doubleday, 1971). Author entries include biographical data and in some cases fuller biographies (taken primarily from standard reference sources) and can be searched by document type—letters, diaries, memoirs, or manuscripts. The user can also search for authors, sources, battles, or events by entering search terms in fields that are specific to each of these categories. A third path through the database is to search the text by word or phrase or by choosing one of several other text search options: Simple, Letters, Diaries, Memoirs, and Advanced. A Simple search can be limited by author, year written, document type, or subject headings. Advanced Search offers even more fields, including age, religion, occupation, marital status, battle, whether the author was killed or survived the war, time and place of writing, and subject headings, just to name a few. There are no drop-down menus showing the available terms within each field, but in many cases users can copy terms from designated lists and paste them into search boxes. Search results can be sorted and formatted in a variety of ways and are hyperlinked to each document's bibliographic details.

North American Women's Letters and Diaries, Colonial–1950 (NAWLD) contains approximately 50,000 pages of diaries and letters from 245 sources that record the "immediate experiences" of more than 400 women. The editors looked for "materials that illustrated the role and status of women, personal attitudes and reactions to specific historical or personal events or individuals, and descriptions that conveyed the life and times of the past." Content was gleaned from sources such as *The Published Diaries and Letters of American Women: An Annotated Bibliography* (G. K. Hall, 1987) and *Women's Diaries, Journals, and Letters: An Annotated Bibliography* (Garland, 1989). Authors range from the famous, such as Susan B. Anthony and Clara Barton, to the obscure but prolific. Letters must have been written before 1950, but diaries that were begun before 1950 are included in full. For the most part, memoirs are excluded because they do not record "women's thoughts at the time they thought them."

Except for some small differences (for example, Battles is dropped as a browse category but Historical Events is added), structure is similar to that of CWLD. Again, the Advanced search mode is extremely powerful. One can search for letters written between 1800 and 1850 by Quaker women who lived in New England, or diary entries about courtship written by teachers, or any documents written about the New York City draft riots in 1863, to give just a few simple examples.

Though not particularly exciting to look at, these databases are well organized and easy to use. Besides the sheer amount of material to which they provide access, sophisticated indexing is their great strength. One of the few frustrations a user is likely to encounter is that the many search possibilities currently outstrip the content, and very refined searches often result in zero hits, but this will change as the databases grow. Recommended for academic libraries and large public libraries with relevant research collections.

Andrew Johnson: A Biographical Companion. Ed. by Glenna Schroeder-Lein and Richard Zuczek. 2001. 354p. bibliogs. index. ABC-CLIO, $55 (1-57607-030-1); e-book, $75 (1-57607-586-9). 973.8.

In a unique approach to biography, ABC-CLIO has been developing a series of encyclopedic guides to influential figures of the Western world. This volume treats Andrew Johnson, who remains a mysterious and complex man and president. Both of the editors spent several years working on the University of Tennessee collection of Johnson's papers, and to a large extent they have relied on the papers and other primary sources in preparing this resource.

A short introduction to Johnson sets the tone for the work, explaining his significance and impact. Most of the volume consists of about 260 alphabetically arranged entries varying in length from a half-page to ten pages. Coverage seems appropriate in light of the book's objective to "examine Johnson's place in the history of the United States" and "place his ideas and actions within historical context to help explain his attitudes and decisions." Topics cover people, documents, events, places, and laws. Representative entries include *Alta Vela* (a small but surprisingly significant Caribbean island); *Farewell address* (1869); *Homestead Act*; *Masonic Order*; *Nephews*; *Slaves, owned by Johnson*; and many major and minor personalities. In each case, the topic is defined and introduced, then detailed in terms of its relationship to Johnson. Cross-references and a list of source materials conclude each entry. Several appendixes enhance the volume: congressional acts and bills (including the Articles of Impeachment), a four-page chronology, and an extensive bibliography. Writing is clear and accessible, authoritative without being pedantic.

With the impeachment of Bill Clinton, there may be greater interest in the only other impeached U.S. president. This resource provides an interesting counterpart to other works on the era, particularly for academic and large public library settings.

Chronology of American Indian History through Time: The Trail of the Wind. By Liz Sonneborn. 2001. 442p. bibliog. glossary. illus. index. map. Facts On File, $60 (0-8160-3977-1). 973.04.

This reference work covers the whole of American Indian history from the theorized migration across the Bering Straight circa 25,000 B.C. to the January 20, 2001, entry noting President Clinton's denial of a pardon for Leonard Peltier. Entries are arranged chronologically within 10 chapters beginning with "Before 1492: Emergence" and ending with "1980 to the Present: Into the Future." Most entries are less than two paragraphs in length.

It is difficult to perceive any bias in the entries because they are presented factually with a recognizable deference to maintaining the integrity of the American Indian point of view on their own history. Special detail is applied to interactions with the U.S. government in terms of such events as legal actions (water rights, American Indian Civil Rights Act, etc.), government agencies (Bureau of Indian Affairs, Department of the Interior), and also Indian government bodies (Alaskan Eskimo Whaling Commission, American Indian Movement). The black-and-white photographs interspersed throughout display outstanding quality and authenticity. These include portraits, news photos, paintings, engravings, and handbills. A small glossary is included along with an index and bibliography.

More current than Gale's *Chronology of Native North American History: From Pre-Columbian Times to the Present* (1994), this book is recommended for large public, secondary, and college libraries. It gives straightforward initial information that might entice a college or secondary student to investigate further and find a suitable topic for a research paper.

The Columbia Guide to America in the 1960s. By David Farber and Beth Bailey. 2001. 508p. bibliogs. index. Columbia, $50 (0-231-11372-2). 973.923.

This convenient handbook to a watershed decade in U.S. history is a hybrid combining the information bytes that characterize a reference source and the narrative approach of a book that would be more at home in a library's circulating collection.

Part 1, "The American Sixties: A Brief Overview," presents concise essays on such topics as the civil rights movement, the Vietnam War, and sixties culture. This is followed by another series of essays that present different viewpoints on some of the issues that helped define the era; examples are "Losing Ground? The Great Society in Historical Perspective" and "The Women's Movement: Liberation for Whom?" Part 3, "The Sixties A to Z," offers brief entries for people (Spiro Agnew, H. Rap Brown, Betty Friedan) and terms (*Black power*, *Green Berets*, *New Frontier*). Part 4 consists of topical essays on religion, popular music, sports, and more. Part 5 contains statistics, quotes, and factoids (top 10 TV shows in 1964, percentage of Americans who opposed women going to work if their husbands could support them in 1969). Winding up the volume are a chronology, a bibliography, and an index. The chronology includes an "Introduced in" list delineating when such phenomena as the felt-tipped pen and the Trimline phone first appeared.

There are a number of other reference sources on the 1960s. Like the Columbia offering, H*istorical Dictionary of the 1960s* (Greenwood, 1999) and the more comprehensive, three-volume *Sixties in America* (Salem, 1999) cover a wide spectrum of topics. *The ABC-CLIO Companion to the 1960s Counterculture* (1998) is more focused in its coverage, and Grolier's highly visual U.S.A. *Sixties* [RBB Mr 1 01] is designed for a high-school audience. All of these take a strictly A–Z approach. *The Columbia Guide to America in the 1960s* provides a variety of ways of looking at the decade and is recommended as a good overview for academic and public libraries—whether in the reference or circulating collection.

Complete American Presidents Sourcebook. 5v. By Roger Matuz. 2001. 1,632p. bibliogs. glossary. illus. indexes. UXL, $199 (0-7876-4837-X). 973.

Arranged chronologically from George Washington to George W. Bush, each of these five volumes provides a reader's guide, a time line of the American presidents, a glossary, research and activity ideas, a table of contents for the set, suggested resources for learning more, and a cumulative index. Each presidential entry presents biographical information in terms of a general overview of the president's term(s) in office, his life until and after the presidency, and outstanding events and issues of his presidency. Sidebars offer biographical summaries, a time line, "Words to Know," lists of Cabinet members for each administration, president-related landmarks, and profiles of people connected with the president or his era (e.g., Harriet Beecher Stowe is featured in the entry on Millard Fillmore). Following each president's information are a biography of the First Lady and at least one primary source such as a speech, executive order, or proclamation that clearly highlights the president's agenda. For each document, there is an introduction placing the document in historical context, followed by background information and central ideas, subsequent events, related facts, and a further reading list.

Each volume has approximately 70 black-and-white photographs or illustrations. A mini–table of contents introduces each presidential section, and a brief bibliography concludes it. Unfamiliar terms are defined in context, either in parentheses or in the margins (in the case of primary source documents).

Although aimed at report writers in grades five through ten, the material also makes excellent supplemental material for classroom instruction. Grolier's heavily illustrated, eight-volume *The Presidents* (1996) serves a similar audience but is not as up-to-date. *Complete American Presidents Sourcebook* is recommended for school libraries. Public libraries might also consider this easily accessible set for their patrons.

Encyclopedia of American Cultural and Intellectual History. 3v. Ed. by Mary Kupiec Cayton and Peter W. Williams. 2001. 2,436p. bibliogs. illus. index. Scribner, $325 (0-684-80561-8). 973.

Librarians familiar with the E*ncyclopedia of American Social History* (1993, also edited by Cayton) and other titles in the Scribner American Civilization series will recognize the way in which this new set tackles its subject. The introduction describes the approach as a "systematic 'reference essay' genre" that explores a subject "more thoroughly than the usual encyclopedia entry and more accessibly than the typical academic journal article."

In this case, the subject is "the ever-changing character and rich variety of American thought and expression." Content is organized in 17 parts, within which there are more than 221 essays contributed by scholars representing a variety of academic fields. The first eight parts constitute a chronological survey of American intellectual and cultural development, beginning with the colonial period and extending through the start of the twenty-first century. Examples of the essays found here are "Conflicting Ideals of Colonial Womanhood," "Thought and Culture in the Free Black Community," "Transcendentalism," "The Harlem Renaissance," and "Vietnam as a Cultural Crisis." The remaining nine parts of the encyclopedia are more thematic, examining such broad topics as "Cultural Groups," "The Political Order," and "The Pursuit and Exchange of Knowledge" and, within these divisions, discussing "Latinas and Latinos in the United States," "Socialism and Radical Thought," and "The Internet and Electronic Communications," to cite just a few examples. Part 10, "Geography and Cultural Centers," includes essays on major regions (New England, the Southwest) as well as major "clusters," such as Chicago, Southern California, and Mormon Utah.

Essay length averages around 10 pages. Each concludes with *see also* references and a bibliography. Sidebars offer quotations or highlight important individuals and interesting facts. Each volume has a table of contents for all three volumes, a comprehensive alphabetical table of contents, and a set index. A chronology in volume 1 links historical with cultural and intellectual events.

This set brings together a remarkable array of material and interpretation from across a number of disciplines. Although some of the essays are heavy going, others make fascinating reading. It will be most at home on the shelves of large public and academic libraries.

The Encyclopedia of American Political History. Ed. by Paul Finkelman and Peter Wallenstein. 2001. 494p. appendix. bibliog. illus. index. CQ, $135 (1-56802-511-4). 973.

This encyclopedia embodies the quality that reference librarians have come to expect from CQ Press. More than 240 signed articles by prominent scholars address the people, organizations, parties, political movements, statutes, and events that have shaped American political history. Coverage begins with events leading up to the American Revolution and continues through the Clinton-era scandals. Current developments are reflected in many of the articles: *Social Security*, for example, discusses proposals to invest a portion of the fund in the stock market; *Reform Party* discusses friction between Jesse Ventura and Ross Perot.

Articles range from less than a column in length (*Cloture; Harrison, William Henry; Liberty Party*) to five pages (*Democratic Party; Treaties: Peace, Armament, and Defense*). They clearly define and describe the subject and its importance to the nation's political history. Entries focus almost exclusively on the political aspects of the topic, but bibliographies at the end of each article lead interested readers to additional sources for in-depth research. Cross-referencing is comprehensive, and photographs and cartoons add visual interest. A descriptive time line of political events in U.S. history and an appendix of acronyms and abbreviations complete the volume.

The editors have ensured a consistent level of quality throughout the work and a writing style that makes it accessible to readers beginning at the high-school level. As stated in the introduction, teachers will find this volume useful in preparing lessons relating to the *National Standards for United States History*. Students will find it a helpful supplement to course texts, and researchers at all levels will find it a good starting point.

Encyclopedia of American Studies. 4v. Ed. by George T. Kurian and others. 2001. 2,000p. bibliogs. illus. index. Grolier, $399 (0-7172-9222-3). 973.

Barbie and baseball, Henry Ford and the Fourth of July, jazz and Jim Crow, the presidency and Elvis Presley, states' rights and the Statue of Liberty, Watergate and Woodstock, and many other improbable pairings can be mined and made from this encyclopedia's table of contents. The variety of topics illustrates both the challenge and the solution the editors faced in deciding what to include. The conundrum of American studies is that it is a discipline but one made up of borrowings from a number of other disciplines. The editors acknowledge this in the encyclopedia's preface by directly posing the question, "What is American Studies?" Their answer reflects the field's expanding boundaries, once narrowly drawn to synthesize the study of American history and literature but today elastic enough to encompass popular culture and the application of current academic theories to the American experience. They identify "*culture*, taking that term in the broadest sense" as the central unifying concept of American studies.

Within that conceptual unity, 660 entries ranging in length from 500 to 5,000 words describe and analyze American cultural phenomena. Some, such as D*isneyland*, F*ederalist Papers*, *Ghost Dance*, *Levittowns*, *Mount Rushmore*, *Reader's Digest*, and *Wall Street*, are distinctively—even emblematically—American. Others, such as A*nti-Semitism*, E*vangelicalism*, H*ighways*, *Marxism*, *Museums*, *Schooling*, and *Vegetarianism*, are universal, albeit colored by American cultural values. Those values become evident in the article-specific discussion of the significance of each topic. The contributors explain what a thing, event, institution, or person was or is; but they also consistently explore their meaning in American culture. In a sense, every article, through its examination of some aspect or artifact of American culture, contributes to answering the question about what American studies is.

Contemporary scholarship informs some articles and the approaches used in others. The influence of women's studies is, of course, evident in the article *Stereotypes and stereotyping*. So is the influence of the broader field of gender studies; the article touches lightly on stereotypes of males, a topic a future edition of the encyclopedia will have opportunity to expand and update. Considerations of the roles of race, class, and gender are woven throughout the encyclopedia.

Beginning with its A–Z arrangement, this set offers the apparatus to help readers make optimum use of its contents as well as to extend their quest for knowledge beyond its pages. A thematic guide to contents complements the alphabetical organization. An extensive subject index facilitates a more granular approach to the articles' contents. Entries in the subject index differentiate citations to any of the 600 illustrations. The signed articles conclude with brief bibliographies.

Students of the formal discipline of American studies will be the primary beneficiaries of the encyclopedia's analyses of the significance of phenomena as familiar as the home and as specialized as the sentimental tradition in literature. However, anyone with an interest in the richness and diversity of American culture will also enjoy and learn from it. Other sources that examine some of the same topics, such as the *St. James Encyclopedia of Popular Culture* (Gale, 2000), do not consider those topics within the academic American studies context. *Encyclopedia of American Studies* is recommended for large public and academic libraries.

Encyclopedia of the Clinton Presidency. By Peter B. Levy. 2002. 402p. illus. index. Greenwood, $65 (0-313-31294-X). 973.929.

The press release for this title describes it as a "spin-free" source on the Clinton presidency, one that offers an unbiased look at our forty-second president. It is designed to provide readers with in-depth information on major figures such as Al Gore, Janet Reno, and Ken Starr; insights into Clinton's role as a politician and pop icon; coverage of domestic policy issues such as health-care reform, gays in the military, and gun control; scandals from Whitewater to Travelgate to Monica Lewinsky; and foreign policy issues including the Middle East, the Balkans, and Northern Ireland. Author Levy also wrote *Encyclopedia of the Reagan-Bush Years* (Greenwood, 1996).

The 230-plus entries are presented with boldface cross-references, *see also* references, and brief lists of suggested readings. Depending on the complexity and importance of the subject, entry length runs from a half page for Jacob A. Stein (attorney for Monica Lewinsky) to more than two full pages for his famous client. Broad topics such as foreign policy receive the longest treatment. Other entries cover people (Ruth Bader Ginsburg, Rush Limbaugh, George Stephanopoulos), themes (A*ssassination attempts*, *Campaign finance reform*), major legislation (F*amily Medical Leave Act*, *Internal Revenue Overhaul Act*), and specific historical events (*Election of* 1992). The volume contains a relatively small number of graphs, charts, and black-and-white photos. It concludes with a six-page time line and an index.

Undoubtedly, other specialized encyclopedias covering the Clinton years will be published in the future, and authors of those works will benefit from a historical perspective that comes with time. However, at present, this source has no competition, and it will lend solid reference support to academic, public, and secondary-school libraries.

History

The Encyclopedia of the Great Depression and the New Deal. 2v. By James Ciment. 2001. 936p. bibliog. glossary. illus. indexes. maps. Sharpe, $189 (0-7656-8033-5). 973.917.

Covering the years from 1929 to 1941, this encyclopedia is divided into six parts. In part 1, five thematic essays cover broad topics, such as government and business. The entries in part 2, "General Entries," treat more than 140 mainly social and cultural topics, ranging from *Advertising and consumption* to *Youth.* Examples of other entries include *Brotherhood of Sleeping Car Porters, General Motors, Hispanic Americans,* and *Wizard of Oz.* U.S. government topics, such as *Federal Art Project, Gold standard,* and *Social Security Act,* are examined in part 3; and international topics, such as *Atlantic Charter, China,* and *Refugees,* are discussed in part 4. Part 5 has more than 130 biographical entries for individuals as diverse as Cab Calloway, Al Capone, Francisco Franco, J. Edgar Hoover, and Mae West. Part 6 contains more than 55 documents, some excerpted and some printed in full.

Entries are the work of more than 75 contributors with academic affiliations. Length ranges from one-half page to several pages for *Unions and union organizing; Supreme Court;* and *Roosevelt, Franklin Delano,* to name a few. Each entry concludes with cross-references and a bibliography, and many are accompanied by well-reproduced black-and-white photos or illustrations. At the end of the set are a glossary, a general bibliography, and three indexes: "Subject Index," "Biographical Index," and "Legal Index," which lists government bills, acts, court cases, laws, and so forth.

The set's multipart organization can be confusing, and cross-referencing and indexing do not always help. Tracing *see also* references requires some guesswork because the various parts of the encyclopedia are not clearly indicated in the cross-reference lists. It would be convenient to have an all-inclusive general index in addition to the three that are provided.

Despite its awkward arrangement, this set has much to recommend it, including the wide range of topics and the selection of documents. Another recent title, Grolier's *Depression America* [RBB Ag 01] is designed for high-school students. *The Encyclopedia of the Great Depression and the New Deal* serves an older audience and will be useful in academic and public libraries.

Encyclopedia of the Industrial Revolution in America. By James S. Olson. 2002. 313p. appendix. bibliog. illus. index. Greenwood, $65 (0-313-30830-6). 973.

The Industrial Revolution changed how people worked and lived in the U.S. This reference work is designed to help students understand the concepts, events, and persons that brought about those all-encompassing changes.

The alphabetically arranged entries are enhanced by suggested readings (including Web sites), black-and-white illustrations, and cross-references. Readers can learn about such diverse topics as the *American Bimetallic League,* the *Gold Standard Act of* 1900, the *Haymarket Riot,* the *Molly Maguires,* and the panics of 1819, 1837, 1857, 1873, and 1907. Inventors, industrialists, politicians, and other key players are profiled, as are major corporations that led the way. Concepts like *Infrastructure* and *Vertical integration* are explained, and significant legislation and landmark cases related to industrialism in the U.S. are reported.

The chronology (from the opening of the first coal mine in America in 1756 to 1922's landmark *Bailey v. Drexel Furniture Company* decision) and the bibliography (arranged by topic) help put the period in perspective.

Although this is a useful resource for persons already knowledgeable about the topic, its index makes it difficult to hone in on specifics. For example, Richard Hoe, who revolutionized newspaper printing, merits a lengthy article and is mentioned in the entry on the printing press, but the index does not include a heading for *newspapers.* Frederick W. Taylor has his own entry, which calls him the "leading efficiency engineer of the Industrial Revolution in the United States," but the researcher not knowing his name cannot find him as there is no index heading for *efficiency.* And, because students frequently need to find significant inventions and inventors, it would have been nice to have them clustered in the index.

Nevertheless, this is a handy compilation of information about a significant period in our history. It should be available to people studying that era, along with *The Industrial Revolution: Opposing Viewpoints* (Greenhaven, 1998). Recommended for high-school, public, and undergraduate libraries.

Encyclopedia of the Spanish-American and Philippine-American Wars. Ed. by Jerry Keenan. 2001. 467p. bibliogs. illus. index. maps. ABC-CLIO, $85 (1-57607-093-X). 973.8.

At the end of the nineteenth century, as at the end of the twentieth and the beginning of the twenty-first, the U.S. became involved in wars that featured terrorism, Muslim animosity toward "infidels," guerrilla warfare, atrocities, serious infighting among various critical agencies, and illnesses that plagued the warriors who returned. The brief, but popular, Spanish-American and Philippine-American Wars also showed the world that the U.S. had become a leading power.

This encyclopedia's more than 300 A–Z entries are written "to provide students and other interested readers with basic information . . . names, dates, and summaries of the significant events related to those wars." Numerous biographical sketches of military and political leaders on all sides offer some background, then concentrate on the important contributions and accomplishments of the subjects during the period in question. *See also* references and suggestions for further reading direct users to more detailed information. Most of the illustrations are portraits or group photographs. There are some maps, but researchers might also wish for detailed photos or drawings of uniforms, flags, and weapons. There is an entry for *"Civilize 'em with a Krag,"* which is a line from an army song that originated during the Philippine-American War, but there is no picture of the Krag-Jorgensen rifle.

An extensive bibliography of print monographs, dissertations, and journal articles follows the entries. There is also an interesting list of relevant motion pictures.

Most Americans learn little about this period unless they major in American history. Libraries wanting to fill that gap will want to add this item to their collections so that readers can learn how U.S. signal balloons were used, who the "immunes" were, and why the U.S. Navy Flying Squadron was called that. A similar resource, Brad Berner's *The Spanish-American War: A Historical Dictionary* (Scarecrow, 1998), is not illustrated and does not devote so much attention to the Philippine-American War. Libraries that do not have Berner's book will certainly want to consider Keenan's; those that do will want to decide whether the photos and additional coverage justify duplication.

Ethics in U.S. Government: An Encyclopedia of Investigations, Scandals, Reforms, and Legislation. By Robert North Roberts. 2001. 392p. Greenwood, $65 (0-313-31198-6). 973.

This new encyclopedia provides "a ready reference source on political ethics controversies, investigations and public ethics reforms throughout American history." While other reference sources on American politics, such as the *Oxford Guide to the United States Government* [RBB N 1 01], discuss a few key controversies, this volume focuses exclusively on political scandals and reform. Entries treat organizations, terms, concepts, court cases, and individuals. Emphasis is on the period since World War II, with coverage ending in January 2000. The most significant and well-known ethics controversies throughout U.S. history, such as Watergate, Whitewater, and the Monica Lewinsky case, are included. Minor events with little press coverage, such as the FDA's 1989 "Chilean Grape Scare," or partially unauthenticated affairs, such as the "October Surprise" 1980 election controversy, are excluded.

Author Roberts, a professor in the political science department of James Madison University, has arranged the 264 entries alphabetically. A time line appears at the beginning of the volume to help readers place the entries into historical context. Other reader aids include an acronym list, more than 65 photographs, and heavy cross-referencing. In addition, there is a brief list of "Suggested Readings" after each entry, usually listing two or three sources from major newspapers (often the *New York Times* or *Washington Post*), journals, or monographs. Index entries such as *sexual harassment controversies* help pull together related material.

The recent explosion of government-related scandals has led to the publication of several like-minded books, but most lack the scope and impartiality of *Ethics in U.S. Government.* Some focus exclusively on recent scandals, like Robert Williams' *Political Scandals in the USA* (Fitzroy Dearborn, 1998). Others focus on only one branch of government, like *Congressional Ethics: History, Facts, and Controversy* (Congressional Quarterly, 1992), or focus on one area of corruption, such as Bruce Felknor's *Political Mischief: Smear, Sabotage, and Reform in U.S. Elections* (Praeger, 1992). Still others are radical in the level of corruption they assert, like Rodney Stichs' *Defrauding America: Encyclopedia of Secret Operations by the CIA, DEA, and Other Covert Agencies* (Diablo Western Press, 1998). *Ethics in U.S. Government* is a unique reference source for those interested in the seedier side of American government. Individual entries provide patrons with quick, validated, easy-to-follow explanations, with the option of pursuing more detail through the suggested readings. Taken as a whole, the encyclopedia offers a fascinating look at the role of ethics controversies in the evolution of the national government. Recommended for public and academic libraries.

Experiencing the American Civil War. 2v. By Kevin Hillstrom and Laurie Collier Hillstrom. 2002. 406p. illus. index. UXL, $90 (0-7876-5585-6). 973.703.

Discussing 25 original works (novels, nonfiction, short stories, poems, plays, films, and songs), this set serves as an introduction for young adults to the wide range of creative treatments of the Civil War. With the help of an advisory board of school librarians and media specialists, the Hillstroms tried to select works with teen protagonists and to present a balanced view of the war—North and South, white and black, male and female. The selections include classics such as *The Red Badge of Courage*, "Battle Hymn of the Republic," "An Occurrence at Owl Creek Bridge," and "O Captain! My Captain." Also included are lesser-known works such as William B. Becker's play B*rady of Broadway* and current titles such as the film *Glory* and Gary Paulsen's YA novel *Soldier's Heart*.

The volumes are arranged by genre. Every chapter begins with an overview essay and a list of representative titles (between 8 and 24 annotated items). Between 2 (for plays and films) and 7 (for novels) works are given in-depth treatment. Each entry includes a brief summary of the work being discussed; a biography of the author, composer, etc.; historical background; a summary of plot or subject matter; themes and stylistic characteristics; a few starter research ideas or activities for students; a short annotated list of related titles in various genres; and a list of sources providing additional information. Essays average 15 pages and usually include black-and-white illustrations or photographs. Occasional sidebars provide interesting details, such as the recent controversy over the novel *The Wind Done Gone*.

At the beginning of the first volume, a time line ranging from 1775 to 2000 refers to events and people discussed in the essays. At the end of each volume is a short list of books and Web sites for middle-and high-school study, as well as an index for the set.

Although one might not agree with all of the Hillstroms' choices, their selections do represent an interesting mix of ideas. Librarians will find this a nice addition to school library and curriculum-oriented public library collections.

George Washington: A Biographical Companion. By Frank E. Grizzard Jr. 2002. 434p. bibliog. illus. index. ABC-CLIO, $55 (1-57607-082-4); E-book, $65 (1-57607-558-3). 973.4.
James K. Polk: A Biographical Companion. By Mark E. Byrnes. 2001. 280p. bibliog. illus. index. ABC-CLIO, $55 (1-57607-056-5); E-book, $65 (1-57607-535-4). 973.6.

New titles in the ABC-CLIO Biographical Companions series, these volumes offers the user a wealth of information on two U.S. presidents, one an icon and the other relatively unknown and underappreciated.

"The first encyclopedic work devoted exclusively to Washington" surveys Washington's personal life, family, business dealings, and correspondents as well as his roles as military leader and president. Most of the alphabetically arranged entries cover three categories of information: people (*Jefferson, Thomas; Lafayette; Washington, Mary Ball*); events (*Boston, siege of; Whiskey Rebellion; Yorktown, battle of*); and interests (*Balloons; James River Company; Last will and testament*). Many entries are three or four pages long, allowing fairly detailed treatment. All conclude with cross-references and suggestions for further reading that are primary materials. Following the A–Z entries are selections from Washington's writings; a chronology; lists of family connections, "military family members," and principal executive officers during Washington's presidency; and a bibliography.

The Polk volume is similarly arranged. Following A–Z entries covering people, events, and concepts important to understanding Polk's life and times, there are selected primary documents, a chronology, a bibliography, and an index. The researcher can better comprehend Polk's personality, political acumen, and accomplishments after reading entries such as *Assassination threats; Boyhood and early education; Cuba; Dueling; Friends; Health; Polk, Sarah Childress; Smithsonian Institution;* and *Wilmot Proviso* as well as those describing significant historical figures of the times. Each entry is followed by *see also* references and a bibliography of primary and secondary sources.

Younger researchers might have benefited from annotations of both the primary documents and the general bibliographies in the two volumes. Black-and-white illustrations and color portraits on the front covers further enhance the works, which should prove helpful to anyone interested in these presidents or the periods during which they lived and served. Recommended for high-school, public, and academic libraries.

The Oxford Companion to United States History. Ed. by Paul S. Boyer. 2001. 940p. bibliogs. index. maps. Oxford, $60 (0-19-508209-5). 973.

Every library should have at least one up-to-date, single-volume reference companion to U.S. history. Considering its prestigious Oxford University Press parentage and its reasonable price, this one will be hard to beat.

Exercising a praiseworthy degree of common sense, Oxford has avoided cumbersome arrangement by topical area or chronology. Instead, all 1,400 signed entries are presented in alphabetical order. Therefore, readers may move easily and quickly to any desired topic. Easy access to the mass of information presented in this source is also facilitated by *see* and *see also* references and an index.

Coverage begins with the colonial period. More than 900 scholars have contributed entries on people, places, events, ideologies, historical and social processes, inventions, technological changes, economic developments, conflicts, arts, and religion. Examples include B*usiness cycle; Coolidge, Calvin; Donner party; Drugs; Faulkner, William; FBI; Freedmen's Bureau; Immigrant labor; Mardi Gras; Mexican War; Pony Express; Vaudeville;* and *Women's rights movements*. The entry *Hispanic Americans* is typical of the longer entries. In 2,500 words it describes the Hispanic-American community; traces its history from colonial times to 2000; notes prominent Hispanic American politicians, artists, and athletes; and characterizes the contemporary Hispanic American experience.

It is convenient that so much information is contained in one volume. However, the trade-off is the small font size, and even researchers young enough to do without reading glasses will appreciate a reader's magnifying glass whenever they may be using the book for more than a few minutes at a time. Also, this is not a good choice if illustrations are important because, other than 25 black-and-white maps, the volume is not illustrated.

There are a few comparable reference sources on U.S. history. *The American Heritage Encyclopedia of American History* (Holt, 1998), though not quite as current, has 500 illustrations, which might make it a preferred choice for junior and senior high schools. It also has a broader chronological range, because its coverage begins with pre-Columbian times. Facts On File's *Dictionary of American History: From 1763 to the Present* [RBB Je 1 & 15 01] has fewer and generally shorter entries. *The Oxford Companion to United States History* is highly recommended for high-school, public, and academic libraries needing an authoritative single-volume resource on the topic.

The Revolutionary War. 10v. By James R. Arnold and Roberta Wiener. 2002. bibliog. glossary. illus. index. maps. Grolier, $269 (0-7172-5553-0). 973.3.

Elementary-and middle-school students studying the American Revolution will find this set a valuable resource. The information is arranged in a chronological sequence from the events leading up to the war, through the years of fighting, to the founding of the new nation.

Each volume is highly illustrated with pictures of significant people and places as well as maps. The battle maps are clear and explain the strategies of the commanders. Sidebars with supplemental information are placed throughout the text. Reference aids include a chronology, bibliography, glossary, Web sites, and lists of places to visit. With the exception of a few general electronic resources, these aids are specific to each volume. The last volume adds a brief overview of what became of the men on both sides who distinguished themselves in the war. Each volume also contains a comprehensive index.

With its chronological structure and wealth of illustrations, this set complements UXL's *American Revolution Reference Library* (UXL, 2000), which offers a selection of biographies and primary documents as well as thematic essays. Recommended for school and public libraries.

War of 1812. By Kelly King Howes. 2002. 318p. illus. index. maps. UXL, $52 (0-7876-5574-0). 973.5.

Who needs a book on the War of 1812? It's sometimes called "The Forgotten War," about which most libraries have enough material in encyclopedias and other U.S. history reference works. However, this volume is full of information not found in more general sources. Much of the text is accompanied by material taken directly from primary source documents (papers and letters), adding interest and context in an attractive and inviting typical UXL format. The author has written several other well-researched nonfiction titles.

The purpose of the work is to provide "students with a clear understanding of the issues . . . as well as the motivations" behind the war. Text is arranged in two sections: the "Almanac," consisting of six chronological sections, and "Biographies," covering individuals from Isaac Brock to William Weatherford. Every chapter lists books and Web sites for more information. There are lots of useful *see* references in the text and a thorough index at the end. Extra features found at the front of the volume are research and activity ideas that seem more appropriate for a teacher's guide as well as a glossary and time line.

Readable text and excellent illustrations (many maps and National Archives photos) make this useful for public and school library collections from upper elementary through high school. For the high-school level and up, E*ncyclopedia of the War of 1812* (ABC-CLIO, 1997) is a good choice.

Australia: The Complete Encyclopedia. Ed. by Mary Halbmeyer. 2001. 912p. illus. indexes. maps. Firefly, $60 (1-55297-543-6). 994.

This book is a very colorful, fast-paced guide to all that is Australia. The first part covers general topics—natural history, human history, government, and culture. Sections on the Aboriginal population and on Australian-claimed Antarctica are particularly well put together. Extensive photographs make turning the pages an adventure. Although the chapters are not very in-depth, there is enough information to satisfy most readers.

The second part is divided into chapters on each of the states and territories that make up Australia. Each chapter has a wonderful group of maps so that locating the many described places is quite easy. Descriptions of national parks, wineries, and off-road trips make the encyclopedia useful for travel collections. Though the mainland Northern Territory is included, no mention is made of external territories that Australia governs, such as Norfolk or Christmas Island.

In addition to a subject index, there is a gazetteer to locate the numerous towns and villages discussed in the text. The lack of bibliography or references and of attribution of text to authors is a shortcoming. Not as academic or far-reaching as *The Cambridge Encyclopedia of Australia* (1994), *Australia: The Complete Encyclopedia* serves as a very good introductory geographic encyclopedia.

Antarctica and the Arctic: The Complete Encyclopedia. By David McGonigal and Lynn Woodworth. 2001. 608p. illus. index. maps. Firefly, $60 (1-55297-545-2). 998.

Antarctica is the coldest, highest, driest, windiest, loneliest place on Earth. It is the source of the world's weather and has been called the last great wilderness on the planet. It is owned by no nation but is overseen jointly by the 44 signatories to the Antarctic Treaty that designates it as a "nuclear free continent for science and exploration."

This encyclopedia, replete with more than 1,000 stunning color photographs and more than 80 thematic maps, will surprise, delight, and educate anyone who wishes to know more about Antarctica. The Arctic comprises less than 10 percent of the book and is used mainly to illustrate the difference between the two ends of the earth. Arrangement is thematic, with sections covering geography, geology, ecology, animal life, polar environment, scientific research, history of exploration, and conservation of the continent itself as well as the sub-Antarctic islands. The most extensive section, "Polar Wildlife," includes information about each animal's behavior, history, and habitat as well as a distribution map and an overview of current scientific research.

The authors are both Antarctic veterans of many years, and the contributing writers are experts in their fields. The "Resources" section of the book includes a copy of the Antarctic Treaty, wildlife conservation status, a vocabulary of Antarctica's unique terminology, a guide to museums and sites associated with Antarctica, and 50 Web sites that were available at the time of this review. The encyclopedia concludes with a thorough gazetteer and index. There is also an accompanying CD-ROM that is searchable and contains many of the same maps and photographs as the book as well as sound and animation for such topics as the development of the ozone hole and the movement of Adelie penguins.

This is an excellent resource for information about Antarctica. It will also prove useful to anyone with questions about weather phenomena, biodiversity, oceanography, animal behavior, and the global environment. Libraries that have older titles about the continent will want to update their resources with this encyclopedia. It is highly recommended for both public and academic libraries.

Subject Index

Italics indicate special features. Items that are followed by "Web" in parentheses are sites that were reviewed in Reference on the Web.

ACTING
Acting. 80
Solo Performers. 83

AFRICA
Africa. 99
Encyclopedia of African History and Culture. 99

ALTERNATIVE MEDICINE
Complementary and Alternative Medicine Information Source Book. 72

AMERICAN STUDIES
Encyclopedia of American Studies. 103

ANIMALS
Animal Sciences. 69
Endangered Animals. 54
International Wildlife Encyclopedia. 70
Magill's Encyclopedia of Science. 70
Storey's Horse Lover's Encyclopedia. 75

ANTARCTICA
Antarctica and the Arctic. 106
Exploring Antarctica (Web). 31

ARCHAEOLOGY
Encyclopedia of Archaeology. 95

ARCHITECTURE
Encyclopedia of Architectural and Engineering Feats. 77

ART
A to Z of American Women in the Visual Arts. 76
Artists. 77
Artist's Illustrated Encyclopedia. 76
Illustrator in America. 78
Masters of Traditional Arts. 77
Oxford Companion to J. M. W. Turner. 78
Oxford Companion to Western Art. 77
Schirmer Encyclopedia of Art. 76

ASTRONOMY
Cambridge Encyclopedia of the Sun. 66
Great Atlas of the Stars. 66

ATLASES
DK Concise Atlas of the World. 92
Where and What: Current World Atlas and Dictionary Roundup. 18

AUSTRALIA
Australia. 106

AVIATION AND SPACE
Cambridge Dictionary of Space Technology. 74
Distinguished African Americans in Aviation and Space Science. 74
Encyclopedia of Flight. 74

BASEBALL
Baseball Players' Best Seasons. 83
Baseball Timeline. 83
Baseball's Best Careers. 83
Best of Baseball. 83
Major League Baseball Transactions, 1946. 83
This Day in Yankees History. 83

BIBLE
Oxford Guide to People and Places of the Bible. 45

BIOGRAPHY
American Scene. 93
Biography Book. 39
Biography Reference Bank. 93
Making It in America. 94
Top 10 Biography Reference Sources. 17

BIOLOGY
Biology. 68

BIRTH CONTROL
Encyclopedia of Birth Control. 58

BLACK HISTORY
Digitizing Black History (Web). 30
Pan-African Chronology III. 90
W. E. B. Du Bois. 50

BUDDHISM
Illustrated Encyclopedia of Zen Buddhism. 46

BUSINESS
Core Collection: E-Commerce. 7
Grey House Directory of Special Issues. 40

CANCER
Gale Encyclopedia of Cancer. 70

CD-ROMS
Britannica 2002. 3
Grolier Multimedia Encyclopedia Year 2002. 3
Microsoft Encarta Reference Library 2002. 4
World Book Encyclopedia Deluxe 2002. 4

CENSORSHIP
Censorship. 58
Forbidden Films. 59

CHEMISTRY
Nature's Building Blocks. 66

CHILDREN
Adolescence in America. 48
Boyhood in America. 48
Child Development. 48
Girlhood in America. 50
Infancy in America. 48
Statistical Handbook on the World's Children. 50

CHRISTIANITY
Dictionary of Asian Christianity. 45
Historical Atlas of Christianity. 45

CIVIL WAR
Civil War and Reconstruction. 47
Experiencing the American Civil War. 105

COMMUNICATION
Encyclopedia of Communication and Information. 47

COMPUTERS
World of Computer Science. 39

CONSTITUTION
Constitutional Amendments. 55

CRIME
Encyclopedia of Crime and Justice. 60
Encyclopedia of Crime and Punishment. 55
Murders in the United States. 59

CULTURES
Countries and Their Cultures. 51

DEATH
Celebrities in Los Angeles Cemeteries. 80
Encyclopedia of Death and Dying. 51
Resting Places. 80

DICTIONARIES
Brewer's Dictionary of Modern Phrase and Fable. 84
Dictionaries (Web). 29
First School Dictionary. 62
Junior Dictionary. 62
Microsoft Encarta College Dictionary. 62
New Oxford American Dictionary. 63
Unabridged and Online: Merriam-Webster Unabridged. 27
Where and What: Current World Atlas and Dictionary Roundup. 18

DINOSAURS
Dinosaur Encyclopedia. 68
Encyclopedia of Prehistory. 66

DISASTERS
Dangerous Planet. 58
Natural Disasters. 89

DRUGS
Encyclopedia of Drugs and Alcohol. 72

EARTH SCIENCE
Atlas of the Evolving Earth. 67
Exploring Earth and Space Science. 67
Oxford Companion to the Earth. 67

EDUCATION
Encyclopedia of American Education. 60
World Education Encyclopedia. 60
World of Learning Online. 42

ELECTIONS
America at the Polls: 1960-2000. 53
Atlas of American Politics 1960-2000. 53
Statistical History of the American Electorate. 53

ENCYCLOPEDIAS
Another Look at . . . : Childcraft. 22
Britannica 2002. 3
Compton's Encyclopedia. 1
Encyclopedia Americana. 1
Encyclopedia Americana Online. 1
Grolier Multimedia Encyclopedia Online. 2
Grolier Multimedia Encyclopedia Year 2002. 3
Microsoft Encarta Reference Library 2002. 4
New Book of Knowledge. 2
New Book of Knowledge Online. 2
New Standard Encyclopedia. 3
Nupedia (Web). 33
World Book Enciclopedia Estudiantil Hallazgos. 42
World Book Encyclopedia. 3
World Book Encyclopedia Deluxe 2002. 4
World Book Online. 3

ENVIRONMENT
Environment Encyclopedia. 59
Environmental Activists. 59
Environmental Resource Handbook. 54
Environmental Resources (Web). 30
Whole New Environment: Environmental Reference Resources in Print. 21
World Atlas of Coral Reefs. 69

ETHICS
Encyclopedia of Ethics. 43
Encyclopedia of Ethics in Science and Technology. 43
Ethics in U.S. Government. 104

ETHNIC STUDIES
American Ethnicity (Web). 29
American Ethnicity Reference Sources. 5

FASHION
For Appearance' Sake. 76
In an Influential Fashion. 60

FIRST LADIES
Wives of the Presidents. 27

FOLKLORE
Encyclopedia of Folk Heroes. 61
Encyclopedia of Urban Legends. 61

Mythical West. 61
Urban Legends (Web). 36

FOOD
Food Safety Information Handbook. 59
Junior Worldmark Encyclopedia of Foods and Recipes of the World. 75
New Complete Book of Herbs, Spices, and Condiments. 75

FUNDAMENTALISM
Encyclopedia of Fundamentalism. 44

GAMBLING
Gambling in America. 83

GARDENING
Annuals and Biennials. 74
Encyclopedia of Gardens. 75
Perennials. 74

GENEALOGY
Genealogy Gold Mine: Ancestry Plus. 24

GENETICS
Gale Encyclopedia of Genetic Disorders. 73
World of Genetics. 68

GEOGRAPHY
Columbia Gazetteer of the World Online. 91
Encyclopedia of World Geography. 91
Rivers of the World. 92
World Geography. 92

GREAT BRITAIN
British Political Leaders. 97
Encyclopedia of the Wars of the Roses. 97

HEALTH AND MEDICINE
Cornell Illustrated Encyclopedia of Health. 72
Encyclopedia of Fertility and Infertility. 73
Encyclopedia of Sleep and Sleep Disorders. 73
Magill's Medical Guide. 71
Oxford Companion to the Body. 71
Oxford Illustrated Companion to Medicine. 71
Staying Healthy (Web). 36

HINDUISM
Illustrated Encyclopedia of Hinduism. 46

HISTORY
Encyclopedia of World History. 89
Facts about the Twentieth Century. 90
History Resource Center. 94
New York Times Twentieth Century in Review: The Cold War. 90
New York Times Twentieth Century in Review: The Gay Rights Movement. 90
World Eras: European Renaissance and Reformation. 97

HISTORY, ANCIENT
Ancient Egyptians. 93
Ancient History. 95
Ancient Rome. 96
Encyclopedia of the Ancient World. 95
Encyclopedia of Women in the Ancient World. 49
Greek and Roman Mythology. 96
Handbook to Life in the Ancient Maya World. 100
Oxford Encyclopedia of Mesoamerican Cultures. 100
Who's Who in the Roman World. 94

HISTORY, U.S.
Beacham's Encyclopedia of Social Change. 50
Columbia Guide to America in the 1960s. 102
Encyclopedia of American Cultural and Intellectual History. 102
Encyclopedia of American Political History. 103
Encyclopedia of the Great Depression and the New Deal. 104
Encyclopedia of the Industrial Revolution in America. 104
Encyclopedia of the Spanish-American and Philippine-American Wars. 104
Encyclopedia of Women in American History. 49
Oxford Companion to United States History. 105
Revolutionary War. 105
War of 1812. 105

HOLIDAYS
Christmas Encyclopedia. 61
Encyclopedia of Easter, Carnival, and Lent. 61

HOLOCAUST
Bearing Witness. 39
Encyclopedia of Jewish Life before and during the Holocaust. 96
Holocaust Encyclopedia. 97

HORROR
Dark Reference. 11
Horror (Web). 32
Horror Reference Shelf. 11

IMMIGRATION
American Immigration. 47
Encyclopedia of American Immigration. 47
Facts about American Immigration. 48

INTERNET
Internet Resources and Services for International Finance and Investment. 41

ITALY
Regions of Italy. 98

JAPAN
Encyclopedia of Contemporary Japanese Culture. 99
Kodansha Encyclopedia of Japan. 99

KOREAN WAR
Korean War: Almanac and Primary Sources. 98
Korean War: Biographies. 98

LANGUAGE
British English A to Zed. 62
Facts On File Dictionary of Foreign Words and Phrases. 62
Nazi-Deutsch/Nazi German. 98
Wimmin, Wimps & Wallflowers. 51

LATIN AMERICA
Encyclopedia of Contemporary Latin and Carribean Cultures. 100
Handbook to Life in the Ancient Maya World. 100
Oxford Encyclopedia of Mesoamerican Cultures. 100

LAW
Biographical Directory of the Federal Judiciary 1789-2000. 55
Encyclopedia of American Law. 56
Historic U.S. Court Cases. 56
Homosexuality and the Law. 55

LIBRARIES
Dictionary for School Library Media Specialists. 41
International Directory of Library Histories. 41

LIFE SCIENCES
Encyclopedia of Life Sciences. 68

LITERATURE
Encyclopedia of Life Writing. 88
Gothic Writers. 85
MagillOnAuthors. 85
Who's Who of Twentieth-Century Novelists. 85
World Literature and Its Times: British and Irish Literature and Its Times: Celtic Migrations to the Reform Bill (Beginnings-1830s). 88
World Literature and Its Times: British and Irish Literature and Its Times: The Victorian Era to the Present (1837-). 88
World Literature and Its Times: Spanish and Portuguese Literatures and Their Times (The Iberian Peninsula). 89
Encyclopedia of Literary Translation into English. 63

LITERATURE, CHILDREN'S
Cambridge Guide to Children's Books in English. 87
Continuum Encyclopedia of Children's Literature. 84
Dictionary of American Children's Fiction, 1995-1999. 87

LITERATURE, U.S.
American Naturalistic and Realistic Novelists. 87
Companion to Southern Literature. 86
Dictionary of Midwestern Literature. 86
Eugene O'Neill. 40
Merriam-Webster's Dictionary of American Writers. 86
William Faulkner A to Z. 87

MARTIAL ARTS
Martial Arts of the World. 84

MATHEMATICS
Mathematics. 65

MENTAL HEALTH
Encyclopedia of Depression. 72
Encyclopedia of Mental Health. 73

MIDDLE AGES
Daily Life in the Middle Ages. 96
Encyclopedia of Women in the Middle Ages. 50
Medieval World. 90

MILITARY HISTORY
America's Military Adversaries. 56
Magill's Guide to Military History. 57
Military History (Web). 33
Oxford Companion to Military History. 57
Reader's Guide to Military History. 57
Warfare and Armed Conflicts. 89
Weapons and Warfare. 74
Who's Who in Twentieth-Century Warfare. 57

MOTION PICTURES
Encyclopedia of Alfred Hitchcock. 80
Encyclopedia of Filmmakers. 81
Encyclopedia of Science Fiction Movies. 81
Encyclopedia of Stanley Kubrick. 80
Espionage Filmography. 81
Feature Films, 1960-1969. 40
Filmography of American History. 81
Films of the Nineties. 40
Photography and Filmmakers. 78
Wallflower Critical Guide to Contemporary North American Directors. 82

MUSIC
American Musical Traditions. 79
American Song. 79
Music Since 1900. 79
New Grove Dictionary of Jazz. 79

MYSTERIES
More Sites on Sleuths: Women of Mystery. 12

MYTHOLOGY
Handbook of Norse Mythology. 46

NATIVE AMERICANS
Chronology of American Indian History through Time. 102
Encyclopedia of American Indian Contributions to the World. 100
Native American Women. 94

NURSING
Gale Encyclopedia of Nursing and Allied Health. 71

OCEANS
World Atlas of the Oceans. 92

ONLINE DATABASES
America the Beautiful. 101

American Civil War, The: Letters and Diaries. 101
Biography Reference Bank. 93
booksinprint.com. 39
Desktop Library: ebrarian for Libraries. 24
Electronic Encyclopedia of American Government. 52
Encyclopedia Americana Online. 1
Encyclopedia of Life Sciences. 68
Genealogy Gold Mine: Ancestry Plus. 24
Grolier Multimedia Encyclopedia Online. 2
History Resource Center. 94
Keeping Up with What's New (Web). 32
Library-in-a-Dorm Room: Questia. 25
MagillOnAuthors. 85
New Book of Knowledge Online. 2
North American Women's Letters and Diaries, Colonial-1950. 101
Science Reference Center. 63
Sixty-Thousand Page Giant: Oxford Reference Online. 26
Unabridged and Online: Merriam-Webster Unabridged. 27
World Almanac Reference Database@FACTS1. 41
World Book Online. 3
World of Learning Online. 42
xreferplus (Web). 38

PARANORMAL
Greenhaven Encyclopedia of Witchcraft. 42
Satanism Today. 43

PEACE
Peace Movement Directory. 54

PHILOSOPHY
Encyclopedia of Asian Philosophy. 44

PHYSICS
Physics Matters!. 66

POETRY
Another Look at . . . : The Columbia Granger's Index to Poetry in Anthologies. 23
Encyclopedia of American Poetry. 86
Masterplots 2: Poetry Series. 85

POLITICS AND GOVERNMENT
Electronic Encyclopedia of American Government. 52

Encyclopedia of American Foreign Policy. 53
Encyclopedia of Political Thought. 51
Ethics in U.S. Government. 104
Oxford Companion to Politics of the World. 52
Oxford Guide to United States Government. 52

POPES
Dictionary of Popes and the Papacy. 45
Papacy. 46

PRESIDENTS
Andrew Johnson. 102
Complete American Presidents Sourcebook. 102
Encyclopedia of the Clinton Presidency. 103
George Washington. 105
James K. Polk. 105
Lives of the Presidents (Web). 33

PROPHECY
Encyclopedia of Prophecy. 42

PSYCHOLOGY
Dictionary of Psychology. 43

PUBLIC HEALTH
Encyclopedia of Public Health. 57

QUOTATIONS
Other People's Words: Recent Quotation Books. 13
Quotations (Web). 34

RADIO
Great Radio Audience Participation Shows. 82

RAINFORESTS
Encyclopedia of Rainforests. 69
Rain Forests of the World. 69

RELIGION
Religion (Web). 34

RELIGION, U.S.
Encyclopedia of American Religious History. 44

RETIREMENT
Facts about Retiring in the United States. 48

RUSSIA
Encyclopedia of Russian Women's Movements. 49

Russia and Eastern Europe. 98

SAINTS
Encyclopedia of Saints. 45

SCIENCE
Nature Yearbook of Science and Technology. 64
Science Q&A (Web). 35
Science Reference Center. 63
UXL Encyclopedia of Science. 64
Visual Science Encyclopedia. 64

SCIENCE HISTORY
Core Collection: History of Science. 8
Encyclopedia of the Atomic Age. 66
Groundbreaking Scientific Experiments, Inventions, and Discoveries of the 17th Century. 64
Makers of Science. 65
Scientific Revolution. 65

SCOTLAND
Collins Encyclopedia of Scotland. 97

SHAKESPEARE
Oxford Companion to Shakespeare. 88
Shakespeare (Web). 35

SHIPWRECKS
Encyclopedia of Western Atlantic Shipwrecks and Sunken Treasures. 89

SOCCER
Encyclopedia of American Soccer History. 84

SPANISH LANGUAGE MATERIALS
Reference Books in Spanish for Children and Adolescents. 15
World Book Enciclopedia Estudiantil Hallazgos. 42

SUPREME COURT
Justices of the United States Supreme Court. 55
Supreme Court of the United States. 56

TELEVISION
Hi There, Boys and Girls!. 82
Performers' Television Credits, 1948-2000. 82
Terror Television. 78

UNITED NATIONS
Great Debates at the United Nations. 54

UNITED STATES
America the Beautiful. 101
County Name Origins of the United States. 92

URBAN STUDIES
Core Collection: Urban Studies. 9

WEATHER
Encyclopedia of Weather and Climate. 67
Macmillan Encyclopedia of Weather. 67

WOMEN
A to Z of American Women in the Performing Arts. 80
Ahead of Their Time. 93
Encyclopedia of One's Own: Women in World History. 23
Encyclopedia of Russian Women's Movements. 49
Encyclopedia of Women and Gender. 49
Encyclopedia of Women in American History. 49
Encyclopedia of Women in the Middle Ages. 50
Encyclopedia of Women Social Reformers. 47
Encyclopedia of Women's Health Issues. 72
Encyclopedia of Women's Travel and Exploration. 91
International Women in Science. 65
Out of the Shadows: Women Building Chicago, 1790-1990. 26
Women's History (Web). 37

WORLD WAR I
History of World War I. 96

WORLD WAR II
Encyclopedia of World War II Spies. 53

WRITING
Sites for Writers (Web). 35
Writer's Tool Kit. 22

ZOOS
Encyclopedia of the World's Zoos. 70

Title Index

This index is for titles found in the "Reviews" section beginning on p.39.

A to Z of American Women in the Performing Arts. 80
A to Z of American Women in the Visual Arts. 76
Acting. 80
Adolescence in America. 48
Africa. 99
Ahead of Their Time. 93
America at the Polls: 1960-2000. 53
America the Beautiful. 101
American Civil War, The: Letters and Diaries. 101
American Immigration. 47
American Musical Traditions. 79
American Naturalistic and Realistic Novelists. 87
American Scene. 93
American Song. 79
America's Military Adversaries. 56
Ancient Egyptians. 93
Ancient History. 95
Ancient Rome. 96
Andrew Johnson. 102
Animal Sciences. 69
Annuals and Biennials. 74
Antarctica and the Arctic. 106
Artist's Illustrated Encyclopedia. 76
Artists. 77
Atlas of American Politics 1960-2000. 53
Atlas of the Evolving Earth. 67
Australia. 106
Baseball Players' Best Seasons. 83
Baseball Timeline. 83
Baseball's Best Careers. 83
Beacham's Encyclopedia of Social Change. 50
Bearing Witness. 39
Best of Baseball. 83
Biographical Directory of the Federal Judiciary 1789-2000. 55
Biography Book. 39
Biography Reference Bank. 93
Biology. 68
booksinprint.com. 39
Boyhood in America. 48
Brewer's Dictionary of Modern Phrase and Fable. 84
Britannica 2002. 3
British English A to Zed. 62
British Political Leaders. 97
Cambridge Dictionary of Space Technology. 74
Cambridge Encyclopedia of the Sun. 66
Cambridge Guide to Children's Books in English. 87
Celebrities in Los Angeles Cemeteries. 80
Censorship. 58
Child Development. 48
Christmas Encyclopedia. 61
Chronology of American Indian History through Time. 102
Civil War and Reconstruction. 47
Collins Encyclopedia of Scotland. 97
Columbia Gazetteer of the World Online. 91
Columbia Guide to America in the 1960s. 102
Companion to Southern Literature. 86
Complementary and Alternative Medicine Information Source Book. 72
Complete American Presidents Sourcebook. 102
Compton's Encyclopedia. 1
Constitutional Amendments. 55
Continuum Encyclopedia of Children's Literature. 84
Cornell Illustrated Encyclopedia of Health. 72
Countries and Their Cultures. 51
County Name Origins of the United States. 92
Daily Life in the Middle Ages. 96
Dangerous Planet. 58
Dictionary for School Library Media Specialists. 41
Dictionary of American Children's Fiction, 1995-1999. 87
Dictionary of Asian Christianity. 45
Dictionary of Midwestern Literature. 86
Dictionary of Popes and the Papacy. 45
Dictionary of Psychology. 43
Dinosaur Encyclopedia. 68
Distinguished African Americans in Aviation and Space Science. 74
DK Concise Atlas of the World. 92
Electronic Encyclopedia of American Government. 52
Encyclopedia Americana Online. 1
Encyclopedia Americana. 1
Encyclopedia of African History and Culture. 99
Encyclopedia of Alfred Hitchcock. 80
Encyclopedia of American Cultural and Intellectual History. 102
Encyclopedia of American Education. 60
Encyclopedia of American Foreign Policy. 53
Encyclopedia of American Immigration. 47
Encyclopedia of American Indian Contributions to the World. 100
Encyclopedia of American Law. 56
Encyclopedia of American Poetry. 86
Encyclopedia of American Political History. 103
Encyclopedia of American Religious History. 44
Encyclopedia of American Soccer History. 84
Encyclopedia of American Studies. 103
Encyclopedia of Archaeology. 95
Encyclopedia of Architectural and Engineering Feats. 77
Encyclopedia of Asian Philosophy. 44
Encyclopedia of Birth Control. 58
Encyclopedia of Communication and Information. 47
Encyclopedia of Contemporary Japanese Culture. 99
Encyclopedia of Contemporary Latin and Carribean Cultures. 100
Encyclopedia of Crime and Justice. 60
Encyclopedia of Crime and Punishment. 55
Encyclopedia of Death and Dying. 51
Encyclopedia of Depression. 72
Encyclopedia of Drugs and Alcohol. 72
Encyclopedia of Easter, Carnival, and Lent. 61
Encyclopedia of Ethics in Science and Technology. 43
Encyclopedia of Ethics. 43
Encyclopedia of Fertility and Infertility. 73
Encyclopedia of Filmmakers. 81
Encyclopedia of Flight. 74
Encyclopedia of Folk Heroes. 61
Encyclopedia of Fundamentalism. 44
Encyclopedia of Gardens. 75
Encyclopedia of Jewish Life before and during the Holocaust. 96
Encyclopedia of Life Sciences. 68
Encyclopedia of Life Writing. 88
Encyclopedia of Literary Translation into English. 63
Encyclopedia of Mental Health. 73
Encyclopedia of Political Thought. 51
Encyclopedia of Prehistory. 66
Encyclopedia of Prophecy. 42
Encyclopedia of Public Health. 57
Encyclopedia of Rainforests. 69
Encyclopedia of Russian Women's Movements. 49
Encyclopedia of Saints. 45
Encyclopedia of Science Fiction Movies. 81
Encyclopedia of Sleep and Sleep Disorders. 73
Encyclopedia of Stanley Kubrick. 80
Encyclopedia of the Ancient World. 95
Encyclopedia of the Atomic Age. 66
Encyclopedia of the Clinton Presidency. 103
Encyclopedia of the Great Depression and the New Deal. 104
Encyclopedia of the Industrial Revolution in America. 104
Encyclopedia of the Spanish-American and Philippine-American Wars. 104
Encyclopedia of the Wars of the Roses. 97
Encyclopedia of the World's Zoos. 70
Encyclopedia of Urban Legends. 61
Encyclopedia of Weather and Climate. 67
Encyclopedia of Western Atlantic Shipwrecks and Sunken Treasures. 89
Encyclopedia of Women and Gender. 49
Encyclopedia of Women in American History. 49
Encyclopedia of Women in the Ancient World. 49
Encyclopedia of Women in the Middle Ages. 50
Encyclopedia of Women Social Reformers. 47
Encyclopedia of Women's Health Issues. 72
Encyclopedia of Women's Travel and Exploration. 91
Encyclopedia of World Geography. 91
Encyclopedia of World History. 89
Encyclopedia of World War II Spies. 53
Endangered Animals. 54
Environment Encyclopedia. 59
Environmental Activists. 59
Environmental Resource Handbook. 54
Espionage Filmography. 81
Ethics in U.S. Government. 104
Eugene O'Neill. 40
Experiencing the American Civil War. 105
Exploring Earth and Space Science. 67
Facts about American Immigration. 48
Facts about Retiring in the United States. 48
Facts about the Twentieth Century. 90
Facts On File Dictionary of Foreign Words and Phrases. 62
Feature Films, 1960-1969. 40
Filmography of American History. 81
Films of the Nineties. 40
First School Dictionary. 62
Food Safety Information Handbook. 59
For Appearance' Sake. 76
Forbidden Films. 59
Gale Encyclopedia of Cancer. 70
Gale Encyclopedia of Genetic Disorders. 73
Gale Encyclopedia of Nursing and Allied Health. 71
Gambling in America. 83
George Washington. 105
Girlhood in America. 50
Gothic Writers. 85
Great Atlas of the Stars. 66
Great Debates at the United Nations. 54
Great Radio Audience Participation Shows. 82
Greek and Roman Mythology. 96
Greenhaven Encyclopedia of Witchcraft. 42
Grey House Directory of Special Issues. 40
Grolier Multimedia Encyclopedia Online. 2
Grolier Multimedia Encyclopedia Year 2002. 3
Groundbreaking Scientific Experiments, Inventions, and Discoveries of the 17th Century. 64
Handbook of Norse Mythology. 46

Word processors and the writing process 142
World directory of modern military vehicles 117
World economic survey 1984 142
World human rights guide 142
World of science 142

INDEXES
Adult video index '84 121
Audiovisual resources in food and nutrition 123
Combined retrospective index to book reviews in humanities journals, 1802-1974 125
The computer information series 40
Computers and information processing world index 40
DataMap 44
Dissertations in the history of education, 1970-1980 128
Federal register 129
Find that tune 62
Fine and applied arts terms index 63
The great song thesaurus 65
A guide to critical reviews 66
Index to America 72
Index to international public opinion, 1982-1983 72
An index to microform collections 72
Index to poetry for children and young people, 1976-1981 72
Index to poetry in popular periodicals, 1955-1959 73
Indexed journals 73
Iran media index 133
Literary criticism index 134
Music psychology index 86
National Geographic index 1947-1983 135
News bank 120
Perspectives of new music 93
Population information in nineteenth century census volumes 95
Print index 97
Twentieth-century author biographies master index 109
Women novelists, 1891-1920 115

SOURCEBOOKS
America the quotable 24
American landmark legislation 122
Choreography by George Balanchine 124
The computer data and database source book 125
Conway's all the world's fighting ships, 1947-1982 42
Design on file 127
Drug use and abuse 51
The encyclopedia of second careers 57
The Eugene O'Neill companion 59
Everyday legal forms 129
Festivals sourcebook 61
Follies and foibles 130
Gary Null's nutrition sourcebook for the '80s 64
The Guinness book of Olympics facts and feats 131
The home how-to sourcebook 70
International development resource books 133
Literature searching in science, technology, and agriculture 134
The London stage, 1920-1929 80
Mutual fund sourcebook 135
The new book of American rankings 87
The new book of world rankings 88
New Iberian world 89
Opposing viewpoints sources 91
Paris Opera 93
A pictorial history of Blackamericans 94
Presidential also-rans and running mates, 1788-1980 138
Reader's Digest 101 do-it-yourself projects 99
A reference companion to the history of abnormal psychology 99
Research guide to philosophy 101
Statistical information on the financial services industry 105
Tests supplement 140
Who's who in Wagner 141
Women composers, conductors, and musicians of the twentieth century 115
Women filmmakers 142
Women in development 142